COLLECTING
Case® Knives
IDENTIFICATION AND PRICE GUIDE

Steve Pfeiffer

Published by

700 East State Street • Iola, WI 54990-0001
715-445-2214 • 888-457-2873
www.krausebooks.com

Our toll-free number to place an order or obtain
a free catalog is (800) 258-0929.

Cover photography by Kris Kandler.

On the cover, clockwise from the top: Case XX USA 5172, "Bulldog" transition stamping, 5-1/2", **$450**; Case Tested 61098, "Large Texas Toothpick," green bone, 5-1/2", **$900**; and Case XX 6185 "doctor's knife," red bone, 3-3/4", **$350**.

Library of Congress Control Number: 2009923189

ISBN-13: 978-1-4402-0238-4
ISBN-10: 1-4402-0238-9

Designed by Katrina Newby
Edited by Kristine Manty

Printed in China

DEDICATION

This book is dedicated to my late father, Russell J. Pfeiffer, the sharpest knife trader I ever knew.

And to the late George Goring Sr. of Michigan, my mentor and friend who introduced me to the wonders of Case pocket knife collecting in 1973.

And finally to the late author Dewey P. Ferguson, who blazed this trail before me.

ACKNOWLEDGMENTS

I would like to thank the good folks at W.R Case & Sons Cutlery Company for graciously providing me with access to the archives at the Case factory, for the fine plant tour, for providing much useful material, and for generally being such gracious hosts. Shirley Boser, Case historian, was a valuable guide for this effort, as were Lisa Miller, coordinator of the Case Collector's Club, and John Sullivan, Case's director of marketing. And thanks to Andy Norcross of the Case Art Department and to Katie Shonts, the new Case historian. And, finally, thanks to Tom Arrowsmith, president of WR. Case & Sons, for supporting this effort.

I would also like to extend a warm thank you to each and every associate of W.R Case & Sons Cutlery Company for the talent and enthusiasm they display in every step of the manufacture of Case pocket knives.

I would like to thank a number of fellow knife collectors who provided support and encouragement for this book, including "Uncle Jim" Prather, Ed Olson, Theron Eckard, Bob Picklesheimer, and Gary Moore.

And many thanks to my dear friend Sheila for transcribing much of the material I copied from the Case factory archives.

CONTENTS

FOREWORD

There's a story behind every Case knife. That may sound like the usual marketing blather, but turn the pages of this book, and you'll see what I mean. Handle materials, blade steels, pattern by pattern, the story of the Case knife comes to light.

For those of us who work for W.R. Case & Sons, there's more to the story. It is not just about the knives, it's about the people. My career with the company began in 1994, a few months after Case Wall of Fame member Mary Petro retired with seventy years of service. Mary started on Bank Street, the first Case factory in Bradford. I had the privilege of actually working with another Case Legend, model maker Tom Hart, the designer of the Texas Lockhorn (page 257). Our marketing team developed the CopperLock®, the RussLock®, and the concept that led to the Pocket Worn® knives. Tom, by the way, had fifty years of service. I mention Mary and Tom, but there have been so many. Generation after generation, skilled Case artisans continue the knife-making traditions started by the Case Brothers more than a century ago.

W.R. Case & Sons Cutlery Company has a rich legacy – something we work very hard to preserve. There have been many changes in the knife industry in recent years. Old-line knife factories like Imperial Schrade and Camillus have closed. More knives are being imported from China and other countries. These economic times are challenging for any American manufacturing company. But the real reward comes because we are lucky enough to make a product – a pocket knife - that people care about. That brings me to the other "people" story at Case – our customers, enthusiasts and collectors.

There's just something about a Case knife – it brings the stories to life. If I'm traveling and mention that I work for Case, invariably I'll learn about a favorite pocket knife or the hunting knife that was a gift from their Dad or Granddad. Our repair department gets so many wonderful letters. Stories of knives used on the farm or carried to war in Vietnam. At the factory, hardly a day goes by without Case Collectors touring the facility. I can't begin to tell you how much that means to all of the Case Associates. Families travel together on their summer vacations, building memories with their children and grandchildren. That probably doesn't happen at many other factories.

It was certainly an honor to be asked by Steve Pfeiffer and the folks at Krause to write the foreword for this book. I offer my congratulations on the tremendous effort and research he put into this book. Whether you are a new or veteran Case collector, it will be a great reference. Case collecting is a great hobby – one to last for a lifetime. Just remember rule number one: Collect what you like – and enjoy.

John Sullivan
Director of Marketing
W.R. Case & Sons Cutlery Co.
Bradford PA

INTRODUCTION

It is with great pleasure and pride that I present this book to the Case pocket knife collecting community.

When I initially conceived this project, I set out to write a book about Case pocket knives that would be significantly different than other books on the market that cover the Case brand.

There are a number of fine books available that thoroughly cover the history of W.R Case & Sons Cutlery Company, including rare information and photos that trace the history of Case and related firms and the lineages of the families involved.

Likewise, there are many stories that have been documented regarding the often colorful personalities involved in the cutlery industry in and around Bradford, Pennsylvania during the early years of operation of W.R Case & Sons and their rivals including the Case Brothers Cutlery Company and the Cattaraugus Cutlery Company.

Rather than "reinventing the wheel" and covering this information again, I chose a different focus for this book. This is a book about the knives themselves. It is a book about staghorn and steel, about pocket knife construction details, handle materials, and the "DNA" of the historic pocket knife patterns that have been in and out

of the Case pocket knife line over the course of many years. Given the vast number of pocket knife patterns and variations produced by Case during the World War I era, the pre-World War II years, the post WWII years, and up to the present day, naturally not everything can be covered.

I have endeavored to include information on various topics related to the Case brand that will be of maximum interest to Case pocket knife collectors, and (I hope) to the collectors of other brands and types of knives as well.

The history of the W.R. Case & Sons Cutlery Company mirrors the history of the modern cutlery industry itself, and American industry in general.

It is my sincere hope that in writing this book I have accomplished the task I set out to do, and that knife collectors of all experience levels in the United States and around the world will gain much valuable information from the study of what is contained herein.

Steve Pfeiffer
AKA "Knifeaholic"
February 2009

THE CASE COLLECTORS CLUB

Listening to collectors is ever so present at Case with one of the best suggestions offered almost 30 years ago. An avid knife collector wrote to a past Case president about forming a knife collectors association. This resulted with the introduction of the Case Collectors Club in 1981.

Since that time, the Case Collectors Club (CCC) has pledged to be the premier association for knife collectors and enthusiasts worldwide. The CCC helps beginning collectors and serious aficionados learn more about the history and rich heritage of Case knives. Collectors are rewarded with unparalleled customer service and quality, handcrafted knives worthy to be labeled "Made in the USA." Case continues to raise the value of membership by offering a quarterly magazine that shares information on new products soon to hit the market, Case history, featured collector stories, annual consumer events, and much more.

Additional membership benefits include free tours of the Case knife factory, special Club events, an exclusive member forum, and options to buy limited edition knives.

The CCC strives to keep the family tradition of Case collecting alive from generation to generation. When an established collector has the opportunity to pass down their collection to a family member, they both share the satisfaction of learning about and acquiring a true masterpiece of American craftsmanship. Sponsoring a junior member in the CCC is a great way to keep the tradition alive by introducing a child or grandchild to the fun of knife collecting.

Club members are a part of the world's largest knife collecting association! For additional information or to join the club, call (800) 523-6350, write to W.R. Case & Sons Cutlery Company, Owens Way, Bradford, PA 16701, or visit www.wrcase.com.

MAXIMS FOR THE CASE POCKET KNIFE COLLECTOR

If it's *your* knife:

It has "regular" bone handles or bone handles with a "red tint."

The stag handles have a "crack."

And it has a steel blade pin in a nickel silver bolster, then it was "crudely repinned with a nail."

It has "visible rust spots."

It has "significant rust and tarnish."

It has "50 percent blade wear" and has been heavily "buffed and polished."

It has "significant blade wobble."

And it has weak backsprings, it has "lazy blades."

And it has a blade that has been reshaped, it is a "broken blade."

It is a phony.

It is a modern counterfeit.

If it's *my* knife:

It has "cherry red bone" handles.

The stag handles have a "natural stress line."

And it has a steel blade pin in a nickel silver bolster, it was a "special factory order" made that way for "extra strength."

It has "specks."

It has "developed a nice patina."

It has "been lightly used and cleaned to near mint."

It has a "hint of blade play."

And it has weak backsprings, they are "easy on the thumbnail."

And it has a blade that has been reshaped, it is a "special tool blade" that "came from the factory" that way.

It is an "authorized reproduction."

It is "new old stock" from a "warehouse find."

Yep, if you have followed the "knife business" for any length of time, you must know that over in Solingen, Germany (or as I heard one "ole timer" once call it, "Sloe Gin Germany"), there are any number of old cutlery warehouses packed with "new old stock" knives, or "old parts," just waiting to be discovered. And many of these knives and blades will have the tang stampings of older American knife companies. Imagine that! I am going to have to go over to Solingen one of these days. I wonder if there are any "old stock" Case pocket knives over there. And don't get me started on "sandbar stag." Please, don't. And how many times have you heard the expression that "that knife came out of the factory" when referring to an old knife. Um...yeah...I think that they ALL came "out of the factory" at some point.

OK gang, here is a little secret to make your "knife collector" lives easier. We have no doubt all been in a situation where we were at a knife or gun show and we want to alert one of our buddies to the fact that we think a knife on a dealer's table is a "phony" or a "counterfeit." Oftentimes this becomes an awkward situation as we want to point this out to our friend, yet it may be considered "bad form" to publicly use the terms "phony" or "counterfeit" out loud in front of the dealer. In addition to this being "bad form," the dealer usually has larger and sharper knives available within easy reach, if you get my drift.

So, in order to remain "incognito," use one of the following statements:

"Why, that knife looks to me like an *artificial leg joint.*" Or "That knife looks like a *cabinetmaker's success* to me.

OK, so what does this gibberish mean? Well, I prefer to think of it as "secret code," but here is the explanation:

Artificial = Faux

Leg Joint = Knee

Artificial Leg Joint = *Faux Knee*

"The cabinetmaker was successful in my kitchen; he made the counter fit."

Cabinetmaker's Success = *Counter Fit*

Get those? If not, ask your wife (if you are a man) or your children (if you are a woman). I know your next question. What, pray tell, is the difference between a "phony" knife and a "counterfeit" knife. Well, here is the difference as I see it: A "phony" is so bad that it won't fool anyone. A "counterfeit" at least attempts to look like the real thing.

CASE XX CUTLERY

*is nationally known for its high standard of
quality, and its original and practical designs*

———

The essential requisites in the manufacturing of High Grade Cutlery are:
KNOWLEDGE of what is necessary to produce it.
EXPERIENCE gained by the old methods, coupled with many of the scientific developments of the present era.

———

We now offer you a line that surpasses anything that we have been able to furnish you in the past.
Our entire line of Hunting Knives, Butcher, Slicing and Paring Knives, Pocket Knives and Razors are manufactured from our High Grade CHROME Vanadium steel in our own factories.
Our blades are all "double tested"—first after hardening and again after tempering—to insure uniform quality. This is why CASE CUTLERY is marked, "Tested XX".

The above text is an excerpt from the introduction to a 1930s-era product catalog published by W.R Case & Sons Cutlery Company. Today, as then, Case continues to research and improve the methods of cutlery manufacture so that Case pocket knife collectors and users can continue to have the finest available pocket knives made in the proud CASE tradition.

CASE POCKET KNIVES
THE MOST POPULAR BRAND AMONG KNIFE COLLECTORS

While pocket knives were manufactured in the United States as early as the mid-1800s, the idea of pocket knives as a collectible began in the post-WWII era of the 1950s. It was probable that the increase in personal wealth and leisure time in the more industrialized years after the war led to a rise in nostalgia for items associated with the Depression years and earlier.

Pocket knives are in many ways a "natural" collectible. The knife is said to be man's earliest and most basic tool. The pocket knife, particularly in the years prior to WWII, was a universal item treasured by men and women, boys and girls. In those days, virtually everyone either carried a pocket knife or had one or more readily available in a tool box or desk drawer. Pocket knives knew no social boundaries. Farmers, laborers, clerks, office workers, dock workers, fishermen, and outdoorsmen all carried and prized pocket knives as the most basic of working tools.

For a young person, the acquisition of the first pocket knife was an important rite of passage. A young boy's or girl's first knife might be an inexpensive new one or a hand me down. Pocket knives in those days were often kept and used until the blades were sharpened down to thin narrow spikes and the handles were worn smooth.

These well used but still serviceable pocket knives were often handed down to the next generation to be used again, and then often retired and put away as valued keepsakes—remembrances of a father or grandfather who may have carried and used the knife for 40 years or more. Cigar boxes or drawers filled with the well used and cared for pocket knives of previous generations were in essence the first knife collections.

The 1890s through the early 1940s can be viewed as the first "golden age" of pocket knife manufacturing in the United States. During that era, literally hundreds of cutlery companies produced pocket knives. Many of these companies were in existence for short periods before either failing or being purchased by new owners or absorbed by other cutlery manufacturers. Other cutlery firms prospered and produced millions of pocket knives that were distributed to every state of the union. The American cutlery industry battled imports, lived through good times and through periods of economic distress, and ultimately retooled to

The Case 62009 "Barlow" pattern was popular as an inexpensive working knife, especially during the pre-WWII years. These three 62009 patterns with the Case Tested stamping exhibit nice sawcut green bone handles. Closed length is 3-3/8". From top: 62009 with spear master blade, 62009 1/2 with clip master blade, and 62009 Sh with sheepfoot master blade. All have pen secondary blades and iron bolsters and liners.

provide millions more knives of all types for the United States government during World War II.

During these years, the American cutlery industry produced some of the finest pocket knives that have ever been manufactured. All cutlery factories of that time relied a great deal on highly skilled cutlers to perform many operations by hand in the manufacture of fine pocket knives, a tradition that continues today in the best knife factories.

Pocket knives manufactured in the early years of the cutlery industry in the United States in the mid- to late 1800s were often relatively simple in design, construction, and materials. Ebony wood and simple undyed cattle bone were often the handle materials of choice on the simple, sturdy, unadorned jack knife patterns of the day. There were few manufacturers of pocket knives in the United States in those days, as most pocket knives and other cutlery items were imported, usually from Sheffield, England.

American pocket knife manufacturers were fully capable of making elegant well-adorned pocket knives that would rival the best knives made in Sheffield. Indeed, the early American manufacturers often made up special displays of pocket knives with handles of tortoise and pearl and with elegant file work, for display at the industrial exhibitions of that era. But by and large, the majority of pocket knives that were widely sold by American manufacturers were simple sturdy one- and two-blade jack knives of various sizes. The "Russell Barlow," manufactured in great quantities by the John Russell Company of Turners Falls Massachusetts, is a classic example of the relatively simple American-made jack knives of the era.

The imposition of tariffs on imported cutlery in the late 1800s provided a significant boost to the then-fledgling domestic cutlery industry in the United States. Domestic production capacity for pocket knives increased with additional firms entering the business and setting up new factories or buying out existing cutleries. From the 1890s through World War I, American cutlery manufacturers expanded the range of pocket knife patterns produced. Pocket knife designs during this era expanded beyond the simple jack, pen, and cattle knife patterns to include more elegant and distinctive designs including the now classic "premium stockman" pattern that has since been widely produced in a variety of sizes and styles by virtually all American cutlery firms.

If the tariffs of the 1890s set the stage for the first "golden age" of American cutlery manufacturing, the end of WWI seemed to provide further impetus to the then-growing domestic cutlery industry. Giant industrial concerns like Remington and Winchester, both experienced in manufacturing and each facing the loss of military contracts, each decided to jump into the manufacture of cutlery for the civilian market, including pocket knives, in a big way.

Large hardware wholesalers grew in the post-WWI era, and typically these firms contracted with existing American cutlery factories to produce private branded lines of pocket knives and other cutlery. One large hardware wholesale house, E.C. Simmons, actually bought a large established cutlery company outright for the supply of its in-house KEEN KUTTER brand of pocket knives.

The era between the two world wars saw the blossoming of the domestic cutlery industry in the United States. Intense competition and a strong domestic market led to broad expansion of the pocket knife lines of each of the major American cutlery firms. Cutlery companies produced a dazzling array of pocket knife patterns, with a seemingly infinite number of variations in sizes, shapes, and blade combinations.

Handle material choices were also expanded during these years. In addition to the more traditional materials such as ebony and cocobolo woods, jigged and dyed bone, and mother of pearl, celluloid handle materials were introduced in a rainbow of colors and in a plethora of patterns. I have long believed that the sheer variety of pocket knife patterns, handle materials and companies/brand names in the business during these years laid the groundwork for the future collectibility of pocket knives.

This first golden age of pocket-knife manufacturing in America continued through the Depression years of the 1930s and early 1940s. While the Depression did claim a number of cutlery firms, others expanded and modernized production to remain competitive. World War II was the catalyst for further change and consolidation in the American cutlery industry, in particular for the cutlery manufacturers whose lines included pocket knives.

Whereas in the period between WWI and WWII there were over 30 major American cutlery firms (in addition to many smaller ones) that were active in the manufacture of pocket knives, by the end of WWII there were only ten major firms that produced quality pocket knives in the United States. When these ten firms retooled and geared up for production for the civilian market after the war, they faced both increased foreign competition and a vastly changed marketplace for cutlery; pocket knives in particular.

Gone were the days of a single cutlery manufacturer producing 600 or more different pocket knife patterns, as a number of the larger firms had done in the earlier years. Gone, too, were some of the traditional pocket knife handle materials that had been routinely used by these companies.

While most pocket knife manufacturers continued to use genuine bone as a handle material after the war, synthetic imitation bone handle materials were increasingly in use. The use of synthetic replacements for bone as a handle material began prior to and during WWII, due to material shortages and the difficulties involved in obtaining bone from overseas during these years. By about 1960, almost every pocket knife manufacturer in the United States had phased out genuine bone handles in favor of synthetics.

Likewise, other traditional handle materials including mother of pearl, colorful celluloid and wood were replaced with modern plastics by many cutlery manufacturers as they trimmed their product lines and cut costs in the face of changing market conditions. As compared to natural handle materials, the more modern plastics were less expensive to process since they could be molded to shape, and they required fewer steps in the manufacturing process. The synthetic materials were also more resistant to cracking and warping, with the result that pocket knives could be manufactured by more automated methods with less skilled hand labor involved.

Despite these changes in the cutlery industry, there was still a significant market for traditional pocket knives during the 1950s and 1960s. The market for pocket knives was largely intact in the rural areas of the South and West in particular, and in other areas where farming, hunting, fishing, and outdoor pursuits continued as part of the local culture.

During the mid- to late 1960s, the introduction and popularity of single-blade lockback folding knives with stainless steel blades began to diminish the market nationally for traditional pocket knives. However, in certain parts of the country, in particular the rural South and Midwest, pocket knives made in traditional patterns with carbon steel blades were still highly regarded among knife users.

It was in these areas of the United States in the late 1960s that organized pocket knife collecting as we know it today began. Guns and pocket knives had always been closely associated with each other and in those days, guns were sold not only in gun and sport shops, but in rural hardware stores and pawn shops. These businesses generally always had large displays of pocket and hunting knives as well, and gun shows and trade days were fertile ground for the trading and selling of pocket knives. Increasingly restrictive gun control laws enacted in the late 1960s caused many gun traders to focus their efforts more on pocket knives rather than guns. As a result of the increased interest in pocket knives, the first guide books and price guides devoted to collectible pocket knives were published in the late 1960s.

As pocket knife collecting took root in the South, Midwest, and other parts of the country, the pocket knives that garnered the most interest were made by one particular company, W.R. Case and Sons Cutlery Company

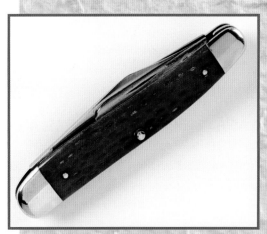

This Case XX 6380 whittler, front and back views, has blood red bone handles that are nicely pocket worn. Pocket wear seems to bring out the deep color of the bone handles.

of Bradford, Pennsylvania. Collectors typically shorten the name of the company to simply "Case." From the inception of pocket knife collecting in the post-WWII years through the present day, Case has been by far the most collected brand. The reasons for this are manifold, and the following represents my personal view as to why Case pocket knives are and have been *Number One* with knife collectors.

1. CASE POCKET KNIVES ARE, AND ALWAYS HAVE BEEN, QUALITY WORKING TOOLS

While Case has always produced well-finished pocket knives, beautiful to look at and with stunning natural handle materials, every one is first and foremost a practical working tool. Whether a Case pocket knife is the tool of choice for a hunter, fisherman, stockman, factory worker, or office worker, every pattern is designed and manufactured first and foremost to be used, and to be used hard. Case pocket knives have been well respected by generations of knife users, and are often handed down from one generation to the next. The quality and popularity of Case knives with users over many years helped lay the foundation for the company being known as the "king" of collectible pocket knives.

As this excerpt from the back cover of a 1974 Case factory catalog says:

The cost of cutlery is relative…relative to what the blade is expected to do; the amount of craftsmanship derived, quality desired in the end product and the time to accomplish it, but most of all the safety in performing the task. Any use of cutlery that ends with the user injured can be the most expensive knife ever purchased.

Our cutlery will not guarantee you against injury but because of its design, balance, quality, of material, and workmanship, it is a much safer tool whether one is using a CASE Pocket Knife, Hunting Knife, Household Knife, Scissor, or Shear.

2. CASE AS A COMPANY WAS, AND IS, AN ANACHRONISM

After World War II, while other cutlery companies tended to abandon the "old ways" of manufacturing cutlery, Case stuck with many of the traditional methods. While many companies went to synthetics, Case continued to use natural handle materials like genuine bone, genuine

stag, mother of pearl, and real wood. Some of the more complex pocket knife patterns were abandoned by other companies in an effort to simplify and cut costs, while Case continued to manufacture them. The continued use of natural handle materials, and the production of a broad product line with many patterns offered, meant that Case had to rely more on skilled hand labor than on automated machinery. The emphasis on skilled hand labor continues to this day in the Case factory.

Beginning in the late 1960s and continuing into the 1970s, the increase in demand for Case pocket knives by the knife collecting fraternity combined with the already significant demand among knife users to outstrip Case's production capacity. By the early 1970s, the word was that Case was only able to fill about half of its orders. Due to the many hand operations involved in production, it was very difficult for Case to ramp up production. Case explained this directly to its dealers in this note from President J. Russell Osborne excerpted from the 1968 Case factory catalog:

TO OUR CUSTOMERS:

In the face of greatly increased demand for our knives, CASE simply refuses to compromise its quality. We will continue to insist on the many hand operations required to produce quality knives. Perhaps we are a hundred years behind the times, but any other means of manufacture would not be CASE.

We do appreciate your indulgence and understanding if we cannot fill your order complete. You may rest assured that we are doing everything possible to speed up production without jeopardizing CASE quality. Thank you!

3. CASE HAS ALWAYS PROVIDED TOPNOTCH CUSTOMER SERVICE

During the years prior to WWII and the decades after the war, most cutlery manufacturers relied on jobbers or on wholesale hardware companies to distribute their products to individual retailers, usually small-town hardware stores, pawn shops, and gun shops. Many of the larger pocket knife manufacturers routinely sold a high percentage of their annual production through regional hardware wholesale companies.

During this era, Case relied on a factory-trained sales force of people who had a detailed knowledge of the Case product line. These sales people would call on individual retailers personally, assisting the dealers in maintaining the best assortment of Case pocket knives and other cutlery products. The cutlery display cases designed and provided by Case were always the finest in the industry.

The following is quoted from a W. R. Case & Sons Cutlery Company price list dated Jan. 1, 1934:

One of the market advantages of the permanent display is that it enables you to keep before your customers an attractive assortment. It enables you to make your purchases in such quantities from time to time upon the patterns that are your best sellers. Statistics of our business show where our customers have adhered to the permanent displays and checked their stock regularly it has enabled them to more than treble their turnover on cutlery.

Case's fine product displays have helped to increase the popularity of the brand over the years. The furniture grade display cabinets with the knives displayed precisely arrayed in an artistic fashion have always attracted attention in any store in which they are placed.

Case cutlery displays, both in the early years and in the modern era, have helped to fuel collector interest in the brand. Case traditionally wired each individual pocket knife to the display board that was mounted in the display cabinet. These knives would often remain in the display wired to the board long after tang stamps had been changed, so the display board knives were often collectible. Many Case pocket knife collectors used to explore old hardware stores in the search for older Case display boards, intact with the older pocket knives still wired in place.

While the cutlery industry in the United States has changed considerably even since the 1970s, Case has maintained a commitment to support knife collectors and users with arguably the finest customer service in the knife business. Case today produces a full-color product catalog every year that is provided to both dealers and consumers. Case maintains an informative Web site and a collectors club. Quarterly newsletters from the Case Collector's Club provide up-to-date information regarding new collectible Case pocket knives.

4. CASE HAS ALWAYS EMPHASIZED THE USE OF NATURAL HANDLE MATERIALS

While other cutlery companies switched to synthetics, Case continued to use a wide variety of natural handle materials. Natural handles on pocket knives are highly prized by collectors due to the inherent beauty of the materials themselves and to the fact that, literally, no two natural handles are alike.

In the decades after World War II, Case continued to use genuine bone as a standard pocket knife handle material, with mother of pearl used on a variety of smaller knife patterns. While Case has used synthetic handle materials as well, natural materials have always dominated the Case pocket knife line. Case is one of a very few cutlery manufacturers to make extensive use of Sambar stag as a handle material. Sambar stag is arguably the handle material most prized by knife collectors due to its beauty and relative scarcity.

In recent years, as Case has increasingly responded to the knife collecting community, the use of natural handle materials has expanded. Using sophisticated manufacturing methods, Case today uses a wide variety of natural handle materials. Some of the newer variations include laser-engraved bone, natural woods, natural minerals, various colors of genuine stag, and exotic mother of pearl. The crafting of pocket knife handles from these materials requires the significant use of skilled hand labor. With the hand operations involved in crafting Case pocket knives using these beautiful natural materials, the Case factory today resembles a custom

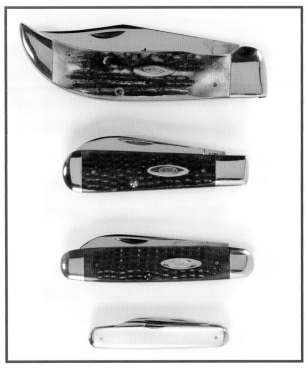

Examples of some Case natural handle materials, from top: Case XX USA 5172 with exceptional burnt stag handles, Case Tested 6299 jack knife with stunning green bone handles, Case XX 6294 cigar jack with light red bone handles, and 7 dot, 1973, 8364 Scis SS with fiery genuine pearl handles.

knife shop more than it does a cutlery factory.

In summary, Case has always relied on the quality of the company's products to in effect be the primary advertising medium, as shown in the following letter to Russ Case from a Case dealer in Illinois, published in a 1948 employee newsletter:

Dear Mr. Case:

I know that you are a busy man, but even so here is a little story that no doubt will be of interest to you.

I have been away from the store for the past seven weeks, undergoing a major operation. The store has been operating under the guidance of my son, Jack, the one to whom you sent the fine trench knife when he was shipped abroad, and another young chap just breaking into the hardware business.

Well, here's the story: Last Saturday Jack tells me that a stranger, well-dressed, and of very business-like appearance popped into the store and asked Don, our assistant, to show him a kitchen knife. This he proceeded to do but the customer became abusive and hard to deal with and kept getting louder and more unreasonable as the prospective sale got underway. Jack was busy at the rear of the store with his own customer, but was soon free and at once to came up to see what the fuss was over. It became apparent at once that the customer putting on the blustery front knew not too much about cutlery, testing the steel in the blades by blowing on them and several old fogy stunts. Said he had never owned but one good knife in his life. "Well," Jack said, "just what kind of knife was that?" "Have it right here in my pocket." Whereupon he threw it out on the counter, a two bladed knife of trim appearance, but well worn. Upon opening the blade the name CASE showed very plainly on the heel of the blade. The boys showed him this and compared it with the name on the slicing knives, etc. Well, that settled the argument and the customer picked out a large steak knife, one of those hollow ground slicing knives, a kitchen knife and then picked out a nice pocket knife for himself. Not satisfied with these purchases he turned around to a display table and picked out several pieces of expensive "Club Aluminum Ware" to take along. The man was on his way to California, therefore, the reason he would not listen to "refund of his money" when the argument started.

Now this is a true story from one of your old dealers. With the best regards to yourself and Mrs. Case, we are,

Very truly yours,
CUSTER & ALLEN
(signed) H.C. Allen

The "hallmark" of the Case cutlery brand is the famous TESTED XX trademark, also referred to simply as XX. In the early years of the cutlery industry, many cutlery manufacturers used simple symbols or letters as trademarks. In the 18th and 19th centuries, the mediums available for communication were limited, and often the early English cutlery manufacturers sold their wares world wide. In order to effectively communicate across language barriers and create brand awareness, cutlery firms often used one or several letters or symbols to represent the brand. Examples include the I*XL trademark used by Wostenholm, the "Star and Cross" used by Rodgers, and the "Twin Logo" used by Solingen-based Henckels.

For W.R Case & Sons, the symbol XX has become famous both with collectors and users. Many collectors are familiar with the introduction of the famous XX and TESTED XX brands by Case Brothers Cutlery Company. W.R. Case & Sons acquired these trademarks from Case Brothers in 1914.

My understanding of the origin of the TESTED XX trademark is as follows: In those days, heat treating of knife blades was an inexact science. Then, as now, each blade requires two heat-treating steps. The first step is hardening, where the blade is heated up and then quenched or rapidly cooled down. This increases the hardness of the steel but leaves the blade in a brittle state. After that, tempering is done where the blade is heated up again and cooled slowly, to decrease the brittleness of the blade.

Each step in those days was controlled largely by the experience of the factory worker and judgment based on the color of the heated blade played an important role in the process. Case Brothers indicated that in its factory, each knife blade was individually tested twice, once after hardening and once again after tempering. Blades at that time were batch heat treated in pans. When all of the blades in a given pan had been tested, an "X" was inscribed on the end of the pan with a grease pencil. The blades went on to be tempered and again each individual blade was tested. After each blade had been tested again and returned to the pan, a second "X" was inscribed on the pan to indicate that those blades were then ready to be ground and polished and assembled into completed knives.

While the "X" marks were actually made on the blade pans and not the blades themselves, Case Brothers adopted the TESTED XX trademark, which was stamped into the steel of each blade prior to the start of the heat treating process. The TESTED XX trademark symbolized the quality of the brand.

After W.R. Case & Sons acquired the TESTED XX trademark from the Case Brothers firm, the brand achieved even greater recognition all over the United States and today the XX trademark continues as a symbol of Case quality.

The following is excerpted from a W. R. Case & Sons Cutlery Company price list dated Jan. 1, 1934:

Case Cutlery is sold to the trade at a fair margin above the cost of production. We have in the past and shall continue in the future to maintain the highest standard of quality, and all goods bearing our name are made from the best materials obtainable. Our steel is made to our own analysis, said analysis having been developed by years of experience.

The uniform quality found in our products is due to the use of our high grade Chrome Vanadium Steel. Our heat treating process is the most modern known to science. In order to have a uniform quality it is necessary to have a uniform hardness. Blades cannot have a uniform temper that do not have a uniform hardness before they are tempered. Tempering is a drawing back process. After our blades are hardened they are put under a Rockwell testing machine to determine the correctness of the hardening. After the temper is drawn they are again put under a Rockwell testing machine to prove the correctness of the temper. This is why Case Cutlery is marked "Tested XX". These tests are gone through as a second check up to prevent any possible errors in the process of hardening and tempering. For that reason we are doubly sure that each and every article bearing our name is of uniform quality.

W.R. Case & Sons Cutlery Company has always had to zealously guard the Case brand name and the famous XX and TESTED XX trademarks from unscrupulous competitors who would try to profit from the time honored name of CASE on cutlery.

The following letter, found in the Case archives, is a bit of a mystery. I have never seen any other documentation regarding the resurrected "Case Brothers" firm that is mentioned in the letter, signed by John O'Kain.

MEMORANDUM

From: W.R. CASE & SONS CUTLERY COMPANY - Bradford, Pennsylvania
To: All Salesmen
Subject: "Case Brothers" Cutlery
Date: November 15, 1948

As you probably know, a new company calling themselves "Case Brothers" is now manufacturing cutlery direct to the retail trade.

For your confidential information we have discussed this matter with the Federal Trade Commission and they will m[ake] a thorough investigation of this steal of the Case name providing we can furnish them with evidence that one or more ultimate users have purchased a knife or knives under this brand in the belief that they were purchasing W.R. Case & Sons Cutlery.

If this evidence cannot be obtained they will probably accept evidence that some retail dealer has purchased this brand of cutlery under the same misapprehension.

We are watching for any of this to appear locally to try to get such evidence. In the meantime, if you are able to locate any of this on the market and trace a sale through a retail store to an ultimate customer please do so at your earliest convenience. If you are unable to trace such a sale please try and find some retailer who is willing to say that he bought this cutlery under such a misapprehension.

We feel that this is really urgent since allowing one firm to capitalize on the Case name will be an open invitation for others to do the same thing.

Yours very truly,
W.R. Case & Sons Cutlery Company
John O'Kain, President

CASE POCKET KNIFE LORE

This section contains a potpourri of information on various aspects of Case pocket knives, from the materials and construction methods used to the quirks of the pattern numbering system and the origin of many of the pattern names.

In putting this section together, I have tried to include material that will provide answers to many of the questions commonly asked by Case collectors. In the process, I believe I have also included much material that will be of interest to all knife collectors, knife users, and others interest in learning about the Case brand.

To the right is the text from an older Case pocket knife wrapping paper that includes care instructions. Case pocket knives were traditionally shipped in bulk boxes, with six individually wrapped knives per box. In later years (circa 1985), Case went to individual boxes for all pocket knife patterns. Today each knife is wrapped in a blank wrapper and packed in an individual box with a separate "Use and Care" pamphlet.

PROPER CARE OF YOUR POCKET KNIFE

Case Pocket Knives are precision-made and hand-crafted by American workmen from the finest American steel – none better the world over! We take pride in producing a knife which will hold a keen, lasting edge that will give perfect satisfaction if cared for properly.

OIL JOINTS – From time to time the joints or working parts should have a drop or two of light machine oil. This will promote smooth operation, prevent rust and wear, wash out dirt particles, and insure longer satisfactory service.

HOW TO SHARPEN – Hold blade at an angle of 10 to 15 degrees on stone. DO NOT LAY BLADE FLAT WHEN SHARPENING. Draw cutting edge against stone from heel to point (as tho' to cut a thin slice of stone), alternating first on one side of blade then the other. Use good oil stone. DO NOT USE A COARSE EMORY WHEEL.

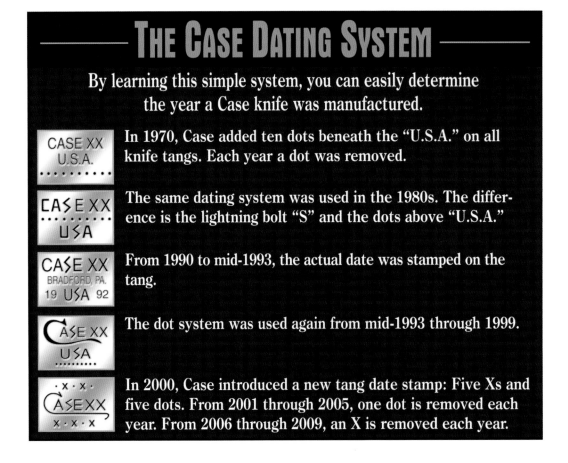

THE CASE DATING SYSTEM

By learning this simple system, you can easily determine the year a Case knife was manufactured.

In 1970, Case added ten dots beneath the "U.S.A." on all knife tangs. Each year a dot was removed.

The same dating system was used in the 1980s. The difference is the lightning bolt "S" and the dots above "U.S.A."

From 1990 to mid-1993, the actual date was stamped on the tang.

The dot system was used again from mid-1993 through 1999.

In 2000, Case introduced a new tang date stamp: Five Xs and five dots. From 2001 through 2005, one dot is removed each year. From 2006 through 2009, an X is removed each year.

CASE POCKET KNIFE TANG STAMPING AND PATTERN NUMBERS

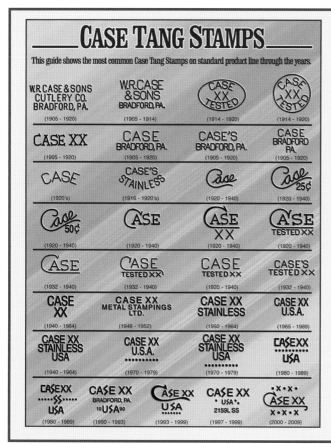

This chart illustrates the more recent Case tang stampings used from 1970 to the present, enabling the determination of the exact year that a blade was stamped.

The charts to the left and on P. 16 outline the tang stampings used by W.R. Case & Sons Cutlery Company over the years. The Case pocket knife numbering system is also explained. The drawings and charts were graciously provided by W.R. Case & Sons Cutlery Company for use in the book.

TANG STAMPS

The chart at left provides an illustration of each of the older Case pocket knife tang stampings with the approximate years of use shown for each stamping. The photos below and on P. 18 also show various tang stampings

HOW TO IDENTIFY A CASE POCKET KNIFE

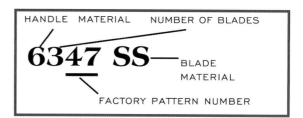

This is an illustration of the Case pocket knife pattern number as it will be found on the tang of a Case pocket knife blade. In this example, 6347 SS is a #47 factory pattern knife with a jigged bone handle, three blades and a surgical steel blade. Had the blade been made of chrome vanadium, the pattern number would have been 6347 CV.

W.R. Case & Sons tang stamping on an 83109 pearl "three-backspring whittler."

Case Tested tang stamping – this variation is the "long tail C" often used on larger knives.

In 1977 and 1978, some tang stampings had the dots spaced widely apart. This example is on a 1978 6254 SSP Trapper.

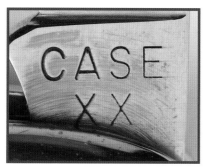

Case XX stamping variation – large tang stamp on a 6318 stock knife.

Case XX stamping variation – small tang stamp on a 6318 stock knife.

Tang stamping on a W.R. Case & Sons 5205 RAZ jack pattern.

Case XX tang stamping.

Case Bradford tang stamping on a 6345 cattle knife pattern.

Unusual variation of a Case Tested tang stamping, often used on smaller knives.

Case XX USA tang stamping variations. The smaller tang stamping, left, and large tang stamping, right. Both are from 3220 Peanut patterns.

Case 9 dot 1981 tang stamping; this is the "lightning S" tang stamp that was used from 1980 to 1989.

Case 10 dot 1980 tang stamping from a stainless steel knife. The "lightning S" tang stamp was used from 1980 to 1989.

Case 2000-2010 tang stamping with dots and Xs.

SHARPENING UP ON CASE BLADE STEELS

From the early days of pocket knife manufacturing into the 1970s, when a person bought a pocket knife, it was virtually a guarantee that the knife would have *carbon steel* blades. Yes, stainless steel was offered as a blade steel on pocket knives by Case (and other) manufacturers as early as the 1920s, but the early stainless steels were not well accepted by knife users in those days. The science for heat treating and manufacturing blades of stainless steel at that time was not well developed and the early pocket knives with stainless steel blades developed a reputation as poor performers in terms of edge holding. Stainless steel was also used as a backspring material on these stainless bladed pocket knives and the stainless backsprings had quite a tendency to break.

Case did offer pocket knives with stainless steel blades during the 1920s and into the Case Tested era. There are a few patterns that will be observed in stainless from these years but in general the use of stainless was limited to the "Fisherman's" pattern pocket knives and some small pen knife patterns, which were often made with fancy celluloid handles. Many of the Tested era stainless pocket knives were made with the regular CASE TESTED "long tail C" tang stamping while others had the tang stamping CASE'S STAINLESS. I have also observed some examples of pen knives with the CASE BRADFORD tang stamp on one blade, CASE'S STAINLESS on the other, and an oval shield stamped with the word STAINLESS.

THE "CARBON VS. STAINLESS" DEBATE

After WWII and into the 1960s, stainless steel blades improved significantly; however, the knife using public was wary and the words "stainless steel" were anathema to the average knife user. Stainless steel knives continued to maintain a reputation for poor edge holding due to past problems. Beginning in the Case Tested era (and possibly earlier) Case's "carbon steel" pocket knives have been made with a carbon steel variation known as *chrome vanadium.* Pocket knives with chrome vanadium blades dominated the Case pocket knife line into the 1960s and 1970s.

While stainless steel blades have over the years since become the "norm" in the cutlery industry, a lively debate continues to this day among some knife users as to the merits of "carbon steel" versus "stainless steel." This debate started a long time ago, as evidenced by the following excerpt from a Case factory price list dated Jan. 1, 1934:

There are two distinct classes of Stainless Steel, one known as low grade stainless with a carbon content of around twenty to thirty-five point. This is commonly known and is sold by the manufacturers of stainless steel as Stainless Iron. The majority of so called stainless steel on the market is this class of stainless and is not of the high grade stainless which is about ninety point carbon. The high grade stainless found in our line is the best that we can procure and will hold a very satisfactory cutting edge, but not as good a cutting edge as found in our high grade Chrome Vanadium Steel.

The word "Stainless" has been very much abused for the reason that the low grade stainless as well as the high grade stainless can both legally be stamped Stainless Steel. For your information, high grade stainless steel has a tendency towards brittleness while the lower grades are all soft.

An article of cutlery in the Butcher and Slicer lines in order to hold a good edge should have a hardening point of not less than fifty-five point Rockwell C test. A Pocket Knife should have a hardening point of not less than fifty-eight point Rockwell C test. A Razor should have a hardening test of not less than sixty-two point. The hardest hardening point obtainable in the so called low grade stainless is forty-five point hardness. Forty point hardness is dead soft.

CASE STAINLESS STEEL POCKET KNIVES POST WWII

In the years after WWII and into the 1950s, Case offered a limited number of pocket knife patterns in stainless steel. Unlike some other cutlery companies, Case has always used stainless steel backsprings on knives that were made with stainless steel blades. In the mid-1950s, Case offered 140 pocket knife patterns, of which 23 were made in stainless steel. Of these 23, the majority (17) were small pen knife and "lobster" patterns. The balance were the 4100 and 6296 X "melon tester" patterns, the 32095 "Fisherman," the Fly Fisherman, and the

5347 Sh Sp SS and 6347 Sh Sp SS "stockman" pattern knives. These knife patterns were all made with mirror polished stainless steel blades and springs.

The older-style mirror polished stainless steel blades appeared identical to the chrome vanadium blades, other than the tang stamping and pattern number. From left: polished stainless steel main clip blade from a Case XX USA-stamped 5347 Sh Sp SS, and polished chrome vanadium main clip blade from a Case XX USA-stamped 5347 Sh Sp.

The six patterns included in the original SSP group of knives, top row, from left: 06263 SSP (3-1/8") and 6318 Sh Sp SSP (3-1/2"); middle row, from left: 6347 Sh Sp SSP (3-7/8") and 61048 SSP (4-1/8"); bottom row, from left: 62048 SSP (4-1/8") and 6254 SSP (4-1/8").

THE NEW SSP LINE – MADE LIKE THE ASTRONAUT'S KNIFE

Stainless steel pocket knife offerings by Case continued at this general level until 1965, when a new line of pocket knives and hunting knives with stainless steel blades was introduced. These knives were a bit different as compared to previous offerings, in that the blades and springs had a glazed finish and the blades were final sharpened with what Case referred to as its new *Polished Edge* treatment. The *Polished Edge* was said to be a final sharpening process where the final honed cutting edge was thinned using a pumice-coated buffing wheel. The *Polished Edge* treatment was designed to produce a much finer sharp edge as compared to the conventional honed blade edges used on most Case pocket knives.

The formulation of stainless steel used in the new SSP line was not revealed by Case. However, Case product information indicated that the knives in the new *Polished Edge* line were made with the same steel and the same edge treatment as the famous Case Astronaut's Knife that was made for inclusion in space capsule survival kits in the 1960s.

The six pocket knife patterns included in this new series included the 06263 SSP, 61048 SSP, 62048 Sp SSP, 6318 Sh Sp SSP, 6347 Sh Sp SSP, and 6254 SSP. Each knife had the words TESTED XX RAZOR EDGE etched lengthwise across the master blade. There were some earlier examples of these knives made with mirror polished blades and with the blade etching TESTED XX STAINLESS; however, the "standard" production version ended up being as described above. Later, in the early 1970s, the 06263 F SSP was added to this line. A limited number of pattern 5347 Sh Sp SSP were made with nine dots (1971). Both of these later knives also had the TESTED XX RAZOR EDGE blade etch. The 6254 SSP introduced in 1965 represented Case's first ever production of the 54 "Trapper" pattern in stainless steel.

One interesting tidbit about Case's use of stainless steel in those days relates to the retail prices of the stainless steel patterns. Today, Case pocket knife collectors and users are used to the idea that a particular pattern with stainless steel blades will have the same retail price as the identical pattern made in chrome vanadium. This was not always true. In the 1970s, for any Case pocket knife pat-

Glazed finish stainless steel blade with etching, "TESTED XX RAZOR EDGE," from a 9 dot 1971 5347 Sh Sp SSP. This etching was used on the main blade of each knife in the SSP series.

tern that was offered in both blade steel choices, the stainless steel version would have a significantly higher retail price. For example, in 1974 the 6254 (chrome vanadium) had a retail price of $11.50, while the 6254 SSP had a retail price of $16.50. Similar price differentials applied to other patterns that were offered in both steels.

MORE OFFERINGS IN STAINLESS STEEL

The "SSP" knives were well received and as Case progressed into the 1970s, more patterns in stainless steel were introduced. While the older stainless pocket knife patterns that remained in the line from the early 1960s were still made with mirror finished stainless blades, all of the new stainless pocket knives introduced in the 1970s were made with glazed blades and most were made with polished edges. Some of these new introductions including the Shark Tooth, Mako, and Hammerhead, had special blade etchings. Others, like the 051 pattern lockbacks, had plain glazed blades with no etching. Even though most of these new stainless knives had polished blade edges with the "SSP" pattern number suffix, the use of the TESTED XX RAZOR EDGE blade etch was limited to the original patterns in the "SSP" line.

By 1978, after the introduction of the Mako and the Hammerhead, there were 97 patterns in the Case standard product pocket knife line, of which 21 were made in stainless steel. Case also made all annual stag sets and almost all other limited edition knives in stainless during these years. The transition of the Case pocket knife line to stainless steel accelerated from 1981 to 1985. During this period, a number of Case's older patterns in chrome vanadium were discontinued and all new patterns introduced were in stainless. In 1981, many of Case's smaller pocket knife patterns that had been in production in chrome vanadium were changed over to production in stainless steel, as mentioned in this excerpt from the *Case Collector's Club*

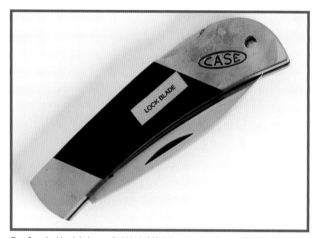

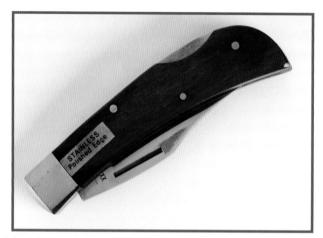

Two Case lockback knives, a P10051 L SSP, left, and a P1051 1/2 L SSP. The stickers on the knives indicate that both knives were mounted on Case display boards. At that time, the majority of Case pocket knives had chrome vanadium blades, so stainless-bladed knives had stickers affixed to identify that they were stainless steel.

Newsletter from June 1981:

Several patterns of pocket knives that now have Chrome Vanadium blades will be changed to Tru-Sharp™ Surgical Steel. The patterns that will be changed are: SR 62027, 63027, 63033, A62033, 92033, A6208, A62009 1/2, A6235 1/2, A62042, 92042, 92042R, SR6220, SR6225 1/2, SR6347 1/2, SR6244, 6344, 22087, 62087, 23087, 03244, and 03244R. The transition will be gradual and may not be seen on the market for a few months.

While 21 patterns are noted in the above text, I believe that the SR62027 and 63027 patterns were discontinued prior to the changeover and that the 03244 and the 03244 R were never actually changed over and remained in production in chrome vanadium. When the above knives were changed over to stainless, they were made with glazed stainless blades with conventional honed edges and with the "SS" suffix after the pattern number.

The pattern number designations on Case stainless steel pocket knives made during the late 1970s and into the 1990s tend to be a bit confusing. Some patterns were made with the "SSP" pattern number suffix but had conventional honed edges. Some patterns made with the "SS" suffix were made with glazed blades while others had polished blades. On the SSP knives, the new introductions did not have the TESTED XX RAZOR EDGE blade etch, while the six original patterns continued to have the etch. By 1991, use of the TESTED XX RAZOR EDGE blade etch had been eliminated while the "SSP" suffix continued in use for several years on some patterns before all were changed over to "SS." While glazed stainless blades were still standard on

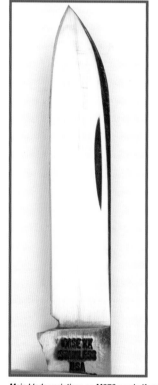

Main blade variations on M279 pen knife patterns, from left: older-style polished blade and glazed finish blade.

some patterns, both glazed and mirror polished stainless knives then had the "SS" suffix.

Beginning in 1997, the glazed finish was dropped in favor of a mirror polished finish on all "standard product" pocket knives that were made with natural handle materials. This is a standard that continues to the present day. Glazed finish stainless blades are still used but only on the "Working Knives" series with synthetic handles and on some lockback patterns.

In 1981, Case changed many patterns from chrome vanadium blade steel to stainless steel. The Appaloosa and Satin Rose patterns were part of this change, and CASE oval shields were added to the smooth bone knives at the same time. Top row from left: A6235 1/2 and A62009 1/2 in chrome vanadium. Bottom row, from left: A6235 1/2 SS and A62009 1/2 SS in stainless steel. Closed length is 3-3/8" on all knives.

In recent years, Case has differentiated between stainless steel and chrome vanadium by variations in the pattern number and the tang stamping. The tang stamping on the left is on a 6207 Sp CV made in 1996; note the regular rounded "S" in the word CASE. The tang stamping on the right is on a 6207 Sp SS made in 1999; note the "lightning S" in the word CASE.

CHROME VANADIUM –
THE DECLINE AND REEMERGENCE

As the number of patterns offered in stainless steel increased, the pattern selection in chrome vanadium decreased. The low point for the chrome vanadium offerings in the Case pocket knife line was in 1991, when only 13 patterns were offered (nine in bone, three in yellow, and one in delrin). During the 1990s and after 2000, Case steadily increased the number of patterns offered in chrome vanadium blade steel, with new patterns offered in various handle materials. Traditionally, Case Chrome vanadium pocket knives bore no special markings designating the steel used, since chrome vanadium had been the norm from the early days of Case. Beginning in 1997, Case added the pattern number suffix "CV" to all Case pocket knives made with chrome vanadium blade steel.

There is a myth regarding Case's chrome vanadium steel that the pocket knife blades are chrome plated. This is not true; chromium is an element of the steel itself but the blades are not chrome plated. The high polish on the finished blades results from Case's final grinding and polishing steps. It is true that beginning in the 1930s Case manufactured household knives and hunting knives with blades of chrome-plated chrome vanadium steel. However, to the best of my knowledge, no Case pocket knifes have ever been made with chrome plated blades. Evidently pocket knife users expected a patina to develop on the blades while household knife and hunting knife users did not. Case dropped the use of chrome plating on household knives in the mid-1960s in favor of polished stainless steel blades. The same was done with the hunting knife line by 1983.

THE MODERN ERA –
SOME OTHER CASE BLADE STEELS

Beginning in the late 1980s, Case began to use some different blade steels on pocket knives that were made in limited production runs; 1989 saw the first use of Damascus steel blades and various types of Damascus have been used in limited quantities since that time. In the 1990s and after 2000, some new stainless steels were also introduced, including ATS-34 and 154 CM. Even today with the availability of these new "exotic" blade steels, Case's "old fashioned" chrome vanadium steel has remained popular with knife users. Some enjoy the ease of sharpening and the fact that the steel takes on a lovely "patina" with use, just like pocket knives did in the "old days."

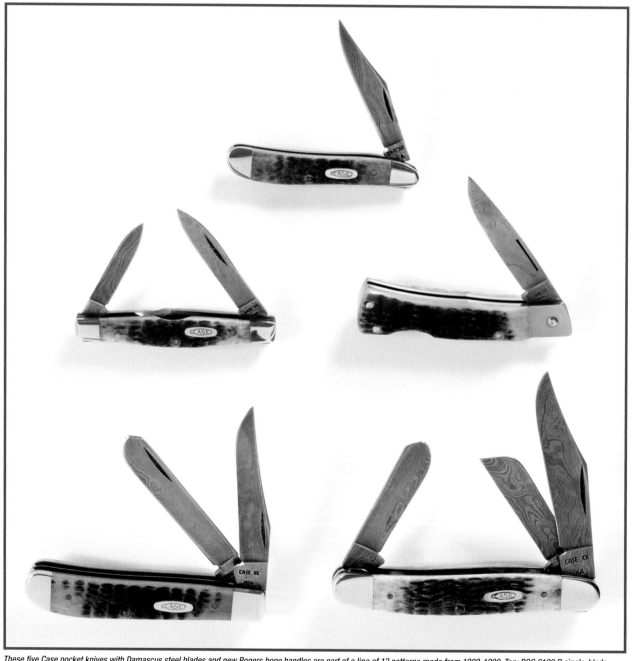

These five Case pocket knives with Damascus steel blades and new Rogers bone handles are part of a line of 12 patterns made from 1989-1990. Top: ROG 6120 D single-blade Peanut; middle: ROG 62042 D pen knife, and ROG 61059 D lockback; bottom: ROG 6207 Sp D Mini Trapper and ROG 6347 Sh Sp D stock knife.

CASE POCKET KNIFE SHIELDS – EMBLEMATIC OF THE BRAND

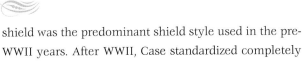

One of the important long-standing traditional features on Case pocket knives is the emblem or *shield* found on the front handle. While some basic jack patterns and some smooth handle knives have been made without shields, the majority of Case pocket knives observed in the traditional patterns will have the classic oval CASE shield installed in the handle.

Case's standard use of the CASE shield across its pocket knife line represented an innovation when it was implemented beginning in the 1920s or earlier. It may come as a surprise to some collectors to know that prior to WWII, Case was virtually the only American pocket knife manufacturer to effectively use the shields on pocket knives as a means to display the brand name. Most manufacturers chose to install a blank shield and some manufacturers would also etch the mark side of the master blade with the company name or trademark. Case and Union Cutlery/Kabar were the only two major cutlery firms during this era that made widespread use of the shield to display the brand name. Robeson Cutlery Company also effectively used "brand" shields on its Pocketeze and Mastercraft lines, though these lines were relatively limited in scope.

I believe that putting the brand name on the shield was a stroke of marketing genius. The blade etch on a pocket knife would look nice while the knife was in a showcase in a store, but after some use and patina, the etch would disappear. Having the brand name on the shield virtually guaranteed that a lot of people, including the owner of the knife and those in close proximity, would constantly be exposed to the Case brand name. Having the brand name on the tang of a pocket knife's blades is of course a good idea, but the shield is a much more visible location when the knife is in use. Since there is a cost involved in the installation of a shield whether the shield is blank or branded, the use of a branded shield is in effect a form of free advertising. More manufacturers eventually got on the bandwagon and in the post WWII years, the use of "brand name" pocket knife shields on American made pocket knives became more widespread.

THE "CASE OVAL" SHIELD – A CLASSIC

Case used a number of different shields during the Case Tested era and in earlier years, but the classic "oval" shield was the predominant shield style used in the pre-WWII years. After WWII, Case standardized completely on the oval shield for many years into the 1970s. There were several key variations of the oval shield used over the years.

CASE TESTED ERA – "CLOSED C" SHIELD

During the Case Tested era and on earlier knives, an oval shield that Case collectors refer to as the "closed C" shield was used. The "C" in the word CASE will be formed in a circular shape with the two end points drawing close together. This shield will also be found on some early CASE XX-stamped knives.

Case Tested-era Case oval shield, closed "C."

CASE XX ERA – "TALL S" SHIELD

The Case XX era saw the introduction of a Case oval shield with two differences. The "C" is no longer "closed" as the points are spread out, each at an angle of about 45 degrees. This is often called the "open C" shield, but the "S" is also taller than the later "open C" shield introduced during the mid-1960s. Many knives with the CASE TESTED tang stamping will also be found with this "open C" shield. In my observation, many CASE TESTED-stamped knives with rough black handles will have the "open C" shield; however, others will also be observed.

Case XX-era Case oval shield, open "C" and tall "S."

CASE XX USA ERA

On these shields the "C" will still be "open" and the "S" will be flatter at the top as compared to the "tall S" shields of the XX era. Again, the transition must have taken some years as both the "tall S" and the "flat S" shields will be found on CASE XX and CASE XX USA stamped knives. Use of the "flat S" design continued into the 1970s.

Case XX USA-era Case oval shield, open "C" and flat top "S."

1974 – THE "COMPOSITION" SHIELD

In the early 1970s two things happened at Case: 1, the use of delrin handles as a substitute for bone handles was on the increase; 2, Case began to notice and respond to the growing community of Case pocket knife collectors. Many new collectors at the time were confused about the appearance of bone handles as compared to handles made of delrin, and Case wanted to emphasize their use of bone and stag handles.

So, beginning in 1974, a change was made that affected all Case pocket knives made with handle materials other than stag and bone. On all knives with walnut, black, yellow, and white composition, jigged brown

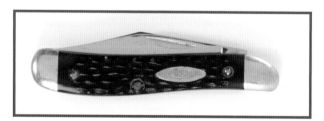

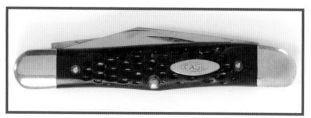

Case 1970s delrin-handled knives with the "conventional" shield, produced prior to the changeover to the "composition" shields. From top: 6 dot 1974 6220 Peanut, 2-2/3"; and 7 dot 1973 6208 "half whittler," 3-1/4".

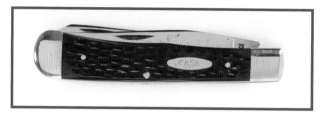

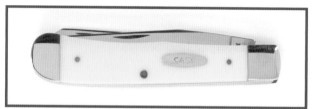

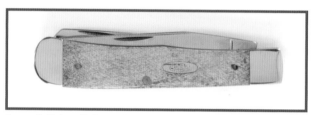

Case pocket knives with "composition" shields, introduced 1974. From top: 6254 Trapper 6 dot, 1974, delrin handles; 3254 Trapper 5 dot, 1985, yellow handles; 7254 SS Trapper 5 dot, curly maple, 1985. Closed length 4-1/8".

Pakkawood, and jigged brown delrin handles, Case went to a shield that had a slightly different appearance. Where the classic Case oval shield had an oval around the word CASE, on the new "composition" shield the oval was eliminated. A few examples of the delrin/wood/composition-handled knives made in 1974 will be found with the "regular" shield since 1974 was the "transition" year.

"Composition" Case oval shield, without the oval around CASE.

During the early years of using the new "composition" shields, the shields that were installed on the composition- and wood-handled knives were in actuality the "normal" shields (with the oval) but then on these knives the oval was removed from each knife as the assembled knife went through the final hafting process, leaving the word CASE intact. In later years, I believe that the "composition" shields were stamped out without the oval.

SHIELD CHANGES IN THE 1980S

During the later 1970s and into the 1980s, Case continued the use of the traditional oval shield in both the "normal" and the "composition" varieties. As will be discussed later in this section, in the late 1970s, Case ended the use of pinned-on shields and all shields were glued. In the mid-1980s, beginning in 1985, Case dropped the number of different sizes of oval shields that were used. It appears that for a time, only one size of shield was made and used on all patterns from the small pen knives up to the folding hunter patterns. These smaller-size shields looked a bit unusual when installed on the larger pocket knife patterns.

Note the extra small CASE oval shield on this 1986 6375 large stock knife.

Then in 1987, Case made a radical change to the new "raised letter" shield, which had the "long tail C" Case logo. The new "raised letter" shields continued to be glued on and the same style shield was used across the entire Case pocket knife line. The use of the "composition" shields ended and all knives with bone, stag, wood, delrin, and composition handles were made with the same style "raised letter" shield. One exception to this was that the three "outsourced" patterns – the 61011, 62031 L R, and 640045 R – all continued to be made with the older style oval "composition" shields.

"Raised Letter" shield used from 1987 through mid-1989.

Appearance wise, the "raised letter" shields were a major departure from tradition. I am not certain of this, but I believe that the first "raised letter" shields used may have actually been made of plastic with a chrome color. Later ones were made of metal. The new shields were used through 1987 and 1988 and into 1989. At that time, apparently due to requests received from Case collectors and dealers, the change was made back to the older style metal oval shields. Again, though, there were no special "composition" shields used this time around. All knives across the product line would have the same shield with the oval around the word CASE (again with the three exceptions as noted above, which continued to be made with the older style oval "composition" shields).

THE LATE 1990S

In 1996, Case introduced a new oval-shaped shield with the CASE XX logo stamped as the standard shield to be used on all pocket knives made with natural handle materials. In 2000, this style was dropped and a new oval shield with a Case "long tail C" logo was introduced. During these years and to the present day, the use of the older style traditional oval shield has continued on all patterns with smooth composition, jigged brown delrin, and jigged brown Pakkawood handles.

CASE XX oval shield, late 1990s era.

PINNED SHIELDS VS. GLUED

Traditionally, each Case oval shield was installed and held in place by being pinned to the liner of the knife upon which it was installed. The oval shields were made in an elongated shape with space for the pin holes at each end. After the shield was installed into the handle recess and the nickel silver shield pins were installed, the pins were peened over. The rough ends were removed and the shield was polished during the final hafting and buffing, so that the shield pin material would blend perfectly with the flat shield. Sometimes these shield pins will begin to "show" after the knife has been carried. On stag-handled knives, the shield pins are often more readily visible, even on mint knives. This may be due to the thickness of the stag handles and the potential for expansion and contraction of the handle due to temperature variations. Shield pins on older Case pocket knives are almost always visible inside of the knife, if you examine the interior of the liner carefully under strong light.

For many years, Case used pinned shields on all pocket knives including those with bone, stag, wood, and smooth composition handles. When delrin handles were introduced (both the smooth yellow and black varieties and jigged brown delrin), Case began installing the shields on these knives by "melting" the shield into the plastic of the front handle. Of course, these shields were made without holes for the pins, since pins were not used. The shields when melted in were held in place by the tight seal formed as the plastic cooled.

A 1970s-era shield (bone handle) from a 1978 6383 whittler (pinned shield).

Case oval shield from 1995. Note that since the shields are no longer pinned, the shield is designed differently with less space at each end of the oval.

Beginning in the late 1970s, Case began to discontinue the use of pinned shields. The new process for bone, stag, and wood-handled knives was to use an epoxy glue to hold the shields in place without the use of pins. I have not been able to determine the exact time that this change was made, but evidently it was phased in over time. I recently examined some Case stag-handled pocket knives from the 1978 "Red Scroll" set. About half of them were observed to have glued-on shields, while the balance had pinned shields. I have observed examples of Case bone-handled knives from 1978 and 1979 with pinned shields and others from the same years with pinned shields. I do believe that by 1980 the pinning of shields was discontinued completely and all shields were glued on.

KNIVES MADE WITHOUT SHIELDS

While a few Case pocket knife patterns had always been made without shields (for example, the 6202 1/2), from the Case Tested and Case XX eras, some examples of patterns that were normally made with shields will be found that were made without the shield. These knives may have been made during WWII or during the years preceding or immediately following the war. During those years, materials were often scarce, and the shield, being an embellishment, could be left off. It is most common to find bone and rough black patterns without shields, but occasionally stag-handled knives will also be found from this era that do not have the CASE shield. Many smooth composition-handled knife patterns in the Case line during this era were routinely made both with and without shields. The 6235 and 6235 1/2 jack patterns continued to be made both with and without the shield into the late 1960s.

An example of Case 35 jack patterns, 3-3/8", made with and without the CASE shield. Top knife is a Case XX-stamped knife and the lower knife is a Case XX USA-stamped knife, both with bone handles.

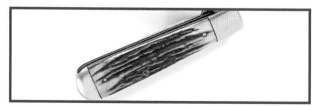

Case Tested 5299 1/2 large jack patterns. The knife at the top was made with a shield and the knife on the bottom was made without a shield. Case stag handled knives made without the CASE shield are rare.

THE LINE ON CASE LINER MATERIALS

In the construction of a traditional pocket knife, the "liner," sometimes referred to as a "scale," is the flat strip of metal that forms the base for the handle, with the bolsters and the handle slabs affixed to the liner using pins (on the vast majority of knives) or epoxy (the handles on very few knives). Liners are also used inside of the knife on certain patterns, and these are often referred to as "side scales," "double liners," "center liners," and "center scales." Some knives are made without liners, in particular metal-handled knives where the metal handle slab also serves as the liner. Traditionally, Case used three liner materials in the manufacture of pocket knives: iron, brass, and nickel silver.

Iron: Iron was used quite a bit for liners in the early days of Case. On knives made prior to the Case Tested era, many of the standard patterns were made with iron liners. Some knives from this era will be found with a mix of materials; for example brass side liners and an iron center scale.

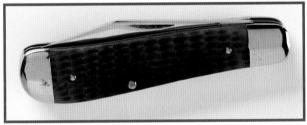

This Case Tested 62028 dogleg jack has iron bolsters and liners and was made without a shield. It was likely a wartime knife.

Some patterns in the early years were actually cataloged with a choice of either iron liners or brass liners, and the "I" suffix was used to designate a pattern with iron liners where the pattern was normally lined with brass. For example, the 6116 I was an iron-lined version of the 6116 single-blade jack knife pattern. This is an example of the unusual steps that were often taken in those times to reduce the costs on lower-priced knives. Iron was always the least expensive liner material used.

Iron bolsters and liners on Case Tested-stamped 62028 dogleg jack knife.

During the Case Tested years, the use of iron liners was generally limited to the "Barlow" and the "Granddaddy Barlow" patterns, but some other CASE TESTED- and CASE XX-stamped knives from the WWII era will have iron bolsters and liners. Beginning during the later Case XX era in the 1950s, the only pattern to be made with iron liners was the 6143 "Granddaddy Barlow." This tradition continued into the 1970s when the 6143 was changed over to brass liners. Iron liners have not been used by Case since then.

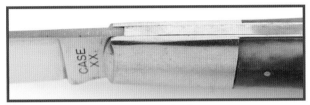

Iron bolster and iron liner on a Case XX-stamped 6143.

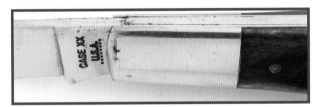

Nickel silver bolster and iron liner on a 6143 made in 1972 (8 dot).

Brass: Brass has long been the "workhorse" liner material on Case pocket knives. Traditionally from the Case Tested era onward, the basic jack patterns that were sold at lower price points had brass liners. Other patterns have also been made with brass liners and for a number of years brass was the only liner material used.

Nickel silver: Nickel silver was always the "deluxe" liner material used by Case and by other pocket knife manufacturers. Many manufacturers traditionally used nickel silver liners on the better stockman pattern pocket knives. It is possible that the reasoning was that since these knives might be used for "veterinary" purposes, nickel silver was better since it does not easily oxidize.

There has long been confusion about the use of nickel silver as a liner material. In the post-WWII era, Case was one of the few companies to use nickel silver as most pocket knife manufacturers had switched exclusively to brass for lining pocket knives. Some less expensive knives used base metal liners that were brass plated. Since solid brass was seen as the most common lining material on better knives, many knife users mistakenly thought that since nickel silver did not have the appearance of brass, it must be an inferior lining material, when in fact the opposite is true. Likewise, today some knife aficionados look at a knife with nickel silver liners and assume that the material is stainless steel.

From the Case XX era onward, Case used nickel silver as a lining material on most patterns in several general categories of pocket knives. Most three-blade stockman patterns were made with nickel silver liners, as were some of the two-blade jack knife patterns that were made on the same frame styles as the stockman knives. The small pen knife patterns were also (with a few exceptions) made with nickel silver liners, as were the "Trapper" and "Muskrat" patterns.

Case factory catalogs from the 1950s through 1980 listed the liner material used on each pocket knife pattern. Things get a bit confusing as a few patterns seemed to switch back and forth between nickel silver and brass depending on the catalog. As a quick reference guide for collectors, the chart below lists the patterns that were cataloged only with nickel silver liners in the Case factory catalogs from the XX era through the 1977 catalog. Also in the chart is a separate list of patterns that showed either nickel silver or brass depending upon the catalog.

Most of the patterns listed in the right-hand column of the chart were switched from nickel in the earlier catalogs to brass by the 1977 catalog. Some (6269, 6292, 6227, and 6279) switched from nickel silver to brass and then by the 1970s back to nickel silver. Other than those patterns listed in the chart, all Case pocket knives from the XX era through 1977 were cataloged as having brass liners. The one exception to this as noted previously is the 6143 (iron lined). There were other random exceptions as a few examples of some of the "100 percent nickel silver" patterns will be observed with brass liners. It is possible that Case ran out of nickel silver supplies at various times and that brass was used to complete production runs. For example, some 54 patterns with the CASE XX USA stamping will be found with brass liners, but this variation is scarce.

The 1977 catalog was used as a "cutoff" for the chart because beginning in 1977-1978, Case began to transition the nickel silver-lined patterns over to brass liners. By 1980, the change was complete and in the 1980 catalog, virtually all pocket knife patterns were listed as having brass liners. The only exceptions were the four patterns with imitation pearl handles and the 21051 L SSP, which were still listed as being lined in nickel silver. In the late 1990s, Case returned to the use of nickel silver as a lining material on pearl-handled pocket knives and on some other "premium" pocket knives.

Patterns With Nickel Silver Lining Case XX Era Through 1977		Patterns Which Varied Brass Or Nickel Silver Lining
4100 SS	6347 Sh Sp	6227
4200 SS	6347 Sp P	62042
3201	6347 Sp Pen	92042
6201	6347 Sh Sp SSP	06244
9201	64047 P	6344 Sh Pen
6208	54052	6344 Sh Sp
6308	62052	6269
3318 Sh Pen	64052	6279 SS
4318 Sh Sp	3254	22087
6318 Sh Sp	5254	62087
6318 Sh Pen	6254	23087 Sh Pen
6318 Sp Pu	6254 SSP	63087 Sp Pen
6318 Sh Sp SSP	9261	6292
6327 Sh Sp	05263 SS	
9327 Sh Sp	06263 SS	
3233	06263 F SS	
5233	06263 SSP	
6233	5375	
6333	6275 Sp	
9233	6375	
9333	6380	
62042 R	5383	
92042 R	6383	
33044 Sh Sp	53087 Sh Pen	
06247 Pen	5392	
53047	6392	
63047	33092	
3347 Sh Sp	62109 X	
5347 Sh Sp	MUSKRAT	

PINNING DOWN
CASE PIN MATERIALS

On most traditional pocket knives, the handle slabs are pinned to the liners with two or more pins on each side, in addition to the "main pin" or "lower pin," which goes through the scales and the backsprings to hold the knife together. As with the liner materials, Case has used various materials for these pins over the years. The Case factory catalogs listed the liner material for each pattern but not the pin material. Some collectors assume that the pin material must match the liner material on a particular knife or the knife is "suspicious." While this can be true in some instances, there are some important exceptions.

A general rule that does seem to hold is that a Case pocket knife with nickel silver liners will also have nickel silver handle pins and main pin. Having said that, I will say that very few exceptions will be observed where a brass main pin was used on a nickel silver-lined knife, but these examples are scarce enough that they may be viewed as "factory errors." On the other hand, *many* Case pocket knives with brass liners from the Case XX era through 1979 will have nickel silver handle pins and a nickel silver main pin. Less commonly observed is a brass-lined knife that has a nickel silver main pin and brass handle pins.

As examples, I have a CASE XX-stamped 6488 with long pull blades and brass liners that has brass handle pins and a nickel silver main pin. Another CASE XX-stamped 6488 in my collection has brass liners but all pins are nickel silver. As a later example, I have a 6254 SSP with the two dot 1978 tang stamping. This knife has brass liners, brass handle pins, and a nickel silver main pin. When Case was fully transitioned to the use of brass liners on almost all patterns in 1980, my observation is that the pin material went to all brass as well, except for on the few remaining nickel silver lined patterns.

A further note applies to the older iron-lined Case pocket knives made up to the WWII era, which were often made with a combination of brass and iron pins.

Another interesting note relates to the finishing of the handle pins on Case pocket knives. Traditionally, a "spinning tool" has been used to finish both ends of the main blade pin on a Case pocket knife after it has been installed in the knife. The spinning tool forms a "crown" or mushroom head on each side of the pin, enabling the pin to permanently hold the knife together. On older Case pocket knives, the handle pins will also be "spun." After installation of the handle and a peening of the pin, a smaller diameter spinning tool would be used to form a "crown" on each handle pin. Beginning in the early 1980s, it appears that Case went to the use of "cold headed" handle pins (similar to a nail with the head pre formed in the pin material), which eliminated the spinning of the handle pins. This change may have taken place earlier on delrin- and composition-handled knives.

BACK TO BASICS ON CASE BACKSPRINGS - AND POCKET KNIFE CONSTRUCTION

The intent of this section is not actually to discuss Case pocket knife backsprings per se, but to review some typical construction details used on the various styles of Case pocket knife patterns and the construction changes that have been made over the years.

For purposes of this discussion, I will define the following terms. Note that this is my personal terminology and it may or may not match the terms that will be found in other sources.

- **Single-end backspring:** The single-end backspring is a backspring that is designed for a blade to be installed at one end only.
- **Double-end backspring:** The double-end backspring is a backspring that is designed for a blade to be installed at each end.
- **Scale:** The scale is the outside handle liner on a pocket knife. The bolsters and the handle slabs will be directly affixed to the scale.
- **Center scale:** On pocket knives that are constructed with multiple backsprings, a center scale is often, but not always, used. The center scale is either a full height center scale, identical to the outer scales, or it may be cut down center scale, designed to leave the center of the knife open.
- **Side scale:** Some pocket knife patterns will have a side scale, which is identical to the "cut down center scale." The difference is that the side scale will be installed inside on one side of the knife, laid flat on the inside of the scale. Knives that incorporate a side scale are often referred to as being "double lined."

An interesting note on Case pocket knife liners is that Case has always stamped a slight crease lengthwise along each liner during the fabrication process. The purpose of the crease is to add rigidity to the liners, strengthening the overall knife.

TRADITIONAL CONSTRUCTION OF CASE POCKET KNIFE PATTERNS

The purpose of the scales on a pocket knife is relatively obvious. The metal scales essentially form the pocket knife handle and enable the attachment of the handle slabs. Most metal-handled knives will not be made with scales since the metal handles essentially take the place of the scales. A Case single-blade jack knife with either natural or composition handles will generally be made with two scales and with one single-end backspring.

The center scale on a pocket knife can have several purposes. On a two-blade jack knife pattern, the center scale adds some rigidity to the knife and keeps the two-blade tangs separated and in alignment. A Case two-blade jack knife with either natural or composition handles will generally be made with two scales, one full height center scale, and with two single-end backsprings.

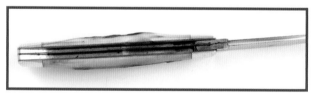

Inside view of a Case XX-stamped 5232 jack knife showing two backsprings with a full center scale.

All Case three-blade "stockman" patterns were traditionally made with two scales, one cut down center scale, one single-end backspring, and one double-end backspring. On a Case stockman pattern, the cut down center scale provides an additional function in that it acts as a "spacer," providing additional space for the secondary blades to fall inside the knife.

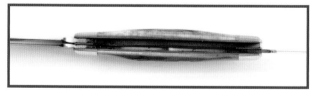

Inside view of a Case XX USA-stamped 5332 stock knife showing two backsprings with a cut down center scale.

Four-blade stockman patterns and four-blade "congress" patterns as traditionally constructed by Case will be similar with two backsprings and a cut down center scale, but for a four-bladed knife, both backsprings would be of the double-end design. On three- and four-blade patterns made with thicker blade stock, the cut down center liner will also be thicker, to provide additional space for the blades to fall inside the knife.

Inside view of a 10 dot 1970 54052 Congress showing two backsprings and a cut down center liner. Note the extra thickness of the center liner.

Back of a Case XX-stamped 6488 Congress pattern showing the two backspring construction. Note the extra thick brass center scale.

Many stockman patterns that included a punch blade were traditionally "double-lined," with a second cut down center scale installed flat against the inside of one scale. This second liner will be found installed on the side of the knife that has the punch blade installed. The Case 64047 P is one example of a double-lined stockman pattern. On these knives, the double liner serves to provide extra space for the punch blade to fit in when closed, and increases the strength of the blade.

Inside view of a Case XX USA 64047 Punch stock knife showing two backsprings and a cut down center liner, with double lining on the punch blade side.

Case "pen knife" patterns as traditionally constructed had a few quirks. Many were constructed simply with two scales and one double-end backspring. Both blades and the backspring would be made with stock of identical thickness. This arrangement works on pen knives where the main blade is relatively short as compared to the length of the handle. The master blade and the pen blade can be ground so that they fall past each other with no interference. Examples of Case pen knife patterns that were traditionally constructed in this manner include the 63 Eisenhower pattern, the 042 pattern and the 079 1/2 "sleeveboard" pen knife.

Inside view of a Case XX-stamped 05263 SS pen knife showing the single backspring construction.

This style of two-blade pen knife pattern was occasionally modified to be "double-lined" pattern with a cut down center liner installed as a "side liner." This was done on some patterns that were made with a long file or a scissors as the secondary blade in addition to the long spear master blade. Since both of the long blades were configured to operate on a single backspring, the file or scissors side would be "double-lined" to accommodate the longer blade.

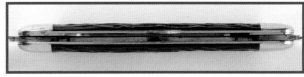

Inside view of a Case XX-stamped 6279 F SS pen knife showing the single backspring construction with double lining on the file side to accommodate the long file blade.

There have been other pen knife patterns made by Case where an additional piece was required. For a knife with a longer wider master blade (like the 33 pattern), there would be a "catch bit" installed at the small pen blade end of the knife. The pen blade on a knife with a catch bit would be made of thinner blade stock as compared to the main blade and the backspring. The catch bit is in effect a small spacer that would be installed next to the pen blade to provide additional space for the tip of the master blade to fall. Other examples of Case pocket knife patterns traditionally made with a catch bit include the 62109 X "Baby Copperhead" and the 62131 "Canoe."

Inside view of a Case XX-stamped 06244 pen knife showing a single backspring with a "catch bit" at the pen blade end.

There are two more major types or styles of pocket knives that differ in construction details from those already discussed. The first pattern is a "split-back whittler," with three blades and two backsprings. The "split-back" or "split-backspring" designation is used by collectors to refer to a specific blade and backspring arrangement. This arrangement includes a relatively thick master blade at one end with a pair of small blades at the opposite end.

Back of a 6308 Whittler showing the split backspring construction.

Back of a 6383 whittler showing the split backspring construction.

The pattern is constructed with the main blade riding on both springs. Each of the two smaller blades rides on one spring. In order to provide space for the main blade to fall between the two small blades, a partial center liner or "wedge" is installed between the backsprings at the small blade end of the knife. Examples of Case "whittler" patterns that were traditionally made with this construction include the 6308, the 6383, and the 6380. Other "whittler" patterns have been made with similar construction but without the "wedge." On these knives, the two backsprings are flat and parallel to each other and the two small blades will be separated by a small metal spacer that is similar to a "catch bit."

Back of a 6380 whittler showing the split backspring construction

The last major general category of pocket knives as traditionally constructed by Case is a style of knife that is sometimes referred to as a "double-end" knife. This style is differentiated by the use of two full-length blades, hinged at opposite ends with each operating on its own backspring. Double-end knife

patterns as made by Case would include two scales and two single-end backsprings, with no other interior liners. Examples of knives made on the double-end style in the Case pocket knife line include the famous Muskrat and 6275 Sp Moose patterns.

Inside view of a Case XX Muskrat showing traditional two-backspring construction with no center liner.

There is actually one other general style to discuss that was traditionally only used by Case on a few patterns offered in the pre-WWII era. This style of construction is similar to that of the "double-end" knife but the knife will have three long blades and three backsprings. Some collectors refer to this style knife as a "three-spring whittler" or as a "three-spring cattle knife." The most well-known older Case pocket knife pattern that was constructed in this style was the 109 pattern.

WR Case & Sons 83109, "Three Backspring Whittler," Pearl, 3-5/8", $1,500.

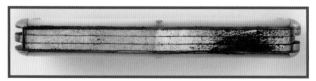

Three-backspring construction of the 83109.

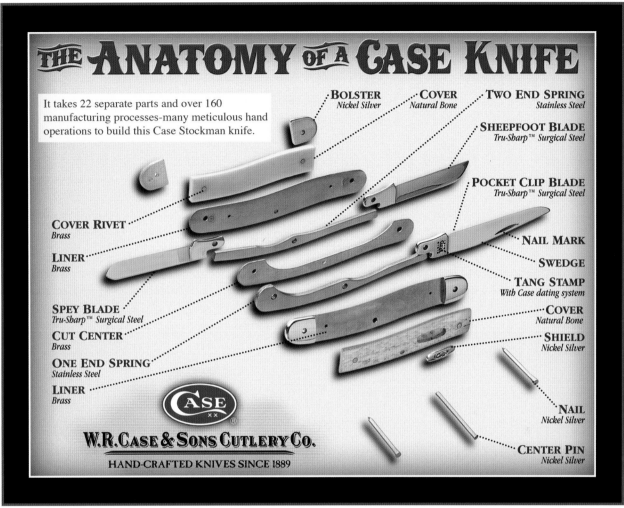

The above exploded view of a typical Case stockman pattern is provided by W.R. Case and Sons.

CONSTRUCTION CHANGES ON SOME MODERN CASE PATTERNS

The previous descriptions are intended to cover the way that the various "traditional" pocket knife patterns were made by Case from the early years of the company until the end of the 1970s.

Beginning in the early 1980s and continuing to the present day, Case has made modifications to some of the "standard" Case pocket knife tooling to changes the basic construction of some patterns. The Pattern Guide section of this book covers most of these in detail, but here are some highlights:

- In the mid-1980s, Case added a cut-down center scale to the Muskrat pattern. This change only lasted for a few years and then the center scale was removed.

- In the early 1990s, Case changed the 47 and the 33 "stockman" patterns to use three backsprings (one single end spring per blade) and no center or side liners.

- In the late 1980s to early 1990s, some 052 four-blade "congress" patterns were made with a side liner added to each side of the knife.

- Beginning later in the 1990s, the 052 four-blade "congress" pattern was changed over to the use of four backsprings (one single end spring per blade) and no center or side liners. Two-bladed 052s were changed to two separate backsprings.

- Beginning in about 1985, the 131 "Canoe" pattern was changed over to two backsprings (one single end spring per blade) with the "catch bit" eliminated.

• In 1981, Case decided to change over some pen knife patterns with the addition of a "side liner" even though these patterns were made with a long master blade and a short pen blade. This is mentioned in the following excerpt from the Case Collector's Club Newsletter of March 1981:

In order to improve the action of certain pocket knives, Case Cutlery will be adding center sales of the following patterns: 06263, 05263, M279, 82079 ½, A62042, 92042, 52042, 62131, A6208, 6201, 9201, 6250, and 06247.

This will be a gradual transition and may not be seen on the market for sometime yet.

Regarding the last item, I believe that some of the 13 patterns shown were discontinued prior to the implementation of this manufacturing change.

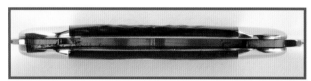

Inside view of a 7 dot 1973 62131 Canoe showing the traditional single backspring construction with a catch bit.

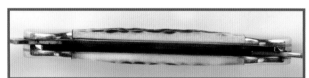

Inside view of a newer 62131 Canoe showing the newer two-backspring construction with no catch bit.

Inside view of a Case Muskrat from 1982 showing two backspring construction with a center liner added.

Inside view of a new style 64052 showing the newer four-backspring construction (individual backspring for each blade) with no center liner.

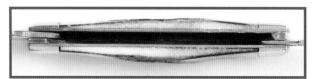

Inside view of a 5233 from 1995 showing the newer two backspring construction with no catch bit.

AN ABBREVIATED LOOK AT CASE PATTERN NUMBER ABBREVIATIONS

Let's start out this discussion by asking...given its meaning, why is the word *abbreviation* such a long word? Well, I do not know the answer to that question, but Case has used many individual letters and abbreviated words as both prefixes and suffixes to pocket knife pattern numbers.

In general, the prefixes to pattern numbers have been used only in more recent years (beginning in the late 1970s) primarily to designate bone- and stag-handle variations. For example, the prefix letter "A" has been used to designate appaloosa-colored bone (for example, A6208) and the prefix "DR" has been used for dark red bone (for example, DR62131 SS). These handle material prefixes will not be further discussed here as they have been well documented in Case factory catalogs and product guides in recent years.

Case has used a number of suffixes to designate blade styles and other features on various pocket knives. The chart below provides an explanation of the more commonly used suffixes including some that were only used on very early knives.

Pattern # Suffix	What It Denotes	Pattern # Example
SAB	Saber Ground Blade	2231 1/2 SAB
Sh	Sheepfoot Blade	11031 Sh
Sp	Spay Blade	1116 Sp
P Or Pu	Punch Blade	64047 P
Pen	Pen Blade	23087 Sh Pen
RAZ	Razor Style Blade	62009 RAZ
F	File Blade or Hook Sharpener	06263 F SS
1/2	Clip Master Blade	6225 1/2
L	Lockback	6111 1/2 L
EO	Easy Opener (notch cutout in handle)	620035 EO
Scis	Scissors Blade	8364 Scis
Shad	Shadow Pattern (no bolsters)	82053 Shad R SS
SS	Stainless Steel Blades And Springs	5347 Sh Sp SS
SSP	Stainless Steel Blades And Springs (blades have polished edges)	6254 SSP
DR	Bolster Drilled for Lanyard	6265 SAB DR
T	Tip Bolsters	8364 T
CC	Concave Ground Blades	11031 Sh CC
X	Extension Bolster	62109 X
I	Iron Lining	6116 I
K	Cap Lifter (Bottle Opener)	M1218 K
J	Two Long Blades	6294 J
Bud	Budding Blade	6104 Bud
B&G	Budding And Grafting Blades	04245 B&G
C (prefix)	"Cap" Bolster At The Lower End	C61050 SAB

The suffixes shown in the chart were used in Case factory catalogs and price lists. As an example, the 6347 with sheepfoot and spay secondary blades would be listed in a catalog or price list as 6347 Sh Sp. A "Barlow" pattern with a clip master blade would be listed as 62009 1/2, while the same knife with a razor master blade would be a 62009 RAZ, and a spear master blade version was a 62009. In the case of the 1/2 suffix, it could be said that the spear blade version of any jack pattern was the "default" version that had no suffix.

A question often arises as to why only some knives that have a given feature will have the pattern number suffix while others with the same feature will not. Let's use 6347 Sh Sp as an example for comparison. Both the 6347 Sh Sp and the 6392 are "stockman" patterns that have sheepfoot and spay secondary blades, but the 47 pattern has the suffix Sh Sp while the 92 pattern does not. In general the rule here is that if a particular pocket knife pattern was offered *only* with a certain option, then the suffix letter or abbreviation for that option was *not* included in the pattern number.

Since the 6392 was offered *only* with sheepfoot and spay secondary blades, it was listed as the 6392 and not the 6392 Sh Sp. As another example, the 62009 1/2 "Barlow" with clip and pen blades was listed with the 1/2 suffix to differentiate it from the spear blade and razor blade variations of the same pattern. By contrast, the 6232 never needed the 1/2 suffix since it was offered with the clip blade as the *only* master blade option. A final example is the 9261. Even though the 9261 was made with "tip" bolsters, the pattern number did not include the letter "T" since the 61 pattern was never made with full bolsters. These conventions were in place as of the Case Tested era and possibly earlier.

When pattern numbers were stamped on the rear tangs of Case blades, they were often abbreviated due to space limitations. Examples include the 6225 1/2, which had only 25 1/2 stamped as the pattern number, and 82079 1/2, which had the pattern number abbreviated to 079 on the blade tang. Some pattern numbers were abbreviated on CASE XX stamped knives and into the 1970s but then later examples will have the full pattern number. This may have been due to improvements in the technology for making dies and stamping the more detailed numbers on the blade tangs.

Often only the pattern number suffixes were abbreviated when stamped on blade tangs. As an example, we will use the 6318 pattern. This pattern was made with a

number of secondary blade combinations. The secondary blades used on Case stockman patterns (with their standard abbreviations shown) are the Sheepfoot (Sh), Spay (Sp), Pen (Pen), and Punch (Pu). It is quickly apparent that if Case attempted to use just the first letter of each of these blade designations in an abbreviation, things would get confusing due to the fact that there are four different blade styles, but only two different first letters. So, in stamping the blades on the tangs, Case would abbreviate each pattern number using the second letter of each blade designation as follows:

6318 Sh Sp	6318 HP
6318 Sh Pen	6318 HE
6318 Sp Pu	6318 PU

Pattern number on a Case XX-stamped 6318 Sh Sp stock knife with sheepfoot and spay secondary blades.

Pattern number on a Case XX-stamped 6318 Sh Pen stock knife with sheepfoot and pen secondary blades.

Pattern number on a Case XX-stamped 6318 Sp Pu stock knife with spay and punch secondary blades.

There were a number of other shortened abbreviations (or would that be abbreviated abbreviations?) used on Case pocket knife tangs. As examples, the 5347 Sh Sp SS became the 5347HPS. The abbreviation "Shad" was shortened to "S," Scis was shortened to Sc, and RAZ was sometimes shortened to R. There are other examples but these should give you an idea of how and why these abbreviations were used.

Pattern number on a 10 dot 1970 5347 Sh Sp SS. Note that the full pattern number is abbreviated as 5347HPS.

Abbreviated pattern number on the rear tang of a Case XX-stamped 82063 SHAD SS pattern.

A note on bails: A number of Case patterns were manufactured with the bail or shackle as standard, with the pattern having an "R" suffix. I can only speculate that "R" was derived from the word "ring" to mean a bail or shackle in a "ring" shape. Patterns that were traditionally made with bails include the "scout" and "electrician" pattern variations and the "rigger's knife" and others.

Occasionally, older examples of Case pocket knives will be found that were made with factory installed bails even though the pattern as listed in Case factory catalogs and price lists was not offered with a bail as standard. The answer to this apparent quandary is found in older Case factory price lists from the Case Tested

A group of Case XX-stamped 6318 stock knife patterns illustrating secondary blade variations, 3-1/2", from top: 6318 Sh Sp (6318 HP) with sheepfoot and spay secondary blades; 6318 Sh Pen (6318 PE) with sheepfoot and pen secondary blades; and 6318 Sp Pu (6318 PU) with spay and punch secondary blades.

era. This is excerpted from a 1941 price list: *A charge of $1.20 per dozen net will be made for the addition of a bail to any pattern not made as regular stock with bail.*

So based on this, any Case Tested pocket knife pattern could in theory be found with a bail installed. This practice evidently continued after WWII as I have a copy of a Case factory sheet from 1966 that lists sales aids available. One of the items listed on the sheet is that a "shackle" (bail) could be *added to any pocket knife pattern on special order for $0.50 per knife, with a minimum order of 1/3 dozen knives."*

I have observed one example of a bone-handled Case XX 6265 SAB with a factory-installed bail. This particular knife was part of an intact Case counter display and was still wired to the display board just as it had left the Case factory. I have also seen examples of the 11031 Sh and the 6217 with bails with 1970s tang stampings. Collectors are advised to be careful though, as many Case pocket knife owners modified their knives by installing crude home made bails to enhance the knives for their own use. A Case factory bail will be made of nickel silver wire and will be neatly pinned to the bolster of the knife with the pin ends "spun" with a rivet spinner.

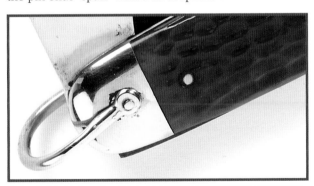

Factory-installed bail on a Case XX-stamped 6445 R scout/utility knife. Note the spun finish on the end of the pin that holds the bail on.

For Flesh Only (Ouch!): An interesting detail on some older Case "Stockman" patterns with a spay secondary blade is that the etching "FOR FLESH ONLY" will be observed on the spay blade. The "stockman" pattern was conceived as a knife for those who work with livestock, and the spay blade was often used for "veterinary" purposes. While Case began to use this etching on some patterns after WWII, it was one of those traditional "touches" that some other manufacturers applied in the years prior to WWII. I have

observed examples of stockman and "cattle knife" patterns with the KEEN KUTTER and WINCHESTER brand names that had FOR FLESH ONLY etched on the spay blade. I have also observed a Cattauragus "cattle" pattern with the words FOR FLESH ONLY actually stamped into the tang of the spay blade.

Case used this etching on the spay blades installed in the 47 and 18 stockman patterns, and on the spay blade in the 63087 Sp Pen. These etchings on the 47 and 18 patterns were discontinued circa 1983. I believe that the practice of etching the spay blade on the 087 pattern was dropped by the early 1970s, or earlier. I have never seen any documentation as to why the FOR FLESH ONLY etching was used on some Case stockman patterns and not on others. For example, the 92 and the 75 stockman patterns (and others) were never made with the etched spay. Frankly, even the reason for the etching in the first place is a mystery, as the "stockman" patterns were generally purchased as general purpose knives. It is possible that the 47 and the 18 patterns had spay blades with a more aggressive concave blade grind, but I do not know this for a fact.

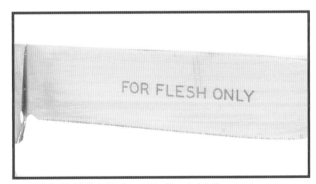

The "FOR FLESH ONLY" etching from a 47 pattern stock knife.

The "FOR FLESH ONLY" etching from an 18 pattern stock knife.

Pattern number locations: On many very early Case pocket knives, the pattern numbers were often stamped on one of the secondary blades of a multi-blade pattern. During the Case Tested era, pattern numbers were generally not actually stamped on the knives but a few will be found with pattern numbers. Case standardized on the use of pattern numbers during the Case XX era after WWII; however, some CASE XX-stamped knives were made without pattern numbers.

Pattern number on the pen blade of the W.R. Case & Sons stamped 5205 RAZ. Many early Case pocket knives were marked with pattern numbers, often on the secondary blades.

From the Case XX era onward, the standard practice was to stamp the pattern number for each knife on the rear of the main blade tang. This rule was changed a bit later in the 1960s and the early 1970s, when many of the newly introduced stainless steel pocket knife patterns with multiple blades would have the pattern number stamped on the tang of one of the secondary blades. The practice of putting the pattern number on a secondary blade seemed to become a standard for all patterns in the late 1970s, beginning on some patterns in 1978.

ZEROING IN ON THE ZEROES IN CASE PATTERN NUMBERS

Some Case pattern numbers include a "0" as a digit either at the beginning of the pattern number (example: 06247 Pen) or in the middle of the pattern number (example: 63047). Case often used the "0" to designate that the pattern was a modification of an existing or an earlier one. Collectors who study the older Case pattern numbers will find many exceptions to this "rule," but it does apply on some patterns. For example, the 6347 pattern was always made with a "standard" clip master blade, while the 63047 was the same knife but with a "California clip" master blade. So the pattern number 63047 represents a modification to the 6347 pattern where there was not a suffix defined to represent the change. Another example is the 06247 Pen where the "0" at the beginning of the pattern number represented a change to a two-blade variation with a single backspring.

There are many instances, however, where the "0" in the pattern number does not represent a modification but instead a completely different pattern. As examples, the 61050 large swell center folding hunter bears no resemblance to the 6250 "Elephant Toe Nail," and the 6111 1/2 L Cheetah bears no resemblance to the 61011 "Hawkbill." The 06263 Eisenhower is an equal end pen knife with a spear master blade, while the 62063 pen knife is a completely different "sleeveboard" pattern. Such are the mysteries of the Case pocket knife numbering system.

And the Strange Case of the Double Zero: A few Case pattern numbers are configured with two zeroes in a row in the middle of the pattern number (example: 640045 R). In some respects this could be said to represent a "further" modification of a pattern that already had a single zero (610050 vs 61050). I do not know if this could be considered a "rule" but in my experience the "double zero" knives were generally lower grade or less expensive versions of the standard patterns upon which they were based.

The 610050, for example, was similar to the C61050 or 61050 patterns in that it was a 5-1/4" swell-center folding hunter with a clip blade. However, the 610050 had thinner bolsters and thinner blade stock as compared to the 050 knives and the 0050 was sold at a lower price point based on the Case Tested era Case factory price lists. Likewise, during the Case Tested era, the 6347 and the 6392 had lower priced variations in the line, the 630047 and the 630092. These "double zero" stockman patterns had brass liners in place of nickel silver and were made without shields to keep the prices reduced.

The examples just listed are from the Case Tested era. More modern examples of some "double zero" pattern knives include the 620035 and 620035 1/2 jack patterns (variations of the 6235 and the 6235 1/2) and the 640045 R (variation of the 6445 R). These knives were designed and built less expensively so that they could be priced at lower price points as compared to the "standard" Case pocket knife patterns that were similar.

"BACK TO THE OLD GRIND" - CASE "NEW GRIND" OR "SHOULDERLESS GRIND" BLADES

From 1983 to 1985, Case attempted to make a somewhat radical change to the manner in which blades were ground. Traditionally, all pocket knife blades had a "square" grind with a straight corner or "shoulder" where the ground portion of the blade met the flat tang area. The new grinding process eliminated the "shoulder" at the tang and instead there was a radius or "filet" at the tang area. Case at the time indicated that the change was made to improve the strength of the blades, as explained in the following excerpt from the *Case Collector's Club Newsletter* of September 1983. Please note that while the illustrations that are referenced in the excerpted write up are not reproduced here, some photographs are included to illustrate some blade styles.

"New grind" or "shoulderless grind" main blade of a 1983 6254 SS Trapper (polished blade).

Case is making a change which will have an effect on all our pocket knives, as well as hunters and household.

For as long as Case has been making knives, blades have been ground in a manner to create what is called a shoulder. The shoulder is the edge of the tang (SEE DIAGRAM A).

CASE is now proceeding to switch over to what is referred to as the shoulderless grind (SEE DIAGRAM B).

This change was proposed by the Engineering Department to upgrade the quality of the blade. It seems that the Manufacturing process to create the shoulder was actually weakening the blade similar to what a glass cutter does to glass. By converting to the shoulderless grind, it increased the strength of blades by 70%, not to mention the fact it also enhances the blades appearance.

The conversion has already occurred on all blades having a polished finish. This changeover will take months to complete before you start seeing all patterns with the shoulderless grind, due to the inventory of the old style shoulder grind finish.

Currently, test runs of glazed finished blades are being sent through the plant. However, there will have to be further modifications done to the glazed finished blades before it becomes a standard feature. So in the meantime, all glazed finished blades will revert back to the shoulder ground finish. This will only be a temporary change.

We will advise you when the changeover becomes permanent, but to date, the test runs have produced quantities of the following patterns (See Below).

6208 SS	6347 1/2 SS
6318 Sh Sp SSP	6104S SS
6225 1/2 SS	62048 Sp SS
62033 SS	6254 SSP
63033 SS	06263 SSP
52033 SS	M279 SS
62042 SS	22087 SS
6244 SS	62087 SS
6344 Sh Pen SS	63087 Sp Pen SS
6347 Sh Sp SSP	

The shoulderless grind of the test run patterns will be different from the finalized version when the modification is complete.

Evidently as Case transitioned over to the new grinding process in 1983, there were problems associated with the use of the "shoulderless grind" process in the production of the glazed finish or "machine ground" blades, as indicated in this excerpt from the *Case Collector's Club Newsletter* of April 1984:

In a previous Newsletter we did an article on the changeover to shoulderless grind on standard stock items. (Shoulderless grind is being shown in the diagram below.)

The article mentioned we were proceeding with the changeover on all standard patterns having mirror polished blades. This changeover is continuing on all knives with polished blades.

All machine ground finished blades, inadvertently referred to as glazed finished blades, will maintain the square shoulder appearance until an evaluation is made by the Engineering Department on the test run of knives mentioned in the previous newsletter.

For various reasons, the new "shoulderless grind" blades on Case pocket knives were not well accepted in the marketplace. Frankly, I question the original

Regular square grind polished stainless steel blades on a 1985 5254 SS Trapper pattern.

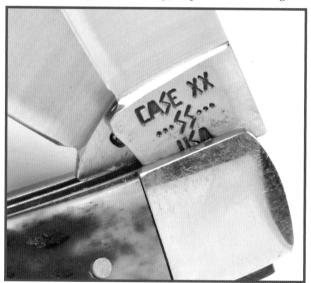

Regular square grind glazed finish stainless steel blades on a 1984 6254 SSP Trapper pattern.

"New grind" or "shoulderless grind" grind-polished chrome vanadium blades on a 1984 6254 Trapper pattern.

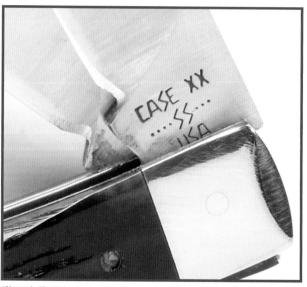

"New grind" or "shoulderless grind" grind-glazed finish stainless steel blades on a 1983 6254 SSP Trapper pattern.

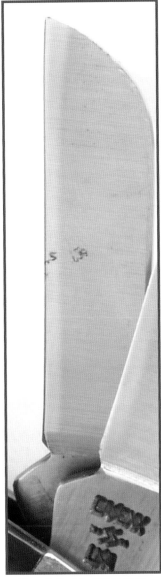

"New grind" or "shoulderless grind" sheepfoot blade from a 53032 SS stock knife made in 1985. This is a polished stainless steel blade.

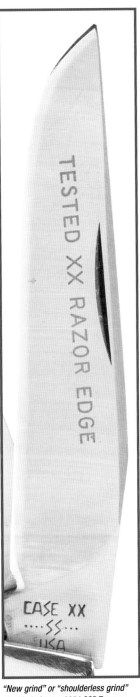

"New grind" or "shoulderless grind" clip blade from a 6254 SSP Trapper made in 1983. This is a glazed stainless steel blade.

premise of "improving the strength" of Case blades since I have never observed Case blades to be at all "weak" or easily broken. So, Case phased out the new process and went back to the traditional "square" blade grind. This excerpt is from the *Case Collector's Club Newsletter* of April 1985:

Almost a year and a half ago, we announced the introduction of the shoulderless grind. This change was to increase the blade strength of the tang area.

We made the change with good intentions of improving the quality of our product. However, many people did not see the change as an improvement.

So, in an effort to meet the demands of the knife user, CASE will initiate a manufacturing change to again produce the traditional square cut shoulder on all the products. This should take about 6 months to accomplish before it is seen on the field.

The important point for the collector of Case pocket knives is that some scarce and unusual variations were created by the process of Case changing over to the "shoulderless grind" blades and then back again.

My own observations on knives with the "shoulderless grind" blades are as follows:

- The exact patterns made and released to dealers with shoulderless grind blades were not documented, so it is not known whether examples of all Case pocket knife patterns made during the years of 1983-1985 will be found with shoulderless grind blades.
- Due to the apparent manufacturing difficulties as noted in the excerpts on the previous page, far fewer knives with glazed finished blades will be found with shoulderless grind blades as compared to the polished chrome vanadium and polished stainless knives.
- Shoulderless grind was used for only about half of the year 1983 and about half of the year 1985, so both square grind and shoulderless grind knives will be found with the tang stampings from those years.
- 1984 was the only full year that shoulderless grind was in use. I do not know whether all knives made in 1984 were made with shoulderless grind but it does seem that a majority were, and it is possible that all polished finish pocket knives made that year were made with shoulderless grind.

THE NAME GAME: CASE POCKET KNIFE PATTERN NICKNAMES

Today Case provides a name for each pocket knife pattern in the line. Collectors have come to know various patterns by these names in addition to the pattern numbers and the product codes used by the company. This was not always so.

A review of cutlery catalogs issued by American cutlery manufacturers prior to the 1960s reveals that pattern names were not often used in catalog descriptions. Some manufacturers would etch the main blades of some patterns as a marketing tool, but by and large it appears that pocket knife pattern names were only used by the sales representatives of the firms to communicate orders to the factories.

One early US pocket knife manufacturer, Holley, of Lakeville, Connecticut, did publish a catalog just prior to the WWI era in which each pocket knife pattern was named.

Collectors today would be amused at some of the names in this catalog since they were generally much different than the marketing and collector names that are used today. Examples include the Michigan Pen, Capped Shiner, and President.

A review of Case factory catalogs reveals that Case in general did not list any pattern names from the early days of the company through the Case XX era.

The few exceptions are the patterns that had names in place of pattern numbers, such as the Muskrat and the Fly Fisherman.

Case's first inclusion of names for some patterns was in Catalog #70, published in 1968. In this catalog Case named a number of patterns (but not all) and these were still just "nicknames," and not considered to be "official" pattern names.

I suspect that Case added the nicknames at that time due to the burgeoning collector interest in the CASE brand. It appeared that Case put together the various pattern nicknames based on what the "old time" collectors and users called the patterns.

There seemed to be two categories of names applied – "collector" nicknames (usually based on the handle shape) and "usage" names related to the way that the patterns were put to work by knife users. Each knife had either one or both types of name included, or none at all.

Given the plethora of pocket knife pattern names today that are dreamed up by knife company marketing people, I thought that collectors might enjoy seeing the "original" names that appeared in the 1968 catalog. These are shown in the chart on P. 45.

Pattern	Knife Nickname(s)	Knife Usage
61048		STOCKMAN'S-TRUCK FARMER'S-SPORTSMAN'S
2138	"SOD BUSTER"	SPORTSMANS'S-FARMER'S-STOCKMAN'S-CAMPER'S
61093		SPORTSMAN'S
5143	"GRANDADDY BARLOW"	
52009	"BARLOW"	
6205 RAZ		ONE ARM MAN'S
62048 Sp		STOCKMAN'S
6249	"VIET NAM"	
6292	"TEXAS JACK"	
M279 SS		PHYSICIAN'S
62131	"CANOE" "JUNIOR RED EYE"	
6275 Sp	"MOOSE"	HEAVY SPORTSMAN'S
6327 Sh Sp		STOCKMAN'S SUNDAY DRESS
6308		MILLWORKER'S-WHITTLER'S
6383		MILLWORKER'S-WHITTLER'S
6380		CARPENTER'S-WHITTLER'S
94052		CARPENTER'S-WHITTLER'S-TOBACCO
6445 R		JANITOR'S-ELECTRICIAN'S-CAMPER'S
640045 R		JANITOR'S-ELECTRICIAN'S-CAMPER'S
64047 P		STOCKMAN'S
6488		CARPENTER'S-WHITTLER'S-TOBACCO
1116 Sp		CASTRATING-VETERINARIAN'S-BUDDING
61011		PRUNER'S-ELECTRICIAN'S-LINOLEUM-ROOFER'S-DAIRYMAN'S-NURSERY
4100 SS		CITRUS-SAUSAGE-MELON TASTER
4200 SS		CITRUS-SAUSAGE-MELON TASTER
6217		LOOM-CARTON-ELECTRICIAN'S
1199 Sh R SS		COAST GUARD-SAILOR'S-GRAFTING
6250	"ELEPHANT TOE NAIL" "SUNFISH" "RED EYE	OLD ENGLISH ROPE KNIFE USED ON SAILING VESSELS
12031 L R		ELECTRICIAN'S-JANITOR
13031 L R		ELECTRICIAN'S-JANITOR
MUSKRAT	"MUSKRAT"	STOCKMAN'S-VARMINT
6254		TRAPPER'S-HEAVY STOCKMAN'S
5172		IDEAL SKINNING KNIFE
6318 Sh Sp SSP		STOCKMAN'S
6347 Sh Sp SSP		STOCKMAN'S
6254 SSP		STOCKMAN'S

GETTING A HANDLE ON CASE HANDLE MATERIALS

Perhaps the most attention-grabbing characteristic of a well-crafted traditional pocket knife is the handle material used, the finest of which are those that combine durability and "sure-grip" characteristics with the inherent beauty of a natural material.

During its long history, Case has used a vast number of both natural and synthetic handle materials on pocket knives, and bone, stag, pearl, and wood have been the mainstays in the "natural" category. Synthetic handle materials have included fancy and colorful celluloid in the pre-WWII years, and modern composition and plastic materials. Metal handles have also graced Case pocket knives, including handles made from nickel silver, stainless steel, sterling silver, and modern aluminum alloys.

In the early years of Case, many of the sought-after variations in handle materials happened due to random manufacturing changes or changes in the suppliers of materials. In later years, as Case catered to the collector market, many innovative handle material variations were introduced by design to provide variety for collectors and knife users.

Beginning in the late 1980s and in particular after the mid-1990s, the variety of handle materials used has blossomed. During these years, Case changed its manufacturing processes to include more accurate dyeing of bone colors and the methodologies necessary to produce much shorter product runs so that more handle varieties can be included. Currently used handle materials at Case run the gamut from stag to myriad variations of bone, to mother of pearl, exotic woods, and precious minerals. Synthetic and metal handle materials are also still in use.

The intent of this section is to acquaint collectors with some of Case's older "classic" handle materials and provide information about the use of these materials that will answer some common questions about handle variations. Many of these "classic" handle materials are still in use by Case today and continue to define the brand.

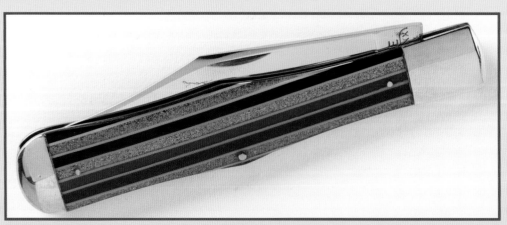

This Case Tested B10050 swell center has glitter stripe celluloid handles.

HANDLE KEY NUMBER 1: WALNUT

Smooth walnut was used to handle Case pocket knives beginning in the Case Tested era. Case used walnut handles on a relatively narrow range of "working knife" patterns, which included the 1116 Sp, 11031 Sh, 12031 and 13031 "electrician's" knives, the 1199 Sh R SS Whaler, and 11011 hawkbill. On walnut-handled knives made with shields, Case used the "composition" shields (without the oval around CASE) beginning in 1974.

The use of walnut as a handle material seemed to end as the older patterns on which it was used were discontinued by Case. The last knives to be made with the traditional walnut handles (and the handle key number 1) were the 12031 L H R "electrician" and 1199 Sh R SS Whaler, which were discontinued in the mid-1980s.

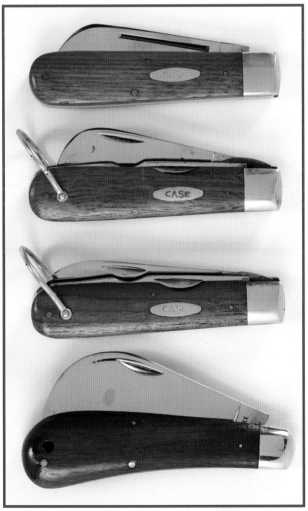

Case pocket knives with smooth walnut handles, from top: 3 dot, 1977, 11031 Sh; 3 dot, 1977, 12031 L H R "electrician"; and 4 dot, 1976, 12031 L R "electrician"; all three are 3-3/4". Bottom knife, Case XX USA 11011 "Hawkbill," 4".

HANDLE KEY NUMBER 2: SMOOTH BLACK

Smooth black, also known as "black composition," goes back to the early years of Case. The early smooth black material may have been a type of celluloid; however, I have never known older Case smooth black handles to decompose or exhibit the "self destruct" characteristic often experienced with celluloid. Likewise, neither the early nor the more recent Case smooth black materials seem to exhibit a tendency to shrink. Since the mid- to late 1960s, Case's smooth black handle material has been made of delrin plastic.

Case Tested pen knife, unknown pattern number, smooth black, 3-5/16".

The 2137 Sod Buster Junior, 3-5/8", left, and the 2138 Sod Buster, 4-5/8", right, are both popular Case "working" pocket knives with smooth black composition handles.

In general, Case has made a relatively small variety of pocket knife patterns in smooth black. Examples from the past include the 2220 "Peanut," 2231 1/2 SAB jack knife, 22055 "cigar" jack, and 23087 Sh Pen "small stockman." The use of smooth black delrin on knives continues today. Two of the more popular smooth black-handled patterns are the Sod Buster and Sod Buster Junior.

HANDLE KEY NUMBER 3: SMOOTH YELLOW

Smooth yellow has always been a popular handle material on Case pocket knives, and the 3254 yellow-handled "trapper" in particular has long been popular with knife users. Smooth yellow goes back to the early years of Case. One interesting point is that in all Case factory catalogs from the 1930s to the 1970s, the material was referred to not as yellow but as "cream composition" in the early catalogs and "cream plastic" in the 1974 and the 1977 catalogs.

Based on my observations, there are at least three major variations or vintages of the smooth yellow handle material. During the Case Tested to the early Case XX eras, the material was yellow celluloid and will have a bright, almost lemon-yellow color, as well as a "white liner"; that is, the edge of the handle where it meets the liner will be a distinct layer of white. The appearance is such that it looks like the bright yellow outer handle material layer was deposited on a sheet of white substrate material.

As many knife collectors are aware, this older celluloid material has a tendency to rapidly decompose if stored improperly and many knives will be found with the handles either "crazed" with cracks or partially or completely disintegrated, even on a knife that does not exhibit much use or abuse. In fact, this "spontaneous decomposition" of yellow celluloid handles is often observed on unused knives with unsharpened blades.

The next variation of smooth yellow handle material appears on most Case XX-era yellow-handled knives. This material has a muted yellow color, which is more of a "cream" color as opposed to bright yellow. I do not know the composition of this material but it does *not* seem to be a plastic material; it seems more

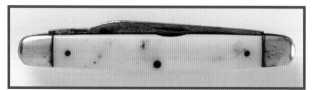

Yellow celluloid handles, with white liner, on a Case XX 3201 pen knife.

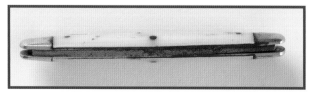

Back of a Case XX-stamped 3201 pen knife showing yellow celluloid handle "white liner."

like celluloid even though this material was used through the 1950s and into the 1960s. All I can say is that this material is even *worse* than the older yellow celluloid in exhibiting the problem of "spontaneous decomposition."

I have seen a number of intact Case XX-era display boards, where all of the knives were mint except for the smooth yellow knives, and the handles on those had completely disintegrated and were in pieces. As this material decomposes, it "outgases" and the result can rust the blades of the yellow-handled knife itself and any other knives in the vicinity; many of the adjoining knives on these display boards exhibited rust coatings on the blades and springs. I have also observed individual yellow-handled knives from this era where the decomposing handles had actually caused the brass liners to corrode and split right down the middle, so the whole knife could literally be pulled apart into two pieces.

The last major smooth yellow-handle variation is yellow delrin. I do not know the exact year of transition; however, the use of jigged brown delrin as a substitute for bone on Case pocket knives began circa 1967, so it would be logical to assume that the previous smooth yellow material had been changed over to smooth yellow delrin by that time frame. Smooth yellow delrin is still in use by Case today.

There was a fourth type of yellow handle material used on Case pocket knives that collectors refer to as "flat yellow," used during the Case XX to Case XX USA eras. The term "flat" does not refer to the geometry of the handle but rather the color itself. Many collectors think Case pocket knives with "flat yellow" handles were made specifically for use on factory-assembled display boards shipped to Case dealers. The majority of "flat yellow"-handled knives observed have wire marks from where the knife was wired to a display board.

The appearance of flat yellow handles is different from that of yellow delrin handles, but the differences are difficult to describe in words. Likewise, the differences do not readily show up in photographs. Basically on flat yellow handles only the tops of the handle pins are visible, while the yellow delrin handles have a slight translucence which allows the rest of the pin to show a little bit and it shows up as a dark ring or circle on the handle. Case pocket knives with "flat yellow" handles are scarce and in the more collectible Case patterns "flat yellow" handles are highly sought after.

One note about yellow delrin handles is that the material had the tendency to develop cracks at the handle pins, and these cracks are commonly observed on knives made from the Case XX USA era into the 1980s. Case abruptly discontinued a number of the smaller yellow-handled knife patterns in 1975. My speculation is that this was done due to the high scrap rate of the smaller knives due to the thinner handles cracking more easily. In recent years, the cracking of the yellow delrin handle material does not seem to be a problem, possibly due to improvements in the material itself.

HANDLE KEY NUMBER 4: SMOOTH WHITE

Smooth white, also known as "white composition," goes back to the early years of Case. The early smooth white material may have been a type of celluloid; however, I have never known older Case smooth white handles to decompose or exhibit the "self destruct" characteristic often seen in celluloid. The early smooth white material used during the Case Tested era and part of the Case XX era often had an off-white color and the appearance of fine grain lines in the material. Some collectors mistake this material for genuine ivory, but Case traditionally never used ivory as handle material. The only exceptions are some recent (1980s and newer) limited edition knives with mammoth ivory handles.

The smooth white handle material used by Case from the Case XX era through the mid-1970s seems

A comparison of two Case XX USA 3254 pattern Trappers, 4-1/8", with yellow composition handles. Top knife has regular yellow composition handles, $100; bottom knife has "flat yellow" composition handles, $175.
Photo courtesy Gary Moore

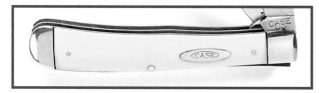

Case pocket knives with yellow composition handles. Top knife is a Case XX 3254 Trapper, 4-1/8", and the bottom knife is a 10 dot, 1970, 3254 Trapper, 4-1/8". The bottom knife has yellow delrin handles.

This Case Tested 18 pattern stock knife, 3-1/2", has been rehandled with modern yellow delrin handles. Note the newer style shield, which is not pinned. This is likely a knife that was sent back to the Case factory for replacement of the handles. Case repairs knives with no intent to deceive collectors; the company is providing a valuable service to knife owners in restoring valued keepsakes and "user" knives. However, collectors should be aware that such repaired knives exist.

to be a different material, with no grain and with a brighter white color. This material does exhibit a tendency to shrink badly and I have seen examples of Case knives with smooth white handles from 1965 to 1974 with severely shrunken handles, even on unused knives, so evidently the white material used even during these later years was not delrin. I have never seen delrin handles exhibit shrinkage.

Historically, Case made a relatively small variety of pocket knife patterns in smooth white. Examples from the past include the 4100 and 4200 "Melon Testers" and 4318 Sh Sp "stockman." The use of smooth white as a handle material seemed to end as the older patterns on which it was used were discontinued by Case. The last of the older patterns to be made with the material were the 4100 and 4318, which were discontinued in the mid-1970s.

The Texas Lockhorn, introduced in 1980, was made with white delrin handles during part of the time it was in production. Another later pattern handled in smooth white was the two-bladed "78" pattern introduced in 1979.

In 1992, Case temporarily revived smooth white as a pocket knife handle material. Four patterns, the "Peanut," "Mini Copperhead," "Trapper," and 01 pen knife, were made with a smooth white handle material that Case indicated was a "polyester-based, simulated ivory." Instead of the "4" handle code number, Case used the letter "I" as an indication of simulated ivory; I 254 SS, I 2109 X SS, I 220 SS, and I 201 SS were the actual pattern numbers. Only the "Trapper" from this series was carried over to 1993 then it, too, was discontinued for 1994.

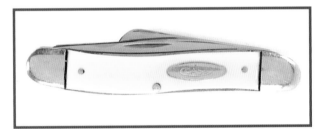

This 8 dot 1972 4318 Sh Sp stock knife exhibits significant shrinkage of the white handle material. The blades on this knife are unused.

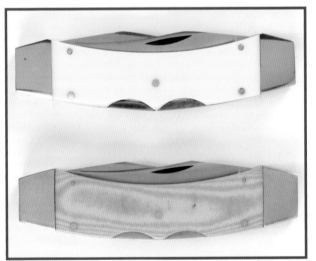

These two Texas Lockhorn knives from 1981 exhibit white delrin handles, top knife, and ivory micarta handles, bottom knife. Closed length is 4-1/2".

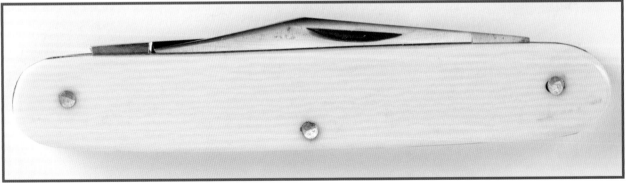

Older grained white composition handle on a Case XX-stamped 4257 pattern.

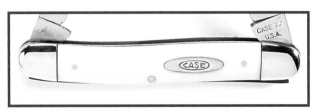

Smooth white composition handle material on a Case XX USA 04247 Sp stock knife. This knife has a pinned shield.

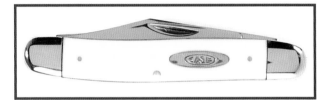

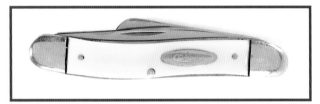

These knives illustrate the shrinkage that can occur with older white composition handles, from top: Case XX USA-stamped 04247 Sp and 8 dot 1972 4318 Sh Sp with mint blades and shrunken handle material.

HANDLE KEY NUMBER 5: GENUINE STAG

Genuine stag, usually referred to simply as "stag," has long been one of the most, if not THE most, sought after handle materials to be found on Case pocket knives. It could be said that no other handle material defines W. R. Case & Sons Cutlery Company as does stag. Stag-handled Case knives have a certain mystique about them that perhaps is matched only by bone in its many variations. The use of stag as a handle material goes back to the early years of Case, and Case's one-time rival, Case Brothers Cutlery Company, also produced stag-handled pocket knives. Stag, when processed by Case for knife handles, has a distinctive look and feel, and the maxim that "no two stag handles are ever alike" is certainly true. Stag is an imported material and as such, it has often been in limited supply due to various factors. The following informative article on stag is from the December 1981 edition of the *Case Collector's Club Newsletter*:

Staghorn from India is one of the most popular materials for knife handles. As popular as it is though, relatively little is known about it by the average knife collector. Not that this information is vitally important to the future of knife collecting, but it may be interesting to know.

The Staghorn used for knife handles comes mainly from two types of Indian deer, the Sambar and the Chital. The Sambar produces horns more suitable for slabs while the Chital's horns are preferred for making rounds that are better suited for carving sets or hunting knives.

These deer live in wildlife preserves in India. When the horns are dropped by the deer, natives in the parks collect them under supervision of park officials. After being collected by hand, they are shipped to stag markets that are anywhere from 50 to 200 miles away. The Staghorn is then sold at auctions supervised by the Indian government. The auction system maintains the value of this raw material.

Manufacturers that convert the horn into the rough handle material can be as far away as 600 miles from the auction site. One such manufacturer is located at the port of shipment in Bombay. This long journey that the raw Staghorn makes is one factor that slows delivery.

Another problem that faces the suppliers and users of Staghorn is the short gathering season. The monsoon rains usually limit the collecting of the horns to December through June. Early or usually long monsoon seasons can limit the procurement even more, making the availability of Staghorn even less than it normally is. This, of course, increases the price of the raw material.

Other problems that occur are embargos at the port of shipment or the port of entry into this country. Securing adequate shipping space and the miles of red tape also contribute to the delays in the delivery of this product.

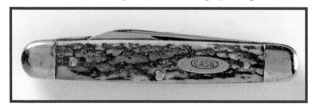

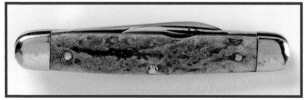

This Case XX 5279 SS pen knife has what I refer to as "snakeskin" stag, often observed on Case Tested and early Case XX-era knives.

This should give you a better idea of the journey that these little pieces of horn must take before they become the beautiful handles that you admire so much. Hopefully, this will also help to understand the price that one has to pay for a genuine stag handled knife.

Stag has been used by Case to handle pocket knives and hunting knives, as well as premium quality table carving sets, which often include a meat carving knife, a carving fork, and a sharpening steel, all with stag handles. Stag-handled steak knife sets have also been part of the Case product line.

There are a number of reasons for the mystique associated with stag as a handle material. First, when properly finished as a handle material, it has a stunning natural beauty that cannot be matched or duplicated using synthetics or other natural handle materials. There are variations that can be found in the stag used by Case over the course of many years. These variations include the Case Tested era "snake-skin" stag, which had a pebbled surface texture, the "red" stag found on Case Tested to Case XX-era knives, "second cut" stag, and the classic "burnt" stag that is found on more modern Case knives.

A second reason for the particular appeal of Case stag-handled knives to collectors is that W.R Case & Sons is, and has been, one of a very few American cutlery companies to widely use stag for handling knives. I have reviewed many old American cutlery and hardware company catalogs from circa 1890 to the 1970s and during those years, a number of firms produced pocket knives and hunting knives in the US. Based on the catalogs and on my observation of countless thousands of antique pocket knives over

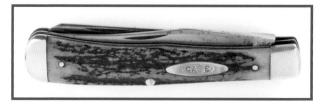

This Case Tested 5254 Trapper has stag handles that are typical of Case Tested-era stag.

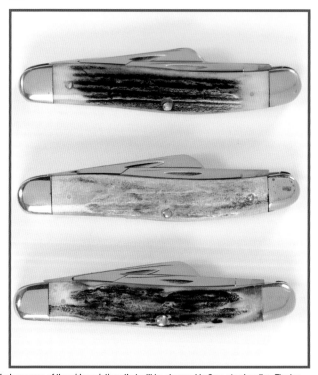

The front and back of these three Case XX USA-stamped 53047 stock knife patterns, 3-7/8", show some of the wide variations that will be observed in Case stag handles. The top knife has light colored stag, almost white in spots. The center knife has medium golden color stag. The lower knife has the more classic burnt color stag. No two Case stag handles are ever quite alike.

many years, I have come to the conclusion that Case and Union Cutlery/KABAR were the only two American cutlery firms to offer a significant variety of stag-handled pocket and hunting knife patterns from 1900 to the 1960s. Other companies did use stag, but not to the extent that it was used by these two firms.

Particularly from 1920 to 1940, other cutlery firms including the industry giants Remington and Winchester, as well as the smaller firms like Utica, Schrade, Western, and Robeson, did indeed offer stag-handled pocket knives. However, Case seemed to offer stag handles on a significantly wider range of patterns as compared to these other firms. Then, too, the stag used by other knife companies often fails to match the beauty of Case stag. I do not know whether this was due to different sourcing or different processing of the stag, but Case stag handles seem to have a unique beauty.

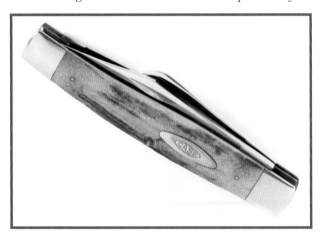

A Case XX USA 5375 large stock knife has smooth stag on the front and gnarly stag on the back. Often the smoother pieces of stag were used for front handles in order to facilitate installation of the CASE shield.

In the post-WWII period, both Case and KABAR continued to manufacture broad lines of stag-handled knives, while stag was all but abandoned by other American cutlery companies. Robeson Cutlery Company did use some stag on knives made during the late 1940s through the 1950s, but other pocket knife manufacturers opted for the use of bone and/or synthetic materials during this time frame.

Beginning in the late 1970s, stag made a modest comeback as some American cutlery firms reintroduced stag handles due to the burgeoning popularity of knife collecting and the appreciation of stag among collectors. As an example, Queen Cutlery Company to the best of my knowledge never made any stag-handled pocket knives from the immediate post-WWII years through the 1970s, but beginning in the 1980s and to today, Queen has made a number of them intended for the collector market.

CASE STAG HANDLE VARIATIONS

From the Case Tested era through the Case XX USA era, there were two important variations of stag used by Case as a handle material. As with many handle variations from that era, the use of these two stag variations was a random manufacturing change, as neither of the variations was ever indicated in any Case factory catalog or price list.

Red stag: "Red stag" was a stag handle variation that will be observed on some examples of knives with the CASE TESTED and CASE XX tang stamps. Red stag has a red tint, which can vary from very subtle to a more definite red color. This color can affect one or both handles on a particular knife. I have never read any documentation that explains the origin of red stag. It may have been a natural stag variation or it is possible that Case dyed some of the stag during those years.

Case pocket knife patterns handled in red stag are scarce, and not every stag-handled knife pattern will be found in red stag. Red stag seems to have disappeared after the early Case XX yeas and is often observed on older Case patterns that have "long pull" master blades. Beginning in the 1990s, Case introduced a new red stag as a handle material, which is dyed to achieve the red tint.

Second cut stag: "Second cut stag" is one of the more interesting and unusual of the older handling materials used by Case and in general is stag that has been formed into slabs and jigged. There is some controversy as to the origin of the second cut stag that was used on older pocket knives from the pre-WWII era until about 1970.

"Regular" stag handles are formed from the outer layer of the stag antler and the natural antler surface is largely left in place as the handles are attached to the knife scales and hafted and finished. Second cut stag by contrast is made from a piece of antler that is finished into a flat slab and then machine jigged to provide a textured surface, as is done with bone handle material. When Case used second cut stag as a handle material, it was also dyed, whereas regular stag handles are flame-treated to enhance the natural colors.

There are two different stories that circulate among Case collectors as to the origins of the older Case second cut stag. One story asserts it was made from thicker stag pieces and that once the outer layer was removed to make a handle, there was an inner layer that could be sawed out in the form of a slab and these slabs were then jigged and dyed to make second cut stag handles.

The other story is that whenever Case received a shipment of stag, there were always individual pieces that had smooth outer layers that lacked the "character" and texture necessary to make a completed stag handle. These smooth pieces of stag were saved up and then quantities were slabbed, jigged, and dyed to make handles.

I personally have never seen any documentation that would serve to support or refute either story.

Many Case knife collectors and dealers assert that second cut stag was used during the Case Tested era on the larger folding hunter patterns, primarily the 65 and 72 patterns. Personally, I do not know how to discern the difference between second cut stag and green bone

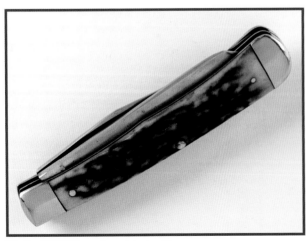

This Case XX 5254 Trapper has red stag handles.

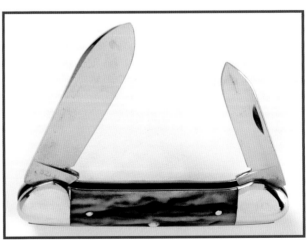

Case XX 52131 Canoe with red stag on the front and dark stag on the back.

on these older Tested-era patterns, as a variety of jig patterns were used on Case green bone handles during these years and if second cut stag was indeed used, it resembles the green bone handles from the period.

Case used second cut stag on a number of knives during the Case XX USA era, and this is readily discernible from both bone and stag. Second cut stag was predominantly used on several larger patterns including the 54 "Trapper," 88 "Large Congress," and 75 "Jumbo Stockman." Second cut stag used during the Case XX USA era has a different jig pattern as compared to the bone handles made during those years. The second cut stag jigging has longer "worm groove" style grooves.

This Case XX 5375 large stock knife with long pull has light-colored red stag handles.

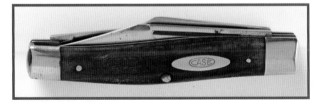

This Case XX 5375 large stock knife with long pull has dark red stag on the front and very dark stag on the back. Stag handles often vary significantly from the front to the back on a particular knife.

Case R5318 stock knife made in 1997 with new red stag handles.

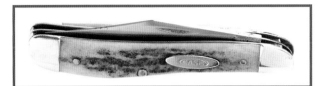

Case XX 5220 Peanut with stag handles; note the variation in the stag handles front to back.

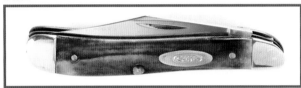

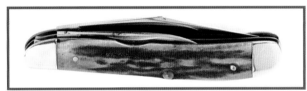

Case XX 5220 Peanut with red stag handles on the front and back.

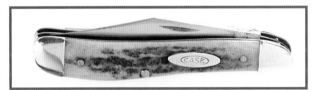

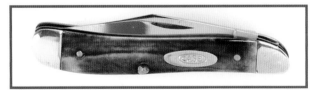

Case XX-stamped 5220 Peanuts, 2-3/4", showing a comparison of "regular" stag handle (top knife) and red stag handle (bottom knife).

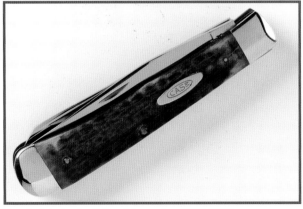

Second cut stag handle with "bone" dye, on a Case XX USA 6254 Trapper.

During the Case XX USA era, some of the second cut stag produced was dyed with a yellow-tinted dye and used on stag-handled patterns with the handle key number "5." At other times, the second cut stag was dyed with a dark red- or wine-colored dye and used on bone-handled knives with the handle key number "6." Both of these variations are relatively rare and highly desired by collectors. Beginning in the 1980s, Case reintroduced second cut stag handle material for use on some limited-edition pocket knives.

STAG-HANDLED KNIVES AND THE RISE OF KNIFE COLLECTING

Whereas most other knife manufacturers in the USA generally limited or dropped stag as a handle material after WWII, Case continued to manufacture a relatively broad line of stag-handled pocket and hunting knives as part of its general product line through the 1950s and 1960s. Case's continued use of natural handle materials in general, and genuine stag in particular, contributed significantly to the rise in popularity of Case pocket knife collecting in the mid- to late 1960s.

However, the use of stag was often curtailed due to the fact that the export of stag was sometimes embargoed by the Indian government for periods of time. My understanding is that these embargoes were intended to fight the poaching of deer to obtain stag instead of the collection of naturally shed antlers. It is perhaps a twist of fate that the timing of one of these stag embargoes contributed significantly to the demand for Case stag-handled knives and the

A comparison of two Case XX USA 54 pattern Trappers, 4-1/8", with second cut stag handles. Top knife is a second cut 6254, dark dye, and the bottom knife is a 5254 second cut, lighter yellowish dye; $1,000 each. Photo courtesy Gary Moore

popularity of Case pocket knife collecting in general.

During the time period of the late 1960s and into 1970, the collecting of Case pocket knives was rapidly gaining popularity. There were several reasons for this. Due to the increasingly stringent gun control laws enacted in the late 1960s, many gun traders and collectors began to abandon or limit their activity with guns, and some even sold off their gun inventories and became knife collectors or dealers. Gun and knife trading and collecting had traditionally gone hand in hand, as much knife trading activity happened at gun shows and trade days where guns were traded. In those days, gun and pawn shops were often dealers for pocket and hunting knives and Case was a premium brand often sold at the better gun shops.

The fact that Case had recently changed tang stampings, from CASE XX to CASE XX USA, also promoted a lot of interest in the brand, as collectors bought up the older knives with the CASE XX tang stampings. The next tang stamp change in 1970 to the "ten dots" stamping created further interest. At the same time, the first knife books were being published and while the early knife books did cover multiple brands, Case knives were prominent and generally documented in the most detail.

Each of these factors contributed to a significant rise in the popularity of Case pocket knives among collectors in the early 1970s. It should also be considered that knife *users* were still the "bedrock" market for Case pocket and hunting knives at the time, so the overall demand for Case products, combined with the company philosophy of providing a hand-crafted product, meant that Case had a difficult time supplying enough knives to meet the market demand at the time. Stag-handled knives in particular were popular with both collectors and users.

While bone was also a popular handle material among collectors, stag is much more distinctive. While bone handles can be either light or dark, and the colors can vary from "plain" to "dazzling," stag handles on Case knives have always been stunning in appearance. That, plus the fact stag-handled patterns were always in the minority in the Case line, led to the buildup of a certain "mystique" surrounding genuine stag-handled Case knives. The term "Case stag" was universally understood among knife collectors, as in, "He just bought a collection of Case stags," or "I just traded that knife for a Case stag."

It just so happened that while collector interest was rising, the supply of Case stags was about to nosedive. In mid-1970, Case announced it was "temporarily" discontinuing stag-handled pocket and hunting knives. Case had gone into 1970 producing a total of 20 stag-handled pocket knife patterns and 10 stag-handled hunting knife patterns. This was in addition to some stag-handled carving sets and steak knife sets in the household cutlery line.

I believe this discontinuance was due to an embargo, but I do not know this for a fact. It may have been due to a slowdown rather than a complete shutdown in the supply of stag. While stag supplies may have been interrupted prior to this, the 1970 interruption represented the first time in Case's history that the entire stag-handled knife line was officially discontinued. Beginning with the 1971 Case factory price list, these 20 pocket knife patterns and nine of the ten hunting knife patterns were listed as "discontinued."

Case did continue to use some stag through the early 1970s, but for standard catalog products, it was limited to the Kodiak Hunter hunting knife and several carving and steak knife sets. The 1974 Case factory catalog (Catalog #71) included the Kodiak Hunter in stag, along with four stag-handled carving sets and two stag-handled steak knife sets. As these were all relatively low-production volume items, evidently Case was able to obtain enough stag to keep them in the standard product line.

When Case discontinued the use of stag on pocket knives in 1970, the news created a surge of interest in Case stags and in the collecting of Case pocket knives in general. Knife collectors scoured Case dealers to purchase the last Case stags that were shipped from the factory in 1970 with the "ten dot" tang stamping. Likewise, the older stags with the CASE XX USA and CASE XX stampings were sought after and knife dealers could often double their money quickly on these.

While Case stag-handled pocket knives had always retailed for a bit higher price than the same knives in bone, in 1970 the retail prices on Case stags were relatively modest, and ranged from $6 for the 5220 "Peanut" to $13 for the 5172 Bulldog. Retail prices for stag-handled hunting knives at the time ranged from $5.50 for the little M5 FINN to $40 for the 561 Deluxe Knif-Ax. The Kodiak Hunter retailed for $25. So for "collector" values on Case stags, the only direction was "up."

THE 1973 STAG COLLECTOR'S SETS

In response to burgeoning collector interest, Case announced the release of a "Stag Collector's Set" of Case stags in 1973. There is some misunderstanding by collectors regarding these sets, which are often called the "1973 Stag Sets." Due to the year of release, some collectors assume the knives were made with the 1973 Case tang stamping (seven dots). This is incorrect. The actual story is somewhat detailed and there are a few nuances. The following represents my understanding of the genesis of these sets.

When Case ceased the production of the general line of stag-handled pocket and hunting knives in mid-1970, the company stopped taking orders for these from dealers. At the time, there were some completed stag-handled knives in stock at Case, and there were many blades that were stamped out and completed with "5" pattern numbers that could not be assembled into completed knives due to the interruption in stag supplies. These blades were stamped with the CASE XX USA and the CASE XX USA (ten dots) tang stampings. So Case kept the completed knives, as well as the leftover stag numbered blades, in stock. As smaller supplies of stag were obtained from 1970-1973, Case used these "old stock" blades to assemble stag-handled pocket and hunting knives. These completed knives were also kept in stock at Case. Apparently Case began planning the release of the 1973 collector's sets during this time.

In 1971, while the production of the additional stags was in process, Case did stamp out some additional new blades for the manufacture of stag-handled knife patterns for the sets. These blades had the 1971 (nine dot) tang stamping. Two of these were special knives that had not been previously produced. The 5111 1/2 L SSP Cheetah and 5347 Sh Sp SSP were both produced just for inclusion in the 1973 stag sets.

Both of these knives featured glazed-finished stainless steel blades with Case's Polished Edge final sharpening. The 5347 Sh Sp SSP featured the "TESTED XX RAZOR EDGE" blade etch found on some other stainless pocket knives. Case had previously produced a similar stainless pattern, the 5347 Sh Sp SS; however, this knife had mirror polished blades with no etching on the main blade. The 5111 1/2 L SSP featured a CHEETAH blade etching. While the CHEETAH was based on the 6111 1/2 L, a long-time standard Case pattern, it was significantly different, with the stainless blade and etching. The CHEETAH could be considered the first Case pocket knife designed specifically for the "collector" market.

Other stag-handled pocket knife patterns produced in 1971 with nine dot blades include the 5220, 5232, 5332, and 53087 Sh Pen. These were general production knives that were identical to the same patterns in the USA and ten dot stampings. My guess is that Case needed these additional knives to round out the sets due to a lack of leftover knives/blades in these particular patterns.

The chart below outlines the patterns of stag-handled pocket knives produced by Case from 1965 up to and including 1970, when they were discontinued. The chart shows the patterns that were discontinued during the Case XX USA era prior to 1970 and indicates the 20 patterns that were still in production in 1970.

One important note is that the 5172 Bulldog was never made with ten dots. In fact, since the 5172 with the Bulldog blade etch and box was last made in 1970, it was never made with the "dots" dating system at all. The 5172 patterns in the sets had the CASE XX USA-era stamping used on the 5172, with CASE XX over 5172 on the front tang and HAND MADE over IN U.S.A. on the rear tang.

Case accumulated stag and manufactured additional stag knives until 2,000 sets were available, with 17 pocket knives and five hunting knives per set. While it is believed the majority of the pocket knives included in these sets (other than the special nine dot runs) were 1970 ten dot knives, it is possible that some knives shipped in the sets had the CASE XX USA tang stamping. With the exception of the Cheetah and 5347 Sh Sp SSP as already described, none of the pocket knives or hunting knives in these sets had any special blade etch or other identifier. The knives were standard production Case stag-handled knives and are indistinguishable from other stag-handled pocket and hunting knives bearing the CASE XX USA and CASE XX USA (ten dot) tang stampings. Since Case stags were in regular production through mid-1970, many ten dot stags had previously been shipped to dealers as standard stock.

The 1973 stag sets also included five patterns of stag-handled hunting knives. Since hunting knives were not made with the "dots" dating system, all of the stag hunting knives included in the sets had the CASE XX USA tang stamping. Each stag set was shipped from the factory in a box with a packing list. Based on information obtained from an undated

Case Stag Pocket Knives 1965 - 1970	Pattern	CASE XX USA 1965 To 1969	CASE XX USA Ten Dots 1970	Comments
One Blade	5165 SAB "Folding Hunter"	x	- - -	Discontinued 1/1/66 and rare with the USA stamping
Knives	5172 "Bulldog"	x	- - -	Was produced in 1970 but not stamped with dots
Two Blade	5220 "Peanut"	x	x	
Knives	5232	x	x	
	5233	x	x	
	05247 Sp	x	- - -	Discontinued 4/1/67 and scarce with the USA stamping
	5254 "Trapper"	x	x	
	05263 SS "Eisenhower"	x	x	
	5265 SAB "Folding Hunter"	x	x	
	5279 SS	x	- - -	Discontinued 1/1/66 and rare with the USA stamping
	52087	x	x	
	5299 1/2	x	x	
	52131 "Canoe"	x	x	
Three Blade	5332	x	x	
Knives	5347 Sh Sp	x	x	
	5347 Sh Sp SS	x	x	Polished Blades - Scarce in 1970 ten dot stamping
	53047	x	x	
	5375	x	x	
	5383 "Whittler"	x	x	
	53087 Sh Pen	x	x	
	5392	x	x	
Four Blade	54052 "Congress"	x	x	
Knives	5488 "Large Congress"	x	x	
All stag handled pocket knives were "temporarily" discontinued in mid 1970.				

Case factory letter, apparently each set consisted of one of the two assortments shown in the chart below.

An interesting note is that there were certain patterns (shown at the bottom of the chart) that were not shown as included in either of the two assortments. It is possible these two assortments were not "absolute" as the only two shipped and that the other patterns were included in some assortments. Another possibility is that the stock of the five patterns not included in either assortment had been depleted and there were no leftover blades for these knives, so they were simply left out of the sets. That would mean the only ten-dot examples of these knives in circulation would be the ones manufactured in 1970 and shipped prior to the discontinuance of stag. The

fact that all of the "47" patterns are in this list could explain why Case chose to produce the 5347 Sh Sp SSP as a special pattern for inclusion in the sets.

These sets were well accepted in the marketplace and were sent to the Case sales representatives on allotment, with each rep being allocated a fixed number of sets to sell. Case collectors scoured Case dealers to acquire these sets. Since there were no serial numbers or other special attributes, the sets were usually broken up for resale. The demand for Case stags had skyrocketed since 1970 and these sets were eagerly anticipated by collectors. I recall one dealer who tried to corner the market on the Cheetah pattern and at one time was known to have accumulated more than 125 of them.

THE 1976 STAG COLLECTOR'S SETS

The saga of Case stags with ten dot, nine dot, and USA-stamped blades did not end after the release of the 1973 stag sets. After the release of the 2,000 1973 sets, Case still had many of the older blades left in stock, and the company was still acquiring stag

Assortment #1	Assortment #2
5111 1/2 L S S P (1)	5111 1/2 L S S P (1)
5220 (2)	5220 (1)
5233 (1)	5232 (1)
5332 (1)	5233 (1)
5347 Sh Sp SSP (1)	5332 (1)
54052 (1)	5347 Sh Sp SSP (1)
5254 (3)	54052 (1)
05263 SS (1)	5254 (2)
5265 S AB DR (2)	05263 SS (1)
5375 (2)	5265 S AB DR (1)
52087 (1)	52131 (1)
52131 (1)	5172 (1)
M5 FINN (2)	5375 (1)
5361 (1)	5392 (1)
523-6" (2)	53087 Sh Pen (1)
	5488 (1)
	M5 FINN
	523-3 1/4"
	516-5"
	523-5"
	523-6"

Patterns Made In 1970 Not Shown In Either Assortment	
	5299 1/2
	5347 Sh Sp
	5347 Sh Sp SS
	53047
	5383 "Whittler"

Case XX USA 9 Dot, 1971, 5111-1/2 LSSP CHEETAH, 4-3/8", $450.

		Pattern	Tang Stamping
Case Stag Sets Released January 1976	Pocket Knives	5111 1/2 L SSP "Cheetah"	Case XX USA Nine Dots
		5172 "Bulldog"	Case XX USA
		5220 "Peanut"	Case XX USA Ten Dots
		5254 "Trapper"	Case XX USA Ten Dots
		5265 SAB "Folding Hunter"	Case XX USA Ten Dots
		52131 "Canoe"	Case XX USA Ten Dots
		5347 Sh Sp SSP	Case XX USA Nine Dots
		5375	Case XX USA Ten Dots
	Hunting Knives	M5 FINN	Case XX USA
		516-5"	Case XX USA
		523-6"	Case XX USA

Approximately 700 of these sets were released in early 1976.
The knives were produced using blades that were stamped with CASE XX USA
and with the CASE XX USA ten dot and nine dot stampings.
These older blades were left over from the production of the 1973 stag sets.
Each set as relased did not have all of the patterns shown, but included a total of seven pocket knives and five hunting knives.

and manufacturing completed stag-handled knives using these blades. In January of 1976, Case released approximately 700 additional stag sets. The knives in these sets were made up between 1973 and late 1975 using the leftover "old stock" blades. As with the 1973 sets, there were no identifying markings or etches that identified these knives as being part of the 1976 sets. They were identical to the 1973 release knives.

The 1976 stag sets included fewer patterns as shown in the chart above.

Again these sets were allocated to the Case sales reps, with the allocations varying in different sales territories. A review of some internal Case sales documents indicated that the different allocations added up to a total of 700 sets. There was no exact documentation available as to the "assortments" that may have been included in each set as shipped. However, the following is excerpted from a Case sales memo dated Jan. 30, 1976:

We have now decided to release the remaining Genuine Stag Knives blanked prior to the August 1970 termination date of the Genuine Stag line. These are the balance of patterns left after our original Genuine Stag Collector's Assortment offered in the Fall of 1973.

The total is about a third as many assortments with not as many Pockets though there are some real valuable collector's items in them. Each assortment contains a variety of medium and large pocket knives having from nine to ten dots and a few with just the "U.S.A." and no dots.

Each assortment will have at least one #5172 "Bulldog" and #5111 1/2 L "Cheetah" and #5254 "Trapper." As a matter of fact, almost all sets will have two Cheetahs, but the few that do not (approx. 100 of them) will have a #52131 "Canoe" as a substitute for the second Cheetah. In all, seven Pockets and five Hunters.

Again, these knives were well received, although at the time, some collectors and dealers got a bit upset at the fact that all of a sudden in 1976 there was a new release of knives with older USA, 1970, and 1971 tang stampings. This release tended to depress the prices of the Cheetah and the 5347 Sh Sp SSP in particular. Whereas these two patterns had been considered to be scarce, now there was a small flood of new ones with the same nine dot tang stampings. Gradually the market absorbed them all and like all older Case stags they are highly sought after by collectors.

MORE STAG LIMITED EDITION KNIVES AND ANNUAL SETS, 1976-1981

Beginning in 1976, Case seemed to have a better supply of stag available as more stag-handled "limited edition" knives were manufactured and released during that year. The 5137 Kentucky Bicentennial

Knife, the third and final release in that series, was made in 1976 in a quantity of 30,000. This knife was a Sod Buster Junior with stag handles. Other limited editions made in 1976 include the American Spirit 5165 SAB SSP folding hunter (10,000 made) and Double Eagle 523-7 hunting knife (2,500 made). These last two were designed to commemorate the USA Bicentennial in 1976.

Also beginning in 1976, annual stag sets were released. For each of the years 1976-1981, a new "limited production" stag set was produced. Each set was made with the "dots" stamping for that year on the pocket knives and each had a special blade etch. All of the pocket and hunting knives made for these sets had glazed finish stainless steel blades with Case's "polished edge" so each pattern number ended in SSP.

These stag sets were again allocated to the Case representatives each year. My understanding is that unlike standard catalog knives, Case dealers could not order the stag sets directly from Case; instead they had to be ordered through the reps. Most of the knives were not serialized but for the years of 1977-1981 a serialized "mint set" with scrolled bolsters was released for each year. The chart on P. 62 shows the patterns made and the quantities released for these annual stag sets.

There are some additional details to note relative to these annual stag sets. Other then the "Mint Sets," these stag knives were released individually wrapped and bulk packed in the Case "pumpkin" boxes, with six pocket knives or three hunting knives to a box. For some reason, each annual set was released to the market the year after the knives were produced. So the 1976 stamped knives (four dots) were actually released in 1977, the 1977 knives in 1978, etc. It appears that the 1981 stamped knives were released in late 1982 to 1983.

This led to at least two anomalies in the sets. The 1977 "Blue Scroll" release includes some examples of the 52087 SSP pattern that were stamped with two instead of three dots. Also in the "Blue Scroll" knives, there were two variations of the "33" pattern made. The tooling for the "33" pattern changed in 1976-1977

from the old style with a narrow master blade to the new "033" pattern with the different frame and the wider master blade. So instead of just the 5233 SSP there were also a number (about 20 percent of the total production) of the 52033 SSP released.

As to the quantities of knives produced as noted in the chart on P. 62, most of this information came from an undated Case factory letter. This letter was apparently a "form letter" that Case sent out to collectors in response to inquiries about stag handled knives. I have seen other sources that present somewhat different production quantities. There has been some confusion in particular as to the quantities of hunting knives released in the 1979 "Bradford Centennial" sets. Information from the Case archives reveals that initially there were to be no hunting knives produced for these sets, due to the limited availability of stag. Then more supplies were procured and the final release was 2,500 each of four different hunting knife patterns,

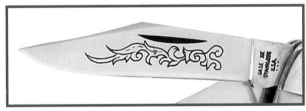

Blade etching—1977 "blue scroll" stag set.

Blade etching, 1978 "red scroll" stag set.

Blade etching, 1979 "Bradford Centennial" stag set.

Blade etching, 1980 "Case 75th Anniversary" stag set.

Case Limited Production Annual Stag Sets With Quantities Made - 1976 To 1981			
Year Made	1976	1977	1978	1979
Tang Stamping	Case XX USA 4 Dots	Case XX USA 3 Dots	Case XX USA 2 Dots	Case XX USA 1 Dot
Blade Etching	Case XX "Gray Scroll"	"Blue Scroll"	Case XX "Red Scroll"	"1879 Bradford Centennial 1979"
Pocket Knives	15,000	19,000	14,000	7,500
Hunting Knives	5,000	7,500	2,500	2,500
Mint Sets	None	1,000	1,000	1,000
Pocket Knives	Pattern	Pattern	Pattern	Pattern
	5111 1/2 L SSP	5111 1/2 L SSP	5220 SSP	5207 Sp SSP
	5172 SSP	5172 SSP	52032 SSP	52027 SSP
	5233 SSP	5233 SSP	5254 SSP	5249 SSP
	5254 SSP	5254 SSP	5279 SSP	5275 SSP
	5265 SAB SSP	5265 SAB SSP	52087 SSP	5292 SSP
	52087 SSP	52087 SSP	MUSKRAT SSP	5318 Sh Sp SSP
	5347 Sh Sp SSP	52131 SSP	5347 Sh Sp SSP	
		5347 Sh Sp SSP		
Hunting Knives	516-5 SSP	516-5 SSP	516-5 SSP	
	523-5 SSP	523-5 SSP	523-5 SSP	
	5 FINN SSP	5 FINN SSP	5 FINN SSP	
	M5 FINN SSP	M5 FINN SSP	M5 FINN SSP	

Year Made	1980	1981
Tang Stamping	Case XX USA "Lightning S" 10 Dots	Case XX USA "Lightning S" 9 Dots
Blade Etching	"1905 75th Anniversary 1980"	No Etch
Pocket Knives	7,500	Not Known
Hunting Knives	None	None
Mint Sets	1,000	1,000
Pocket Knives	Pattern	Pattern
	5207 Sp SSP	5149 SSP
	5208 SSP	52027 SSP
	5235 1/2 SSP	5235 1/2 SSP
	5244 SSP	5254 SSP
	5275 Sp SSP	MUSKRAT SSP
	52109 X SSP	53131 SSP
	5318 Sh Sp SSP	

as explained in this excerpt from the *Case Collector's Club Newsletter* of June 1981:

In the March issue of this newsletter there was an article on page 8 about genuine stag sets. In that article, under the 1979 Bradford Centennial stag set, there was no mention made of stag hunters. This is because at that time Case had no genuine stag available to make 1979 series hunters. However, this has changed.

We were able to locate some suitable genuine stag, so we are able to make a 1979 I-dot Genuine Stag Set photo-etch. There will be four patterns made in a quantity of 2,500 each. M5 FINN SSP, 5 FINN SSP, 516-5 SSP, and 523-5 SSP.

These stag hunters will be available sometime around the end of September or early October. By the September issue of this newsletter, a definite date of release should be available.

Note from the above excerpt that the 1979 hunting knives were actually released in late 1981. Other interesting information was revealed relative to the 1981 stag sets. Apparently, Case decided to handle the release of these particular sets a little differently. They were not considered as "limited" edition knives but as standard product pocket knives. This is explained in this excerpt from the *Case Collector's Club Newsletter* of September 1982:

1981 (9 DOT) Stag Pockets: Every year since 1978, CASE has issued a Stag Pocket knife Collector's set. This included 7,500 regular sets and 1,000 serial numbered mint sets.

In the past few years, the demand for stag pocket knives has changed. Therefore, CASE is changing to meet the demand.

Instead of the 7,500 regular sets of pocket knives we will be adding six patterns of stag-handled knives to our regular line. The knives will be available to our dealers in late October. We will ship them as available.

We will continue to issue 1,000 mint sets. This edition promises to be extra special. WE will have full details and photos in the December newsletter.

The patterns in open stock and in mint set are 52027 SS, 5235 1/2 SSP, 5149 SSP, 5254 SSP, STAG MUSKRAT and 53131 SSP. In addition to the Stag handles, all will have glazed finish stainless steel blades with polished edges, stainless steel springs, brass liners and nickel-silver bolsters.

Evidently it took awhile for these knives to be released. This is an excerpt from the Case Collector's Club Newsletter of March 1983:

9 DOT STAGS – they are now available as an open stock item through your local dealer. Hurry and get yours! The patterns are 52027 SSP, 5235 1/2 SSP, 5149 SSP, 5254 SSP, Stag Muskrat SSP and 53131 SSP.

Based on the above, no information as to the quantities made of the 1981 stag knives (other than the mint sets) was published as the knives were not considered to be "limited." These patterns were only in production for one year with the "lightning s" nine dot stamping. Due to the release of the mint sets and the fact the general release stags were only made in 1981, Case collectors generally consider the 1981 stag knives to be an "annual set" in the same vein as the 1976-1980 sets.

OTHER STAG LIMITED RELEASES AND BACK TO STANDARD PRODUCTION

From 1979 through 1983, Case released a number of additional limited edition knives and special factory order or SFO knives in stag. Limited editions included stag-handled versions of the "shark" series lockback knives (5158 L SSP, 5159 L SSP, and 5197 L SSP). There were also some additional limited edi-

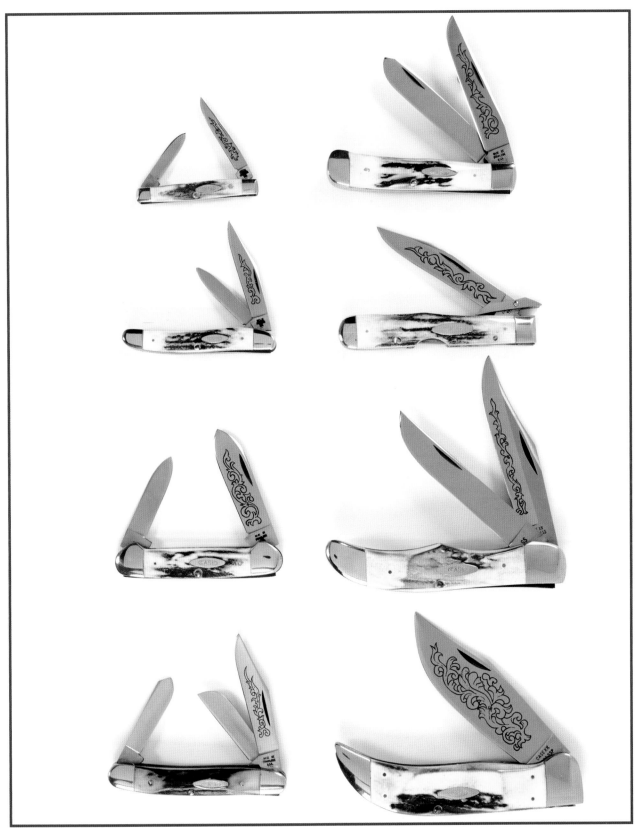

Pocket knives from the "blue scroll" stag set made in 1977 and issued in 1978. Left row, from top: 5233 SSP pen knife (2-5/8"), 52087 SSP jack knife (3-1/4"), 52131 SSP Canoe (3-5/8"), 5347 Sh Sp SSP stock knife (3-7/8"). Right row, from top: 5254 SSP Trapper (4-1/8"), 5111 1/2 L SSP (4-3/8"), 5265 SAB SSP (5-1/4"), 5172 SSP (5-1/2").

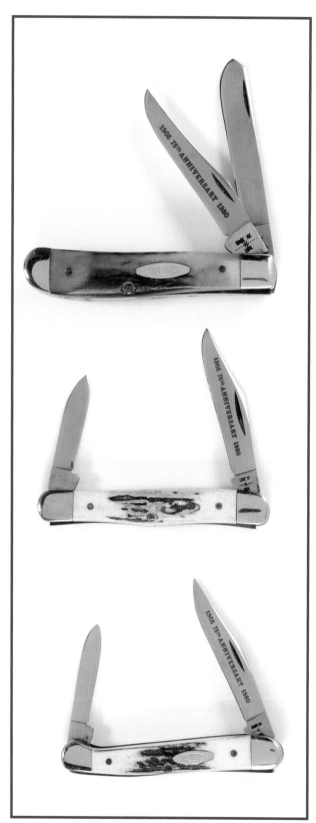

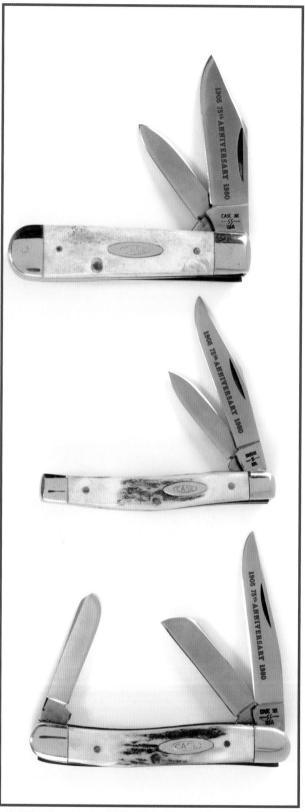

Pocket knives from the Case 1980 "Case 75th Anniversary" stag set, made in 1980 and released in 1981. Left row, from top: 5207 Sp SSP, 3-1/2"; 5208 SSP, 3-1/4"; and 52109 X SSP, 3-1/8". Right row, from top: 5235 1/2 SSP, 3-3/8"; 5244 SSP, 3-/4"; and 5318 Sh Sp SSP, 3-1/2".

Pocket knives from the Case 1979 "Bradford Centennial" stag set, made in 1979 and released in 1980. At left, from top: 52027 SSP, 2-3/4"; 5207 Sp SSP, 3-1/2"; and 5249 SSP, 3-15/16". At right, from top: 5275 Sp SSP, 4-1/4"; 5292 SSP, 4"; and 5318 Sh Sp SSP, 3-1/2".

Four of the pocket knives from the 1978 "Red Scroll" stag set, made in 1978 and released in 1979. Left, from top: 52032 SSP, 3-1/2"; 52087 SSP, 3-1/4". At right, from top: 5347 Sh Sp SSP, 3-7/8", and MUSKRAT SSP, 3-7/8".

tion stag hunting knives made with round stag handles instead of the traditional "scale tang" handle construction with stag slab handles. SFO releases that were made for Case customers in limited runs included a 5185 SSP stag "doctor's knife" and two different sets of pocket knives with second cut stag handles that were made in 1983 and 1984.

All of the mentioned stag knives and sets released from 1973 to 1983 were limited or SFO knives that were not considered part of the Case "standard product" line. As noted, the 1981 stags were technically an exception to this, but were nonetheless only in production for one year. Each year beginning in 1971, there were no stag-handled pocket knives in the standard product line, and only one hunting knife (the Kodiak Hunter).

Beginning in 1979, Case added stag-handled pocket knives to the standard product line in a small way. The new Gentlemen's Line, introduced in 1979, included a 5120 R SSP "Peanut" and a 52042 R SSP pen knife, both with stag handles. The following year, the 52033 R SSP and 05263 R SSP pen knives were also added. A small stag-handled hunting knife, the 523-3 1/4" small game knife, was also introduced in 1980. These four patterns of pocket knives and one hunting knife represented the first true production of "standard product" stag-handled knives by Case since 1970.

Beginning in 1984, Case made a permanent addition of open stock (not limited production) stag-handled pocket knives to the standard product line. There were six new stag-handled pocket knife patterns introduced that were added to the line in addition to the 5120 SSP, 52033 SSP, and 05263 SSP that were still in production (without bails) after the Gentlemen's Line had been dissolved. The patterns produced are shown in this chart:

Case Stag Pocket Knives 1984 "Open Stock" Standard Product Line 1984-1986	
Pattern	Notes
5225 1/2 SS	Polished
52032 SS	Blades
5254 SS	With Shields
5318 Sh Sp SS	"Jigged"
53032 SS	Stag
53033 SS	1984-1985
	"Regular"
	Stag
	1985-1986
5120 SSP	Glazed
52033 SSP	Blades
05263 SSP	No Shields
	"Regular"
	Stag

The three former Gentlemen's Line patterns had glazed blades and were made without Case shields. The six newly introduced stag pocket knife patterns were made with polished stainless steel blades and were produced in an unusual stag variation. The stag was processed in a manner similar to that used for bone, but rather than leaving the natural texture and "burl" in place on the antler slabs as had been traditionally done, Case smoothed the stag slabs, removing the natural texture. Then the slabs were jigged

Case Stag Pocket Knives Standard Product Line 1987-1990	
Pattern	Notes
5220 SS	Polished
52032 SS	Blades
52033 SS	All With
05263 SS	Shields
5254 SS	"Raised Letter"
52087 SS	Shields
5318 Sh Sp SS	1987-1989
53032 SS	Oval Shields
53033 SS	Mid 1989-1990

Pocket Knives With Damascus Blades Stag Handles 1989-1990	
	5120 D
	5125 1/2 D
	51059 L D
	511098 D
	51405 L D
	5207 Sp D
	5215 D
	52033 D
	52042 D
	5254 D
	52131 D
	5347 Sh Sp D

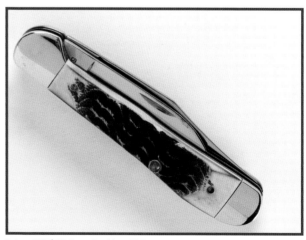

An example of mid-1980s-era jigged stag handles, with front and back handle shown. The knife is an SFO 5249 Copperhead from 1985.

with a special jig pattern and the oval opening for the shield was milled out. The slabs were either dyed or flame treated (I do not know the exact process) so that the finished handles had a resemblance to stag. These jigged stag handles are considered by collectors to be a form of second cut stag, though they were presented and marketed by Case at the time as stag.

While this jigged stag was an attractive handle material in its own way, unfortunately, at least in my opinion, the finished handles did not really resemble the genuine stag handles that had traditionally graced fine Case stag-handled pocket knives. Other collectors must have agreed with me, because by 1986 the use of the jigged stag had been dropped and Case went back to the use of stag handles that were processed in the traditional manner. Since the jigged stag knives were in production during the years of 1984-1985, they will be found with the "shoulderless grind" blades in addition to the traditional square grind blades.

The nine stag pocket knife patterns in the chart on P. 67 remained in the Case line through 1986. Beginning in 1987, the three smaller knives with glazed blades were discontinued and three patterns were added to the line with polished blades, as shown in the chart. The knives made in 1987-1988 will have the "raised letter" shields. In 1989, the use of the "raised letter" shields continued but midway through the year a change was made back to the older style "oval" shield. It is therefore possible that both style shields will be found on a particular stag pattern made in 1989.

Also in 1989-1990, Case produced pocket knives with Damascus steel blades for the first time, 12 of which were produced in stag; see chart near top right on P. 67. Again these will be found with both the "raised letter" shield, as well as the old-style oval shields.

While the Damascus-bladed knives (see chart P. 67) were considered to be standard product knives, their production was limited due to the high retail prices (suggested retail prices ranged from $60 to $130 per knife in 1989).

From 1989-1990, Case management introduced a bewildering number of knives in both new and old patterns, many in limited production. Some of these releases were stag-handled knives, including a large percentage of patterns in the Case Centennial series.

Beginning in 1991, Case was under new management again and the standard product line was revamped.

From 1991 through 2000, Case continued to produce a standard product line of stag-handled pocket and hunting knives each year. The patterns produced varied but in general from seven to 15 patterns of pocket knives and lockback folders were included, as well as several hunting knives.

During this period, Case introduced some new stag variations including Vintage Stag, Midnight Stag, and a new Red Stag. The production of stag-handled knives was interrupted by a new embargo after 2000, which lasted for several years, but Case has resumed production in recent years.

Another example of mid-1980s-era jigged stag handles. The knife is an SFO 5254 SS Trapper from 1985 that was made as a club knife for a local knife club.

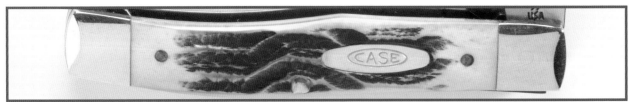

"Jigged stag" handle from a 53032 SS stock knife made in 1985.

HANDLE KEY NUMBER 6:
BONE (ALSO ROUGH BLACK, PAKKAWOOD, AND DELRIN)

In addition to stag, bone has always been a significant handle material on Case pocket knives and continues today to be a defining handle material for W.R. Case & Sons. The use of jigged bone as a handle material goes back to the earliest years of Case, and bone has been made in myriad variations of color and jig pattern over the years. The term "bone" as applied to Case pocket knife handle material refers to the shin bone of cattle, sourced from South America and processed by jigging and dying at the Case factory.

From the earlier years of Case up into the 1970s, the variations in bone handles were all due to random manufacturing changes. Beginning in the late 1970s, and accelerating after the mid-1990s, Case has produced bone handles in specific colors and specific jig patterns, creating many new series of collectible bone-handled knives in a wide variety of colors.

From the late 1800s until the advent of WWII, jigged bone was without a doubt the most widely used handle material on pocket knives made by American cutlery firms. "Jigging" refers to the patterns that are cut into the surface of the bone handle slabs prior to their assembly on a knife. While smooth bone handles were sometimes used, most bone handles were dyed and jigged. Jigging of bone is done so that the finished pocket knife handle will have a better gripping surface. The story is often told that the bone was dyed and jigged so that when finished as a pocket knife handle, the material would resemble stag. I do not know whether this is the true origin of the jigged bone handle idea, but jigged bone was referred to by various names in the early cutlery catalogs including "bone stag," "patent stag," "stag" and others.

Most of the jigged bone handles produced by American cutlery firms in the pre-WWII era had a brown or tan color and are often referred to by collectors as "brown bone" handles. Each cutlery firm had its own particular jigging pattern, and experienced collectors can often identify the brand of an older pocket knife by examining the bone color and jig pattern. Case and Union Cutlery/KABAR were two firms that used a dark greenish-tinted bone during this era that collectors refer to as "green bone."

Chestnut-colored bone handle on a Case XX-stamped 06247 Pen.

Red worm groove bone on a Case XX 6265 SAB folding hunter.

While bone was a widely used handle material prior to WWII, its use began to wane in the post-WWII era. During these years, there were fewer cutlery firms in business manufacturing pocket knives, and the number of pocket knife patterns produced declined significantly. Cutlery companies looked to modernize their operations and reduce costs. One result of this was the widespread change to the use of synthetic handle materials on pocket knives.

The shift to synthetics was also due to the improved synthetic materials available after the war. Before the war, celluloid handles were used, but celluloid was flammable and had the tendency to spontaneously disintegrate when the knife was carried and used. After the war, various plastics became available and cutlery companies could use molded handles that resembled the texture of jigged bone. Delrin was developed in the 1960s and proved to be a better and more durable handle material than either celluloid or the earlier plastic and hard rubber handle materials. Delrin offered another advantage in that delrin handles could be molded in subtle color variations so that bone and stag handles could be more closely imitated.

Based on a review of older cutlery catalogs, it appears almost all American cutlery firms had phased over completely to the use of synthetics in place of bone by the early 1960s. Some of these firms resumed the use of bone on a limited basis in the 1970s in response to the emerging market for limited edition "collector's" knives, but the use of bone on standard production pocket knives

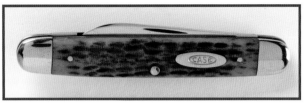 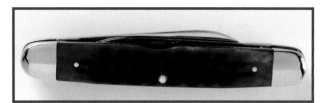

A Case XX 6279 F SS pen knife with the front handle faded from being on a store display board. Note that the front handle has the appearance of green bone, while the back handle is red bone.

was ended by most companies. The lone exception was W.R Case & Sons. Case did begin to use Pakkawood and delrin during the 1960s, but only on a few patterns. Case continued the use of bone as a primary handle material on "standard product" pocket knives into the 1970s and 1980s and on to the present day.

BONE HANDLE VARIATIONS, PRE-WWII THROUGH CASE XX ERA

Case today has the ability to produce bone handles in a wide variety of different color variations and jig patterns. However, an important fact is that from the early years up through the late 1970s, Case *never* produced any bone-handled knives sold or marketed as having any specific color or jig pattern. Many knife collectors new to the hobby might be surprised to find this out, since the terms "green bone," "red bone" and others are commonly used to describe Case bone handles of various vintages.

The fact is that all Case factory catalogs and price lists from the early years pre-WWII on through the 1950s to the 1970s listed the key handle number 6 or 06 as designating "bone stag," the term Case traditionally used for jigged bone. No mention of bone color or jig pattern was ever made in these documents. All of the early bone variations from "dark bone," "tan bone," "green bone" and "red bone" that have been identified by collectors were evidently random variations that were due either to changes in the bone itself over the years or (more likely) changes to dyes used. I have never seen any evidence that any of the bone colors or changes to the coloring or jigging patterns were intentional during these years.

Jig patterns can also vary somewhat randomly for several reasons. First, the jigging of bone is an inexact science to begin with, so the patterns can vary depending on variations in the particular bone slab, the orientation of the bone as it is jigged, and the control of the process by the operator. Second, the jig pattern can change somewhat as the jigging tools wear during production, and more significant changes can occur due to the breakage of a tool. Lastly, it is possible that Case over the years fabricated new jigging tools to replace those that were broken or worn out and the new tools may have had slight variations as compared to the old ones.

During the Case Tested era, Case produced a wide variety of pocket knife patterns. One Case factory price list from the late 1930s lists almost 500 pocket knife patterns, of which about 50 percent had bone stag handles. In 1955, the Case pocket knife line included about 140 pocket knife patterns. Again about half of these had bone stag handles. By June of 1975, the pocket knife line had dropped to an even 100 patterns, of which 70 were handled in bone (or in delrin or Pakkawood simulating bone). This information, obtained from Case factory price lists, indicates the percentage of bone-handled knives in the Case pocket knife line increased after stag was discontinued as a handle material while at the same time many patterns handled in smooth yellow and in other handle materials were discontinued.

The rest of this section describes a number of the well known bone handle variations and synthetic bone substitutes used by Case from the early years into the 1970s and 1980s. I would like to note here that some knife collectors are of the belief that the bone handles on any particular Case pocket knife must match exactly in color and texture from front to back or the knife should be considered as "suspicious." I can state from my own experience that on older Case pocket knives, this is NOT true and in fact the two bone handles on a particular knife will *rarely* match.

In my experience, the front handle of an older Case pocket knife *usually* (but not always) will be the handle that will exhibit more color and lighter colors as com-

A Case XX 6380 whittler with a very rare variation: true green bone on the front and true red bone on the back.

An example of dark (black) bone handles on a Case XX 63047 stock knife.

pared to the back handle. This may be due to the extra hafting and finishing that is required on a front handle, since the front handle has the shield installed. This extra hafting and finishing also often flattened out the jig patterns on the front handle, altering the appearance of the jigging as compared to the back handle. I do not believe Case craftspeople ever tried to select specific handles on each knife to try to "match" the handles or to put the more attractive bone on the front of the knife. The simple fact is that the final colors of a particular bone handle do not truly emerge until after the handle is attached to the knife, hafted, and buffed.

By "older" knives, I mean ones that were made from the pre-WWII years until the mid-1990s. By the late 1990s, Case had developed the ability to more closely control the bone colors. However, individual bone handles even on the newer knives are like snowflakes; no two are ever exactly alike even though they may be closer today in color.

In some instances, older Case pocket knives will be found that will exhibit distinctly different bone variations on the same knife. The best example of this is a knife that will have a "green bone" handle on one side and a "red bone" handle on the other side. Some collectors and dealers believe that such knives were made up special by Case as "salesman's samples" intended for Case sales reps to use in showing customers the change to the handle material.

I have personally never believed the "salesman's sample" story in relation to these knives, for several reasons. First, as already noted, Case never sold or

marketed bone-handled knives as having a specific color to the handles. It also seems that if one did, indeed, intend to show different then it would actually be simpler to merely have two "standard" knives and show them side by side. I believe that these knives are simply the result of Case having a number of handle slabs in stock during the dye changeovers and that the old stock handles were used up along with the newer dyed handles.

There is another explanation for some of these green/red bone-handled knives. When Case pocket knives were wired to display boards and they were on display for many years, the front handles on the display knives would often fade due to exposure to sunlight. I have seen some examples of these "board" knives where it appears that the knife handle started out as a red bone handle but after fading, the front bone handle appeared to have a greenish tint. This color looks green but will have a distinctly different look as compared to regular Case green bone.

Dark bone or regular bone: As mentioned previously, from the early years of Case into the 1980s and early 1990s, its line of standard production bone-handled knives were produced with bone stag handles that were not presented as having any specific color. A significant percentage of the bone-handled pocket knives produced during these years will have bone handles that are a dark color. This is what I generally refer to as regular bone.

The color of regular bone handles can vary from solid black to black with some small patches of light coloring at the edges, to very dark brown to very dark red. No two pieces of bone ever seem to take dye in the

Case Tested C61050 SAB swell center with green bone handles.

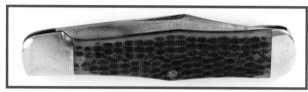

Back handle on the C61050 SAB.

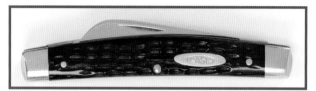

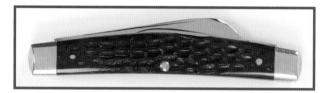

A comparison of Case XX-era dark black bone, top, and green bone on Case XX-stamped 62052 congress pen knife patterns, 3-1/2".

A comparison of the back handles of the congress pen knife patterns.

same manner, so seldom are two bone handles seen that are exactly alike. But generally what collectors consider to be regular bone or just bone will have no significant areas of light coloring or of visible brown or red coloring.

Green bone: During the Case Tested era and into the first years of the Case XX era, a significant number of pocket knives were handled in what Case collectors refer to as green bone. Apparently the dyes used to color bone during this period produced colors ranging from the darker regular bone to the somewhat more colorful green bone. The term green bone is often considered to be a misnomer since some of what is referred to as green bone on these older knives actually has shades of brown and tan. In actuality, the "green" in green bone is not a Kelly green or lime green, but an olive green shade that can vary from dark to light olive.

Sometimes the bone has a tan or deep brown color in addition to the olive green, but collectors still generally refer to this as green bone. Some collectors refer to green bone that has significant tan or brown shades as "honeycomb bone." While it is impossible to pin down the exact years of use for Case green bone, it is generally believed this color ended during the 1950s due to dye changes. There are some pocket knife patterns that (per Case factory price lists) were introduced in the late

1950s to 1960s that will not be found in green bone. Generally, the most desired Case green bone-handled knives will have an even olive green to light olive green color on both the front and back handles. In general, though, knives that have any discernable green in the handles are more desirable than knives with the very dark regular bone handles.

Red bone: During the Case XX era and in later years, a significant number of pocket knives were handled in what collectors refer to as "red bone." The change from green to red bone is generally assumed to have been due to Case changing the formulation of the dyes used, perhaps due to a change of suppliers. To the best of my knowledge, this has never been documented and is speculation only.

An interesting point is that if you study the pocket knife lines of other manufacturers, it seems that several other American pocket knife manufacturers began to use red-colored dyes in processing their bone after WWII. Prior to that, it seems all bone-handled pocket knives had brown, tan, or green bone handles. After WWII and into the 1950s, most of the bone-handled pocket knives produced by the Robeson Cutlery Company and by Boker USA had handles of red bone. Robeson used a red bone handle material that collectors refer to as "strawberry bone" in the 1950s, while

 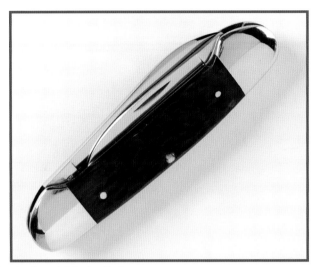

This Canoe from 1973 exhibits dark bone handles on both front and back.

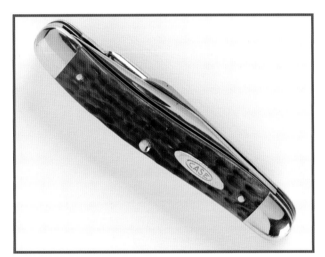 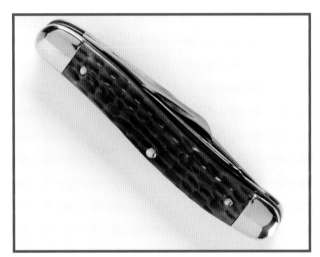

This Case XX 6318 stock knife has outstanding red bone handles that are nicely matched front to back.

 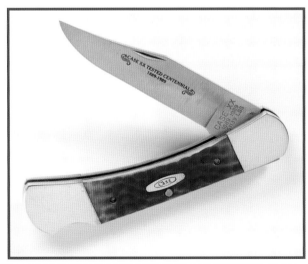

In 1989, Case released a series of knives commemorating the Case 1889-1989 "centennial." These knives had special shields and tang stampings and exhibit "modern" -era Case red bone handles that had a more even "strawberry" red color as compared to older Case red bone-handled knives. From left: 6215 SS "Gunstock," 3"; and 61139 L SS, 5".

A DR624 SS Trapper from 1998, front and back. This knife is an example of newer red bone.

Boker USA used a darker red bone.

Some Schrade Walden-marked knives from the 1950s era will be found with "peach seed" or "worm groove" bone handles in a dark red color. This evidence, while anecdotal, may lend credence to the idea that the change to red bone handles may have been due to a dye change that also affected other manufacturers. Likewise, "late Rogers" bone, which has a red color, seems to appear only on later Case XX-era knives made after WWII, rather than Case Tested-era knives.

Red bone handles on Case pocket knives can vary from a very dark red to a more medium "blood" red to a lighter red, sometimes with white accents. Generally, the most desired Case red bone-handled knives will have an even blood red to light red color on both the front and back handles. In general, though, knives that have any red in the handles are more desirable than knives with the very dark regular bone handles.

Rough black: The synthetic handle material "rough black" was used by Case as a substitute for bone stag in handling pocket knives. Rough black, or "Plastag" as it was referred to by Case, was used during the Case Tested and the early Case XX eras on many pocket knives. In some knife books, rough black is said to be a wartime substitute for bone on pocket knives made during WWII. My personal opinion is that while it is likely that rough black was used on wartime pocket knives, I believe most rough black-handled Case pocket knives were manufactured during peace time. I speculate this because in my observation, a great majority of rough black-handled Case pocket knives are "deluxe" knives with nickel silver bolsters, brass or nickel silver liners, and nickel silver Case shields. As the use of nickel silver and brass was curtailed during the war, true wartime knives would likely have been made with iron bolsters and liners and without shields.

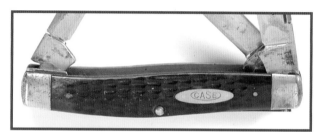

Case Tested 6393 stock knife, 3-15/16", with dark green bone handles.

Case Tested 6253, pen knife, rough black, 3-1/4".

Based on my observations, there were two major variations of rough black handle material used on pocket knives on Case Tested and early Case XX-era knives. The most commonly found variation has a distinctive "worm groove" jigging that is in a random pattern. This material seems to be a type of hard rubber, and it appears that the jigging was done by machine. The second rough black variation appears to be a type of plastic, with a more conventional jig pattern that appears to have been created during the molding of the handle slab.

While the "worm groove" rough black material was used on a variety of Case pocket knife patterns, I have seen the "molded plastic" material only on some examples of the 6445 R scout/utility knife and the 6345 cattle knife. While rough black was used on many Case pocket knife patterns, not every pattern made during

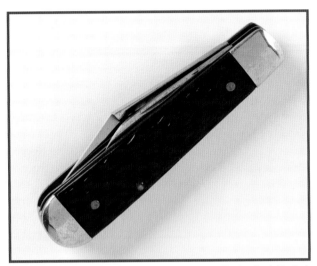

This *KINGSTON*-stamped jack knife with jigged black composition handles is identical to the Case XX-stamped 620035 1/2 jack knife. I believe that the 620035 1/2 was made on contract for Case.

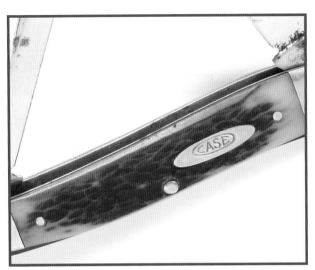

Early Rogers bone handle on a Case XX-stamped 6380 whittler pattern.

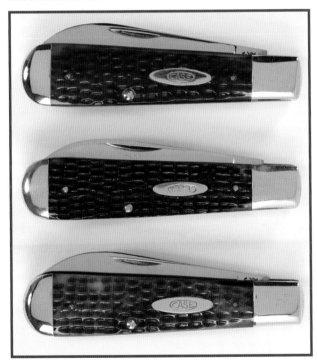

Case Tested green bone variations on the 6299 jack pattern. Note the slightly different coloring and jig patterns from one knife to the next.

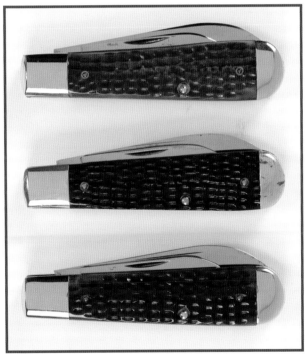

The back handles on the 6299 green bone variations.

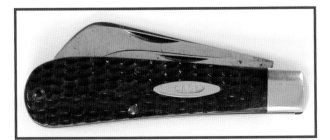

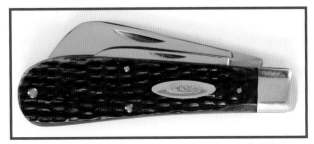

A comparison of green bone to "regular" bone on the Case 6217 pattern, 4". The Case Tested stamped 6217, left, has green bone handles. The Case XX-stamped knife, right, has dark bone handles with a slight brown tint.

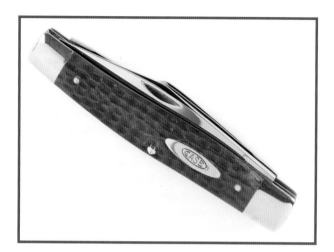
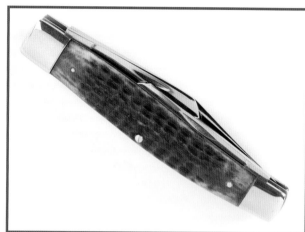

This Case XX 6375 large stock knife has lighter-colored red bone handles on both front and back.

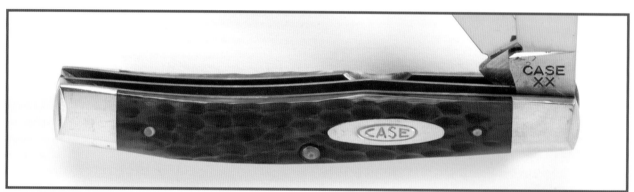

This Case XX 6232 jack knife has "reddish" bone handles that are not quite "true" red bone.

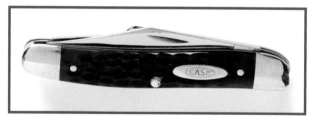
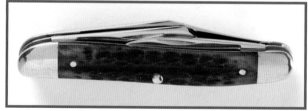

This Case XX 63087 Sp Pen small stock knife has nicely matched dark red bone handles.

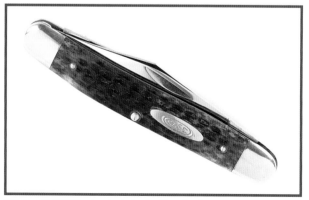
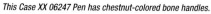

This Case XX 06247 Pen has chestnut-colored bone handles.

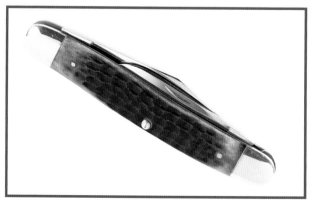

Back handle of the Case XX 06247 Pen.

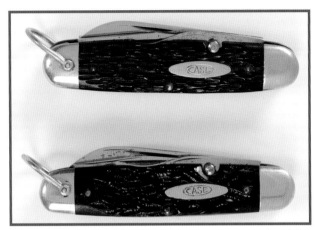

These are two distinct varieties of "rough black" handle material used by Case during the Case Tested and Case XX eras. Top knife is a Case XX-stamped 6445 R with "jigged black composition" handles (appear to be plastic). The bottom knife is a Case Tested 6445 R with "rough black" handles (appear to be hard rubber). The lower variation, which has "worm groove"-style jigging, is by far the more common of the two. Closed length on both is 3-3/4".

A Case XX USA 640045 R scout/utility knife with jigged black composition handles.

the Case Tested and the Case XX era will be found with rough black handles. A few patterns, including the 62031, 62031 1/2, and 6299, are relatively common to find in the "worm groove" rough black handles.

Some pocket knives made later in the Case XX and the Case XX USA eras were made with another variation of jigged black composition handles that could be considered as "rough black." These later patterns include the 620035 and the 630035 1/2 (both jack knife patterns) and the 640045 R scout/utility knife. In my opinion, these patterns were all manufactured on contract for Case by other cutlery firms, and the jigged black composition handles have a different appearance as compared to the older rough black variations.

Rogers bone: Another Case bone stag variation is what collectors refer to as "Rogers bone." My understanding is that this material was purchased by Case from a firm that also supplied other cutlery companies with bone handles, and that the jigging and dying of the bone was done by the vendor, not Case. Rogers bone has a distinctive jig pattern, which is what defines it as a handle material, and there are two color variations found.

So called "early Rogers" bone has a tan or brown

color, while "late Rogers" bone will have a wine red color that is significantly different than the color of most Case "red bone" handles. Early Rogers bone will be found on some pocket knives from the Case Tested era to the early Case XX era. Late Rogers bone will be found primarily on CASE XX stamped knives, although some examples have been observed with the CASE XX USA tang stamping.

The use of both early Rogers bone and late Rogers bone was another "random" variation. Rogers bone was used as a substitute for bone stag-handle material. As was the case with green bone, red bone, and rough black, Rogers bone was never mentioned in any Case factory catalog or price list. It is probable that Case purchased quantities of Rogers bone to make up for shortfalls in in-house bone supplies.

Not every Case pocket knife pattern from the period during which Rogers bone was used will be found handled in the material. In my experience, early Rogers bone is significantly rarer than is late Rogers bone. The 6380 "carpenter's whittler" is one pattern that had significant numbers handled in early Rogers bone, though that particular knife is still considered rare. Some of the patterns more commonly found in late Rogers bone include the 6220, 6233, 6232, 6332, and 6347. All Case pocket knives from this era handled in Rogers bone are considered to be relatively rare. Some patterns, including the Muskrat, are rare and desirable in Rogers bone.

Case in recent years has introduced bone handles that are jigged and dyed in-house with what the company refers to as "Rogers"-style jigging. While this is an attractive handle material, Case has made it different enough that there will be no confusion with the older Rogers bone materials. Another note about Rogers bone is that many knife collectors will refer to any older jigged brown bone pocket knife handles, regardless of the knife's vintage or manufacturer, as "Rogers bone." In my opinion, this is incorrect, since true Rogers bone is the product of one specific handling material company and was processed on the machinery of that company to obtain the distinctive jigging style.

Pakkawood: Pakkawood is a laminated hardwood material, so essentially it has elements of both a natural material (wood) and a synthetic material (plastic resins

Early Rogers bone handle on a Case Tested 6231 1/2 jack knife.

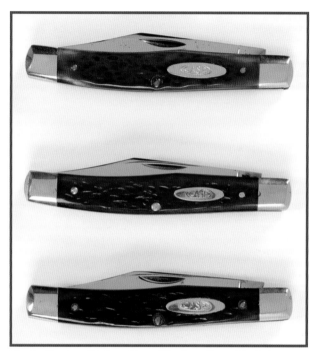

Like other Case bone, "late Rogers" bone will be observed in a variety of color variations, as illustrated by these Case XX 6232 jack knife patterns, 3-5/8"; from top: light color, medium color, and dark color. The back of the knives are shown below.

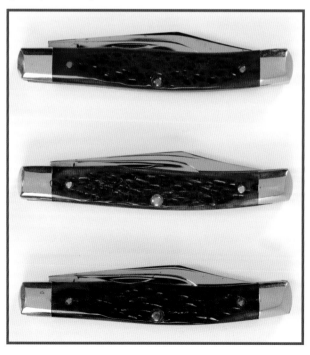

used for the lamination). The use of Pakkawood handle material on Case household cutlery began in the years following WWII. The Pakkawood used on household knives was medium brown in color and hafted and polished to a high-gloss finish. Case introduced the use of Pakkawood to handle some pocket knife patterns in the early 1960s. The Pakkawood handles used for pocket knives were made in a darker brown color and jigged like bone handles.

Case initially used Pakkawood as an occasional substitute for bone handles on the larger folding knife patterns. These patterns were the 61011, C61050 SAB, 6165 SAB, 6250, and 6265 SAB. During the 1960s, both bone and Pakkawood handles were used on these knives. It is probable that Case had difficulty obtaining a sufficient quantity of larger bone slabs for use on these knives, so Pakkawood was substituted in order to maintain production. By the mid-1960s, the use of Pakkawood handles had increased significantly on these patterns and examples with bone handles and with the CASE XX USA tang stamping can be found, but are rare. By some point in the Case XX USA era, all had been switched to 100 percent production in Pakkawood.

In mid-1970, the 6217 pattern was also switched to production 100 percent in Pakkawood. A few additional jigged Pakkawood-handled patterns were introduced in the 1970s, including the 6265 SAB DR SS, 6165 SAB DR L SS, and 61051 L SSP. In some later product catalogs, Case referred to the jigged Pakkawood handle material as Lamistag. The use of jigged Pakkawood has continued to the present day on the 6265 SAB SS "folding hunter" pattern.

Delrin: While Case "smooth composition" handles in yellow, black, and white have been made of delrin, when most collectors refer to a "delrin"-handled knife, they are referring to one made with jigged brown delrin handles as a substitute for bone stag handles. These knives will have the handle key number "6," identical to that used to designate bone stag. In some Case factory catalogs and price lists in the 1970s, Case referred to jigged brown delrin as Delstag. Beginning in the 1980s it was referred to as "jigged brown plastic" or "jigged brown synthetic." In this section (and in this book in general), I refer to this handle material simply as "delrin."

Case introduced the use of delrin as a substitute for bone in handling pocket knives during the Case XX USA era. I have never seen specific documentation as to the exact year of the introduction of delrin, but I personally have never seen a delrin-handled knife with the CASE XX tang stamping. The first use of delrin handles on regular production Case pocket knives was on the "048" pattern. This knife is sometimes referred to by collectors as a "slim trapper" or a "farmer's knife" and was made by Case in a number of blade variations during the Case XX USA era. All of the "6"-numbered variations of the "048" pattern will be found in both bone and delrin handles with the CASE XX USA tang stamping.

I do not know why Case chose the "048" patterns for

the first use of delrin, but by 1969 all 048 patterns had been changed over to 100 percent production in delrin handles. The changeover of this particular pattern to delrin may have been simply to reduce manufacturing costs. The "048" pattern knives were relatively inexpensive knives in the Case line, and the pattern required long thin bone slabs. It is possible that this pattern got to be too expensive to produce in bone due to the extra processing of the bone required and the propensity of thinner bone handles to crack during assembly.

In mid-1970, Case took another group of patterns

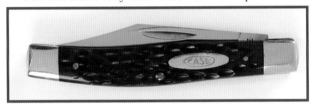

Regular Case XX-era dark reddish bone, top, as compared to "late Rogers" bone, bottom, on Case XX-stamped 6232 patterns, 3-5/8".

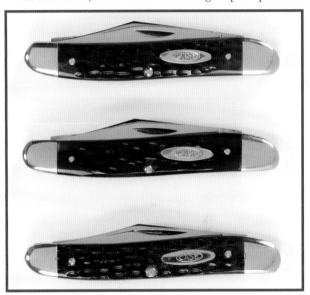

From top: A comparison of Case XX-era dark reddish bone, late Roger's bone and green bone on Case XX-stamped 06244 pen knife patterns, 3-1/4".

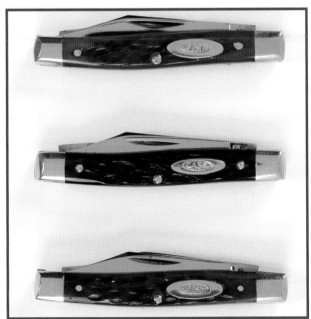

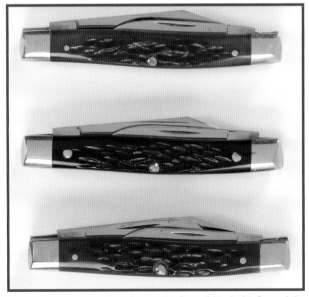

Case "late Rogers" bone color variations, on Case XX-stamped 33 pen knife patterns, 2-5/8", and compared to Case XX red bone. From top: late Rogers light color, late Rogers dark color, and regular red bone.

Jigged Pakkawood imitation bone handle on a 1972 (8 dot) 6265 SAB DR.

Bone handle comparison to Pakkawood handles on 6250 "Sunfish" patterns, 4-3/8". From top: Case XX with red bone handles, and 10 dot, 1970 stamping with Pakkawood handles.

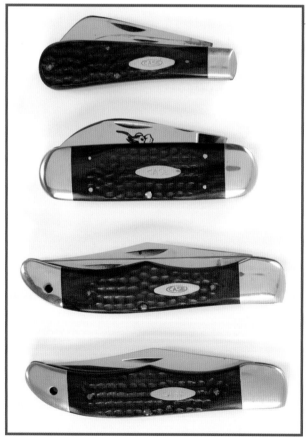

A group of Case pocket knives illustrating jigged Pakkawood handle material, used on larger patterns in place of jigged bone. From top: 7 dot, 1973, 6217 curved jack, 4"; 5 dot, 1975, 6250 "Sunfish," 4-3/8"; 8 dot, 1972, 6265 SAB DR "folding hunter," 5-1/4"; and 1 dot, 1979, 6165 SAB DR "folding hunter," 5-1/4". Note that, depending upon the year made, some knives have the "standard" CASE oval shield and some have the "composition" shield.

and switched them all from bone to 100 percent production in delrin. For this group, both bone and delrin-handled examples will be found with the 1970 ten dot tang stamping. The chart on the next page shows the initial group of "100 percent delrin" pocket knife patterns including the "048" and 1970 patterns. (Note: this chart does not include the 640045R, since that pattern had always been made with jigged composition handles beginning in the Case XX era.)

During the 1970s, the situation regarding Case's use of delrin as a pocket knife handling material got a bit more complex and interesting. At some point during the early 1970s, Case began the "random" use of delrin handles as a substitute for bone handles across the entire product line of bone-handled knives. During the early to mid-1970s, and particularly beginning in 1973, Case's supply of bone evidently became sporadic. One reason that I heard at the time was that there were outbreaks of hoof and mouth disease among cattle in South America, which traditionally had been Case's source of bone. The outbreaks of the disease resulted in limited bone exports. Case's use of delrin during the 1970s was analogous to its use of the "rough back" handle mate-

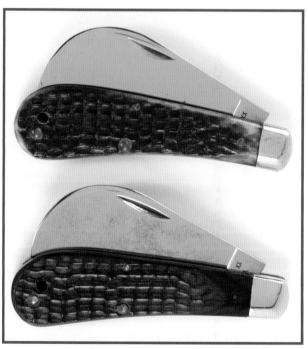

Bone handle comparison to Pakkawood handles on 61011 "Hawkbill" patterns, 4". From top: Case XX USA stamping with reddish bone handles, and 2 dot 1978 stamping with Pakkawood handles.

 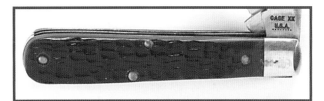

Bone handle comparison to delrin, from left: Case XX 6202 1/2 with dark bone handles, and an 8 dot, 1972, 6202 1/2 with delrin handles.

rial as a substitute for bone during the 1940s and the 1950s.

Just as Case's discontinued use of stag in mid-1970 caused more interest with collectors who sought out these increasingly scarce stag-handled knives, a similar situation occurred as Case expanded the use of delrin as a substitute for bone stag in the early to mid-1970s. As more delrin was used, there was much speculation among collectors that Case would finally follow other cutlery companies and discontinue the use of bone completely. This never happened of course, but in those years, collectors eagerly picked through the stock of knives on hand at Case dealers, searching for the ever more elusive bone-handled specimens.

So for each of the years of 1970 through 1977, it is possible that any Case pocket knife pattern with a "6" number will be found handled in either bone or delrin. As with most things Case-related, there are some exceptions to this. For purposes of this discussion, I will use two categories of delrin-handled knives. The term "100 percent delrin" will be applied to those patterns that Case chose to switch to 100 percent production in delrin. The term "random delrin" will be applied to patterns that were primarily made in bone but would be made in delrin on a temporary basis only when bone supplies ran out. This essentially includes all bone-handled patterns not in the "100 percent delrin" category.

The chart at right shows the initial groups of patterns that became "100 percent delrin" knives. These knives from then on would only be produced in delrin and not switched back to bone. There are two minor exceptions to this in that Case did make some 6202 1/2 and 62009 1/2 patterns in bone in 1975. My speculation on this is that the company actually ran out of the pre-molded delrin handles for these patterns and switched back to bone to complete some production runs.

I believe that as time went on in the 1970s, Case

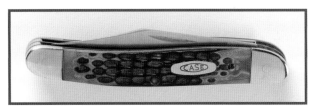

Delrin handles will fade on knives that are exposed to strong light, often as a result of being wired to a store display board. This 62087 SS from 1990 has a faded front handle. The faded delrin will sometimes exhibit a bluish tint.

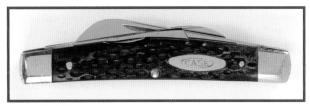

A comparison of delrin handles to bone handles on 64052 congress patterns. Top knife is a 10 dot 1970 knife with bone handles; bottom knife is a 7 dot 1973 example with delrin handles.

Case Pocket Knife Patterns Switched to 100% Production In Delrin 1967-1970	Pattern	Year Changed
	61048	Circa 1967
	61048 Sp	Circa 1967
	61048 SSP	Circa 1967
	62048 Sp	Circa 1967
	62048 Sp SSP	Circa 1967
	6202 1/2	1970 (Mid Year)
	62009	1970 (Mid Year)
	62009 1/2	1970 (Mid Year)
	62009 RAZ	1970 (Mid Year)
	6214	1970 (Mid Year)
	6214 1/2	1970 (Mid Year)
	6220	1970 (Mid Year)
	6227	1970 (Mid Year)
	6327	1970 (Mid Year)
	6233	1970 (Mid Year)
	6333	1970 (Mid Year)
	06244	1970 (Mid Year)
	6244	1970 (Mid Year)
	6344 Sh Pen	1970 (Mid Year)
	6344 Sh Sp	1970 (Mid Year)
	62087	1970 (Mid Year)
	63087 Sp Pen	1970 (Mid Year)

switched some other patterns to the 100 percent delrin category, but there is no available documentation on this. For example, I have personally never observed a 6201 or a 62042 in bone made after 1972, or a 6225 1/2 in bone made after 1973. There are other examples that could be given, but the only way to verify this would be via the observation of actual knife specimens.

Regarding the knives in the random delrin category, it is not a certainty that each pattern will be found in both delrin and in bone in each of the years 1970 through 1977. The random substitution of delrin for bone means that each individual knife pattern may or may not have been made in delrin for each given year or "dots" tang stamping. Again the only way to ascertain this would be by observation of actual knife specimens. My observation is that very few "random delrin" knives were made in either 1970 (ten dots) or in 1971 (nine dots). The use of delrin on the "random delrin" knife patterns seemed to increase somewhat in 1972, became very prolific for the years of 1973 through 1975, and continued significantly through 1976 and 1977.

It seems that for the patterns in the "random delrin" category, some will be found more frequently in delrin than others. My own observation is that examples of the 6254 and 6347 in chrome vanadium are scarce in delrin, while delrin-handled examples of the 6318, 6232, and 6332 patterns are relatively common. I personally have never seen or heard of any examples of the 6445 R or 62131 in delrin, although they may indeed exist.

Beginning in 1978, it appears Case ended the "random" use of delrin handles and beginning that year, some patterns went back to 100 percent production in bone while others went to (or continued with) 100 percent production in delrin. Again this was not documented that I know of, but is based on my personal observation. You should bear in mind that the above discussion only applies to Case pocket knives made during the 1970s. Beginning in the late 1970s and through the ensuing years, many patterns, including the 6201, 6220, 62009 1/2, 6344, etc., have been brought back into production in bone and have been made in a wide variety of bone handle variations. Beginning in the mid-1980s and continuing to today, the use of delrin has been limited to a relatively few "no frills" pocket knife patterns in what Case currently refers to as the Working Knives line.

CASE BONE THROUGH THE 1970S AND 1980S

Among Case collectors, red and green bone are well known as bone handle materials that will be found on Case XX-era knives, in addition to dark or regular bone and Rogers bone. From the Case XX USA era and into the 1970s, the bone coloring seemed to go through a few more "random" changes as the years went by. Green bone was long gone by the Case XX USA era, but bone-handled knives with the CASE XX USA tang stamping will be found in both regular bone and various red bone shades. One observation about USA-era red bone is that more knives will be found with lighter red tint to the bone, and many of the red tinted bone handles will have white accents and/or more of a white color along the edges of the handles.

The deep red to reddish-tinted bone and regular bone continued into the 1970 era. Another observation is that from 1970-1972, some bone handles will have more of a brown color and often have light tan to yellow accents in the bone, particularly around the edges. Some collectors refer to this as "chestnut" bone, but it seems that beginning about 1973, this color went away and a lot of the bone handles observed on knives made from 1973 through 1977 were very dark, almost black in color, sometimes with light-colored spots of white or red along the handle edges.

Even though a lot of dark bone (and delrin) handles were used from 1973-1977, a percentage of the bone-handled knives made in this era will be found with stunning red handles. This seems to be especially true beginning with knives made in 1975. Some of the knives from 1975-1977 will have nice blood red bone handles, while others have almost a red-orange coloring. Case produced some beautiful red bone-handled

This 3 dot 1977 Muskrat has very dark (black) bone typical of many 1970s-era Case pocket knives.

pocket knives during this time frame. Again, remember that since Case was not attempting to color the bone, these variations were random, and many color variations will show up from each year.

Starting in 1978, there may have been another dye change, as the "random" reddish or red bone handle variations seemed to disappear beginning with knives that had the 1978 (two dot) tang stamping. Bone used on standard "6" number pocket knives from 1978 through about 1984 seems to exhibit several variations. The bone is usually dark (black) as the base color, but many handles will have white accents and white edges. Some percentage of the bone handles from the 1978-1984 era will also have a deep olive green tint. While this bone does not resemble the older Case XX-era green bone, it does have an attractive color.

THE BEGINNING OF CASE BONE IN COLORS

To the best of my knowledge, the first time Case issued a knife that was marketed as having a specific bone color occurred in 1978, when the limited edition Appaloosa Peanut was manufactured. This knife was a 6220 pattern handled in a smooth bone that had a mottled brown and white color. The coloring of the bone was said to resemble an Appaloosa horse. The following description of this knife is an excerpt from a Case sales memo dated Feb. 16, 1979:

Attached are special order forms for the No. A6220 "Appaloosa Peanut." Orders will be accepted on the special order form only! Samples are being sent under separate cover.

This is the limited edition run of 15,000. They will be numbered 1 through 15,000 on the bolster. Blades and springs are chrome vanadium. "Case Appaloosa" is electro-etched on the blade.

Handles are bone. The coloring of the handles will be much more varied than our other bone handles, because of a special production process. This variation in color is desirable from a collector's standpoint since it will be seldom that two knives will look the same. Keep in mind, however, that it also means more variation in the two sides of the same knife. This can't be avoided because it doesn't show up until the knife is hafted.

This knife is being made available as a collector's

Case XX USA 2 Dot, A6220, 1978, Appaloosa bone, serial numbered, 2-3/4". The Appaloosa was the first bone handle made to a specific color.

A closeup of the Appaloosa handle.

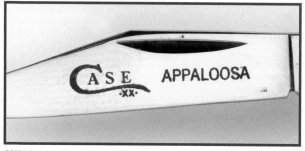

A6220 Appaloosa main blade etching.

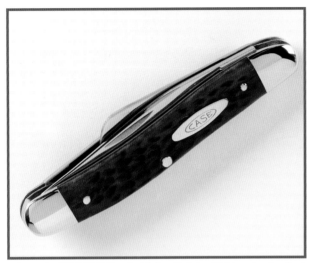 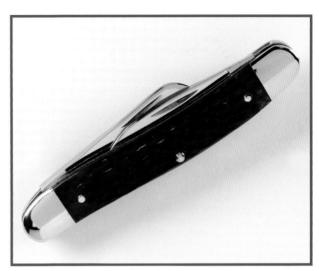

A Case 7 dot 1973 6318 Sh Pen stock knife with dark reddish bone handles, front and back views.

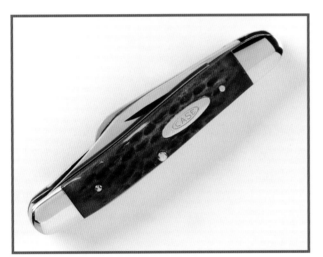 

This 5 dot 1975 6347 Sh Sp SSP stock knife has front and back handles of nice blood red bone—very desirable and hard to find on 1970s-era knives.

This 6254 SSP Trapper from 1972 exhibits dark bone handles on the front and back with light coloring at the edges of the bone.

item to help the younger collector's (who don't have a lot of money) get started.

These knives will be completely shipped by the end of June with over 1/2 shipped by the end of March.

This knife was well received by collectors so in 1979 Case decided to take ten pocket knife patterns from the standard pocket knife line and convert them from jigged bone and delrin to new smooth bone handles in two different color variations. The two colors used were the Appaloosa brown/tan bone that had been used on the A6220 limited edition, and a new color, Satin Rose. The Satin Rose handles had a light red color with the letters "SR" used in front of the pattern number. The chart below shows the existing pocket knife patterns that were discontinued in their previous format and introduced in the new colored smooth bone handles in 1979.

These knives represented the first issue of Case "standard product" pocket knives in specific bone colors. Note that on the 63047, Case changed the pattern number slightly on the new version (SR6347 1/2). My understanding from a review of Case sales memos is that the first 3,000 pieces made of the new SR6347 1/2 actually used the old version of the pattern number and had the pattern number stamp SR63047. Case at the time also made a special limited production version of this pattern with smooth green bone handles.

The G63047 was made in a quantity of 5,500 pieces (these were not serialized).

The listed ten patterns were made with chrome vanadium blades and without Case shields in the smooth bone handles. These knives were made as shown from 1979 through 1981. In late 1981 or early 1982, the SR62027 was discontinued and the other nine patterns were converted to satin finished stainless blades (with SS after the pattern numbers) and Case oval shields were added. This line up was only made for a short period, and then all nine patterns were changed over to delrin handles to provide a lower retail price point.

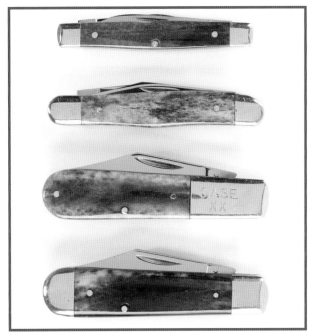

Case pocket knives with Appaloosa bone handles, introduced in 1979, from top: A62042 pen knife (3"), A6208 (3-1/4"), A62009 1/2 (3-3/8"), and A6235 1/2 (3-3/8").

Case Pocket Knife Patterns	Existing Pattern	Existing Handle	New Pattern	New Handle
	6208	Bone	A6208	Appaloosa
	62009 1/2	Delrin	A62009 1/2	Appaloosa
Smooth Bone Handles In Colors	63033	Delrin	A63033	Appaloosa
	6235 1/2	Delrin	A6235 1/2	Appaloosa
	62042	Delrin	A62042	Appaloosa
A - "Appaloosa" Bone	6220	Delrin	SR6220	Satin Rose
SR - "Satin Rose" Bone	6225 1/2	Delrin	SR6225 1/2	Satin Rose
	62027	Delrin	SR62027	Satin Rose
Introduced 1979	6244	Delrin	SR6244	Satin Rose
	63047	Bone	SR6347 1/2	Satin Rose

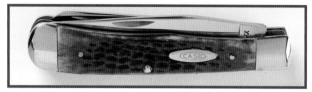
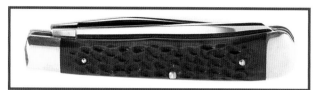

Case 6 dot, 1974, 6254 Trapper has a beautiful orange-red bone front handle and a dark bone back handle. Bone handles on Case pocket knives rarely match from front to back.

This 5 dot 1975 64047 Punch stock knife has front and back handles of nice blood red bone—very desirable and hard to find on 1970s-era knives.

This 2 dot 1978 Muskrat has dark bone handles with light colored edges, another bone variation often seen on late 1970s-era Case pocket knives.

BONE HANDLES IN THE 1980S AND BEYOND

During the 1980s, Case went though a lot of changes as a company, and many of the classic older pocket knife patterns were discontinued. Sometimes during the early 1980s, it seemed that every announcement from Case included a long list of newly discontinued pocket knife pattern numbers. Given that many of the smaller patterns had previously been converted over to delrin handles, by 1983 very few bone-handled pocket knives remained in Case's standard product pocket knife line.

In the 1983 factory catalog, only the following 18 pocket knife patterns remained in the line with bone handles: 6207 Sp SSP "Mini Trapper," 62032, 6249 "Copperhead," 6254 "Trapper," 6254 SSP "Trapper," 6275 Sp "Moose," 6292 "Texas Jack," 62109 X "Baby Copperhead," 62131 "Canoe," Muskrat, 6308 "Whittler," 6318 Sh Sp, 6318 Sh Sp SSP, 63032, 6347 Sh Sp, 6347 Sh Sp SSP, 6375 and 6392.

Both the 62109 X and the 6308 were discontinued circa 1985, so Case went from 1986 to 1990 with only 16 standard bone-handled pocket knives. Beginning in 1989 and continuing into the 1990s, Case added various lines of pocket knives with special bone colors to the standard pocket knife line. For example, in 1991, nine patterns in dark red bone were added, with the letters "DR" added prior to the pattern number (for example, DR6254 SS).

However, a core group of regular bone-handled knives, with no specific bone color, remained in the Case standard product catalog although the pattern selection continued to shrink. By 1995, the line of basic bone-handled knives had shrunk to twelve patterns, eight in chrome vanadium and four in stainless steel. Beginning in 1996, all Case catalog knives in bone were shown in specific bone colors. The older "generic" bone patterns became brown bone in 1996 and then chestnut bone from 1997 on and some additional patterns were added during these years. Case's chestnut bone had a deep brown color, but as with some earlier bone handles the chestnut bone handles sometimes took on a "red bone" hue during final finishing.

Post-2000, chestnut bone was dropped as a standard catalog bone color and amber bone was introduced as Case's "basic" bone color. In the ensuing years up to today, Case has produced a seemingly countless number of bone handle variations.

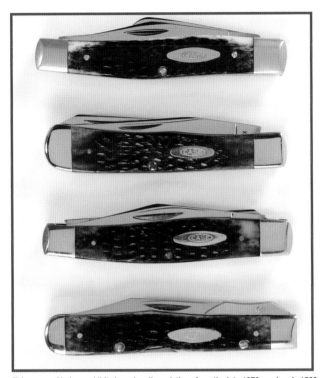

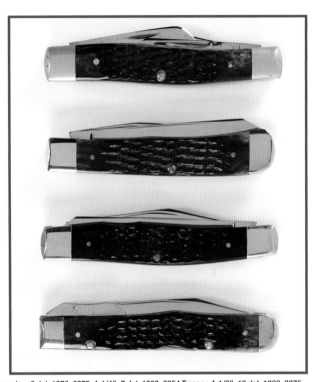

This group of knives exhibits bone handle variations from the late 1970s and early 1980s, from top: 2 dot, 1978, 6375, 4-1/4"; 7 dot, 1983, 6254 Trapper, 4-1/8"; 10 dot, 1980, 6275 Moose, 4-1/4"; and 10 dot, 1980, 6111 1/2 L, 4-3/8".

These two Muskrat patterns exhibit late 1970s bone variations. Top knife is from 1977 with very dark bone; bottom knife is from 1978 and has dark bone with light edges. These are random dye variations.

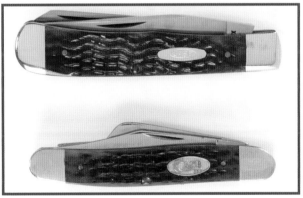

Two knives exhibiting 1980s bone variations. Top knife is a 7 dot, 1983, 6254 SSP Trapper, 4-1/8", and the bottom knife is a 3 dot, 1987, 6347 Sh Sp stock knife, 3-7/8".

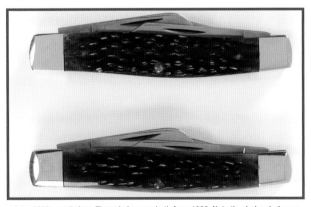

These two 6375 patterns, 4-1/4", exhibit unusual bone variations (coloring and jigging) seen on later 1980s-era knives. These knives are both from 1986. Note the dark coloring on the top knife and the lighter coloring on the bottom knife. Note the very small Case oval shields on these late 1980s knives.

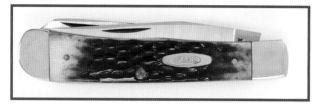

These two 6254 SSP Trapper patterns (4-1/8") exhibit variations of mid-1980s bone. Top knife is from 1984 and the bottom knife is from 1983. The handles on the top knife have light-colored edges; the bottom knife has very dark handles. Again these differences are due to random dye and hafting variations.

HANDLE KEY NUMBER 7: SMOOTH WOOD

During the Case Tested era and earlier, the handle key number "7" was used to indicate imitation tortoise shell (celluloid) handle material. This material was used on very few patterns. The Case factory price lists I have observed from the 1930s to the 1940s listed all of the Case handle materials in use with the handle code numbers, but on all of these lists the number "7" was simply skipped since there were no knives in the line by that point that were made with imitation tortoise shell handles. Likewise the catalogs and price lists from the Case XX era onward simply skipped a listing or description of this handle key number.

In 1972, when Case designed the Shark Tooth lockback folding knife, the number "7" was revived for use to designate the use of smooth curly maple handle material. Case intended to use this material on the regular production Shark Tooth so a number of blades were stamped with the pattern number 7197 L SSP. However, problems developed with the curly maple material prior to the release of the Shark Tooth to the market. Case switched the handle material for the knife to black Pakkawood but the "7" numbered blades that had already been stamped were used in the Pakkawood version. In 1977, about 1,800 of the original Shark Tooth knives with curly maple handles were also released. After that point, the handle key "7" again disappeared for a number of years.

Curly maple handle material on a 7207 Sp SS "Mini Trapper."

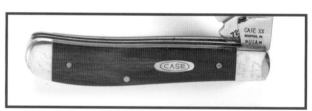

Rosewood handle material on a 7207 Sp SS "Mini Trapper."

The next use of the "7" handle key number occurred in 1989 when Case introduced a line of traditional and modern pocket knife patterns that were handled in curly maple. The following patterns were introduced: 711010L SS, 71405 L SS, 7207 Sp SS, 7215 SS, 7225 1/2 SS, 72033 SS, 72042 SS, 7254 SS, 072087 SS, 7344 Sh Pen SS, and 73087 Sp Pen SS.

This selection of patterns was in production from 1989 to 1990. In 1991, the new curly maple line continued but with fewer patterns. In 1993, the curly maple patterns were replaced with rosewood handled knives but the use of the "7" handle code continued on these knives. Case has in recent years continued to use the handle key number "7" to designate various smooth wood handles.

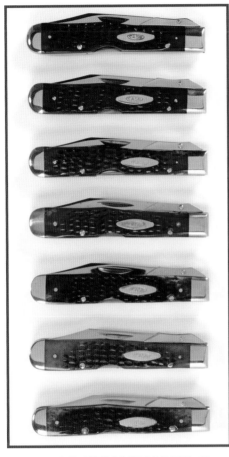

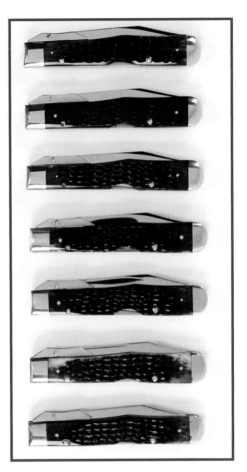

The photo at left is a group of 6111 1/2 L "Cheetah" patterns, 4-3/8", showing bone-handle variations. From top: Case XX USA stamping dark red bone, 8 dot 1972 dark red bone, 6 dot 1974 dark red bone, 3 dot 1977 blood red bone, 1 dot 1979 dark bone with light spots, 1 dot 1979 lighter greenish bone, and 10 dot 1980 dark bone with light edges. The photo at right shows the back handles of the 6111 1/2 L "Cheetah" group. Note the handle differences from front to back. Sometimes the handles will match, but often the back handle will be darker-colored bone.

HANDLE KEY NUMBER 8: GENUINE PEARL

Genuine mother of pearl was in the past one of the most widely used handle materials by many knife manufacturers, in particular on smaller pocket knives. The use of genuine pearl as a handling material goes back to the early years of Case. During the pre-WWII years, pearl was used on many smaller patterns as well as some larger patterns including the 18 "stockman," 65 "folding hunter," and 50 "Elephant Toe Nail."

During the Case XX era, Case used pearl on a number of the smaller pen knife and "lobster" patterns, most of which were made with stainless steel blades. The Case factory catalog from 1955 listed a total of 13 patterns in pearl. These were all smaller pen knife and "lobster" patterns. Production of many of these patterns continued into the 1960s, but most were discontinued by 1966.

Evidently the available supplies of genuine pearl handle material began to diminish in the mid-1960s. Case factory catalogs and price lists from 1968 and through the 1970s did not list any patterns in genuine pearl. Case was, however, still producing some patterns in pearl at this time. The probable explanation for this is that pearl handle material was in short supply and the relatively few pearl-handled knives that were made may have been allocated to the Case sales reps. The last of the older patterns to be produced in genuine pearl from 1968 to 1979 are as follows: 8233, discontinued circa 1974; 82053 S R SS, discontinued circa 1973; 8261, discontinued 1973; 82079 1/2 SS, discontinued circa 1985; and 8364 Scis SS, discontinued circa 1973.

Since these five patterns were not listed in catalogs or in price lists during that era, it is difficult to determine the year that each was discontinued. The years shown above are approximate; I have estimated them based on specimens of actual knives that I have observed. These knives were all made with nickel silver liners and with mirror polished blades of either chrome vanadium or stainless steel as shown. The pearl handles were pinned on, as was traditional for Case. Also, all Case pearl-han-

 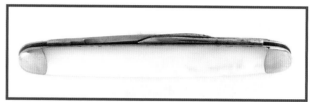

Case Tested 8271 pen knife with pearl handles and dovetailed bolsters; note the lack of handle pins. The dovetailing holds the handles in place.

dled knives from the Case XX era through the 1980s were made without shields. This was also virtually 100 percent true for the older Case pearl-handled knives, but I have seen a very few early Case pearls that had shields.

Of the patterns listed on P. 89, I believe that only the 82079 1/2 SS continued in production through the 1970s, though it may not have been made every year. In 1981, a new pearl-handled pocket knife pattern was introduced, the 8201 SS. This knife is described in the following excerpt from the *Case Collector's Club Newsletter* of June 1981:

A new Genuine Pearl handled pocket knife is being added to the regular line of Case knives. The 8201 SS will have a mirror finished, stainless steel pen and pocket blades and a stainless steel back spring. Both the liners and bolsters will be made of nickel silver.

The 8201 SS, along with the 82079 1/2, are the only two Genuine Mother of Pearl knives in regular production at Case. The 82079 1/2 is a knife that is regularly being ordered engraved for gifts and the 8201 will no doubt follow the same path when it becomes available.

Traditionally, all Case pearl-handled pocket knives were made with the handles pinned on. The only exception was the 8271 pattern, an unusual pen knife pattern made with dovetailing of the pearl-handle material under the nickel silver bolsters, eliminating the need for handle pins. Pinning of pearl was an operation that required a lot of skill, due to the tendency of pearl to crack. In 1981, Case changed its manufacturing process and began making pearl-handled knives without handle pins, with the pearl handles glued on. This was announced in this excerpt from the *Case Collector's Club Newsletter* of September 1981:

On the 82079 1/2 and the new 8201 SS, the handle materials are not changing but the way we are putting them on is. If you come across a new one you will probably notice that there are no pins in the cover. This is because they are now being glued on with a special super strength epoxy.

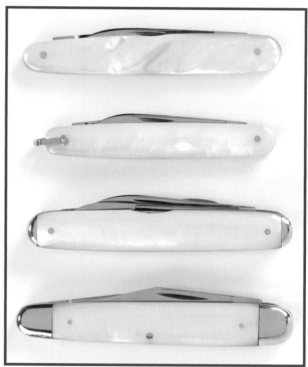

Case Pocket knives with genuine pearl handles, from top: Case XX 82063 SHAD SS, 3-1/16"; Case XX USA 82053 SHAD R SS, 2-13/16"; 7 dot, 1973, 8364 Scis SS, 3-1/8"; 5 dot, 1975, 82079 1/2 SS, 3-1/4". Note that on these knives all handles are pinned on.

This new process for the handles has gone through some rigorous testing including, dropping, hitting and even throwing the knife. In not one instance did the cover come off. It seems that the handle material will break before the glue will let loose. The gluing also makes a stronger cover because the glue covers the entire over surface whereas the rivets only held a small portion of the cover surface.

At that time, the 8201 SS and the 82079 1/2 SS were the only pearl-handled pocket knives in the Case line. In 1982, a pearl handled "Peanut," the 8220 SS, was added and also was made with glued on pearl handles. These three pearl-handled patterns were all shown in the Case factory catalog from 1983 and in the price list dated Jan. 15, 1985. None were shown in the 1986 catalog or price list, so evidently they were all discontinued circa 1985. That marked

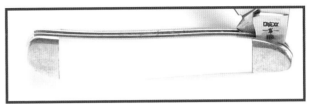

This 8 dot 1982 8220 SS Peanut is one of the pearl-handled knives made with glued-on pearl handles with no handle pins.

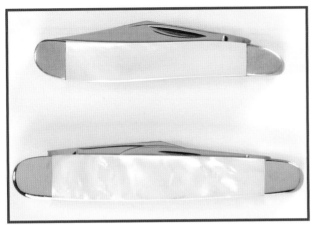

Case Pocket knives with genuine pearl handles that are glued on with no handle pins, from top: 8 dot, 1982, 8220 SS Peanut, 2-3/4", and 8 dot, 1982, 82079 1/2 SS, 3-1/4".

the end of Case's use of genuine pearl on standard product pocket knives for a number of years (though its use was continued on limited edition/SFO knives).

In 1995, Case reintroduced the use of pearl on standard product pocket knives, and pearl-handled knives have been in the product line every year since that time. The 1995 catalog listed five pocket knife patterns in mother of pearl. These knives featured brass liners and handle pins and mirror finished stainless steel blades, and the knives were made without shields. In this new introduction of pearl handled knives, Case returned to the traditional method of pinning the pearl handles on.

Beginning in 1997, the mother of pearl line was enhanced, with the switch to nickel silver liners and handle pins and the installation of a Case shield on each knife. Beginning in 1999, a special "long tail C" Case shield was introduced for exclusive use on pearl-handled knives. Since 1995, Case has produced a wide variety of large and small patterns in pearl, including the popular 54 "Trapper" pattern.

HANDLE KEY NUMBER 9: IMITATION PEARL

Imitation pearl is a synthetic material intended to simulate a genuine mother of pearl handle. The use of imitation pearl as a handle material goes back to the early years of Case, and a number of interesting variations of the material have been used on Case pocket knives over the years. While imitation pearl is in itself an attractive handle material, the earlier generations of this material lacked the iridescence and natural

beauty of genuine mother of pearl. Based on my observations, there were at least four major variations of imitation pearl-handle material used on Case pocket knives from the Case Tested era through the 1980s.

What I refer to as "regular" imitation pearl is the basic material that was used on many knives with the CASE TESTED stamping and on most CASE XX-stamped imitation pearl knives. The use of "regular" imitation pearl during these eras alternated with the use of the "older cracked ice" imitation pearl material. This seemed to be a random variation. The use of "regular" imitation pearl continued through the Case XX USA era and into the 1970s.

"Regular" imitation pearl has a glossy appearance and a smooth, even white color. The "older cracked ice" imitation pearl by contrast has a series of swirls or striations in the material under the smooth surface. Whereas "regular" imitation pearl is always white, the "older cracked ice" handles can vary in color from off white to having a yellowish tint.

During the Case XX era, a relatively small number of pocket knife patterns were offered with imitation pearl handles. Most of these were small pen knife patterns, but Case also offered the 93047 "stockman" and the 9383 "whittler" in imitation pearl. These larger patterns were discontinued in the mid-1950s and are relatively rare. Another sought after pattern in imitation pearl is the 9220 "Peanut," discontinued in 1965.

The use of the "older cracked ice" handle material seemed to end in the late Case XX era and by the Case XX USA era all imitation pearl-handled knives were made with the "regular" imitation pearl. The use of "regular" imitation pearl handles continued into the 1970s. At that time, its use was limited to the 9233, 9261, 92042 and 92042 R pen knives and on the 9333 and 9327 "Stockman's Sunday Dress" knives. Most of these were discontinued by the mid-1970s. It should be noted that none of the imitation pearl-handled knife patterns made from the Case XX era through the 1980s were made with the Case shield in the handle.

By 1977, the 92033 and the 92042 were the only remaining imitation pearl-handled patterns in the Case line. Starting at some point in 1976-1977, Case changed to a new imitation pearl-handle material, which I refer to as "new cracked ice." This new material resembled the older cracked ice with striations under the surface, but the color was a bright white. This new material was used on these patterns for a number of years, but it was found that handles made of this material had a tendency to shrink after installation on a knife. The following is an excerpt from a Case sales memo dated April 14, 1980:

A few problems have developed with our current source for the cracked ice handle material. We have experienced a shrinkage problem with the current handle material we are using; therefore, we are trying to secure additional sources for the cracked ice as well as solve the problems with our current supplier.

Because of these problems, we do not know when we will again have any stock of the #92033 and the #92042. Effective immediately, we will be canceling these two patterns off all open stock and display orders currently in the house. Please do not take any more order for these two patterns until further notice. We will keep you updated on this situation.

Case evidently found a new supplier, as the factory catalog #81 (published in 1981) included the 92033 and the 92042, as well as two additional patterns in imitation pearl, the 9201 R SS and the 92042 R SS in the Gentlemen's Line. While the catalog refers to the handle material on these patterns as "imitation pearl," it appears to be what I refer to as the "new cracked ice" material.

By 1983, another change had been made and Case again went to a different new imitation pearl-handle material. The 1983 Case factory catalog shows the 92033 SS

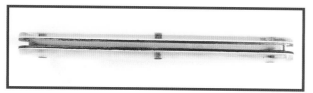

Cracked ice celluloid handle on Case XX-stamped 9279 SHAD SS pattern showing the "white liner."

and the 92042 SS (now with the "SS" suffix as the blade material for these patterns was changed over to polished stainless steel). Both of these knives featured a brilliant looking imitation pearl-handle material that was glued on, so neither knife had handle pins. Note that by that time, Case had also gone to gluing genuine pearl handles on as well.

This new material was still referred to by Case as "imitation pearl," but I refer to it as "acrylic pearl" because it resembles later imitation pearl-handle material that has been made of acrylic. In my opinion, this material provides a fairly close match to genuine pearl in appearance. Both of these patterns were discontinued by March of 1986 and that was the end of the use of imitation pearl handles on standard product Case pocket knives for a period of several years.

In 1992, Case revived imitation pearl as a pocket knife handle material. Four patterns, the "Peanut," the "Mini Copperhead," the "Trapper," and the 01 pen knife were made with a "simulated pearl" handle material that Case indicated was a "polyester-based, simulated pearl." Case continued the use of the number "9" as an indication of simulated pearl (9254 SS, 92109 X SS, 9220 SS, and 9201 SS were the actual pattern numbers). Only the "Trapper" from this series was carried over to 1993 then it, too, was discontinued for 1994. These four knife patterns were made with the Case oval shield.

HANDLE KEY P: PAKKAWOOD

As discussed in the previous section on genuine bone handles, Case began the use of jigged Pakkawood as a substitute for bone on certain large patterns beginning in the early 1960s. Another Pakkawood variation was smooth Pakkawood, first used on the P172 Buffalo when it was introduced in 1969. The use of smooth Pakkawood expanded as Case introduced a number of patterns of modern stainless steel lockback knives in the 1970s, including the P197 L SSP Shark Tooth, the P158 L SSP Mako, and the P159 L SSP Hammerhead. The P137 Sod Buster Junior, the second knife in the Kentucky Bicentennial series, was also handled in smooth Pakkawood. Case continues today to use Pakkawood on a number of lockback knife patterns.

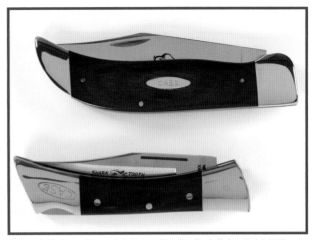

Case pocket knives with smooth Pakkawood handles. Top knife is a 10 dot, 1980, P172, 5-1/2" Buffalo with brown Pakkawood handles, and the bottom knife is a 7 dot, 1973, P197 L SSP, 5-1/4" Shark Tooth with black Pakkawood handles.

These knives illustrate variations in Case imitation pearl handles over the years; from top: Case XX 9279 SS pen knife, 3-1/8", "cracked" ice handles; Case XX 9220 Peanut, 2-3/4", "regular" imitation pearl handles; 2 dot, 1978, 92042 pen knife, 3", "new cracked ice" handles; and 7 dot, 1983, 92033 SS pen knife, 2-5/8", new "acrylic pearl" handles.

Comparison of genuine pearl to imitation pearl handles, from top: 8 dot, 1982, 8220 SS Peanut, 2-3/4", genuine pearl, and 7 dot, 1983, 92033 SS, 2-5/8", with later "acrylic" imitation pearl handles.

HANDLE KEY M: METAL

Various metals have been used as handle materials on Case pocket knives over the years. During the Case Tested Era, both nickel silver and stainless steel were used as handle materials on some pocket knife patterns. By the Case XX era, the letter "M" seemed to be used exclusively to designate stainless steel handles. From 1965-1967, Case produced a pocket knife pattern with sterling silver handles. This knife, pattern number S-2, used the handle key letter "S" to designate sterling silver.

Patterns produced in stainless steel handles from the Case XX era into the 1970s include the M279 SS, the M279 F SS, and the M279 Scis SS, as well as the M3102 R SS and the Fly Fisherman. On earlier Case XX to Case XX USA specimens of these knives, the stainless steel handles will have a polished finish. Beginning in the late 1960s, Case went to a "brushed" handle finish on these metal handled patterns. Beginning in the 1970s, Case also used the "M" handle code on modern lockback knives that were made with lightweight aluminum alloy handles. Examples include the M1051 L SSP and the M1057 L SSP.

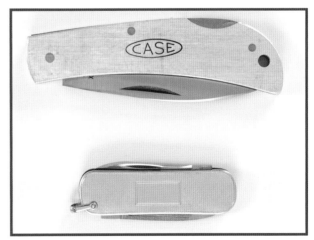

Case pocket knives with metal handles, from top: 9 dot, 1981, M1051 L SSP, aluminum alloy handles, 3-3/4"; Case XX USA S-2, sterling silver handles, 2-1/4".

CASE POCKET KNIFE PATTERN GUIDE

I consider this section to be the "heart" of the book. Over its long history, W.R. Case & Sons has produced a dizzying array of pocket knife patterns in all conceivable shapes and sizes and blade configurations.

Many of the patterns made in the early days of Case and up into the Case Tested era were discontinued and never seen again after WWII. Other early patterns have endured to the present day; indeed, a number of Case pocket knife patterns currently in the line have been in continuous production since the early 1900s.

Pocket knife patterns or "handle dies" truly represent the "DNA" of the Case brand. In recent years, Case has looked to the company's past and many of the older patterns have been resurrected in modern form, with the traditional styling, detailing, and handle materials intact. Case is a company with a rich history and tradition and through many of these patterns, the legend continues.

A complete review of all Case pocket knife patterns new and old is well beyond the scope of a single volume. In assembling the information for this section, I have tried to include many of the most collectable and well known pocket knife patterns that were in production from the post WWII years up to the 1990s. I had a certain logic in mind in making this selection. On the subject of the older pre-WWII Case pocket knives, many interesting variations were made but most of these knives are very rare, and some are downright obscure. Even dedicated collectors may go for many years without coming across actual examples of many of the very old Case pocket knives.

I have chosen to document much information on the wide range of case pocket knife patterns made from the time that Case retooled after WWII and then through the 1960s, 1970s, 1980s and into the early 1990s. This will provide Case pocket knife collectors with information on a wide range of knives, examples of which are often readily available in today's collector market, with some searching of course. Case went through a lot of changes in this time period and the material here will track the myriad changes to the line over several decades.

While information on the older Case pocket knives (1980s and earlier) is often hard to find, the newer knives are much better documented. In the old days, catalogs were published only sporadically, with time spans as long as six years between catalogs. Beginning in 1991, Case began publishing a complete color catalog every single year. These catalogs do an excellent and thorough job of documenting the pocket knives made from 1991 to present day. My intent in assembling this Pattern Guide, together with the previous sections, is to provide the collector with as much information as possible on a wide swath of Case patterns assembled in one place.

It is my contention that if a beginning Case knife collector absorbs the information on the range of patterns illustrated and included in this section, then a solid foundation will be formed for evaluating and learning about the older pre-WWII pattern variations. At the same time, this learning process will illustrate to the collector the history and evolution of many patterns that are in the Case pocket knife line today.

ADDITIONAL NOTES

I have attempted to document to the closest extent possible the years that many patterns were introduced and/or discontinued. This was done using the Case factory price lists and catalogs I have available, as well as my own memory. Catalogs and price lists provide, at best, approximate information. In many instances, knives were discontinued in between the times that a new catalog or price list was issued; at other times, a discontinued pattern may have continued to be shown in price lists even after its production had been discontinued, if the factory still had some stock of the pattern. Then, too, I did not have a price list available for every year.

While I have documented a lot of the minute variations made for many of the patterns, I did not try to list all of them. There are many variations, including rare handle materials, that are seldom seen and often subject to the judgment of the collector (bone handle colors for example). On the older knives from the XX era, I have attempted to include the major variations; however, the small variations collectively are virtually infinite.

Likewise, there are a few better documented variations never mentioned in this section if they affected the entire Case pocket knife line. For example, a number of the patterns listed in this section will be found made with "shoulderless grind" blades (1983-1985), and later with "raised letter" shields (1987-1989). Listing these individual variations for each individual pattern affected would result in a very cumbersome document. You are encouraged to study carefully the previous sections of this book in order to learn how to recognize many of these additional variations.

As is true with the balance of this book, the Pattern Guide section focuses almost exclusively on the pocket knives that were made in Case's "standard product" line. Case has produced enough limited-edition knives and SFOs over the years to fill many volumes the size of this book. I have in a number of instances mentioned some limited or SFO releases in the pattern descriptions, in particular if I believed that mention of the SFO would enhance the description of the evolution of the pattern. Likewise, I have added more descriptive and historical information to several of the "key" patterns that were important to the history of Case and to patterns that have particular collector interest.

PATTERN 00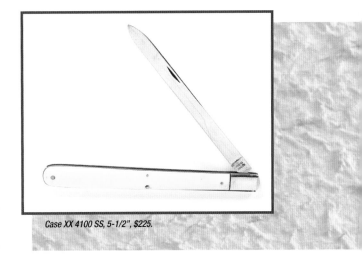

The basic pattern: The 00 pattern is a long slim jack knife pattern generally referred to by collectors as the "Melon Tester." The 00 pattern was introduced by Case in the 1950s and is a "barehead" jack knife, meaning there is a bolster only at the blade end. It was designed to be used for sampling fruits, vegetables and meats. In the 1967 and 1974 Case factory catalogs, the 00 pattern was listed in the Special Purpose Knives section with the caption, "Citrus – Sausage – Melon Tester" under the picture. The closed length of the 00 pattern is 5-1/2".

A number of other cutlery companies have produced similar "sampler" knives, but usually these have been made up as inexpensive single-blade knives with no bolsters, intended for use as advertising or premium knives. The Case 00 pattern is a first-class knife, with nickel silver liners and bolsters and polished stainless blades. Some will be found with imprinted handles often with the names of food and produce companies.

I have always been puzzled as to the exact market for which this type of knife was intended, since it is doubtful that the average person would seek out a special pocket knife with which to test melons. I suspect that fruit growers would have a need for such a knife, or people whose job it is to inspect and buy produce or meats for a market or store chain (or an FDA inspector).

Variations: The 00 pattern was always made with white composition handles and with polished stainless steel blades. During the Case XX era, the following variations were made:

Case XX 4100 SS, 5-1/2", $225.

- 4100 SS, with a polished stainless steel spear blade.
- 4200 SS, with polished stainless steel spear and pen blades.

Case introduced the 4100 SS in 1958. The 4200 SS came later. The first listing of the 4200 SS is found in the Case factory price list dated Jan. 1, 1966 and it is shown as a new pattern.

The 4100 SS and the 4200 SS were both produced through the CASE XX USA era into the 1970s. The 4200 SS was discontinued circa 1973 and the 4100 SS was discontinued as of Sept. 1, 1974.

The 4200 SS was actually first manufactured prior to 1965 in a small quantity with the CASE XX STAINLESS tang stamping. This is a very rare knife. It is probable that a small production run or pilot run of the 4200 SS pattern was done prior to full production of the knife.

Other variations: A few 00 patterns will be found with serrated blades. They were never listed in Case factory catalogs with serrated blades, so this was evidently a special order option. They are rare. I have observed examples of the 4100 SS with a serrated master blade. I have never seen a serrated 4200 SS but it is possible that some were made. During the last years of production in the 1970s, some examples of the 4100 SS were made with glazed finish stainless steel blades instead of polished. This appears to be a random variation.

Newer variations: The 00 pattern has never been reintroduced.

PATTERN 01

The basic pattern: The 01 pattern is a small senator or equal end penknife, constructed with a single backspring and a blade at each end. Closed length is 2-5/8". The 01 pattern goes back to the early years of Case. During the pre-WWII years, it was offered both with and without a bail and with various handle materials including celluloids and genuine pearl, as well as bone.

Blade and handle variations: The 01 pattern has a spear master blade and a small pen blade. No other blade variations have been used.

During the Case XX era, the following principal variations were made:

- 3201, with yellow composition handles.
- 6201, with bone handles.
- 9201, with imitation pearl handles.

The 3201 will be found with the CASE XX stamping in both the older yellow celluloid (with white liner) and with yellow composition handles. Later examples made from the CASE XX USA era and into the 1970s will have yellow delrin handles. Most 3201s were made without shields, but some had shields. This seems to be a random variation. The 3201 was discontinued in 1975.

The 6201 in the CASE XX stamping will be found in several of the Case XX-era bone color variations including green bone, "regular" bone and red bone. The use of bone handles on the 6201 continued into the 1970s. During the 1970s, delrin was substituted for bone on the 6201 on a random basis. It is possible that the 6201 was changed to being handled 100 percent in delrin after 1972. I have personally never seen a bone-handled specimen from the 1970s made after 1972. The 6201 was discontinued in 1976.

The 9201 in the CASE XX stamping will be found with both the older "cracked ice" imitation pearl handles and with "regular" imitation pearl. Cracked ice was not used on the 9201 after the CASE XX era, so later examples made from the CASE XX USA era and into the 1970s will have "regular" imitation pearl handles. The 9201 was discontinued circa 1973.

Blade steel and liner material: From the XX era through the time that the pattern was discontinued in the 1970s, all 01 patterns were only offered with chrome vanadium as the blade steel. The liner material during these years was nickel silver.

Other variations: Most examples of the older 01 pattern will have a groove cut into the back handle for ease in opening the pen blade. However, some examples will be found without the thumb groove. This appears to be a random variation.

Newer variations: The 01 pattern was reintroduced in 1979 as part of the Gentlemen's Line. The following two variations were introduced:

- 6201 R SS, with delrin handles and a bail.
- 9201 R SS, with "new cracked ice" handles and a bail.

Both of these variations had stainless steel blades with a steel finish and brass liners. These knives were only made for a few years and were discontinued in December 1982.

In 1981, the 8201 SS was introduced. This variation was made with genuine pearl handles that were glued on (no pins) and had polished stainless steel blades and brass liners. The 8201 SS was discontinued in 1985.

Beginning in 1991, Case reintroduced the 01 pattern and it has been made in a variety of handle materials and with stainless steel blades.

Case XX 3201, yellow celluloid, 2-5/8", $100.

Case XX USA 1 Dot, 1979, 6201 R SS, Delrin, 2-5/8", $30.

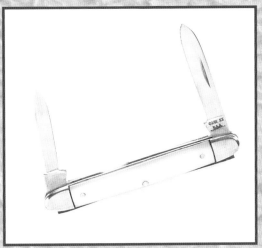

Case XX USA 10 Dot, 1970, 9201, imitation pearl, 2-5/8", $35.

Case XX USA 9 Dot, 1971, 6201, bone, 2-5/8", $65.

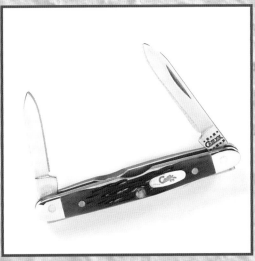

Case XX USA, New-2000 Stamping, 6201, "new green bone," 2-5/8", $35.

PATTERN 02

The basic pattern: The 02 pattern is a basic "swell-end" jack knife, with two blades and two backsprings. Closed length is 3-3/8". The 02 pattern goes back to the early years of Case and is a "barehead" jack knife, meaning there is a bolster only at the main blade end. This was done to reduce the cost of the knife. The 02 was a relatively inexpensive knife in the Case line.

Blade and handle variations: During the Case XX era, the following principal variation was made:

- 6202 1/2, with bone handles and clip master blade and pen blade.

The 6202 1/2 in the CASE XX stamping will be found in several of the Case XX-era bone color variations including green, regular and red, and in rough black. The use of bone handles on the 6202 1/2 continued until mid-1970. The 6202 1/2 was one of a number of patterns that were changed to being handled 100 percent in delrin in 1970, so both bone and delrin examples were made in that year.

Even though the 6202 1/2 was normally handled 100 percent in delrin after 1970, there was a limited number made in genuine bone in 1975, which appears to be a random factory variation. I believe it is possible that Case ran out of the molded delrin handles for the pattern during a production run and had to temporarily go back to bone. The 6202 1/2 was discontinued after 1977.

Blade steel and liner material: From the XX era through the time that the pattern was discontinued in the 1970s, all 6202 1/2 patterns were only offered with chrome vanadium as the blade steel. The liner material during these years was brass.

Newer variations: The 02 pattern has never been reintroduced.

Case XX 6202 1/2, reddish bone, 3-3/8", $100.

Case XX USA 8 Dot, 1972, 6202 1/2, delrin, 3-3/8", $50.

PATTERN 05

The basic pattern: The 05 pattern goes back to the early years of Case and is a "swell-end" jack knife, with two blades and two backsprings. The pattern has an elongated bolster with a "step" at the main blade end and thus is in some respects a variation of the "Barlow" pattern. However, unlike most Barlows, the bone handles on the 05 pattern were traditionally jigged bone as compared to the sawcut bone typically used on the Barlow by most manufacturers. The 05 is a "barehead" jack knife,

meaning that there is a bolster only at the main blade end; closed length is 3-3/4".

The 05 pattern with the "razor" master blade was traditionally referred to by collectors as the "one-armed man," or as the "one-armed man's knife." This is due to the design of the razor-style master blade. With practice, it is possible to open the razor blade with one hand by hooking the tip on a flat surface or on the edge of a pocket or belt. No one has ever figured out how the "one-armed man" is supposed to open the pen blade, however.

Blade and handle variations: During the Case XX era, the following principal variations pattern were made:

- 6205, with bone handles, spear master blade and pen blade.
- 6205 RAZ, with bone handles, razor master blade, and pen blade.

The 6205 with the spear master blade was always made with a regular pull main blade, while the 6205 RAZ had long pull as standard on the main blade. The 6205 and the 6205 RAZ in the CASE XX stamping will be found in several of the Case XX-era bone color variations including green, regular and red. The 6205 was discontinued in 1964; however, the 6205 RAZ remained in the Case line.

During the 1970s, delrin was substituted for bone on the 6205 RAZ on a random basis. Both delrin and bone examples will be found; however, my observation is that bone handles are much scarcer on examples of the 6205 RAZ made after 1972. The 6205 RAZ was discontinued as of Jan. 1, 1978.

Blade steel and liner material: From the XX era through the time that the pattern was discontinued in the 1970s, all 05 patterns were only offered with chrome vanadium as the blade steel. The liner material during these years was brass.

Newer variations: Some 05 patterns with the razor master blades were made as SFOs in the early 1980s with satin finished stainless blades. The 05 pattern with a razor master blade was reintroduced into the Case standard product line in 1989-1990. However, at this time the pattern was retooled to include a lower bolster and was made with polished stainless steel blades. It has been produced in this configuration with both spear and razor master blades as the 005 pattern in recent years.

WR Case & Sons 5205 RAZ, note the master blade has been reshaped by a previous owner, 3-3/4", $900.

Backspring view of the 5205 RAZ showing the iron bolsters and liners.

Case XX 6205, red bone, 3-3/4", $300.

Case XX 6205 RAZ, bone, 3-3/4", $300.

Case XX-stamped 6205 patterns showing the main blade variation. Top: 6205 spear master blade with regular pull; bottom: 6205 RAZ razor master blade with long pull.

PATTERN 07

The basic pattern: The 07 pattern goes back to the Case Tested era and is a "dogleg" jack knife, with two blades and two backsprings. Closed length is 3-1/2". The 07 is a "capped" jack knife, meaning there are bolsters at both the main blade end and the lower end.

Blade and handle variations: During the Case XX era, the following principal variations were made:

- 2207, with smooth black handles, clip master blade and pen blade.
- 6207, with bone handles, clip master blade and pen blade.

The 6207 in the CASE XX stamping will be found in several of the Case XX-era bone color variations including green, regular and red, and in rough black. The 2207 is a relatively rare variation. Based on older Case factory price lists, it appears that the 2207 was discontinued sometime prior to 1955. The 6207 remained as a standard pattern in the Case line.

The use of bone handles on the 6207 continued into the 1970s. During the 1970s, delrin was substituted for bone on a random basis and beginning in 1978, it appears Case went back to handling the 6207 100 percent in bone.

A major change to the 6207 pattern occurred during 1979. During the later part of the year, the standard 6207 was discontinued and replaced with a new variation—the 6207 Sp SSP, also known as the "Mini Trapper." The Mini Trapper was designed on the 6207 frame with bone handles, but the blades were changed to a "California clip"-style main blade and a long spay secondary blade. The blades were satin finished with a polished edge and the main blade was etched with the words "Mini Trapper."

The Mini Trapper was conceived as a smaller version of the popular 54 "Trapper" pattern and soon it became immensely popular with both collectors and users.

Blade steel and liner material: From the XX era through the time that the pattern was changed to the Mini Trapper in 1979, all 07 patterns were only offered with chrome vanadium as the blade steel. The liner material during these years was brass, which was continued on the new Mini Trapper. The new

Case XX 6207, red bone, 3-1/2", $200.

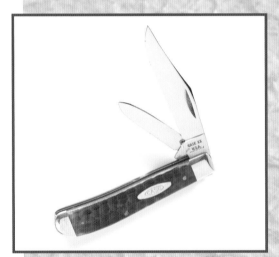

Case XX USA 10 Dot, 1970, 6207, red bone, 3-1/2", $125.

Case XX USA 1 Dot, 1989, Lightning S, ROG 6207 SP, rogers bone, Damascus, 3-1/2", $125.

07 Mini Trapper was made in stainless steel with polished blade edges (SSP) as the only option for a number of years, but later variations have been offered in chrome vanadium as well.

In 1991, a 6207 Mini Trapper with chrome vanadium blades and bone handles was introduced as part of the Case standard product line, but this version was discontinued after 1992. In 1993, a 3207 Mini Trapper with chrome vanadium blades and yellow handles was introduced and has remained in the Case standard product line until the present day.

Other variations: While the basic 6207 was made in both bone and delrin during the 1970s, the 6207 Sp SSP with the Mini Trapper blade etch was never made with delrin handles.

After 1990, the Mini Trapper blade etching was dropped, while the satin blade finish was still used on the "standard product" Mini Trappers. In 1997, Case dropped the use of the satin finish on all knives with natural handle materials, including the Mini Trapper and all blades were polished from that point on.

Newer variations: The "old style" 6207 has not been made since the Mini Trapper was introduced. In the years since 1979, and in particular beginning in the 1990s, the Mini Trapper has been made in a wide variety of handle materials.

Case 1990 Tang Stamp, 6207 SP SSP, bone, 3-1/2", $65.

Case 1990 Tang Stamp, 7207 SP SS, curly maple, 3-1/2", $65.

Case XX USA 10 Dot, 1980, Lightning S, 6207 SP SSP, main blade has "Mini Trapper" etching, 3-1/2", $75.

Case 1990 Tang Stamp, 7207 SP SS, rosewood, 3-1/2", $65.

Case Long Tail C, 1996 Stamp, 6207 SP CV, chestnut bone, 3-1/2", $50.

Case Long Tail C, 1999 Stamp, 6207 SP SS, chestnut bone, 3-1/2", $50.

Case XX USA 1 Dot, 1979, 5207SP SSP, Bradford Centennial, 3-1/2", $100.

Case XX USA 10 Dot, 1980, Lightning S, 5207 SSP, Case 75th Anniversary, 3-1/2", $100.

PATTERN 08

The basic pattern: The 08 goes back to the early years of Case and is a "semi-swell center" or "humpback" frame that was made as both a two-blade penknife (6208) with a single backspring and as a three-blade "whittler" pattern (6308). The 6308 pattern is a "split-back whittler," with three blades and two backsprings. The 6208 is referred to by collectors as the "half whittler."

The "split-back" or "split-backspring" designation is used by collectors to refer to a specific blade and backspring arrangement. The 6308 has a relatively thick master clip blade at one end with a small clip blade and a pen blade at the opposite end. The 6308 has two backsprings, with the main blade riding on both springs. Each of the two smaller blades rides on one spring. In order to provide space for the main blade to fall between the two small blades, a partial center liner or "wedge" is installed between the backsprings at the small blade end of the knife.

Closed length of the 08 pattern is 3-1/4".

Blade and handle variations: During the Case XX era, the following principal variations were made:

- 6208, with bone handles, clip master blade and pen blade.
- 6308, with clip master blade, small clip blade and pen blade.

The 6208 and the 6308 in the CASE XX stamping will be found in several of the Case XX-era bone color variations including green, regular and red, and in rough black.

During the 1970s, delrin was substituted for bone on the 6208 and 6308 on a random basis and both examples will be found; however, my observation is that starting in 1978, both knives were switched back to being handled 100 percent in bone. Production of the 6308 continued until 1985, when the pattern was discontinued.

The 6208 pattern went through the following evolution as Case made changes to its product line in the later 1970s and early 1980s. The 6208 with bone handles and chrome vanadium blades was discontinued in mid-1979 and replaced with the A6208.

Case XX 6208, "half whittler," green bone, 3-1/4", $175.

Case XX 6208, "half whittler," rough black, 3-1/4", $150.

Case XX 6308, "whittler," red bone, 3-1/4", $350.

Case XX 6308, "whittler," rough black, 3-1/4", $350.

This was the same 6208 pattern in chrome vanadium blade steel but with smooth Appaloosa-colored bone handles. This initial variation of the A6208 was made without a shield. The A6208 was one of ten patterns Case introduced in 1979 with smooth genuine bone handles in two colors, Appaloosa and Satin Rose.

The next change took place in mid-1981, when the A6208 was changed to the A6208 SS. This was essentially the same knife but with satin finished stainless steel blades and with a shield added to the smooth Appaloosa bone handles. The A6208 SS was relatively short lived and discontinued in 1982. Later in 1982, the pattern was reintroduced as the 6208 SS with satin finished stainless steel blades and with delrin handles. The 6208 SS in delrin was discontinued in 1985.

Blade steel and liner material: From the XX era through the 1970s, all 08 patterns were only offered with chrome vanadium as the blade steel. The liner material during these years was nickel silver. Beginning circa 1978, Case began changing all pocket knife patterns with nickel silver liners to the standard use of brass as the lining material. This change was complete by 1980. Later examples of the 08 pattern as described above had stainless steel blades (6208 only) and had brass liners.

Newer variations: Case has reintroduced the 08 pattern in recent years in both two-blade and three-blade variations in a variety of handle materials.

Case Tested 6308, "whittler," green bone, 3-1/4", $900.

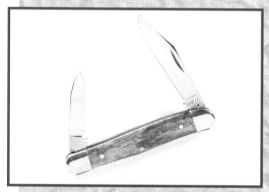

Case XX USA 10 Dot, 1980, Lightning S, A6208, Appaloosa bone, 3-1/4", $50.

Case XX USA 7 Dot, 1973, 6208, delrin, 3-1/4", $50.

Case XX 6308, "whittler," green bone, 3-1/4", $600.

Case XX USA 10 Dot, 1980, Lightning S, 5208 SSP, Case 75th, 3-1/4", $75.

PATTERN 009

The basic pattern: The 009 pattern goes back to the early years of Case and is the classic "Barlow" pattern. The bone handles on the 009 were traditionally "sawcut" rather than jigged bone; closed length is 3-3/8". During the Case Tested era, the 009 Barlow pattern was made with both celluloid and bone handles. During these years, a variety of master blade variations were offered including a clip, spear, razor, spay, and sheepfoot.

Blade and handle variations: During the Case XX era, the following principal variations were made:

- 62009, with sawcut bone handles, spear master blade and pen blade.
- 62009 1/2, with sawcut bone handles, clip master blade and pen blade.
- 62009 RAZ, with sawcut bone handles, razor master blade, and pen blade.

The 62009, 62009 1/2, and 62009 RAZ in the CASE XX stamping will be found in several of the Case XX-era bone color variations including green, regular and red.

A variation of the 009 pattern during the XX era was made with black composition handles and it has a different appearance as compared to most Case Barlows. It is my opinion that the 62009 and 62009 1/2 patterns with the black handles were made on contract by Utica Cutlery Company for Case. Case has always made most of its pocket knives in house, but like most manufacturers, it occasionally had the need to outsource production of certain patterns.

Another variation that was likely made on contract is a XX-era 62009 1/2 with a long pull master blade and with sawcut tan/green bone handles. Again the tooling on these is slightly different and it is my opinion that they were made by Ulster Knife Company for Case.

The use of bone handles on the 62009, 62009 1/2, and 62009 RAZ continued until mid-1970. These three Barlows were among a number of patterns that were changed to being handled 100 percent in delrin in 1970, so both bone and delrin examples were made during that year. The 62009 was discontinued in 1975 and the 62009 RAZ was discontinued as of Jan. 1, 1977. The 62009 1/2 remained in the Case line.

Even though the 62009 1/2 was normally handled

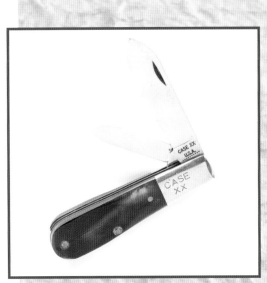

Case XX USA 10 Dot, 1970, 62009 "Barlow," bone, 3-3/8", $80. Note: Master blade in front.

Case XX 62009, "Barlow," bone, 3-3/8", $125. Note: Master blade in back.

Case XX 62009 RAZ, bone, 3-3/8", $150.

100 percent in delrin after 1970, there was a limited number made in genuine bone in 1975, which appears to be a random factory variation. I believe it is possible that Case ran out of the molded delrin handles for the pattern during a production run and the company had to temporarily go back to bone.

The 62009 1/2 pattern went through the following evolution as Case made changes to its product line in the late 1970s and early 1980s. The 62009 1/2 with delrin handles and chrome vanadium blades was discontinued in mid-1979 and replaced with the A62009 1/2. This was the same 62009 1/2 pattern in chrome vanadium blade steel but with smooth Appaloosa-colored bone handles. The A62009 1/2 was one of ten patterns Case introduced in 1979 with smooth genuine bone handles in two colors, Appaloosa and Satin Rose.

The next change took place in mid-1981, when the A62009 1/2 was changed to the A62009 1/2 SS. This was essentially the same knife but with satin finished stainless steel blades and the smooth Appaloosa bone handles. The A62009 1/2 SS was relatively short lived and was discontinued in 1982. Later in 1982, the pattern was reintroduced as the 62009 1/2 SS with satin finished stainless steel blades and delrin handles. The 62009 1/2 SS in delrin was discontinued in 1985.

Blade steel and liner material: From the XX era

Case XX 62009 RAZ, "Barlow," red bone-long pull, 3-3/8", $200.

Case XX 62009-1/2, "Barlow," red bone, 3-3/8", $200.

Case XX 62009-1/2, "Barlow," green bone-long pull, 3-3/8", $250.
Note: Possible contract knife.

Case XX USA 62009 RAZ, "Barlow," bone, 3-3/8", $100.

through the 1970s, all 009 Barlow patterns were only offered with chrome vanadium as the blade steel. The liner material during these years was brass. Later examples as described above had stainless steel blades.

Other variations: Most Case two-blade jack patterns have traditionally been designed and tooled to have the master blade in the front of the knife and the pen blade in the back. Case 009 Barlow patterns in general have followed this rule. However, during the Case XX and CASE XX USA eras, many examples of the 009 Barlow patterns were made with slightly different tooling that put the pen blade in front and the master blade in back.

This appears to be a random tooling variation since examples of the knives will be found both ways. Another variation is that on some 009s with the clip master blade in back, the clip blade shape will be slightly different with the nail pull out further on the blade. Also on some 009s with the razor master blade in back, the razor blade will have long pull instead of the normal regular pull. These variations do not seem to have a significant effect on the collector value of the 009 patterns.

Newer variations: Case reintroduced the 009 Barlow pattern in 2000 and it has since been made in a variety of handle materials with polished stainless steel blades.

Case Tested 62009, "Barlow" spear master, green bone, 3-3/8", $350.

Case Tested 62009SH, "Barlow," sheepfoot master, green bone, 3-3/8", $450.

Case Tested 62009-1/2, "Barlow" clip master, green bone, 3-3/8", $350.

Case XX USA 1 Dot, 1979, A62009-1/2, Appaloosa bone, 3-3/8", $60.

Case XX USA 6 Dot, 1974, 62009 RAZ, Delrin, 3-3/8", $60.

Case XX USA 7 Dot, 1983, Lightning S, 62009-1/2 SS, Delrin, 3-3/8", $45.

Case XX USA 7 Dot, 1983, Lightning S, A62009-1/2 SS, Appaloosa bone, 3-3/8", $60.

PATTERN 11

The basic pattern: The 11 pattern goes back to the early years of Case and is an example of what some collectors refer to as an "English Jack" frame style. Closed length is 4-3/8". During the Case Tested era, it was made in several variations including a two-blade jack and a single-blade jack, and a single-blade lockback version, the 6111 1/2 L. The 6111 1/2 L incorporates a folding hand guard and is the only variation of the 11 pattern that was kept in the Case line after the Case Tested era.

The 6111 1/2 L is sometimes referred to by collectors as a "swing-guard lockback" or as a "floating guard knife." Another collector name for the pattern is the Cheetah. This name was originated by Case when a special run of the pattern was made with stag handles and a Cheetah blade etching in 1971 for inclusion in the 1973 stag collector's sets. While the standard 6111 1/2 L always had a saber-ground blade made of chrome vanadium steel, the Cheetah was made with a hollow ground stainless steel blade. The original Cheetah pattern number is 5111 1/2 L SSP.

For many years, the 6111 1/2 L was the only single-blade locking blade knife in the Case product line, quite a contrast to today when lockback knives are heavily represented in the product lines of Case and other knife manufacturers. In fact, in the early to mid-1970s, most collectors referred to the 6111 1/2 L simply as "the lockback," or "the Case lockback." The 6111 1/2 L was also a very difficult knife to obtain during those years. My understanding is that Case had difficulty producing them in quantity due to the extra hand operations involved in fitting the lockback mechanism and the floating guard.

Blade and handle variations: During the Case XX era, the following principal variation was made:

- 6111 1/2 L, with bone handles, a lockback with a single saber ground clip blade and a folding guard.

The 6111 1/2 L in the CASE XX stamping will be found in several of the Case XX-era bone color variations including green, regular and red. I do not believe that this pattern was ever handled in rough black.

During the 1970s, delrin was substituted for bone on the 6111 1/2 L on a random basis and both examples will be found; however, my observation is that starting in 1978, the pattern was switched back to being handled 100 percent in bone. The 6111 1/2 L was discontinued in late 1981.

Blade steel and liner material: From the XX era through the time that the pattern was discontinued, the 6111 1/2 L was only offered with chrome vanadium as the blade steel. The liner material during these years was brass. The 5111 1/2 L SSP CHEETAH was made with a stainless steel blade.

Other variations: One very rare variation made during the CASE XX USA era had an extra "1" in the pattern number. This was apparently due to an error in the fabrication of the stamping die and this variation is highly sought after by collectors.

Newer variations: Case has recently reintroduced a new version of the 6111 1/2 L. The modern version has been made in a wide variety of handle materials, with a flat ground polished stainless steel blade with the CHEETAH blade etching. A smaller version, the Cheetah Cub, has also been introduced.

Case XX USA 9 Dot, 1971, 5111-1/2 LSSP CHEETAH, 4-3/8", $450.

Case XX USA 6111-1/2 L, bone, 4-3/8", $300.

Case XX USA 1 Dot, 1979, 6111-1/2 L, bone, 4-3/8", $125.

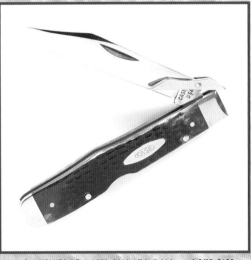

Case XX USA 1 Dot, 1979, 6111-1/2 L, light bone, 4-3/8", $150.

Case XX USA 3 Dot, 1977, 6111-1/2 L, red bone, 4-3/8", $150.

Case XX USA 6 Dot, 1974, 6111-1/2 L, reddish bone, 4-3/8", $140.

Case XX USA 8 Dot, 1972, 6111-1/2 L, reddish bone, 4-3/8", $150.

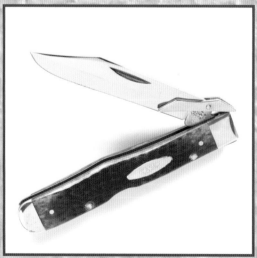

Case XX USA Dotted-10 Dot, 1980, 6111-1/2 L, bone, 4-3/8", $150.

Case XX USA 3 Dot, 1977, 5111-1/2 L SSP, "blue scroll," 4-3/8", $175.

PATTERN 011

The basic pattern: The 011 pattern goes back to the early days of Case and is a curved single blade jack knife. Collectors refer to the 011 pattern as the "hawkbill" due to the shape of the frame; it is also referred to as a "pruner." The design of this pattern is such that it was used for a number of purposes including as a horticultural knife or to cut carpeting, linoleum, or insulation. Closed length is 4".

Blade and handle variations: During the Case XX era, the following principal variations of the 011 pattern were made, with the "pruner" master blade as standard:

- 11011, with smooth walnut handles.
- 61011, with bone handles.

The 61011 in the CASE XX stamping will be found in several of the Case XX-era bone color variations including green, regular and red. The use of bone handles on the 61011 continued into the 1960s. During the CASE XX and CASE XX USA eras, jigged laminated wood, or "Pakkawood," was substituted for bone on the 61011 on a random basis. It is believed that the 61011 was changed over to being handled in Pakkawood 100 percent at some point early in the CASE XX USA era. It is rare to see a CASE XX USA stamped 61011 in genuine bone. Production of the 61011 (in Pakkawood) and the 11011 (in walnut) continued into the 1970s. The 11011 was discontinued as of Jan. 1, 1977.

Blade steel and liner material: From the XX era through the time that the 61011 was changed to the stainless steel (see below), all 011 patterns were only offered with chrome vanadium as the blade steel. The liner material during these years was brass.

Newer variations: Production of the 61011 in Pakkawood continued until late 1981, when it was discontinued; in 1986, it was replaced with a similar 61011 pattern with jigged brown delrin handles and with a chrome vanadium blade. It is my opinion that this replacement 61011 was made on contract for Case by Camillus Cutlery Company. The delrin-handled 61011 remained in the Case product line until recent years. However, it was changed from chrome vanadium blade steel to satin finished stainless steel in 1990-1991. The 61011 SS was discontinued in 2006 when Camillus Cutlery ceased operation.

Case XX USA 61011, "Hawkbill," red bone, 4", $150.

Case XX USA 5 Dot, 1985, Lightning S, 61011, Delrin, 4", $40.

Case Tested 61011 "Hawkbill," green bone, 4", $375.

Case XX USA, 11011, 4", $75.

Case XX USA 2 Dot, 1978, 61011, Pakkawood, 4", $55.

Case's Bradford 61011, "Hawkbill," green bone, 4", $500.

Many early examples (Case Tested and older) of the 61011 "Hawkbill" had unusually thick bone handles. These are the handles on a Case Tested 61011.

Unusual tang stamping variation of "CASE'S BRADFORD." It is believed this tang stamping predates 1920.

PATTERN 14

The basic pattern: The 14 pattern goes back to the early years of Case and is a basic "swell-end" jack knife, with two blades and two backsprings. Closed length is 3-3/8". The 14 pattern is similar to the 02 pattern; however, while the 02 pattern is a "barehead" jack knife (bolster at the main blade end only), the 14 is a "capped" jack knife, with bolsters at both ends.

Blade and handle variations: During the Case XX era, the following principal variations were made:

- 6214, with bone handles, spear master blade and pen blade.
- 6214 1/2, with bone handles, clip master blade and pen blade.

The 6214 and the 6214 1/2 in the CASE XX stamping will be found in several of the Case XX era bone color variations including green, regular and red, and in rough black. The use of bone handles on the 6214 and on the 6214 1/2 continued until mid-1970. The 6214 and the 6214 1/2 were among a number of patterns changed to being handled 100 percent in delrin in 1970, so both bone and delrin examples were made in that year. For the balance of the years made until they were discontinued, both knives were made only with delrin handles. The 6214 and the 6214 1/2 were both discontinued as of June 1, 1975.

Blade steel and liner material: From the XX era through the time the pattern was discontinued in the 1970s, all 14 patterns were only offered with chrome vanadium as the blade steel. The liner material was brass.

Newer variations: The 14 pattern has never been reintroduced.

Case XX USA 9 Dot, 1971, 6214, Delrin, 3-3/8", $50.

PATTERN 16

The basic pattern: The 16 pattern is a basic "swell-end" jack knife, with two blades and two backsprings. Closed length is 3-3/8". It goes back to the early years of Case and is a "barehead" jack knife (bolster at the main blade end only).

Blade and handle variations: During the Case XX era, the following principal variations were made:

- 6216, with bone handles, and spear master blade and pen blade.
- 6216 1/2, with bone handles, and clip master blade and pen blade.
- 1116 Sp, with smooth walnut handles and a single spay blade.

The 6216 and the 6216 1/2 were made with the CASE TESTED tang stamping prior to WWII; after WWII, they were not in the Case line for a number of years but were reintroduced in 1962. The 6216 and the 6216 1/2 were lower-priced knives. When they were put back into the Case line as of March 1, 1962, they replaced the 620035 and the 620035 1/2. These were both lower-priced knives as well that had, in my opinion, been manufactured for Case by another cutlery firm.

The price was kept low on the 16 patterns since they did not have the CASE shield or lower bolsters, and based on my observations, they had somewhat thinner blade and backspring stock as compared to similar other Case jack patterns like the 6235 and the 6235 1/2. The 1962 price list indicates a retail price for the 6216 of $2.50, and $3.25 for the 6235. The 16 pattern, as it was retooled for the Case XX era, is one of a very few Case "jack" patterns designed with the pen blade in front and the master blade in back, as standard for the pattern.

Since most examples of the 16 pattern made during the XX era were made later in the 1960s, the primary bone color variations observed include regular and red. The 6216 and the 6216 1/2 were both discontinued as of March 1, 1968. The 6216 with the CASE XX USA tang stamping is particularly rare.

The 1116 Sp was designed to be a "budding" knife for horticultural uses or as a castrating knife.

Production of the 1116 Sp was continued into the 1970s and discontinued circa 1973.

Blade steel and liner material: From the XX era through the time the pattern was completely discontinued in the 1970s, all 16 patterns were only offered with chrome vanadium as the blade steel. The liner material during these years was brass.

Newer variations: The 16 pattern has never been reintroduced.

Case XX 6216, bone, 3-3/8", $140.

Case XX 6216-1/2, bone, 3-3/8", $140.

PATTERN 17

The basic pattern: The 17 pattern goes back to the Case Tested era and is a "curved" jack knife, with two blades and two backsprings. Closed length is 4". It is a "barehead" jack knife, meaning there is no bolster at the lower end.

The 17 pattern is a heavily constructed working knife, sometimes referred to as a "loom fixer." While this nickname would indicate it may have been used in textile mills, I have never been able to uncover the exact reason for it.

During the pre-WWII era, many cutlery companies made patterns similar to the Case 17 pattern, and several referred to the pattern as the New England Whaler. I have seen examples made by Remington, Landers, Frary, and Clark, Schrade Cutlery Company, and the John Russell Cutlery Company that had "NEW ENGLAND WHALER" either etched on the main blade or imprinted into the front handle of the knife, so it is probable that the Case 17 pattern evolved from rope knives used by sailors.

Blade and handle variations: During the Case XX era, the following principal variations were made:

- 2217, with smooth black handles, sheepfoot master blade and pen blade.
- 6217, with bone handles, sheepfoot master blade and pen blade.

The 6217 in the CASE XX stamping will be found in several of the Case XX-era bone color variations including green, regular and red. The 2217 is a relatively rare variation. Based on older Case factory price lists, it appears that the 2217 was discontinued some time prior to 1955. The 6217 remained a standard pattern in the Case line.

The use of bone handles on the 6217 continued until mid-1970. The 6217 was changed to being handled 100 percent in jigged laminated wood or Pakkawood in 1970, so both examples were made in that year. An interesting fact about the 6217 is that it is one of a very few Case "jack" patterns that has the pen blade in front and the master blade in back, as standard for the pattern. The 6217 was discontinued in 1978.

Blade steel and liner material: From the XX era through the time the pattern was discontinued, all 17 patterns were only offered with chrome vanadium as the blade steel. The liner material during these years was brass.

Other variations: Occasionally examples of the 6217 pattern will be found with a factory-installed bail. Since this

PATTERN 18

variation (would be a 6217 R) was never shown in any Case catalog or price list, I believe it was an option offered as a special factory order for individual retailers. I have seen examples of the 6217 with a bail with 1970s tang stampings.

Newer variations: The "old style" 6217 has not been reintroduced since it was discontinued. However, Case recently introduced a new pattern, the 117, a scaled-down version of the older 17 pattern, designed by Tony Bose.

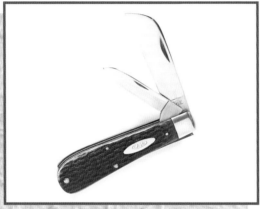
Case XX 6217, "Curved Jack," bone, 4", $250.

Case Tested 6217, "Curved Jack," green bone, 4", $600.

Case XX USA 7 Dot, 1973, 6217, Pakkawood, 4", $100.

The basic pattern: The 18 pattern goes back to the early years of Case and is a medium serpentine stockman pattern with rounded bolsters. Closed length is 3-1/2". It has been primarily manufactured as a three-blade stockman pattern.

Blade and handle variations: The 18 pattern has always been made with either a "California clip" or standard clip as the main blade. During the Case XX era, the following principal variations were made:

- 3318 Sh Pen, with yellow composition handles, and secondary blades sheepfoot and pen.
- 4318 Sh Sp, with white composition handles, secondary blades sheepfoot and spay.
- 6318 Sh Sp, with bone handles, secondary blades sheepfoot and spay.
- 6318 Sh Pen, with bone handles, secondary blades sheepfoot and pen.
- 6318 Sp Pu, with bone handles, secondary blades spay and punch.

In 1965, a stainless steel version was introduced as part of a line of six stainless steel pocket knives introduced that year with the CASE XX USA tang stamping:

- 6318 Sh Sp SSP, with bone handles, secondary blades sheepfoot and spay. Satin finished stainless steel blades with polished edges, main blade etched "TESTED XX RAZOR EDGE."

The 3318 will be found with the CASE XX stamping in both the older yellow celluloid, with white liner, and yellow composition handles. Later examples made from the CASE XX USA era into the 1970s will have yellow delrin handles. The 3318 is still in the Case line today; however, in the early 1980s, it appears the pattern was discontinued for a short time from late 1981 through 1982. In 1983, the 3318 was reintroduced as the 3318 Sh Sp with the secondary blades changed from sheepfoot and pen blades to sheepfoot and spay blades. The 4318 Sh Sp with white composition handles was discontinued circa 1973.

The 6318 variations in the CASE XX stamping will be found in several of the Case XX-era bone color variations including green, regular and red. The use of bone handles on the 6318, including all blade variations, continued into the 1970s. During the 1970s, delrin was substituted for bone on the 6318 on a random basis. My observation is that starting in 1978, all 6318s were switched back to being handled 100 percent in bone.

The 6318 with sheepfoot and spay secondary blades is still in the Case line today, and many variations have been offered in recent years with different bone colors. The 6318 Sh Pen and the 6318 Sp Pu were both discontinued in 1982. The 6318 Sh Sp SSP was gradually changed over to mirror finished stainless blades with no blade etching.

Blade steel and liner material: From the XX era through 1964, all 18 patterns were only offered with chrome vanadium as the blade steel. In 1965, the first version in stainless steel was offered as noted above. Beginning circa 1978, Case began changing all pocket knife patterns with nickel silver liners to the standard use of brass as the lining material. This change was complete by 1980.

Other variations: During the CASE XX era, the 18 patterns were made with the master blade being either a California clip or standard clip. This appears to be a random variation, as the older catalogs never show both blade options. During the CASE XX USA era and through the 1970s, only the California clip master blade was used. The 4318 was made during the CASE XX era with a punch as one of the secondary blades; this is a somewhat rare variation.

The 6318 Sp Pu pattern with spay and punch secondary blades will be observed with two styles of punch blade. The "wraparound" punch blade has a crease with half of the blade at a right angle to the other half. The "flat" punch variation is a simple stamped out blade tapering to a fine point and appears to be a random variation as well.

Beginning circa 1991, the blade etching "TESTED XX RAZOR EDGE" was dropped from the main blade of the 6318 Sh Sp SSP, while the satin blade finish was still used on the "standard product" 6318 Sh Sp SSP. In 1997, Case dropped the use of the satin finish on all knives with natural handle materials, including the 6318 Sh Sp SSP and the blades were polished from that point on.

Newer variations: During the 1980s, a stag-handled version was introduced, 5318 Sh Sp, as part of the Case pocket knife line in 1984 when Case introduced the new "open stock" line of stag-handled pocket knives. The 18 pattern is currently a mainstay in the Case product line. Beginning in the mid- to late 1990s, it has been produced with a wide variety of handle materials. The 18 handle dies has also been used to produce a "Mini Muskrat" pattern. This variation has twin "California clip" blades at opposite ends of the knife and operating on two backsprings.

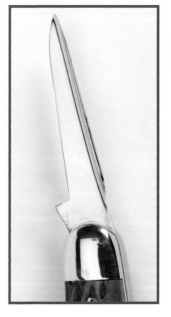

This is the "wraparound" punch blade found on some examples of the 6318 pattern.

"Standard" clip master blade, left, and "California" clip master blade, from Case XX-stamped 6318 stock knives.

Case XX 6318 Sh Sp, red bone, regular clip, 3-1/2", $225.

Case XX 6318 Sp Punch, bone, California clip, 3-1/2", $200.

Case XX 6318 Sh Pen, green bone, regular clip, 3-1/2", $350.

Case XX 6318 Sh Pen, dark reddish bone California clip , 3-1/2", $200.

Case XX 6318 Sh Pu, red bone, 3-1/2", $350. California clip note:
This blade variation was not shown in catalogs or price lists.

Case XX 6318 Sh Sp, light red bone, California clip, 3-1/2", $225.

This Case Tested 18 pattern stock knife, 3-1/2", has been rehandled with modern yellow delrin handles. Note the newer style shield, which is not pinned. This is likely a knife that was sent back to the Case factory for replacement of the handles. Case repairs knives with no intent to deceive collectors; the company is providing a valuable service to knife owners in restoring valued keepsakes and "user" knives. However, collectors should be aware that such repaired knives exist.

Case XX USA 1 Dot, 1979, 3318 Sh Pen, 3-1/2", $60.

Case XX USA 7 Dot, 1973, 6318 Sh Pen, reddish bone, 3-1/2", $80.

Case XX USA 8 Dot, 1972, 6318 SSP, reddish bone, 3-1/2", $80.

Case XX USA, New-1997 Stamp, R5318SS, "new red stag," 3-1/2", $65.

Case XX USA 8 Dot, 1972, 4318 Sh Sp (note handle shrinkage), 3-1/2", $75.

Case 2003 Stamp, 6318 SS, autumn bone, limited shield, 3-1/2", $45.

Case XX USA 1 Dot, 1979, 5318 SSP, Bradford Centennial, 3-1/2", $80.

Case XX USA 10 Dot, 1980, lightning S, 5318 SSP, Case 75th Anniversary, 3-1/2", $80.

PATTERN 20

The basic pattern: The 20 pattern is well known by Case collectors as the "Peanut." It is a small dogleg jack knife with a closed length of 2-3/4" and goes back to the early years of Case.

Blade and handle variations: The 20 pattern traditionally had a clip master blade and a small pen blade. During the pre-WWII years, it was offered with various handle materials including celluloids and genuine pearl, as well as bone and stag. During the Case XX era, the following principal variations were made:

- 2220, with smooth black composition handles.
- 3220, with yellow composition handles.
- 5220, with stag handles.
- 6220, with bone handles.
- 9220, with imitation pearl handles.

The 3220 will be found with the CASE XX stamping in both the older yellow celluloid, with white liner, and yellow composition handles. Later examples made from the CASE XX USA era into the 1970s will have yellow delrin handles. The 2220 and the 3220 were both discontinued in 1975. The 3220 was not part of the Case line for many years but was reintroduced in 1993 in chrome vanadium and is still in production today. The 2220 was never reintroduced.

Production of the 5220 continued through the Case XX USA years and the pattern was discontinued in 1970 when Case stopped regular production of stag-handled pocket knives. The pattern was reintroduced as the 5220 SS with polished stainless steel blades in 1987.

The 6220 in the CASE XX stamping will be found in several of the Case XX-era bone color variations including green regular and red, as well as in rough black and "late Rogers" bone.

The use of bone handles on the 6220 continued until mid-1970. The 6220 was one of a number of patterns changed to being handled 100 percent in delrin in 1970, so both bone and delrin examples were made in that year.

The 9220 in the CASE XX stamping will be found with both the older "cracked ice" imitation pearl handles and with "regular" imitation pearl. Cracked ice was not used on the 9220 after the CASE XX era, so later examples made from this era will have "regular" imitation pearl handles. The 9220 was discontinued as of Feb. 1, 1965, so it is believed it was never made with the CASE XX USA tang stamping.

The 6220 pattern remained in the Case line through the 1970s and went through the following evolution as Case made changes to its product line in the later 1970s and early 1980s: the 6220 with delrin handles and chrome vanadium blades was discontinued in mid-1979 and replaced with the SR6220. This was the same 6220 pattern in chrome vanadium blade steel but with smooth "Satin Rose"-colored bone handles. This initial variation of the SR6220 was made without a shield and it was one of ten patterns Case introduced in 1979 with smooth genuine bone handles in two colors, Appaloosa and Satin Rose.

The next change took place in 1981, when the SR6220 was changed to the SR6220 SS. This was essentially the same knife but with glazed finished stainless steel blades and with a shield added to the smooth Satin Rose bone handles. The SR6220 SS was relatively short lived and was discontinued in 1982; later in 1982, the pattern was reintroduced as the 6220 SS with glazed finished stainless steel blades and delrin handles. This pattern remains in the Case line today as part of the "working knives" series.

Blade steel and liner material: From the XX

Case XX USA 10 Dot, 1970, 5220 "Peanut," 2-3/4", $125.

Case XX, 6220 "Peanut," Bone, 2-3/4", $110.

Case XX 6220 "Peanut," late rogers bone, 2-3/4", $175.

era through the 1970s, all 2220, 3220, 5220, 6220, and 9220 patterns were only offered with chrome vanadium as the blade steel. As already noted, in the 1980s the blade material was changed over to stainless steel for the remaining 20 pattern variations. The liner material during these years was brass.

Other variations: Examples of the 20 pattern made during the Case XX USA era will be found with two different size tang stampings, which appears to be a random variation. While it is generally believed delrin handles were introduced on the 6220 pattern in 1970, some delrin-handled examples will be found with the CASE XX USA tang stamping. These are quite rare and may have been made up as prototypes, or leftover USA-stamped blades may have been used in 1970 after the pattern was switched over to delrin.

Newer variations: A new version of the 20 pattern was reintroduced in 1979 as part of the Gentlemen's Line. The following variation was introduced:

• 5120 R SSP, a single clip blade with stag handles (no shield) and with a bail.

This knife had stainless steel blades with a glazed finish and brass liners. Some 5120 R SSP patterns will also be found with the 1978 tang stamping (two dots). Some of these earlier examples of the

Case XX 6220 "Peanut," rough black, 2-3/4", $200.

Case XX USA 6 Dot, 1974, 6220 "Peanut," delrin, 2-3/4", $60.

Case XX 5220, "Peanut," 2-3/4", $175.

Case XX 5220, "Peanut," red stag, 2-3/4", $450.

5120 R SSP were made with the Case shield. The Gentlemen's Line knives were only made for a few years. However, the 5120 SSP was kept in the Case pocket knife line into the 1980s (the bail was dropped in 1982). In 1987, it was discontinued and Case added the 5220 SS with polished stainless steel blades and a shield to the standard product line.

In 1982, Case introduced a new pearl-handled Peanut, the 8220 SS, which was manufactured with mirror polished stainless steel blades and brass liners. The mother of pearl handles were glued on (no pins). Case used glue rather than pins to attach all pearl handles beginning in 1981. The 8220 SS with glued pearl handles was discontinued in 1985.

Beginning in the 1990s, Case introduced many additional variations of the 20 "Peanut" pattern and it has been offered in many different handle materials with both chrome vanadium and stainless steel blades. A delrin-handled version of the 6220 with chrome vanadium blades was reintroduced in 1991. This version was discontinued after 1992.

Clip and pen blades were used on the 20 pattern as the only blade variations until the late 1980s when the "Trapper Nut" pattern was introduced with a long spay blade as the secondary blade. The "Trapper Nut" has been produced in various configurations for SFO releases and as a standard product.

Case XX 9220, "Peanut," imitation pearl, 2-3/4", $150.

Case XX USA 6220, "Peanut," bone, 2-3/4", $100.

Case XX USA, 3220, large tang stamp, 2-3/4", $65.

Case XX USA, 3220, small tang stamp, 2-3/4", $65.

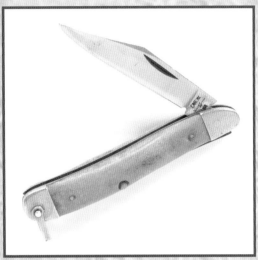

Case XX USA 10 Dot, 1980, Lightning S, 5120 R SS, 2-3/4", $50.

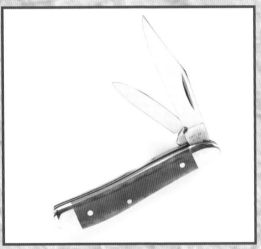

Case XX USA 1 Dot, 1979, SR6220, "Satin Rose" bone, 2-3/4", $55.

Case XX USA 1 Dot, 1989, Lightning S, ROG 6120, rogers bone, Damascus, 2-3/4", $75.

Case XX USA 2 Dot, 1978, A6220, Appaloosa bone, serial numbered, 2-3/4", $80.

Case XX USA 3 Dot, 1977, 6220, Delrin, 2-3/4", $45.

Case XX USA 8 Dot, 1982, Lightning S, 8220 SS, pearl, no pins,
2-3/4", $75.

Case XX USA 6 Dot, 1984, Lightning S, 5120 SSP, 2-3/4", $50.

Case XX USA 8 Dot, 1982, Lightning S, 6220 SS, Delrin, 2-3/4", $35.

Case 1995 Stamp, 5220 SS, 2-3/4", $55.

PATTERN 024

The basic pattern: The 024 pattern goes back to the early years of Case and is a basic "swell-end" jack knife, made in both one- and two-blade versions. Closed length is 3". During the Case Tested era, the 24 pattern was used to designate a 3" closed jack with cap and bolster. The 024 variation of the 24 pattern is a "barehead" jack knife, meaning there is a bolster only at the main blade end. The 024 pattern is a small jack knife pattern. Some collectors refer to this style of smaller jack knife as a "boy's knife."

Blade and handle variations: Based on a review of Case factory price lists, it appears the 024 pattern was introduced to the Case XX-era pocket knife line in 1958. The following principal variations were made:

One-blade variations:

- 31024 1/2, with yellow composition handles, and a single clip blade.
- 61024 1/2, with bone handles, and a single clip blade.

Two-blade variations:

- 32024 1/2, with yellow composition handles, clip master blade and pen blade.
- 62024 1/2, with bone handles, clip master blade and pen blade.
- 220024 Sp, with smooth black handles, master spay blade and coping blade. This is the "Little John Carver" pattern.

The above pattern variations were all made without shields. The 31024 1/2 and the 32024 1/2 in the CASE XX stamping will be found in both the older yellow celluloid, with white liner, and yellow composition handles. The 31024 1/2 was discontinued in 1964. The 32024 1/2 was discontinued circa 1967 and was made with the CASE XX USA tang stamping.

The 61024 1/2 and the 62024 1/2 in the CASE XX stamping will be found in the later Case XX-era bone color variations including regular and red. The 61024 1/2 and 62024 1/2 were both discontinued as of April 1, 1967, and both patterns were made with the CASE XX USA tang stamping.

The 220024 Sp is an interesting version of the 024 pattern. When it was introduced, it was sold both as a standard pocket knife pattern and as part of the Little John Carver, a whittler's kit that included the 220024 Sp jack knife packed in a balsa wood block (the knife was set in a recess cut into the block).

The wood block included an acetate sleeve with a pattern imprinted that could be used to carve a toy boat out of the block. The block with the knife and sleeve were packed in an individual two-piece cardboard box with special graphics. Case pocket knife collectors often refer to the 220024 Sp jack knife as the "Little John Carver"; however, the basic 220024 Sp pattern was evidently sold both individually and as part of the kit. The knife by itself is scarce but a complete Little John Carver whittler's kit with the block, knife, sleeve, and box is extremely rare.

The Little John Carver whittler's kit was listed in the Case factory price lists as "85 Little John Carver." In 1958, the 220024 Sp knife alone had a retail price of $2.25, while the kit retailed for the princely sum of $3.49. Both the knife and whittler's kit were discontinued in mid-1961.

Blade steel and liner material: From the XX era through the time the patterns were discontinued in the late 1960s, all 024 patterns were only offered with chrome vanadium as the blade steel. The liner material during these years was brass.

Newer variations: The 024 pattern has never been reintroduced.

Case Tested R2024-1/2, Jack Knife Glitter Stripe, Celluloid, 3", $300.

PATTERN 25

The basic pattern: The 25 pattern is well known by Case collectors as the "Coke Bottle." It is a small swell-center jack knife with a closed length of 3" and goes back to the early years of Case.

Blade and handle variations: The 25 pattern has traditionally had a clip master blade and a small pen blade. During the Case XX era, the following principal variation was made:

• 6225 1/2, with bone handles, clip master blade and pen blade.

There is another rare variation that was made during the Case XX era, the 6225 RAZ, that had a razor master blade. I have only seen one example of this knife in over 35 years of collecting. Older XX examples of the 6225 1/2 with the clip master blade will sometimes be found with long pull on the master clip blade.

The 6225 1/2 in the CASE XX stamping will be found in several of the Case XX-era bone color variations including green, regular and red, as well as in rough black.

The use of bone handles on the 6225 1/2 continued into the 1970s. During the 1970s, delrin was substituted for bone on the 6225 1/2 on a random basis. It is possible the 6225 1/2 was changed to being handled 100 percent in delrin after 1973. I have personally never seen a bone-handled specimen from the 1970s made between 1973 and 1979.

The 6225 1/2 pattern remained in the Case line through the 1970s and went through the following evolution as Case made changes to its product line in the later 1970s and early 1980s. The 6225 1/2 with delrin handles and chrome vanadium blades was discontinued in mid-1979 and replaced with the SR6225 1/2. This was the same 6225 1/2 pattern in chrome vanadium blade steel but with smooth "Satin Rose"-colored bone handles. This initial variation of the SR6225 1/2 was made without a shield. The SR6225 1/2 was one of ten patterns Case introduced in 1979 with smooth genuine bone handles in two colors, Appaloosa and Satin Rose.

The next change took place in 1981, when the SR6225 1/2 was changed to the SR6225 1/2 SS. This was essentially the same knife but with glazed finished stainless steel blades and a shield added to the smooth Satin Rose bone handles. The SR6225 1/2 SS was relatively short lived and discontinued in 1982; later in 1982, it was reintroduced as the 6225 1/2 SS

Case Tested 62024-1/2, green bone, 3", $275.

Case XX 61024-1/2, bone, 3", $75.

Case XX 62024-1/2, bone, 3", $100.

Case Tested 6225-1/2, "Swell Center Jack," rough black, 3",
$350.

Case XX 6225-1/2, red bone, 3", $275.

with glazed finished stainless steel blades and delrin handles.
The 6225 1/2 SS was discontinued in 1985.

Blade steel and liner material: From the XX era
through the 1970s, all 6225 1/2 patterns were only offered
with chrome vanadium as the blade steel. The liner material during these years was brass.

Newer variations: During the 1980s, a stag-handled
version of the 25 pattern was introduced. The 5225 1/2 SS
was introduced as part of the line in 1984 when Case introduced the new "open stock" line of stag-handled pocket
knives. Beginning in the late 1980s, Case reintroduced the
25 1/2 pattern in bone and other handle materials. It has
since become a mainstay in the Case line and has been
offered in many different handle materials with polished
stainless steel blades.

Case Tested 62025-1/2, "Swell Center Jack," rough black, 3",
$400.

Case XX USA 1 Dot, 1979, SR6225-1/2, "Satin Rose" bone, pilot run
etching, 3", $75.

Case XX USA 1 Dot, 1989, Lightning S, ROG6125-1/2, rogers bone, Damascus, 3", $75.

Case XX USA 10 Dot, 1980, Lightning S, SR6225-1/2, "Satin Rose" bone, 3", $55.

Case XX USA 5 Dot, 1975, 6225-1/2, Delrin, 3", $45.

PATTERN 27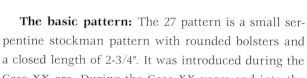

The basic pattern: The 27 pattern is a small serpentine stockman pattern with rounded bolsters and a closed length of 2-3/4". It was introduced during the Case XX era. During the Case XX years and into the 1980s, it was manufactured as both a three-blade "junior stockman" pattern and a two-blade jack pattern. The stockman version, due to its small size, was sometimes referred to as a "Stockman's Sunday Dress" knife.

There is a second Case 27 pattern that is a small two-blade "sleeveboard" pen knife pattern made with a clip master blade at one end and a pen blade at the other. This pattern had a closed length of 2-3/4". The 27 pen knife pattern had a zero in the pattern number (62027 1/2, 92027 1/2). This is one of a number of examples where the "zero" in the pattern number designates a completely different pattern and not just a minor variation of another one. The 027 1/2 pen knife pattern was made during the Case Tested and the Case XX eras.

A further confusing point is that the 27 stockman pattern was later (in the late 1970s) modified to become the 027 pattern while retaining the same basic "stockman" shape. This is explained further on in this section.

Blade and handle variations: The 27 stockman pattern has always been made with a clip as the main blade, although the style of the clip blade changed over the years. During the Case XX era, the following principal variations were made:

Patterns made with the 27 "stockman" frame:

- 6227 jack knife pattern with bone handles, secondary pen blade.
- 6327 stockman pattern with bone handles, secondary blades sheepfoot and spay.
- 9327 stockman pattern with imitation pearl handles, secondary blades sheepfoot and spay.

Patterns made with the 027 "sleeveboard" frame:

- 62027 1/2 pen knife pattern with bone handles, secondary pen blade.

The 6227 and 6327 variations in the CASE XX stamping will be found in the later XX-era bone color variations including regular and red. I do not believe examples will be found in green bone, since the 27 pattern was a later addition to the CASE XX line; however, this is not definite. The 62027 1/2 was listed in Case XX-era factory price lists from July 1, 1963 until Jan. 1, 1966; none were produced with the CASE XX USA tang stamping.

The use of bone handles on the 6227 and 6327 continued until mid-1970. They were two of a number of patterns changed to being handled 100 percent in delrin in 1970, so both bone and delrin examples were made in that year.

The 9327 in the CASE XX stamping will be found with both the older "cracked ice" imitation pearl handles and with "regular" imitation pearl. Cracked ice was not used on the 9327 after the CASE XX era, so later examples made from the CASE XX USA era and into the 1970s will have "regular" imitation pearl handles. The 9327 was discontinued circa 1973.

The shape of the main clip blade on the 27 pattern gradually changed from the Case XX era through the Case XX USA era. The pattern initially had a "standard" clip blade with a pronounced "peak" above the nail pull. During the mid-1960s, the tooling was changed. The new style clip had a slimmer profile with the nail pull further out toward the tip. This shape is similar to a "California clip" blade style.

Production of the 6227 and the 6327 with the slim clip master blades and delrin handles continued through 1976. Beginning circa 1977, the tooling for the 27 pattern was changed somewhat. The new retooled pattern was given the pattern number 027. The new 027 retained the basic shape, but was somewhat of a heftier knife with more substantial blades.

The reason for this change was never documented. However, during this time period, Case redesigned the tooling for a number of pocket knife patterns in order to standardize common parts between patterns. My speculation is that Case changed both the 27 and the 33 patterns so that they could share some common parts.

The 62027 with delrin handles and chrome vanadium blades was discontinued in mid-1979 and replaced with the SR62027. This was the same 62027 pattern in chrome vanadium blade steel but with smooth "Satin

Case XX USA, 6227, bone, 2-3/4", $60. Note: Standard clip blade.

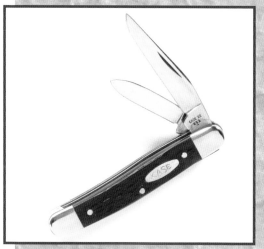

Case XX USA 1 Dot, 1979, 62027, delrin, 2-3/4", $40.

Case XX USA 10 Dot, 1980, Lightning S, SR62027, "Satin Rose" bone, 2-3/4", $50.

The 27 pattern had traditionally been made as a jack knife or as a three-blade stockman. In recent years, Case has also made pen knives using the 27 frame. This example is a 6227 with pocket-worn "old red bone" handles made in 1997. Note that Case has returned the 27 pattern to the original XX-era styling. Closed length is 2-3/4", $40.

Case XX USA 1 Dot, 1979, 52027 SSP, Bradford Centennial, 2-3/4", $75.

Case XX USA 4 Dot, 1976, 6227, delrin, 2-3/4", $45. Note: Slim clip blade.

Back of the 6227.

Rose"-colored bone handles without a shield. The SR62027 was one of ten patterns Case introduced in 1979 with smooth genuine bone handles in two colors, Appaloosa and Satin Rose. The SR62027 was discontinued in late 1981, as was the 63027.

Blade steel and liner material: From the XX era through the time the patterns were discontinued as already noted, chrome vanadium was the only blade steel offered on the 27 stockman and jack patterns. The 27 and 027 "stockman" patterns were traditionally made with nickel silver liners. The 27 "jack" pattern will be found with both brass and nickel silver as the liner material, but the later 027 jack was listed as having nickel silver liners. Beginning circa 1978, Case began changing all pocket knife patterns with nickel silver liners to the standard use of brass as the lining material. This change was complete by 1980, so the later 027 patterns will have brass liners.

Newer variations: Case reintroduced the older style 27 pattern in both two-blade jack and three-blade stockman formats, including the older style "standard" master clip blade, in the late 1980s. In recent years, many variations of the three-bladed stockman pattern have been offered in a variety of handle materials and with stainless steel blades. Case also introduced the 6227 pattern as a pen knife rather than a jack knife. This style was first made as part of the original Pocket Worn series released in 1996.

PATTERN 028

The basic pattern: The 028 pattern goes back to the early years of Case and is a "serpentine dogleg" jack knife, with two blades and two backsprings. Closed length is 3-1/2". The 028 is a "capped" jack knife, meaning there are bolsters at both the main blade end and lower end.

Blade and handle variations: During the Case XX era, the following principal variations were made:

- 22028, with smooth black handles, clip master blade and pen blade.
- 62028, with bone handles, clip master blade and pen blade.

The 62028 in the CASE XX stamping will be found in the early Case XX-era bone color variations including green and regular, and in rough black. Based on a review of Case factory price lists, it appears that both the 22028 and the 62028 were produced in the early 1950s and discontinued prior to 1955. Then in 1958, the 22028 was reintroduced and produced until the end of 1964. The 028 pattern has not been reintroduced.

Case Tested 62028, "Dogleg Jack Knife," Rough Black, 3-1/2", $275.

Case Tested 62028, "Dogleg Jack," green bone, 3-1/2", $450.

PATTERN 29

The basic pattern: The 29 pattern is a "curved" jack knife, with two blades and two backsprings. Closed length is 2-1/2". The 29 pattern goes back to the Case Tested era and earlier and is a "barehead" jack knife, meaning there are bolsters only at the main blade end of the knife.

The 29 pattern is sometimes referred to by collectors as the "Tadpole." It is the shortest (closed length) jack pattern made by Case.

Blade and handle variations: During the Case XX era, the following principal variations were made:

- 2229 1/2, with smooth black handles, clip master blade and pen blade.
- 6229 1/2, with bone handles, clip master blade and pen blade.

The 6229 1/2 in the CASE XX stamping will be found in several of the Case XX-era bone color variations including green, regular and red, and in rough black. The 2229 1/2 was discontinued in the mid-1960s. It is believed no examples of the 2229 1/2 were made with the CASE XX USA tang stamping. The 6229 1/2 remained in the Case line until it was discontinued in 1967. The 6229 1/2 with the CASE XX USA tang stamping is relatively scarce. During these years of production, all 29 patterns were made without shields.

Blade steel and liner material: From the XX era through the time the pattern was discontinued, all 29 patterns were only offered with chrome vanadium as the blade steel. The liner material during these years was brass.

Newer variations: The 29 pattern has never been reintroduced.

Case XX 6229-1/2, "Tadpole," bone, 2-1/2", $175.

PATTERN 31

The basic pattern: The 31 pattern goes back to the early years of Case and is a basic "swell-end" jack knife, with two blades and two backsprings.

There have been special purpose variations made with one and three blades and backsprings as well. Closed length is 3-3/4". The 31 pattern has been made both as a "barehead" jack knife, bolster at the main blade end only, and as a "capped" jack knife, with bolsters at both ends.

The 31 jack pattern is a strongly built pattern with thick blade stock and backsprings. Basic swell end jack knives of this size and style were very common in the years prior to WWII and were widely produced by all of the major cutlery companies.

In the years after WWII, the popularity of the basic "jack" pattern began to wane in favor of the stockman pattern.

Case was the only knife manufacturer to continue producing a wide variety of this style of jack pattern during the years following WWII and into the 1960s and the 1970s.

Case used the 31 pattern tooling for the production of the well-known TL-29 "electrician's" knife before and during WWII. A civilian version of the TL-29 was introduced in the Case line after WWII.

Blade and handle variations: During the Case XX era, the following principal two-blade jack variations were made:

- 22031 1/2, with smooth black handles (no lower bolster), clip master blade and pen blade.
- 2231 1/2, with smooth black handles (with lower bolster), clip master blade and pen blade.
- 2231 1/2 SAB with smooth black handles (with lower bolster), saber ground clip master blade and pen blade.
- 62031, with bone handles (no lower bolster), spear master blade and pen blade.
- 6231, with bone handles (with lower bolster), spear master blade and pen blade.
- 62031 1/2, with bone handles (no lower bolster), clip master blade and pen blade.
- 6231 1/2, with bone handles (with lower bolster), clip master blade and pen blade.

Case XX 62031, red bone, 3-3/4", $250.

Case XX 6231, bone, 3-3/4", $250.

Case XX 62031-1/2, red bone, 3-3/4", $250.

These "special-purpose" variations were also made:

- 12031 L R, with smooth walnut handles (no lower bolster), a bail and with spear master blade and screwdriver/wire stripper blade with a liner lock. This is the classic TL-29 style "electrician's knife."
- 13031 L R, with smooth walnut handles (no lower bolster), a bail, similar to the 12031 L R except with a third backspring added and a third "hawkbill" style blade.
- 11031 Sh, a single-blade version with smooth walnut handles and a sheepfoot master blade.

The bone-handled 31 patterns in the CASE XX stamping will be found in several of the Case XX-era bone color variations including green, regular and red, and in rough black. For the clip master blade versions (also for the 11031 Sh), long pull on the master blade was standard. Long pull will also be found on some older examples with a spear blade. The bone and rough black-handled 31 patterns will sometimes be found made without shields.

There was also a smooth white-handled version of the 31 jack pattern made during the Case XX era. The 4231 1/2 had a master clip blade and pen blade and had the lower bolster.

The examples that I have seen had no shield in the handle and often had advertising imprints in the front handle. This variation is somewhat rare and I have never seen it listed in any older Case catalogs or price lists. It may have been a special-order item.

Most of the bone and smooth black-handled jack knife variations of the 31 pattern were discontinued during the 1960s, during the late Case XX era. The 6231 was made briefly during the Case XX USA era and examples with the CASE XX USA tang stamping will be found but they are quite rare.

By the mid-1960s and into the 1970s, only the 6231 1/2 and the 2231 1/2 SAB remained in the Case line. The 2231 1/2 SAB was discontinued in 1978. During the 1970s, delrin was substituted for bone on the 6231 1/2 on a random basis. It is possible that the 6231 1/2 was changed to being handled 100 percent in delrin after 1976. I have personally never seen a bone-handled

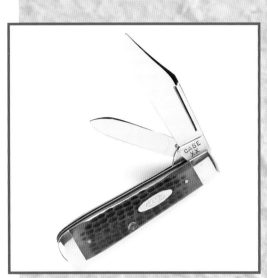

Case XX 6231-1/2, red bone, 3-3/4", $225.

Case XX 62031, rough black, 3-3/4", $200.

Case XX 62031-1/2, rough black, long pull, 3-3/4", $200.

specimen from the 1970s made between 1976 and 1981 when the 6231 1/2 pattern was discontinued.

The 13031 L R three-blade electrician's knife was discontinued in 1974. The 11031 Sh was discontinued in 1978. Production of the 12031 L R with the spear master blade and walnut handles continued into the early 1980s. In 1979, another variation was added, the 12031 L H R. This version was similar but had a "hawkbill"-style master blade in place of the spear master blade. The 12031 L R was discontinued in mid-1982 and the 12031 L H R was discontinued in December of 1982.

Blade steel and liner material: Until the introduction of the 62031 electrician's knife in stainless steel (see below), all 31 patterns were offered only in chrome vanadium blade steel. The standard liner material for all 31 patterns was brass; however, some older examples from the Case XX era may be found with iron liners and bolsters.

Newer variations: The 31 pattern as a jack knife with clip and pen or spear and pen blades has never been reintroduced.

The 31 electrician's knife pattern was reintroduced in 1986 in a different format. The new knife was the 62031 L H R, made with chrome vanadium hawkbill and screwdriver blades and with jigged brown delrin handles. It is my opinion this replacement 62031 L H R was made on contract for Case by Camillus Cutlery Company.

The delrin-handled 62031 L H R remained in the Case product line until recent years. However, it was changed from chrome vanadium blade steel to glazed finished stainless steel in 1990-1991.

The 62031 L H R SS was discontinued in 2006 after Camillus Cutlery Company ceased operation.

Case XX 62031, green bone, long pull, 3-3/4", $375.

Case Tested 2231-1/2, flat blade, 3-3/4", $325.

Case XX 2231-1/2 SAB, saber ground blade, 3-3/4", $125.

Case Tested 6231-1/2, early rogers bone, 3-3/4", $450.

Case XX USA 4 Dot, 1976, 12031 LR, "electrician's knife," 3-3/4", $45.

Case XX USA 3 Dot, 1977, 11031 SH, 3-3/4", $45.

Case XX USA 3 Dot, 1977, 12031 L H R, "Hawkbill," master blade, 3-3/4", $45.

Case XX USA 5 Dot, 1975, 6231-1/2, delrin, 3-3/4", $45.

PATTERN 32

The basic pattern: The 32 pattern goes back to the early years of Case and is a medium stockman pattern with squared bolsters. Closed length is 3-5/8". During the Case XX years and later, it has been manufactured as both a three-blade "stockman" and two-blade jack pattern. Collectors sometimes refer to the 32 pattern as a "gunstock jack" or a "gunstock stockman" since the handle shape bears a resemblance to the shape of the stock of a shotgun or rifle.

Blade and handle variations: The 32 pattern has always been made with a clip as the main blade. During the Case XX era, the following principal variations of the 32 jack and stockman patterns were made:

- 5232 jack pattern with stag handles and secondary pen blade.
- 6232 jack pattern with bone handles and secondary pen blade.
- 5332 stockman pattern with stag handles, secondary sheepfoot and pen blades.
- 6332 stockman pattern with bone handles, secondary sheepfoot and pen blades.

Production of the 5232 and the 5332 continued through the Case XX USA years and both were discontinued in 1970 when Case stopped regular production of stag-handled pocket knives.

The 6232 and the 6332 in the CASE XX stamping will be found in several of the Case XX-era bone color variations including green, regular and red, as well as rough black and "late Rogers" bone. The use of bone handles on the 6232 and the 6332 continued into the 1970s. During the 1970s, delrin was substituted for bone on the 6232 and the 6332 on a random basis, but beginning in 1978, it appears Case went back to handling the 32 patterns 100 percent in bone.

Production of the 6232 and the 6332 continued with delrin and bone handles through 1977. Beginning in 1978, the 32 pattern tooling was changed to a slightly different pattern given the designation 032. The new 032 retained the basic "gunstock" shape of the 32 pattern, but was slightly smaller with a closed length of 3-1/2". The blade tooling was changed to make the blades somewhat smaller and with rounded tangs as compared to the 32 pattern which had definite "half stops."

Case XX 5232, 3-5/8", $250.

Case XX 6232, rough black, 3-5/8", $175.

Case XX 6232, green bone, 3-5/8", $275.

The reason for the change from the 32 pattern to the 032 pattern was never documented. However, during this time period, Case redesigned the tooling for a number of pocket knife patterns in order to standardize common parts between patterns. The 032 pattern is the same length as the 18 pattern, which has always been a popular Case stockman pattern. My speculation is that Case changed the 32 pattern tooling to the 032 so that the 032 patterns could share some common parts with the 18 patterns.

As with other changes to the tooling of Case pocket knives, there were some "transition" models of the 62032 and the 63032 produced in 1978. These knives were manufactured with the new 032 tooling, but had the old pattern numbers, 6232 and 6332. At the time, I had heard unofficial estimates that there were 5,000 to 6,000 of each of these "transition" models produced.

The 62032 and the 63032 with bone handles and chrome vanadium blades have remained in the Case pocket knife line continuously until the present day. Both the 32 and the 032 patterns have always been popular with pocket knife users.

Blade steel and liner material: From the XX era through the 1970s, chrome vanadium was the only blade steel offered on the 32 stockman and jack patterns. The standard lining material for the 32 and the 032 patterns has always been brass.

Newer variations: During the 1980s, stag-handled versions of the two- and three-bladed 032 patterns were introduced. The 52032 SS and the 53032 SS were introduced as part of the line in 1984 when Case introduced the new "open stock" line of stag-handled pocket knives.

Standard production stainless steel variations of the 032 patterns in bone handles, 62032 SS and 63032 SS, were added to the Case pocket knife line in 1991 but were only made during 1991-1992. These knives had glazed finish stainless steel blades.

In recent years, many variations of the two- and three-bladed 032 patterns have been offered in a variety of handle materials and with stainless steel blades.

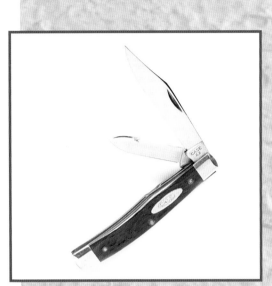

Case XX 6232, late rogers bone, dark color, 3-5/8", $225.

Case XX 6232, late rogers bone, medium color, 3-5/8", $225.

Case XX 6232, late rogers bone, light color, 3-5/8", $225.

These two knives illustrate the change from the old style 32 pattern to the new style 032 pattern. The knife at left is a Case XX-stamped 6232, reddish bone, 3-5/8", $175. Bottom knife is a 62032 with the 1992 tang stamping, bone, 3-1/2", $50.

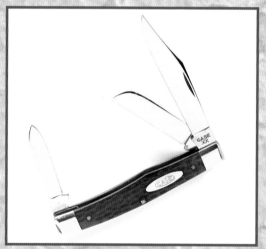

Case XX 6332, reddish bone, 3-5/8", $200.

During the Case Tested era, some 32 patterns were made with "California clip"-style master blades, while others were made with "standard"-clip master blades. From left: Case Tested-stamped 6332, green bone, with "California clip," 3-5/8", $450; and Case XX 6332, light color green bone, standard clip, 3-5/8", $350.

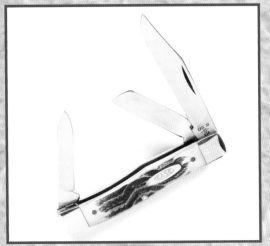

Case XX USA 5 Dot, 1985, Lightning S, 53032 SS, "jigged stag," new grind blades, 3-1/2", $150.

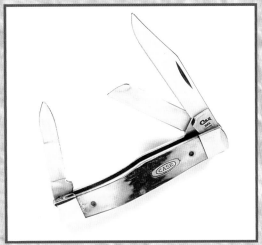

Case 1994 Stamp 53032 SS, 3-1/2", $75.

Case 1995 Stamp 62032, bone, 3-1/2", $50.

Case XX USA 5332, 3-5/8", $150.

Case XX USA 2 Dot, 1978, 52032 SSP, 3-1/2", $80.

PATTERN 33

The basic pattern: The 33 pattern goes back to the early years of Case and is a small serpentine stockman pattern with squared bolsters. Closed length is 2-5/8". During the Case XX years and up to the present day, it has been manufactured as a both a three-blade "junior stockman" pattern and two-blade pen knife pattern.

Blade and handle variations: The 33 pattern has always been made with a clip as the main blade, although the style changed over the years. Secondary blades have always been a pen blade for the two-blade pen knife version, with a sheepfoot blade added for the three-blade version.

During the Case XX era, the following principal variations were made:

- 3233, two-blade pen knife with yellow composition handles.
- 6233, two-blade pen knife with bone handles.
- 5233, two-blade pen knife with stag handles.
- 8233, two-blade pen knife with pearl handles.
- 9233, two-blade pen knife with imitation pearl handles.
- 6333 stockman pattern with bone handles, secondary blades sheepfoot and pen.
- 9333 stockman pattern with imitation pearl handles, secondary blades sheepfoot and pen.

The 3233 will be found with the CASE XX stamping in both the older yellow celluloid, with white liner, and yellow composition handles. Later examples made from the CASE XX USA era and into the 1970s will have yellow delrin handles. The 3233 was discontinued in 1975.

Production of the 5233 continued through the Case XX USA years and the pattern was discontinued in 1970 when Case stopped regular production of stag-handled pocket knives.

The 6233 and 6333 variations in the CASE XX stamping will be found in several of the Case XX-era bone color variations including green, regular and red bone, and in "late Rogers" bone and rough black. The use of bone handles on the 6233 and the 6333 continued until mid-1970. The 6233 and the 6333 were two of a number of patterns that were changed to being handled 100 percent in delrin in 1970, so both bone

Case Tested 6333, Rough Black-Long Pull, 2-5/8", $175.

Case XX 6233, late rogers bone, dark color, 2-5/8", $125.

Case XX 6233, late rogers bone, light color, 2-5/8", $125.

and delrin examples were made in that year.

The 8233 was produced into the 1970s. Genuine pearl-handled pocket knives were not listed in Case factory catalogs or price lists from about 1967 through the 1970s even though they were in production. Based on my observations, I believe the 8233 was discontinued circa 1974.

The 9233 and the 9333 in the CASE XX stamping will be found with both the older "cracked ice" imitation pearl handles and with "regular" imitation pearl. Cracked ice was not used on the 9333 after the CASE XX era, so later examples made from the CASE XX USA era and into the 1970s will have "regular" imitation pearl handles. The 9333 was discontinued circa 1973.

The shape of the main clip blade on the 33 pattern gradually changed from the Case XX era through the Case XX USA era. Older examples of XX-era 33 patterns will be found with regular clip blades with long pull. The main blade tooling then changed to a "standard" clip blade with regular pull and with a pronounced "peak" above the nail pull. This is the most common blade shape to be found on CASE XX-stamped 33s and on some 33s with the CASE XX USA tang stamping. During the mid-1960s, the tooling was changed again. The new-style clip had a slimmer profile with the nail pull further out toward the tip. This shape is similar to a "California clip" blade style. This blade style continued on the 33 pattern into the 1970s.

Production of the 6233 and the 6333 with the slim clip master blades and delrin handles and the 9233 with imitation pearl handles continued through 1976. Beginning circa 1977, the tooling for the 33 pattern was changed. The new retooled pattern was given the pattern number 033. The new 033 retained the basic shape but was somewhat of a heftier knife with more substantial blades.

The reason for this change was never documented. However, during this time period, Case redesigned the tooling for a number of pocket knife patterns in order to standardize common parts between patterns. My speculation is that Case changed both the 33 and the 27 patterns so that these two patterns could share some common parts.

Case XX 6333, red bone, 2-5/8", $125. Note: Standard clip blade.

Case XX USA 3 Dot 1977, 5233 SSP, "blue scroll," 2-5/8", $65. Note: Slim clip blade.

Case XX 6233, green bone, long pull, 2-5/8", $225.

The 62033 with delrin handles and chrome vanadium blades was discontinued in mid-1979 and replaced with the A62033. This was the same 62033 pattern in chrome vanadium blade steel but with smooth Appaloosa-colored bone handles without a shield. The A62033 was one of ten patterns Case introduced in 1979 with smooth genuine bone handles in two colors, Appaloosa and Satin Rose.

The next change took place in 1981, when the A62033 was changed to the A62033 SS. This was essentially the same knife but with glazed-finished stainless steel blades and with a shield added to the smooth Appaloosa bone handles. The A62033 SS was relatively short lived and discontinued in 1982. Later in 1982, the pattern was reintroduced as the 62033 SS with glazed finished stainless steel blades and delrin handles.

The 62033 SS in delrin was manufactured until 1991 when the new tooling was again introduced for the 33 pattern changing the style of the knife back to the older style of the Case XX era with a "standard" clip master blade. The newer-styled 6233 SS with delrin handles has been in the Case line ever since then as part of the "working knives" series.

Production of the 92033 continued in the late 1970s. By 1976, all imitation pearl handle material had been changed over to the "new cracked ice" plastic material. After 1981, the 92033 was changed over to the 92033 SS with mirror finished stainless steel blades and with the newer "acrylic pearl" handles that were attached with glue (no handle pins). The 92033 SS was discontinued in 1985.

The 63033 with delrin handles and chrome vanadium blades was changed over to the 63033 SS with glazed finished stainless steel blades in mid-1981. As with the two-blade pen knife variation, the tooling for the 63033 SS was changed over in 1991 to the 6333 SS and this pattern has remained as part of the "working knives" series.

Blade steel and liner material: From the XX era through the time the patterns were changed over to stainless steel as noted above, chrome vanadium was the only blade steel offered on the 33 stockman and pen knife patterns. During the XX years and up until

Case XX 6333, rough black, 2-5/8", $150.

Case XX 9233, imitation pearl, 2-5/8", $80.

Case XX USA 10 Dot, 1980, lightning S, A62033, Appaloosa bone, 2-5/8", $50.

the late 1970s, nickel silver was the lining material. Beginning circa 1978, Case began changing all pocket knife patterns with nickel silver liners to the standard use of brass as the lining material. This change was complete by 1980.

Other variations: Some 33 patterns with the CASE XX tang stamping were made with a "long pull" nail pull on the master clip blade. These examples were made early in the Case XX era and are fairly rare. Long pull master blades will be observed on both two- and three-blade 33 patterns.

Newer variations: A new version of the 033 pattern was introduced in 1980 as part of the Gentlemen's Line. The following variation was introduced:

- 52033 R SSP, clip and pen blades with stag handles (no shield) and a bail.

This knife had stainless steel blades with a glazed finish and brass liners. The Gentlemen's Line knives were only made for a few years. However, the 52033 SSP was kept in the Case pocket knife line into the 1980s (the bail was dropped in 1982). In 1987, the 52033 SSP was discontinued and Case added the 52033 SS with polished stainless steel blades and with a shield to the standard product line.

In 1984, Case added the 53033 SS, with polished stainless blades and a shield, to the standard product line as part of the new "open stock" stag-handled knife series. The 52033 SS and the 53033 SS continued to be manufactured through 1992. Beginning in 1993, the two patterns were changed to the 5233 SS and the 5333 SS with the older Case XX-style tooling.

During the 1990s, Case changed the tooling on the two-blade 33 pen knife patterns so that the knives have two separate backsprings, one for each blade. Likewise, the three-blade version was changed over to have three backsprings and no center liner. However, the change on the three-blade version does not seem to be 100 percent as some are still made with two backsprings. In recent years, many variations of the 33 three-bladed stockman pattern have been offered in a variety of handle materials and with stainless steel blades.

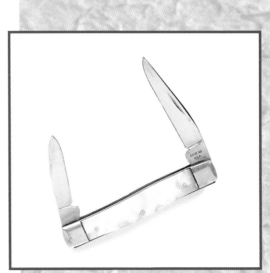

Case XX USA 3 Dot, 1977, 92033, "new cracked ice," 2-5/8", $40.

Case XX USA 4 Dot, 1986, lightning S, 63033 SS, delrin, 2-5/8", $30.

Case XX USA 5 Dot, 1985, lightning S, 62033 SS, delrin, 2-5/8", $30.

Main clip blade variations for the 33 pattern, from left: older style long pull clip blade from the Case Tested to Case XX era; wide clip blade from the Case XX to Case XX USA era; slim clip blade from the Case XX USA era through 1976; and 033 clip blade.

Case XX USA 7 Dot, 1973, 9333, imitation pearl, 2-5/8", $50.

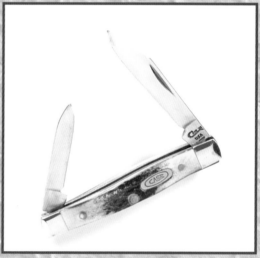

Case 1995 stamping, 5233 SS, 2-5/8", $55.

Case XX USA 7 Dot, 1983, lightning S, 92033 SS, "acrylic imitation pearl," 2-5/8", $40.

Case XX USA 9 Dot, 1981, lightning S, 52033 R SS, 2-5/8", $65.

PATTERN 35

The basic pattern: The 35 pattern is a basic "swell-end" jack knife, with two blades and two backsprings. Closed length is 3-1/4". The 35 pattern goes back to the early years of Case and in the pre-WWII years was made both as a "barehead" jack knife (bolster at the main blade end only) and as a "capped" jack knife with bolsters at both ends. All examples of the 35 pattern made from the later XX era through the 1980s were "capped."

Blade and handle variations: During the Case XX era, the following principal variations were made:

- 6235, with bone handles, spear master blade and pen blade.
- 6235 1/2, with bone handles, clip master blade and pen blade.
- 620035, with jigged black composition handles, spear master blade and pen blade.
- 620035 1/2, with jigged black composition handles, long pull clip master blade and pen blade.

The 6235 and the 6235 1/2 were made both with and without lower bolsters with the CASE TESTED tang stamping prior to WWII. It is possible that some early CASE XX-stamped examples were made without lower bolsters. Both the 6235 and the 620035 were also made with the CASE XX tang stamping as "easy opener" jack knives with a handle cutout to assist in opening the main blade. These are quite rare variations.

The 6235 and the 6235 1/2 in the CASE XX stamping will be found in several of the Case XX-era bone color variations including green, regular and red, and in rough black. The patterns will be found both with and without shields in the CASE XX stamping, which seemed to be a random variation. It appears that starting with the CASE XX USA tang stamping, the shield was used 100 percent and this continued on the 35 pattern until the late 1970s.

The 620035 and the 620035 1/2 were both lower-priced knives and, in my opinion, were manufactured for Case by another cutlery firm, possibly Schrade Cutlery Company. The tooling and handle material on these patterns closely matches that of knives manufactured by Schrade under the Kingston brand.

Case XX 6235, rough black, no shield, 3-3/8", $100.

Case XX 6235-1/2, rough black, no shield, 3-3/8", $100.

Case XX 6235, rough black, with shield, 3-3/8", $100.

The price was kept low on the 0035 patterns since they had composition rather than bone handles and were made without the CASE shield. The blades on the 0035 patterns were tumble polished, and based on my observations they had somewhat thinner blade and backspring stock as compared to the 6235 and the 6235 1/2. The 1957 Case factory price list indicates a retail price for the 6235 1/2 of $3, while the retail for the 620035 1/2 was $2.25.

The 6235 was discontinued as of Jan. 1, 1966, while the 6235 1/2 remained in the Case line. The 6235 with the CASE XX USA tang stamping is particularly rare since it was discontinued soon after that tang stamping was introduced.

During the 1970s, delrin was substituted for bone on the 6235 1/2 on a random basis and both examples will be found; however, my observation is that very few bone-handled examples were made after 1972 and until 1979. Almost all examples of the 6235 1/2 pattern made during these years were handled in delrin. From 1977 to 1979, some examples of the 6235 1/2 in delrin were made without shields.

The 6235 1/2 pattern went through the following evolution as Case made changes to its product line in the later 1970s and early 1980s. The 6235 1/2 with delrin handles and chrome vanadium blades was discontinued in mid-1979 and replaced with the A6235 1/2. This was the same 6235 1/2 pattern in chrome vanadium blade steel, but with smooth Appaloosa-colored bone handles. This initial variation of the A6235 1/2 was made without a shield. The A6235 1/2 was one of ten patterns Case introduced in 1979 with smooth genuine bone handles in two colors, Appaloosa and Satin Rose.

The next change took place in 1981, when the A6235 1/2 was changed to the A6235 1/2 SS. This was essentially the same knife but with glazed finished stainless steel blades and with a shield added to the smooth Appaloosa bone handles. The A6235 1/2 SS was relatively short lived and discontinued in 1982. Later in 1982, the pattern was reintroduced as the 6235 1/2 SS with glazed finished stainless steel blades and delrin handles. The 6235 1/2 SS in delrin was discontinued in 1985.

Blade steel and liner material: From the XX era through the time the pattern was changed over to 100 percent stainless steel as noted above, all 35 patterns were only offered with chrome vanadium as the blade steel. The liner material during these years was brass.

Newer variations: The 35 pattern has never been reintroduced.

This jack knife with the "KINGSTON USA" tang stamping is identical in tooling and handle material to the Case XX 620035 1/2 jack knife pattern. I believe it is possible that Case contracted with Imperial Schrade, owner of the KINGSTON trade mark, to manufacture the 620035 and the 620035 1/2 on contract during the 1960s.

Case XX 6235-1/2, bone, without shield, 3-3/8", $140.

Case XX USA 8 Dot, 1982, lightning S, A6235-1/2 SS, Appaloosa bone, 3-3/8", $60.

Case XX USA, 6235-1/2, red bone, 3-3/8", $80.

Case XX USA 1 Dot, 1979, A6235-1/2, Appaloosa bone, 3-3/8", $60.

Case XX USA 10 Dot, 1980, lightning S, 5235-1/2 SSP, Case 75th, Anniversary, 3-3/8", $75.

PATTERN 37

The basic pattern: The 37 pattern is the "Sod Buster." It is a 3-5/8" knife with a single skinner blade and brass liners. It was introduced in 1970 with the following variations:

- 2137, with glazed finished chrome vanadium blade and smooth black handles.
- 2137 SS, with glazed finished stainless steel blade and smooth black handles.

The above were the only two variations of the 37 pattern offered by Case as part of the standard pocket knife line through the 1970s and the 1980s. The glazed finished blade on each knife includes the etching of a plow with the words, "SOD BUSTER JR." The 2137 SS also includes the word "STAINLESS" at the top of the blade etching. The 2137 in chrome vanadium steel was discontinued after 1990. The 2137 SS has been part of the Case product line up to the present day. In 1993, a yellow-handled version (the 3137) in chrome vanadium steel was added to the product line, and later a 3137 SS was added. These yellow-handled variations have polished blades without the etching.

During the 1980s, a large number of yellow-handled SFO versions of the Sod Buster Junior were made for one of Case's dealers. These knives had glazed finished blades with the usual "SOD BUSTER JUNIOR" blade etching.

Case XX USA 9 Dot, 1971, 2137, "Sod Buster Junior," 3-5/8", $35.

PATTERN 38

The basic pattern: The 38 pattern is a large basic single-blade general purpose working knife known as the "Sod Buster." It was introduced by Case in the late 1960s with the CASE XX USA tang stamping and was first shown in the Case factory price list dated March 1, 1968. The Sod Buster became an instant success both with knife collectors and users and has continued to be popular up to today. To the best of my knowledge, Case was the first American cutlery firm to offer a knife in the style of the Sod Buster, which has been a standard pattern with some cutlery firms in Germany for many years.

It is a 4-5/8" knife with a single skinner blade and brass liners and was initially made in the following variations:

- 2138, with glazed finished chrome vanadium blade and smooth black handles.
- 2138 SS, with glazed finished stainless steel blade and smooth black handles.
- 2138 L SS, with glazed finished stainless steel blade and smooth black handles. The main blade locks open with a split liner lock.

The 2138 SS and the 2138 L SS were both introduced in 1970 with the "ten dot" stamping. The above three variations were the only ones of the 38 pattern offered by Case as part of the standard pocket knife line through the 1970s and 1980s.

The glazed finished blade on each knife includes the etching of a plow with the words "SOD BUSTER." The 2138 SS and the 2138 L SS each also include the word "STAINLESS" at the top of the blade etching. The 2138 in chrome vanadium steel was discontinued after 1990. The 2138 L SS with the liner lock was discontinued in 1985.

The 2138 SS has been part of the Case product line up to the present day. In the 1990s, a yellow-handled version (the 3138) in chrome vanadium steel was added to the product line. The yellow-handled variation was made with a polished blade without the etching. This version, the 3138, has since been discontinued.

During the 1980s, a large number of yellow-handled SFO versions of the Sod Buster were made for one of Case's dealers. These knives had glazed finished blades with the usual SOD BUSTER blade etching.

Case XX USA 1 Dot, 1989, lightning S, 3138 SS, "Sod Buster" etched, 4-5/8", $45.

Case 2006 stamp, 3138 CV, "Sod Buster," 4-5/8", $35.

Case XX USA 10 Dot, 1980, Lightning S 2138 L SS Liner Lock "Sod Buster," 4-5/8", $45. Photo courtesy Gary Moore

Case XX USA 9 Dot, 1981, lightning S, 2138, "Sod Buster," 4-5/8", $40.

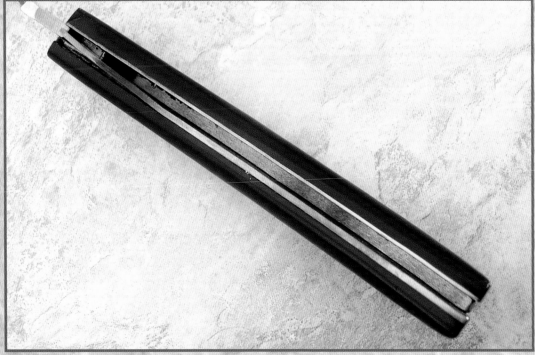

Interior view of a Case 10 dot, 1980, 2138 L SS, showing the liner lock mechanism. Photo courtesy Gary Moore

PATTERN 042

The basic pattern: The 042 pattern goes back to the early years of Case and is a small pen knife with squared bolsters and slight "swell center" shape, constructed with a single backspring and with a blade at each end. Closed length is 3".

Blade and handle variations: The 042 pattern has a spear master blade and a small pen blade. No other blade variations have been used on this pattern. During the Case XX era, the following principal variations were made:

- 62042, with bone handles.
- 92042, with imitation pearl handles.
- 62042 R, with bone handles and a bail.
- 92042 R, with imitation pearl handles and a bail.

The 62042 in the CASE XX stamping will be found in several of the Case XX-era bone color variations including green, regular and red, and in rough black. The use of bone handles on the 62042 and 62042 R continued into the 1970s. During the 1970s, delrin was substituted for bone on the 62042 on a random basis, and it's possible the 62042 was changed to being handled 100 percent in delrin after 1972. I have personally never seen a bone-handled specimen from the 1970s made after 1972. The 62042 R was discontinued as of Jan. 1, 1972.

The 92042 and 92042 R in the CASE XX stamping will be found with both the older "cracked ice" imitation pearl handles and "regular" imitation pearl. Cracked ice was not used on the 92042 after the CASE XX era, so later examples made from the CASE XX USA era and into the 1970s will have "regular" imitation pearl handles. The 92042 R was discontinued as of Jan. 1, 1972.

Production of the 92042 continued in the 1970s and circa 1976, the handle material was changed over to the "new cracked ice" plastic material. After 1981, the 92042 was changed over to the 92042 SS with mirror finished stainless steel blades and with the newer "acrylic pearl" handles that were attached with glue (no handle pins). The 92042 SS was discontinued in 1985.

The 62042 pattern went through the following evolution as Case made changes to its product line in the later 1970s and early 1980s. The 62042 with delrin handles and chrome vanadium blades was discontinued in mid-1979 and replaced with the A62042. This

was the same 62042 pattern in chrome vanadium blade steel but with smooth Appaloosa-colored bone handles. This initial variation of the A62042 was made without a shield and was one of ten patterns Case introduced in 1979 with smooth genuine bone handles in two colors, Appaloosa and Satin Rose.

The next change took place in 1981, when the A62042 was changed to the A62042 SS. This was essentially the same knife but with glazed finished stainless steel blades and with a shield added to the smooth Appaloosa bone handles. The A62042 SS was relatively short lived and discontinued in 1982, and later that year, it was reintroduced as the 62042 SS with glazed finished stainless steel blades and with delrin handles. The 62042 SS in delrin remained in the Case line until it was discontinued after 1998.

Blade steel and liner material: From the XX era through the time the pattern was converted over to stainless steel as described above, all 042 patterns were only offered with chrome vanadium as the blade steel. The liner material from the Case XX era through the mid-1970s was nickel silver. Beginning circa 1978, Case began changing all pocket knife patterns with nickel silver liners to the standard use of brass as the lining material. This change was complete by 1980. Beginning in the 1977 catalog, the 042 patterns were listed as having brass liners.

Newer variations: The 042 pattern was reintroduced in the late 1970s as part of the Gentlemen's Line, with the following variations:

- 52042 R SSP, with stag handles a bail, and glazed finished stainless steel blades.
- 92042 R, with "new cracked ice" handles a bail, and polished chrome vanadium blades.

These knives were only made for a few years. The bail was dropped from the 52042 R SSP in 1982 and the 52042 SSP (without the bail) was discontinued as of Sept. 1, 1983. The 92042 R was changed over to polished stainless steel blades in 1981 and was discontinued as of Sept. 1, 1983.

Beginning in the late 1980s, Case has produced other variations of the 042 pattern, with polished stainless steel blades.

Case XX 62042, Green Bone, 3", $150.

Case XX USA 1 Dot, 1989, lightning S, ROG62042, Rogers bone, Damascus, 3", $85.

Case XX 62042, red bone, 3", $100.

Case XX USA 10 Dot, 1970, 92042, imitation pearl, 3", $60.

Case XX USA 1 Dot, 1979, A62042, Appaloosa bone, 3", $45.

Case XX USA 2 Dot, 1978, 92042 , "new cracked ice," 3", $35.

PATTERN 43

The basic pattern: The 43 pattern is the "Daddy Barlow" pattern also known as the "Granddaddy Barlow." It is a 5" (closed length) knife with a single clip blade and goes back to the early years of Case.

The 6143 was traditionally made with sawcut bone handles and iron bolsters and liners. The 6143 was intended as a relatively inexpensive "work" knife, so iron was used in order to keep the cost low.

Some examples of the 6143 made during the Case XX era were made with smooth black handle material. The pattern number for these knives was still designated as 6143 since the black was used as a substitute for genuine bone when bone was in short supply, similar to the way that "rough black" handles were used as a substitute on other bone-handled knives.

During the Case XX years, the 6143 was made with the traditional iron liners and bolsters.

At some point during the 1960s, the bolster material was changed to nickel silver but iron remained as the lining material.

The use of iron for liners continued into the late 1960s and possibly the early 1970s. At some point in the 1970s, the liner material was changed to brass.

During the 1970s, delrin was substituted for bone on the 6143 on a random basis and both delrin and bone examples will be found; however, my observation is that very few, if any, bone-handled examples were made after 1974.

It is possible the 6143 was changed over to 100 percent production in delrin handles after 1974. The 6143 was discontinued in late 1981.

During all of these years, chrome vanadium was the only blade steel offered on the 6143.

In recent years, Case has reintroduced the 6143 pattern with stainless steel blade material and in various bone handles.

Case XX 6143 "Granddaddy Barlow," red bone, 5", $140.

Case XX USA 8 Dot, 1972, 6143 "Granddaddy Barlow," bone, 5", $75.

Case Tested 6143, green bone, 5", $300.

PATTERN 44

The basic pattern: The 44 pattern goes back to the early years of Case and is a medium stockman with squared bolsters. Closed length is 3-1/4". During the Case XX years and later, it has been manufactured as a three-blade "stockman," two-blade pen knife, and two-blade jack pattern.

Blade and handle variations: The 44 pattern has always been made with a clip as the main blade. During the Case XX era, the following principal variations of the 44 jack and stockman patterns were made:

- 6244 jack pattern with bone handles, master clip blade and secondary pen blade.
- 6344 Sh Pen stockman pattern with bone handles, secondary sheepfoot and pen blades.
- 6344 Sh Sp stockman pattern with bone handles, secondary sheepfoot and spay blades.
- 33044 Sh Sp stockman pattern with yellow handles, secondary sheepfoot and spay blades. This is the "small birdseye" pattern with no bolsters.
- 06244 pen knife pattern with bone handles and secondary pen blade.

The 33044 is a knife made with no bolsters and with large nickel silver washers anchoring the blade pins at each end. This pattern is referred to by collectors as the "small birdseye" pattern due the oversized pins; the 33092 is a similar knife but at 4" long closed, it is referred to as the "large birdseye." The 33044 Sh Sp with yellow composition handles was introduced in 1963 and discontinued in 1978.

The 6244 and 6344 in the CASE XX stamping will be found in several of the Case XX-era bone color variations including green, regular and red. The use of bone handles on the 6244 and the 6344 continued until mid-1970. The 6244 and 6344 Sh Sp and 6344 Sh Pen were three of a number of patterns changed to being handled 100 percent in delrin in 1970, so both bone and delrin examples were made that year. Production of the 6244, 6344 Sh Pen, and 6344 Sh Sp continued with delrin handles through the 1970s. The 6344 Sh Sp was discontinued in 1979.

The 6244 pattern remained in the Case line through the 1970s and went through the following evolution as Case made changes to its product line in the later

Case XX 06244, Late Rogers Bone, 3-1/4", $150.

Case XX 6244, bone, 3-1/4", $100.

Case XX 06244, reddish bone, 3-1/4", $100.

1970s and early 1980s. The 6244 with delrin handles and chrome vanadium blades was discontinued in mid-1979 and replaced with the SR6244. This was the same 6244 pattern in chrome vanadium blade steel but with smooth Satin Rose-colored bone handles. This initial variation of the SR6244 was made without a shield. The SR6244 was one of ten patterns that Case introduced in 1979 with smooth genuine bone handles in two colors, Appaloosa and Satin Rose.

The next change took place in 1981, when the SR6244 was changed to the SR6244 SS. This was essentially the same knife but with glazed finished stainless steel blades and with a shield added to the smooth Satin Rose bone handles. The SR6244 SS was relatively short lived and discontinued in 1982. Later in 1982, the pattern was reintroduced as the 6244 SS with glazed finished stainless steel blades and delrin handles. The 6244 SS was discontinued in 1985.

The 6344 Sh Pen remained in the Case line through the 1970s and into the 1980s. In 1981, the pattern was changed over to glazed finished stainless steel blades as the 6344 Sh Pen SS. The 6344 Sh Pen SS with delrin handles has remained in the Case product line ever since as part of the "Working Knives" series.

The 06244 pen knife is an unusual pattern variation in that it has rounded bolsters, while the other 44 patterns have squared bolsters. The frame or handle die for the 06244 is in actuality identical to the Case 087 frame,

but for some reason, the "44" pattern number was used when the 06244 was put into production during the Case XX era. The use of the pattern number 06244 continued until the knife was discontinued in 1979. At that time, a yellow-handled version, the 03244, was still in production. Circa 1987, Case changed the pattern number on that knife to the correct number, 32087 Pen.

Blade steel and liner material: From the XX era through the early 1980s, chrome vanadium was the only blade steel offered on the 44 patterns. The standard lining material for the 44 "stockman" patterns (and for the 06244) was nickel silver. The 44 "jack" pattern was made with brass liners. Beginning circa 1978, Case began changing all pocket knife patterns with nickel silver liners to the standard use of brass as the lining material. This change was complete by 1980. Beginning with the 1977 catalog, all 44 patterns were shown as having brass liners.

Newer variations: The 03244 R pattern in yellow handles was introduced in the late 1970s as part of the Gentlemen's Line. This pattern was designed with a bail and polished chrome vanadium blades. Later the bail was dropped and the pattern number was changed to 32087 Pen. This pattern is still in the Case line today and is also offered with stainless steel blades.

The 6344 with sheepfoot and pen secondary blades has been widely produced by Case in recent years in a variety of different bone handles.

Case XX 06244, green bone, 3-1/4", $250.

Case Tested 6344, green bone, 3-1/4", $350.

Case XX USA 1 Dot, 1979, 6344 Sh Sp, delrin, 3-1/4", $50.

Case XX USA 5 Dot, 1975, 6344 Sh Pen, delrin, 3-1/4", $50.

Case XX USA 10 Dot, 1980, SR6244, "Satin Rose" bone, 3-1/4",
$50.

Case XX USA 3 Dot, 1977, 33044, 3-1/4", $75.

Case XX USA 10 Dot, 1980, lightning S, 5244 SSP, Case 75th
Anniversary, 3-1/4", $75.

PATTERN 45
(CATTLE KNIFE PATTERN)

The basic pattern: The 45 "Cattle Knife" pattern is an "equal-end" or "cigar" pattern knife, with three blades and two backsprings. Closed length is 3-5/8". The 45 pattern goes back to the early days of Case and most collectors refer to an equal-end three-blade knife as a "cattle" pattern. The origin of this name is not known. However, some knife companies in the pre-WWII years, including Winchester and Keen Kutter, manufactured this style of knife with the words "CATTLE KNIFE" engraved in the composition handles, often with the image of a steer. It is generally assumed this style of knife was popular with those who worked with livestock.

Case also used the "45" pattern number designation on the "scout/utility" knife patterns, 6445 R and 640045 R. However, the frame size on the three-blade 45 pattern "cattle" knives was slightly smaller at 3-5/8" closed while the 45 "scout/utility" knife frame has a closed length of 3-3/4". So in reality, these are two patterns with slightly different tooling but with the same pattern number.

Blade and handle variations: During the Case XX era, the following principal variations were made:

- 2345 1/2 Sh, with smooth black handles, clip master blade and secondary sheepfoot and pen blades.

- 2345 1/2 Pu, with smooth black handles, clip master blade and secondary spay and punch blades.
- 6345 1/2 Sh, with bone handles, clip master blade and secondary sheepfoot and pen blades.

Case also made some variations of the 45 pattern with two blades operating on a single backspring. During the Case XX era, a pattern number 02245 Sh was made as a horticultural knife.

The 6345 1/2 in the CASE XX stamping will be found in several of the Case XX-era bone color variations including green, regular and red, and in rough black. Both the 2345 1/2 Sh and the 6345 1/2 Sh were made into the late 1960s when they were both discontinued as of Jan. 1, 1966. Both patterns are fairly rare with the CASE XX USA tang stamping.

Blade steel and liner material: From the XX era through the time the pattern was discontinued, all 45 "cattle" patterns were only offered with chrome vanadium as the blade steel. The liner material during these years was nickel silver.

Newer variations: The 45 "cattle" pattern has been reintroduced on a limited basis for special factory order knives beginning in the 1980s.

Case Bradford 6345, Punch "Cattle Knife," green bone, 3-5/8",
$1,000.

Case Tested 2345-1/2, "cattle knife," 3-5/8", $250.

Case XX 2345-1/2, "cattle knife," 3-5/8", $175.

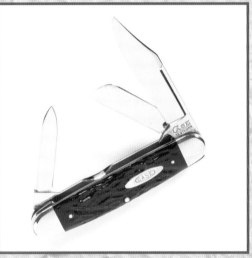

Case Tested 6345-1/2, "cattle knife," rough black, 3-5/8", $400.
Note: This is a used knife that has been polished.

Case XX 6345-1/2, "cattle knife," red bone, 3-5/8", $350.

Case Tested 6345-1/2, "cattle knife," dark green bone, 3-5/8",
$500. Note: This is a used knife that has been polished.

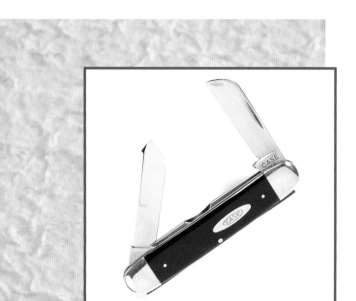

These are all variations of the Case 45 pattern with the Case XX tang stamping. The top knife is a Case XX budding and grafting knife, 02245, with smooth black composition handles, 3-5/8", $175. Center knife is a rare Case XX 06245 pattern, green bone handles, 3-5/8", $400; note: rare variation not shown in XX era catalogs or price lists. For comparison, the bottom knife is a Case XX 6445 R scout/ utility knife, with red bone handles, 3-3/4", $275. Note that for the 45 pattern, the four-blade version is a longer frame, 3-3/4", as compared to two- and three-blade versions, 3-5/8".

PATTERN 45
(SCOUT/UTILITY KNIFE PATTERN)

The basic pattern: The 45 "Scout/Utility Knife" pattern is an "equal-end" or "cigar" pattern knife, with four blades and two backsprings. Closed length is 3-3/4". This pattern goes back to the early days of Case and the term "scout/utility" knife is often used by collectors to refer to a "Boy Scout"-type four-blade utility knife that is not an "official" knife sanctioned by the Boy Scouts of America.

Case used the 45 pattern number designation on the scout/utility knife patterns 6445 R and 640045 R, as well as on similar cattle knife patterns with two and three blades. However, the frame size on the three-blade 45 pattern cattle knives was slightly smaller at 3-5/8" closed, while the 45 scout/utility knife frame has a closed length of 3-3/4". So in reality, these are two patterns with slightly different tooling but with the same pattern number.

Blade and handle variations: During the Case XX era, the following principal variations of the 45 scout/utility pattern were made:

- 6445 R, with bone handles.
- 640045 R, with jigged brown or black composition (imitation bone) handles.

These variations were made with a spear master blade, can opener blade, bottle opener/screwdriver blade, and punch blade. Each included a bail in the handle. The 6445 R in the CASE XX stamping will be found in several of the Case XX-era bone color variations including green, regular and red, and in rough black.

While the 6445 R and 640045 R are similar patterns, the difference between the two is that the 6445 R was made in house by Case, while the 640045 R was a knife always made on contract for Case by other knife companies. During the XX era, it is believed that at various times, the 640045 R was made by Camillus Cutlery Company, Schrade/Ulster, and Utica Cutlery Company. During these years, the 640045 R was always manufactured with composition imitation jigged bone handles. While it was a quality knife, the 640045 R was sold by Case as a lower priced "budget" scout/utility knife, and the knife had relatively thin blade stock, liners, and bolsters.

Case Tested 6445R, "Scout/Utility Knife," with Scout shield, green bone, 3-3/4", $750.

Case XX 6445R, reddish bone, 3-3/4", $275.

Case XX 6445R, jigged black composition, 3-3/4", $200.

By contrast, the 6445 R was built like a tank, with extra thick blade stock and brass liners. The 6445 R was designed and built as a serious tool for the outdoor enthusiast. In my opinion, the Case 6445R was the finest scout/utility pocket knife ever to be manufactured by any American cutlery firm. The 6445 R was made through the 1970s with bone handles. I personally have never seen an example that was handled in delrin. The 6445 R was discontinued in 1978.

For many years, Case included both the 6445 R and 640045 R in the standard product pocket knife line. The 640045 R was sold at a much lower price as compared to the 6445 R. For example, the 1977 Case factory price list shows retail prices of $19.50 for the 6445 R and $11.50 for the 640045 R. I believe Case offered the 640045 R since the scout/utility pattern is popular as a "first knife" and many younger knife buyers are on a budget.

Most knife collectors may be aware that until recent years, Case never made "official" BSA sanctioned Boy Scout knives. Companies that did provide them in the pre-WWII era included Ulster Knife Company, Remington, and New York Knife Company. An interesting fact is that in the 1930s, some Case catalogs and price lists included a pocket knife pattern listed as the "#1502 Official Scout Knife." The #1502 was an official BSA Boy Scout knife manufactured by Ulster Knife Company. It appears that Case purchased these knives from Ulster Knife Company and resold them to Case dealers so that dealers would have access to an "official" BSA Boy Scout pocket knife. These knives would have been sold as purchased with the Ulster Knife Company markings, without any Case markings.

The 640045 R remained in the Case line after the 6445 R was discontinued. Circa 1990, the pattern was changed over to glazed finished stainless steel blades, pattern number 640045 R SS. This version remained in the Case line until recent years. It was discontinued in 2006 after Camillus Cutlery Company, the last contract manufacturer of the pattern, ceased business.

Blade steel and liner material: From the XX era through the time that the pattern was discontinued, the 6445 R was only offered with chrome vanadium as the blade steel. The liner material during these years was brass. The 640045 R has also been made only with brass liners.

Case Tested 6445 R, green bone, without shield, 3-3/4", $375.

Case Tested scout knife, red handles, "birdseye" rivets, 3-3/4", $300.

Case Tested 6445R, rough black, 3-3/4", $375.

Case XX USA 640045R, black composition, 3-3/4", $65.

Case Tested 6445R, with Case oval shield, 3-3/4", $450.

Case 1990 stamp, 640045R SS, delrin, 3-3/4", $40.

Note the differing styles and placement of the can opener blades.

PATTERN 46

The basic pattern: The 46 pattern is the "rigger's" or "sailor's" knife. This is a two-blade pattern with a master sheepfoot blade and a secondary marlin spike blade. The 46 pattern goes back to the Case Tested era.

During most of the Case XX era, the 46 pattern was manufactured in one variation:

- 3246 R SS, with yellow composition handles.

In 1964, a second version of the 46 pattern was added:

- 6246 R SS, with bone handles.

The 3246 R SS will be found with the CASE XX stamping in both the older yellow celluloid, with white liner, and yellow composition handles. The 3246 R SS was never made with a shield. The 3246 R SS was discontinued as of Jan. 1, 1966. The 3246 R SS was not manufactured with the CASE XX USA tang stamping.

The 6246 R SS was introduced in 1964, during the last year that the CASE XX tang stamping was used, so it is relatively rare with the CASE XX STAINLESS marking. During the 1970s, delrin was substituted for bone on the 6246 R SS on a random basis and both examples will be found; however, my observation is that very few, if any, bone-handled examples were made after 1976. The 6246 R SS was discontinued in 1978. The last examples made from 1978 that I have observed had a glazed finish on the sheepfoot blade.

In 1979, another version of the 46 pattern was introduced to replace the 6246 R SS. This new version was, in my opinion, made on contract for Case by Camillus and had jigged brown delrin handles. This version had a locking marlin spike and the pattern number was 6246 L R SS. This version was discontinued at the end of 1982. Case later (after 2000) brought the 6246 L R SS pattern back and it was offered for several years prior to the cease of operations by Camillus Cutlery Company.

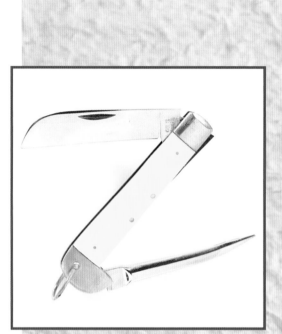

Case XX 3246 R SS, "riggers knife," 4-3/8", $140.

Case XX USA 6 Dot, 1974, 6246 R SS, bone, 4-3/8", $100.

PATTERN 47

The basic pattern: The 47 pattern is a large serpentine stockman pattern with rounded bolsters. Closed length is 3-7/8". This pattern goes back to the early years of Case and has been primarily manufactured as a three- or four-blade stockman pattern. Another variation was a "two-blade stockman" with a blade at each end and a single backspring.

Blade and handle variations: The 47 pattern has always been made with either a "California clip" or standard clip as the master blade. During the Case XX era, the following principal variations of the 47 pattern were made:

Two-blade variations—"standard" clip master blade:

- 04247 Sp, white composition handles with spay secondary blade.
- 05247 Sp, stag handles with spay secondary blade.
- 06247 Pen, bone handles with a pen secondary blade.

Three-blade variations—"standard" clip master blade:

- 3347 Sh Sp, with yellow composition handles, secondary blades sheepfoot and spay.
- 5347 Sh Sp, with stag handles, secondary blades sheepfoot and spay.
- 5347 Sh Sp SS, with stag handles, secondary blades sheepfoot and spay (polished stainless steel blades).
- 6347 Sh Sp, with bone handles, secondary blades sheepfoot and spay.
- 6347 Sh Sp SS, with bone handles, secondary blades sheepfoot and spay (polished stainless steel blades)
- 6347 Sh Pu, with bone handles, secondary blades sheepfoot and punch.
- 6347 Sp Pu, with bone handles, secondary blades spay and punch.
- 6347 Sp Pen, with bone handles, secondary blades spay and pen.

Three-blade variations—"California" clip master blade:

- 53047, with stag handles, secondary blades sheepfoot and spay.
- 63047, with bone handles, secondary blades sheepfoot and spay.
- 93047

Case XX USA 5347 Sh Sp, 3-7/8", $225.

Case Tested M347 Sp Pen, has solid nickel silver handles, 3-7/8", $250.

Case XX 3347 Sh Sp, yellow composition, 3-7/8", $175.

Four-blade variations—"California" clip master blade:

- 64047 Pu, with bone handles, secondary blades spay, pen, and punch (this was a four-bladed knife with two backsprings).

In 1965, a new stainless steel version of the 47 pattern was introduced as part of a line of six stainless steel pocket knives introduced that year with the CASE XX USA tang stamping:

- 6347 Sh Sp SSP, with bone handles, standard clip master blade, secondary blades sheepfoot and spay. Glazed finished stainless steel blades with polished edges, main blade etched "TESTED XX RAZOR EDGE."

The 3347 will be found with the CASE XX stamping in both the older yellow celluloid, with white liner, and yellow composition handles. Later examples made from the CASE XX USA era and into the 1970s will have yellow delrin handles. The 3347 Sh Sp was discontinued in late 1982. The 04247 Sp and the 05247 Sp were both discontinued during the Case XX USA as of April 1, 1967 and both of these patterns are somewhat rare with the CASE XX USA tang stamping.

Production of the other stag-handled 47 pattern variations, 5347 Sh Sp, 5347 Sh Sp SS, and 53047, continued through the Case XX USA years and the patterns were discontinued in 1970 when Case stopped regular production of stag-handled pocket knives. In 1971, Case made a special run of a new stag-handled variation, the 5347 Sh Sp SSP. This knife has glazed finished stainless steel blades with polished edges, with the main blade etched "TESTED XX RAZOR EDGE." The later stag sets from 1976, 1977, and 1978 each included the 5347 Sh Sp SSP as well.

The bone-handled 47 pattern variations in the CASE XX stamping will be found in several of the Case XX-era bone color variations including green, regular and red, as well as in rough black and "late Rogers" bone. The 6347 Sh Pu with sheepfoot and punch secondary blades was discontinued in 1963. The 6347 Sh Sp SS with polished stainless steel blades was discontinued as of Jan. 1, 1966.

The 93047 is a relatively scarce variation of the 47 pattern. It was made early in the Case XX era beginning in 1950 and discontinued in 1956. All examples of the 93047 that I have observed have had "cracked ice" handles.

Case XX 06247 Pen, bone, 3-7/8", $175.

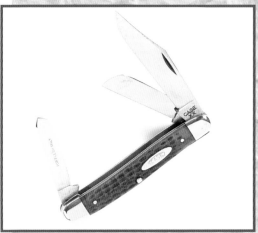

These two Case XX-stamped 47 stock knife patterns, 3-7/8", illustrate differences in Case XX-era bone, as well as the main clip blade style. The top knife is a Case XX 63047 with well matched very dark (black) bone handles, $175. Note the "California clip"-style main blade. The bottom knife is a Case XX 6347 Sh SP with nicely matched blood red bone handles, $325. Note the "standard" clip-style main blade.

The use of bone handles on the 47 patterns, including all remaining blade variations, continued into the 1970s. During the 1970s, delrin was substituted for bone on the 47 pattern knives on a random basis. My observation is that starting in 1978, all 47 patterns were switched back to being handled 100 percent in bone. The 6347 Sp Pu (punch blade) was discontinued in 1974 and the 6347 Sp Pen (pen blade) was discontinued in 1976. The 64047 Punch was discontinued in 1979. The 06247 Pen was discontinued in 1982.

The 6347 Sh Sp and the 63047 both remained in the Case line through the 1970s. The 63047 went through the following evolution as Case made changes to the product line in the later 1970s and early 1980s. The 63047 with bone handles and chrome vanadium blades was discontinued in mid-1979 and replaced with the SR6347 1/2. This was the same 63047 pattern in chrome vanadium blade steel and with a "California clip" master blade but with smooth Satin Rose-colored bone handles. For some unknown reason, Case changed the pattern number designation from the "0" in the middle of the pattern number to designate the California clip blade to using the 1/2 suffix, which was normally used to designate a clip master blade. This is not exactly consistent, but it is what Case did.

This initial variation of the SR6347 1/2 was made without a shield and was one of ten patterns Case introduced in 1979 with smooth genuine bone handles in two colors, Appaloosa and Satin Rose.

The next change took place in 1981, when the SR6347 1/2 was changed to the SR6347 1/2 SS. This was essentially the same knife but with glazed finished stainless steel blades and with a shield added to the smooth Satin Rose bone handles. The SR6347 1/2 SS was relatively short lived and discontinued in 1982; later that year, it was reintroduced as the 6347 1/2 SS with glazed finished stainless steel blades and with delrin handles. The 6347 1/2 SS was discontinued in 1985.

The 6347 Sh Sp with chrome vanadium blades was discontinued in 1990. The 6347 Sh Sp SSP was the last 47 pattern variation to remain in the standard pocket knife line and was gradually changed over to mirror finished stainless blades with no blade etching, and this pattern is still in the Case line today as the 6347 SS. In the mid-1990s, Case retooled the 6347 pattern so that the knife has three separate backsprings, one spring per blade, with no center liners.

Blade steel and liner material: The 47 pattern was one

Case XX 6347 Sp Pen, late rogers bone, 3-7/8", $325.

Case XX 6347 Sh Pu, late rogers bone, 3-7/8", $375.

Case XX 6347 Sh Pu, rough black, 3-7/8", $350.

of the first of the larger Case pocket knife patterns to be offered with stainless steel blades. It appears that stainless steel was first offered as a blade option on the 47 stockman pattern starting just after WWII. The 5347 Sh Sp SS with polished stainless steel blades was listed in a Case factory price list from 1949. Soon after that the 6347 Sh Sp SS was added, again with polished stainless steel blades.

From the Case XX era through the 1970s, the liner material for all of the 47 patterns was nickel silver. Beginning circa 1978, Case began changing all pocket knife patterns with nickel silver liners to the standard use of brass as the lining material. This change was complete by 1980.

Other variations: Some 47 patterns with the CASE XX tang stamping were made with a "long pull" nail pull on the master clip blade. These examples were made early in the Case XX era and are fairly rare. Long pull master blades will be observed on three-blade 47 patterns with the "standard" clip master blade.

The 47 pattern variations with punch secondary blades will be observed with two styles of punch blade. The "wraparound" punch blade has a crease with half of the blade at a right angle to the other half. The "flat" punch variation is a simple stamped out blade tapering to a fine point. This appears to be a random variation. It is my observation that the "flat" punch blade on the 47 pattern will be found only on the early Case XX-era knives that have a long pull on the master blade.

Beginning circa 1991, the blade etching "TESTED XX RAZOR EDGE" was dropped from the main blade of the 6347 Sh Sp SSP, while the glazed blade finish was still used on the "standard product" 6347 Sh Sp SSP. In 1997, Case dropped the use of the glazed finish on all knives with natural handle materials, including the 6347 SS, and the blades were polished from that point on.

Newer variations: The 47 stockman pattern with stainless steel blades and three backsprings is currently a mainstay in the Case product line. Beginning in the mid- to late 1990s, the 47 stockman pattern has been produced with a wide variety of handle materials. It has also been produced in a split backspring "whittler" variation with master clip, small clip, and small coping blades. This variation was introduced in 1998 and has been made in a number of handle materials with polished stainless steel blades.

Case XX 6347 Sp Pu, bone, 3-7/8", $250.

Case XX 64047P, reddish bone, 3-7/8", $325.

Case XX 64047P, green bone, 3-7/8", $750.

Case XX USA 4 Dot, 1976, 5347 Sh Sp SSP, gray etch, 3-7/8", $125.

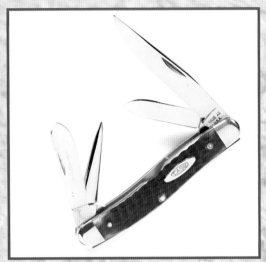

Case XX USA 64047P, bone, 3-7/8", $175.

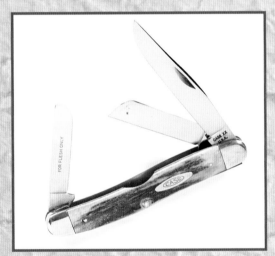

Case XX USA 53047, 3-7/8", $225.

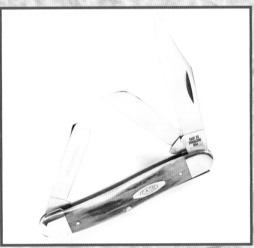

Case XX USA 10 Dot, 1970, 5347, stainless, 3-7/8", $450.

Case XX USA 53047, 3-7/8", $225.

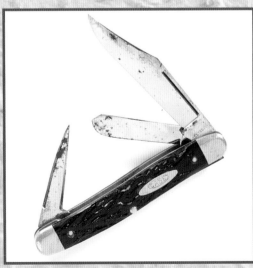

Case Tested 6347 Sp Pu, rough black, 3-7/8", $400.

Case XX USA 3 Dot, 1977, 5347 SSP, "blue scroll," 3-7/8", $125.

Case XX USA 1 Dot, 1989, lightning S, ROG6347, Rogers bone damascus, 3-7/8", $150.

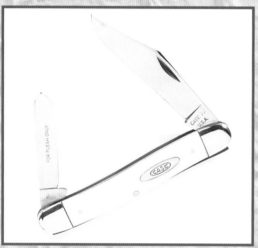

Case XX USA 04247 SP, white composition, 3-7/8", $175.

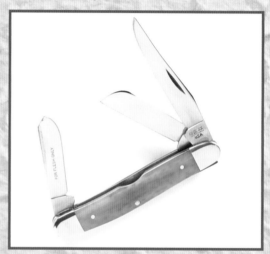

Case XX USA 10 Dot, 1980, lightning S, SR6347-1/2, "Satin Rose" bone, 3-7/8", $75.

Case XX USA 1 Dot, 1979, 06247 Pen, bone, 3-7/8", $75.

Case XX USA 3 Dot, 1987, lightning S, 6347 Sh Sp, 3-7/8", $50.

Case XX USA 5 Dot, 1975, 6347 Sh Sp SSP, red bone, 3-7/8", $125.

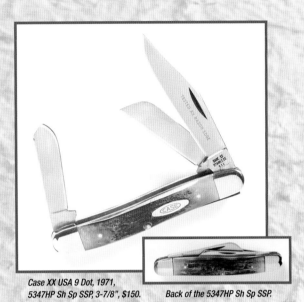

Case XX USA 9 Dot, 1971,
5347HP Sh Sp SSP, 3-7/8", $150.   *Back of the 5347HP Sh Sp SSP.*

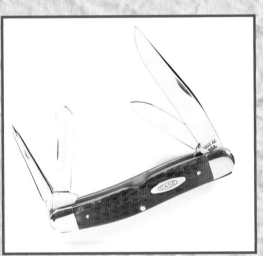

Case XX USA 5 Dot, 1975, 64047 P, red bone, 3-7/8", $140.

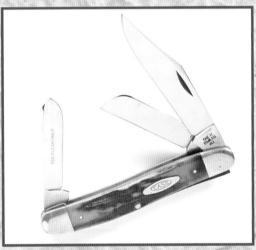

Case XX USA, 5347 Sh Sp SS, 3-7/8", $175.

Case XX USA 8 Dot, 1982, lightning S, SR6347-1/2 SSP, "Satin
Rose" bone, 3-7/8", $75.

Case XX USA 2 Dot, 1978, 5347 SSP, 3-7/8", $125.

PATTERN 048

The basic pattern: The 048 pattern is a slim bare-head jack pattern with a squared top bolster and no lower bolster. Closed length is 4-1/8". The 048 pattern goes back to the early years of Case and has been manufactured as both a one- and two-blade jack pattern. Some collectors refer to the 048 in both one and two blades as a "slim trapper" pattern. The single-bladed 048 pattern has also been referred to as the "farmer's knife," a nickname that may be due to a listing in the Case factory catalogs from 1967 and from 1974. In those catalogs, the listing for the 31048 and 61048 patterns included the description, "STOCKMAN'S – TRUCK FARMERS – SPORTSMAN'S."

Blade and handle variations: During the Case XX era, the following principal variations were made:

One-blade variations:

- 31048, with yellow composition handles and clip master blade.
- 31048 Sp, with yellow composition handles and long spay master blade.
- 31048 Sh R (the "florist's knife"), with yellow composition handles and a short sheepfoot master blade and bail.
- 61048, with bone handles and clip master blade.
- 61048 Sp, with bone handles and a long spay master blade.

Two-blade variations:

- 32048 Sp, with yellow composition handles, a clip master blade and long spay secondary blade.
- 62048 Sp, with bone handles, a clip master blade and long spay secondary blade.

In 1965, two stainless steel versions of the 048 pattern were introduced as part of a line of six stainless steel pocket knives introduced that year with the CASE XX USA tang stamping:

- 61048 Sp SSP, with bone handles, standard clip master blade. Glazed finished stainless steel blade with polished edge, blade etched TESTED XX RAZOR EDGE.
- 62048 Sp SSP, with bone handles, standard clip master blade and long spay secondary blade. Glazed finished stainless steel blades with polished edges,

main blade etched TESTED XX RAZOR EDGE.

Some older 31048 and 32048 Sp patterns will be found with the CASE XX stamping in both the older yellow celluloid, with white liner, and yellow composition handles. The 31048 Sp was introduced in 1958 and the 31048 Sh R in 1963, so these patterns most likely were never produced in the older yellow celluloid handle material.

The 31048 Sh R is known as the "florist's knife" by collectors. It was a horticultural knife pattern used to trim flower stems. The 31048 Sh R was discontinued as of Jan. 1, 1967, but none were made with the CASE XX USA tang stamping. It is probable that the stock of knives with the CASE XX tang stamping was not exhausted until 1967.

Later examples of the yellow-handled 048 patterns made from the CASE XX USA era and into the 1970s will have yellow delrin handles. The 31048 Sp was discontinued as of Jan. 1, 1972. Production of both the 31048 and the 32048 Sp continued into the 1980s. Both of these patterns were discontinued in 1982.

The bone-handled 61048 and 62048 Sp pattern variations in the CASE XX stamping will be found in several of the Case XX-era bone color variations including green, regular and red, as well as "late Rogers" bone. The 61048 Sp was introduced in 1958, so it most

This 5 dot 1975 32048 Sp is 4-1/8" and $50. It has slightly different blade grinds and tooling as compared to most Case 048 pattern knives and it is believed that these slightly different examples were made on contract for Case by another cutlery firm.

likely was never produced in green bone, but this is not definite.

The use of bone handles on the 048 patterns, including all blade variations, continued into the late 1960s. During the Case XX USA era, all bone-handled 048 patterns were switched 100 percent to production in delrin. Both delrin and bone-handled examples of the 61048, 61048 Sp, 62048 Sp, and 62048 Sp SSP will be found with the CASE XX USA tang stamping. From that point through the 1970s and into the 1980s, all standard product examples of theses patterns were made 100 percent with delrin handles.

The changeover of the 048 patterns represented Case's first use of jigged brown delrin handles as a substitute for bone handles on pocket knives. The reason this pattern was selected for the first use of delrin is not known; however, I think it was done as a cost-cutting measure. The 048s were always popular and inexpensive basic work knives, and they would require long thin pieces of bone. That, along with the "barehead" design, may have meant more than usual cracking of the bone handles during assembly.

The 61048 Sp was discontinued as of Jan. 1, 1972. The 61048, 61048 SSP, 62048 Sp and the 62048 Sp SSP all remained in the Case line through the 1970s. Around 1984 or 1985, the TESTED XX RAZOR EDGE blade etchings were deleted from the stainless steel versions, and the chrome vanadium versions were discontinued in this time frame as well. The 62048 SSP was discontinued after 1990. The 61048 SSP (later designated as the 61048 SS) with delrin handles has remained in the Case line to the present day as part of the "Working Knives" series.

Blade steel and liner material: The earlier 048 patterns from the Case XX era were all offered only with chrome vanadium blade steel. Stainless steel was first offered as a blade steel option on the 61048 and the 62048 patterns starting with the introduction of the "SSP" line in 1965. The liner material used for the 048 pattern from the Case XX era onward was brass.

Other variations: An interesting 048 pattern variation is that during the 1970s, some 048 patterns (31048, 61048, 61048 SSP, and 62048 SSP) were produced that had a distinctly different "look" and "feel" as compared

Case XX 61048, green bone, 4-1/8", $200.

Case XX 61048, red bone, 4-1/8", $150.

Case XX 61048, late rogers bone, 4-1/8", $150.

to previously produced 048s and other standard Case pocket knives. The differences are hard to describe, but the blade grinds and finishes are decidedly different and the frame style is slightly different. Most Case collectors are of the opinion that these "different" 048 pattern knives were manufactured on contract for Case by another cutlery firm, most likely Camillus Cutlery Company. If this is true, then only a percentage of the 048 patterns were out-sourced as more examples of the "normal" versions will be found.

Beginning circa 1986, the blade etching TESTED XX RAZOR EDGE was dropped from the main blade of the 61048 SSP and the 62048 SSP, while the use of the glazed blade finish was continued. By 1991, the "SSP" suffix on the 61048 SSP was changed to "SS."

Newer variations: Beginning in the late 1980s, Case has produced numerous versions of the one- and two-bladed 048 patterns as SFOs and as part of the Case standard product line. Some variations were made with "caps" or lower bolsters but retained the 048 pattern number. The 31048 was also reintroduced into the standard product line beginning in 1993.

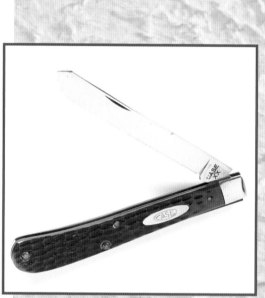

Case XX 61048 SP, dark red bone, 4-1/8", $150.

Case XX 62048 SP, red bone, 4-1/8", $225.

 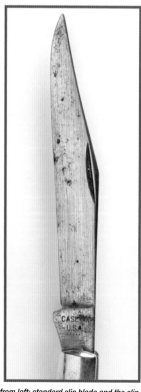

Main clip blade variations on the 048 pattern, from left: standard clip blade and the clip blade that will be found on examples believed to be contract made.

Case Bradford RM1048, Slim Trapper, red/black mingled celluloid, 4-1/8", $450.

Case Tested 62048 SP, green bone, 4-1/8", $450.

Case XX USA 10 Dot, 1980, lightning S, 62048SP SSP, delrin, 4-1/8", $60.

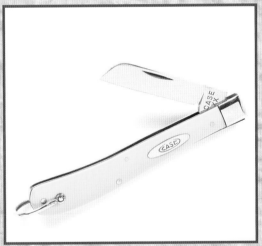

Case XX 31048 Sh R, "florist's knife," yellow composition, 4-1/8", $175.

Case XX USA 61048 SSP, reddish bone, 4-1/8", $80.

Case XX USA 8 Dot, 1982, lightning S, 31048, 4-1/8", $45.

PATTERN 49

The basic pattern: The 49 pattern goes back to the early years of Case and is referred to by collectors as the "Copperhead" pattern. It is a 3-15/16" (closed length) jack knife with a clip master blade and a pen secondary blade. The 49 pattern has a bolster at the blade end and a "cap" at the other end. The pattern is known for the distinctive shape of the bolster at the blade end. The bolster extends upward to cover the sharp corners at the back of the blade tangs.

During the Case XX era, the following principal variation was made:

- 6249, bone handles with clip master blade and pen blade.

The 6249 in the CASE XX stamping will be found in several of the Case XX-era bone color variations including green, regular and red. I do not believe that the 6249 was produced in rough black.

The use of bone handles on the 6249 continued into the 1970s. During the 1970s, delrin was substituted for bone on the 6249 on a random basis and both examples will be found; however, my observation is that starting in 1978, the pattern was switched back to 100 percent production in bone. The 6249 was popular with both collectors and users but was discontinued after 1990. During all of these years, chrome vanadium was the only blade steel offered on the standard production model of the 6249. The lining material was brass.

Collectors and knife users have often given more than one nickname to a particular Case pocket knife pattern. The 1967 and the 1974 Case product catalogs showed the name "Copperhead" for the 6249 pattern and also the name "Viet Nam." The following is excerpted from the June 1981 edition of the *Case Collector's Club Newsletter*:

The nickname "Viet Nam" was never officially given to the 6249 by Case Cutlery. It seems that this particular knife was very popular among the GIs in Viet Nam. Because of this, that nickname caught on. So it was actually named by the consumer.

By the way...I've been asked before about the reason for the swelled head bolster on the 6249 and other Case knives. I'll take this opportunity to explain.

The back side of the blade tang normally sticks above

the knife allowing that edge to ear holes in pockets. By making a larger bolster at the end, the tang is recessed so there is no edge to wear out your pocket.

Newer variations: Limited edition and SFO versions of the 49 pattern were made in stag handles with stainless steel blades. In 1998, Case introduced a 3249 pattern with a Wharncliffe master blade style and chrome vanadium blades. This variation had an "easy opener" cutout in the handle. In recent years, Case has reintroduced the 6249 pattern with stainless steel blade material and various different bone handles.

Case XX 6249 "Copperhead," light red bone, 3-15/16, $350.

Back of the 6249.

Case XX USA 2 Dot, 1978, 6249, bone, 3-15/16, $125.

Case XX USA 5 Dot, 1985, lightning S, 5249 "Copperhead," "jigged stag" handles, 3-15/16", $125.

Case XX USA 6 Dot, 1974, 6249, dark red bone, 3-15/16, $125.

Case XX USA 9 Dot, 1971, 6249, red bone, 3-15/16, $175.

Case XX USA 1 Dot, 1979, 5249 SSP, Bradford Centennial, 3-15/16", $125.

PATTERN 50

The basic pattern: The 50 pattern is referred to by collectors as the "Sunfish" or "Elephant Toe Nail" pattern. It is a 4-3/8" (closed length) knife with a spear master blade and a pen secondary blade at opposite ends of the knife, operating on a single backspring. The 50 pattern goes back to the early years of Case and in the early days of both the WR Case & Sons Cutlery Company and Case Brothers Cutlery Company, the 50 pattern was widely produced. In addition to bone handles, stag and mother of pearl were used on the 50 pattern. Beginning in the Case XX era, bone was the only handle material offered.

During the years prior to WWII, many cutlery companies produced "sunfish" pattern pocket knives similar to the 50 pattern. Case was the only American cutlery firm to continue production of the sunfish pattern after WWII (in recent years, other firms have produced the pattern in response to modern collector demand). The sunfish pattern is an unusual pocket knife pattern, essential a "jumbo pen knife" with heavy duty blades, bolsters, and backspring. There is much speculation as to the purpose for which the sunfish pattern was designed.

The Case product catalog #70 published in 1967 was the first one to indicate pattern nicknames and/or purposes for some of the various pocket knife patterns in the line. This catalog included the usage description "old English rope knife used on sailing vessels" under the 6250 pattern. This has since been debunked, as I do not believe any evidence has been presented that the sunfish pattern was ever used on sailing vessels. Based on my own study of older pocket knife catalogs from a number of manufacturers, I believe the sunfish pattern was first manufactured in the 1880 to 1900 time frame.

My personal opinion is that the "sunfish" pattern was conceived as a heavy duty "work" knife and became popular among workers in the oil fields in the Pennsylvania area. The sunfish pattern with its wide master blade would be useful for working with the heavy timbers and hemp ropes used on the oil derricks of that era.

This usage would also explain the fact that production of the sunfish pattern was associated primarily

Case XX 6250, "Sunfish," red bone, 4-3/8", $750.

with Case, Case Brothers, and other cutlery firms located in the Pennsylvania and New York areas within proximity to the early oil industry. It seemed to be a regional pattern not produced by cutlery firms outside of that geographic area. Other cutlery firms well known for producing the sunfish pattern include Platts Brothers, Crandall, Utica, Camillus, Union, Robeson, New York Knife Company, and Napanoch. Remington and Winchester, located in Connecticut, were arguably two of the most prolific producers of pocket knives during the 1920 to 1940 time period, but neither of these two firms produced the sunfish pattern.

The evolution of "collector" names for various Case pocket knife patterns can be an interesting topic. The 1967 and the 1974 Case product catalogs showed the names "Sunfish" and "Elephant Toe Nail" for the 6250 pattern and also the name "Red Eye." When I began collecting Case pocket knives in the early 1970s, the name "Sunfish" seemed to be the most popular name for the 6250 pattern with collectors. After Case began etching the main blade with the elephant etching as described below, it seemed that the name "Elephant Toe Nail" became much more popular for the 6250 and for the similar pattern knives manufactured by other knife companies.

During the Case XX era, the following variation was made:

- 6250, bone handles with spear master blade and pen blade.

The 6250 in the CASE XX stamping will be found in several of the Case XX-era bone color variations including green, regular and red. It appears that the 6250 was never produced in rough black.

The use of bone handles on the 6250 continued into the 1960s. During the CASE XX and CASE XX USA eras, jigged laminated wood, or Pakkawood, was substituted for bone on the 6250 on a random basis. It is believed that the 6250 was changed over to being handled in Pakkawood 100 percent at some point early in the CASE XX USA era. It is very rare to see a CASE XX USA-stamped 6250 in genuine bone, though some were produced.

Production of the 6250 in jigged brown Pakkawood continued into the 1970s. In 1974, a change was made and an etching of a charging elephant was added to the main blade of the 6250. Blade etchings on Case pocket knives are common on current production knives, but at that time, very few Case pocket knives were made with etched blades. The addition of the etching to the main blade of the 6250 represented one of Case's early efforts to cater to knife collectors. The 6250 will be found both with and without the elephant etching in the 1974 tang stamping, but examples of the plain blade version from that year are scarce.

The "elephant" blade etching on the 6250 continued for every year until 1979. At that time, the blade etching was changed to a picture of an oil well with the words "BRADFORD BONANZA." This version was in production from 1979 on and the 6250 was discontinued in late 1981. During all years of production from the Case XX era up to this point, the 6250 was made only with chrome vanadium blade steel and with brass liners.

Newer variations: In recent years, Case has reintroduced the 6250 pattern with stainless steel blade material and in various different bone handles.

Case XX 6250, "Sunfish," red bone, light color, 4-3/8", $650.

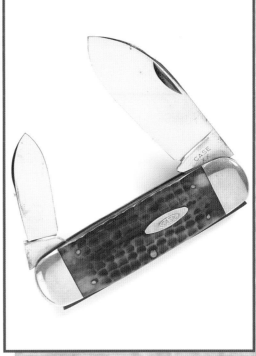

Case XX 6250, "Sunfish," green bone, 4-3/8", $1,500.

Case XX USA 10 Dot, 1970, 6250, "Sunfish," Pakkawood, 4-3/8", $150.

Case XX USA 1 Dot, 1979, 6250, Pakkawood, Bradford Bonanza etch, 4-3/8", $175.

Case XX USA 5 Dot, 1975, 6250, Pakkawood, elephant etch, 4-3/8", $140.

PATTERN 050

The basic pattern: The 050 pattern is a swell-center folding hunter pattern and referred to by collectors as the "big Coke bottle" pattern. It is a 5-1/4" (closed length) knife with a clip master blade. The 050 pattern goes back to the early years of Case and during the years prior to WWII, it was produced in a variety of handle materials including bone, stag, and celluloids. It was produced with both a saber ground clip master blade and a flat ground clip blade, and both with and without a lower bolster. A lockback version was also produced. The C61050 L SAB had a locking saber ground clip blade with an attached folding hand guard.

After WWII and during the Case XX era, the only variation of the 050 pattern produced was the C61050 SAB. This bone-handled knife had a saber ground clip master blade, an extended bolster at the blade end, and a "cap" or lower bolster at the other end of the handle. It is believed that the "C" at the beginning of the pattern number designates the inclusion of the "cap" or lower bolster.

The C61050 SAB in the CASE XX stamping will be found in several of the Case XX-era bone color variations including green, regular and red. It appears that the C61050 SAB was never produced in rough black.

The use of bone handles on the C61050 SAB continued into the 1960s. During the CASE XX era, jigged laminated wood, or Pakkawood, was substituted for bone on the C61050 SAB on a random basis. The C61050 SAB was changed over to being handled in Pakkawood 100 percent at some point later during the Case XX USA era. Both bone and Pakkawood handled examples will be found with the CASE XX stamping. A few bone examples will be observed with the Case XX USA stamping but these are rare. Beginning with the CASE XX USA ten dot stamping and into the 1970s, Pakkawood was used 100 percent. The C61050 SAB was discontinued in 1977.

Newer variations: In recent years, Case has reintroduced the 050 pattern with stainless steel blade material and in various different bone handles and with a flat ground clip master blade.

Case Tested B10050, "Swell Center" Glitter Stripe, 5-1/4", $1,200.

Case Tested 61050, green bone, 5-1/4", $600.Note: This is a used knife that has been polished.

Case Tested C61050 SAB, "Swell Center," green bone, 5-1/4", $600.

Case XX C61050 SAB, red bone, 5-1/4", $450.

Case Tested 61050L SAB, green bone, 5-1/4", $3,000.

PATTERN 051

The basic pattern: The 051 pattern is a modern lockback pattern introduced into the Case line in 1976. The P197 L SSP Shark Tooth, introduced in 1975, was the first modern stainless steel lockback in the Case product line.

Case built upon the success of the Shark Tooth with the introduction of the following three models a year later:

- 21051 L SSP, with glazed finish stainless steel blade and smooth black handles.
- 61051 L SSP, with glazed finish stainless steel blade and jigged brown Pakkawood handles.
- M1051 L SSP, with glazed finish stainless steel blade and lightweight metal handles (this knife was actually first produced in 1977).

Each of these variations had a drop-point blade. Closed length of the 051 pattern is 3-3/4". The 21051 and the 61051 were made without shields, while the M1051 was made with handle slabs of a lightweight aluminum alloy with the CASE logo engraved in the front handle.

Each knife was designed with a hole at the end of the handle for a lanyard. Case never gave an official name to this pattern but it did refer to the M1051 L SSP as the "Trailpacker" in some sales literature. I have heard some knife collectors refer to the 051 pattern as the "Hornet."

After a few years the 61051 L SSP was discontinued (1980) and two new 051 pattern variations were introduced:

- P10051 L SSP, with glazed finish stainless steel drop point blade and a brass frame with smooth black Pakkawood handles.
- P1051 1/2 L SSP, with glazed finish stainless steel clip blade and smooth brown Pakkawood handles.

The P1051 1/2 L SSP was introduced in 1981; the P10051 L SSP was introduced in 1980 and initially produced with an incorrect pattern number. The following explanation of P10051L SSP is from the *Case Collectors Club Newsletter* from March 1981:

In August 1980, Case introduced the 061051L SSP. This knife is slightly different from the normal 51L series in that it has brass bolsters at both ends. This modification is the reason for the second "0" added to the pattern number.

The knife also features smooth laminated hardwood handles, a drop point Case Tru-Sharp™ surgical steel blade, stainless steel back spring, and brass liners.

After the first factory order was produced, the pattern number was found to be in error. The number should have been P10051L SSP.

The reason for the new pattern number is that all knives with the smooth laminated hardwood handles should have P as a prefix. Also, the second "0" should be in the middle of the pattern number.

All the knives are now being produced with the new pattern number However, 5,000 knives were made with the 061051L SSP stamped on them. These were the first knives made in this pattern and should prove to become valuable collectors items.

A limited production run (7,500) of the 51051 L SSP pattern in stag was done in 1980. This knife was made using the same brass frame used on the P10051 L SSP.

The four standard product variations of the 051 pattern (21051, M1051, P1051 1/2, and P10051) remained in the Case product line through the 1980s and all were discontinued after 1989.

The M1051 L SS was reintroduced in 1991 and manufactured through 1996. This version of the M1051 has a slim stainless steel handle without the CASE logo engraved.

Case XX USA 3 Dot, 1977, 21051 L SSP, 3-3/4", $50.

Case XX USA 8 Dot, 1982, lightning S, P10051 L SSP, 3-3/4", $50.

Case XX USA 10 Dot, 1980, lightning S, 051051 L SSP, 3-3/4", $80.

Case XX USA 3 Dot, 1977, 61051 L SSP, Pakkawood, 3-3/4", $50.

Case XX USA 9 Dot 1981 lightning S M1051 L SSP, 3-3/4", $45.

Case XX USA 8 Dot, 1982, lightning S, P1051 1/2 L SSP, 3-3/4", $50.

PATTERN 052

The basic pattern: The 052 pattern goes back to the early years of Case and is a medium "congress" with squared bolsters. Closed length is 3-1/2". During the Case XX years and later, it has been manufactured as both a two-blade pen knife pattern and a four-blade pattern.

Blade and handle variations: During the Case XX era, the following principal variations were made:

- 62052 pen knife pattern with bone handles, master sheepfoot and pen blades operating on a single backspring.
- 64052 four-blade pattern with bone handles, master sheepfoot and master spear blades, pen blade and coping blades operating on two backsprings.
- 54052 four-blade pattern with stag handles, master sheepfoot and master spear blades, pen blade and coping blades operating on two backsprings.

Production of the 54052 continued through the Case XX USA years and was discontinued in 1970 when Case stopped regular production of stag-handled pocket knives.

The 62052 and the 64052 in the CASE XX stamping will be found in several of the Case XX-era bone color variations including green, regular and red. The use of bone handles on the 62052 and the 64052 continued into the 1970s. During the 1970s, delrin was substituted for bone on the 62052 and the 64052 on a random basis. The 62052 was discontinued in 1977, while the 64052 remained in the product line. Beginning in 1978, it appears that Case went back to handling the 64052 pattern 100 percent in bone. The 64052 was discontinued in late 1981.

Blade steel and liner material: From the XX era through the early 1980s when the 64052 was discontinued, chrome vanadium was the only blade steel offered on the 052 pen knife and four-blade patterns. The standard lining material for the 052 pattern during those years was nickel silver. Beginning circa 1978, Case began changing all pocket knife patterns with nickel silver liners to the standard use of brass as the lining material. This change was complete by 1980.

Other variations: The 052 pattern with four blades is unusual in that both the large sheepfoot blade and the long spear blade are considered as "master" blades and each will have the Case logo tang stamping. Due to

this fact, some "transition" examples that have a different logo stamp on each blade will be observed.

Transition models are a result of blades from one year that are left over and used up prior to new blades being stamped out for a particular year. For example, some four-bladed 052 patterns will be found with the CASE XX tang stamp on one large blade and the CASE XX USA tang stamp on the other large blade. There are also transition models with CASE XX USA and CASE XX USA (ten dots) for the 54052 and the 64052 and with various "dots" combinations during the 1970s and the early 1980s for the 64052. Transition models are scarce.

Newer variations: During the 1980s and into the 1990s, the 64052 pattern was reintroduced for some limited editions. Later versions had brass liners and stainless steel blades, usually with "long pull" nail marks on the blades. Earlier versions of the 54052 and 64052 patterns with nickel silver liners had one handle liner on each side and a thick center liner. Later versions were double-lined with brass on each side with a brass center liner. In the 1990s, the pattern was re-tooled with multiple backsprings and no double-side or center liners. This new tooling is designed with a separate backspring for each blade, so a 62052 will have two backsprings and a 64052 will have four backsprings. These new versions are made with no center liners and no double-side liners.

Case XX USA 64052, bone, 3-1/2", $150.

Case XX 62052, dark bone, 3-1/2", $150.

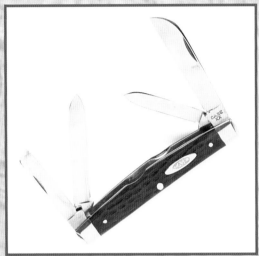

Case XX 64052, dark red bone, 3-1/2", $550.

Case XX 62052, green bone, 3-1/2", $500.

Case XX USA 10 Dot, 1970, 64052, bone, 3-1/2", $225.

Case XX USA 10 Dot, 54052, "Congress," 3-1/2", $300.

Back of the 54052 Congress.

PATTERN 053

The basic pattern: The 053 pattern is a "senator" or equal end pen knife pattern with a closed length of 2-3/4". It is a relatively small and slim Case pen knife pattern similar in shape and appearance to the 63 Eisenhower pattern, but the Eisenhower at 3-1/8" closed is a significantly larger knife. The 053 pattern goes back to the Case Tested era or earlier. During the Case Tested years, a 6253 pen knife pattern was also produced; the 53 was a 3-1/4" senator pen knife so it was larger than the 053.

Blade and handle variations: During the Case XX era, the following principal variations of the 053 pen knife pattern were made:

"Shadow" versions no bolsters:

- 82053 Shad R senator pen knife, spear master blade and secondary pen blade made as a "shadow" pattern with no bolsters, and with a bail.
- 82053 Shad R SS senator pen knife, polished stainless steel spear master blade and secondary pen blade, made as a "shadow" pattern with no bolsters, and with a bail.

With bolsters:

- 62053 SS senator pen knife pattern with bone handles, spear master blade and secondary pen blade.
- 82053 SS senator pen knife pattern with pearl handles, spear master blade and secondary pen blade.

Case XX USA 7 Dot 1973, 64052, Delrin, 3-1/2", $125.

Case 2005 stamp, 64052SS, "barn board" bone, 3-1/2", $50.

Back of the 64052SS.

The 82053 Shad R in the Case XX era was made with both chrome vanadium and with stainless steel as the blade material. Based on a review of available Case factory catalogs and price lists, it appears that the chrome vanadium was offered early in the Case XX era and by the mid-1950s, the pattern was changed over to stainless steel. The pattern number for the 82053 Shad R SS was abbreviated as 82053 S R SS in Case price lists.

The 82053 S R SS was produced into the 1970s. Genuine pearl-handled pocket knives were not listed in Case factory catalogs or price lists from about 1967 through the 1970s, even though they were in production. Based on my observations, I believe the 82053 S R SS was discontinued in 1973.

The 62053 SS and 82053 SS were both introduced in mid-1961. The 62053 SS has the same general appearance as the 06263 SS Eisenhower pattern with a rounded handle shape and elongated bolsters. The 62053 SS is in effect a smaller version of the 06263 SS. It is believed that these patterns were only offered in stainless steel. The 62053 SS will be found in regular and red bone. The 82053 SS was discontinued as of Feb. 1, 1965, and the 62053 SS was discontinued as of Jan. 1, 1966.

Liner material: The standard liner material for the 053 patterns up until the time that the 82053 S R SS was discontinued in the 1970s was nickel silver.

Newer variations: The 053 pattern has never been reintroduced.

Case Tested 6253, pen knife, rough black, 3-1/4", $175.

Case XX 82053 S R, chrome vanadium, 2-13/16", $125.

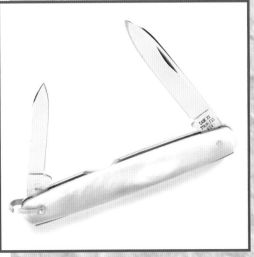

Case XX USA, 82053 S R SS, 2-13/16", $80.

PATTERN 54

The basic pattern: The 54 pattern is the legendary Case "Trapper." It was always popular with knife users and since the late 1970s has gained prominence as arguably the "premier" Case pocket knife pattern in terms of collector interest. The standard 54 pattern is a long "dogleg"-style jack pattern with a closed length of 4-1/8". While in recent years the 54 pattern has been manufactured in a number of blade configurations, the classic and most widely used combination is a long "California clip" master blade and a long spay blade. The basic 54 pattern is a "capped" jack knife, with bolsters at both ends.

History: Due to the prominence of the 54 pattern among collectors, it is interesting to delve into its history. Much of this is speculation based on my long-time study of older cutlery catalogs and the viewing of actual knives. As with most of the older pocket knife patterns, the exact history of the 54 pattern has not been documented and detailed factory records in most instances do not exist.

The 54 trapper pattern is of course a popular pattern today in the Case product line, and in recent years other manufacturers of traditional pocket knives have produced similar patterns. During the pre-WWII years, however, trapper patterns in the 54 style were not widely produced. My best speculation is that the pattern we know today as the Case 54 was introduced in the 1920s. Both Case and Union Cutlery/KABAR produced similar 54 style trapper patterns during this time frame, and it is possible that one of these two cutlery companies designed the pattern.

All of the early Union Cutlery company examples of this style knife have had the KA-BAR shield and tang stamping, so it is probable that the Union Cutlery version was introduced in the mid-1920s after the KA-BAR brand name was created. The KA-BAR versions were usually made with the blade etching *Old-Timer's Trapper's Knife.* The tooling and detailing of these early KA-BAR trapper patterns closely matches that of the Case 54 pattern trappers with the CASE TESTED tang stamping. I have observed that in general, many of the knives in the Case product line from these years seemed to be similar to patterns and knives in the KA-BAR line. This was probably due to the close family ties between these firms.

This early KA-BAR trapper pattern with green bone handles was made by the Union Cutlery Company circa 1925 to 1940s. Note the resemblance of the tooling and detailing to that of the Case Tested-era 54 pattern.

This yellow composition-handled trapper pattern with the "KABAR" tang stamping was made by Kabar Cutlery Company circa 1950s to 1960s. Though a later knife, it retains the lines and detailing of the Case Tested-era 54 patterns. Note the narrow lower bolster.

I do not know of any earlier examples of other brand knives that were similar in tooling to the Case 54 and the KA-BAR trapper patterns. I believe that these trapper patterns grew out of an older pattern made by a number of American cutlery firms from about the 1880s on. This pattern is a long slim "dogleg"-style jack, usually with a closed length of about 3-7/8", and made with a long clip or saber clip master blade and a pen blade. Some collectors refer to this pattern as a "slim dogleg," while it is also referred to as a "pen trapper," a more modern "collector" name for that pattern.

Many of the historic American cutlery companies produced the "slim dogleg" jack with clip and pen blades, including New York Knife Company, Miller Brothers, Schrade Cutlery Company, and Cattaraugus Cutlery Company. Maher & Grosh, a mail order firm, marketed this particular pattern for many years and had them made on contract. The "slim dogleg" jack in this configuration seemed to be a popular pattern as many early examples will be found with a variety of tang stamps.

At some point, some cutlery manufacturers began to produce another variation of the "slim dogleg" jack with a long spay blade as the secondary blade. This variation could be considered the forerunner to the more robust 54 trapper pattern. Early examples of the "slim dogleg" jack with the long spay secondary blade are scarce. I have seen examples made by Challenge Cutlery Company and by Empire Knife Company.

Case also made a "slim dogleg"-style knife (the 048 pattern) but it is not known whether this pattern precedes the 54 pattern in the Case line.

The earliest Case factory price list I have seen is from 1934. This price list includes the 3254 (yellow handles), the 6254 (stag handles), the 6254 (bone) and the 9254 (imitation pearl). The same four variations are shown in the 1941 price list, but the 9254 was listed as being discontinued.

I also have a copy of an unusual document with the title, *W.R. CASE & SONS BRADFORD PENNA. – ANALYSIS OF SALES 1937.* This typewritten document appears to show the patterns in production by Case at that time and the quantities of knives that were sold

This pattern, made by the Challenge Cutlery Company of Bridgeport, Connecticut, circa 1890s to 1930, is referred to as a "slim dogleg jack" or "pen trapper." I believe this pattern eventually evolved into the "trapper" pattern.

This early "Trapper" pattern was made by the Challenge Cutlery Company of Bridgeport, Connecticut, circa 1890 to 1930. This would be considered a forerunner to what we know as the modern 54 trapper pattern. Note the unusual shape of the long spay blade.

(in dozens) for that year. This document also lists the same four 54 pattern variations with the following quantities for each:

Case Analysis of Sales, 1937

Pattern	Quantity
3254	97-9/12 dozen
5254	51-8/12 dozen
6254	44-4/12 dozen
9254	13 dozen

Note the unusual method of reporting quantities at the time, in fractions of dozens. A similar document from 1938 lists the same four 54 patterns again with slightly lower quantities of each shown. An interesting note is that the highest selling pattern listed in the 1937 list was the 62009 1/2 "Barlow" with a sales figure of 1,276 dozen. These figures offer collectors today an idea of the relative rarity of these older 54 patterns as compared to other patterns in the Case line at the time.

Beginning in the late 1930s and into the post-WWII era, both Case and KABAR continued to make "Trapper" pattern pocket knives in similar "54" pat-

This STA-SHARP-marked trapper pattern, made by Camillus Cutlery Company for Sears circa 1940, is typical of the smaller frame trapper patterns that some companies manufactured beginning in the late 1930s and continuing into the 1960s and 1970s. While it is a trapper the tooling is significantly different from that of the Case 54 pattern.

tern tooling. The 1950s- to 1960s-era KABAR trappers continued to be made in the older style tooling that resembled the tooling of the Case Tested-era 54 pattern, with narrow blades and a narrow end bolster. During the period of the 1940s to the early 1950s, Case altered the tooling on the 54 pattern to produce a slightly heftier frame and a wider master blade, and the end bolster grew larger in several increments.

During this time, several other manufacturers, including Camillus and Schrade, began to offer "Trapper" patterns that seemed to be more refined versions of the old "slim dogleg" pattern. These patterns had handle shapes that were more similar to the 54 pattern but they were smaller, usually 3-7/8" in length. Western Cutlery also offered a "Trapper" pattern that was similar to the Case 54.

The "Trapper" pattern in general and the Case 54 in particular have achieved significant popularity in recent years among both collectors and users. Oddly enough, from the 1950s to the early 1970s, the "Trapper" was a bit of a "quiet" pattern. Of the ten or so major American manufacturers of quality pocket knives in the post-WWII era, about seven offered a version of the "Trapper." Each of these manufacturers offered a broad line of pocket knives at the time and the "Trapper" patterns while popular seemed to pale in comparison to the "stockman" pattern in terms of the variations offered and the sheer numbers sold.

During my early years of collecting Case pocket knives in the early to mid-1970s, the Case 54 pattern was not highly sought after as it is today. It had popularity among collectors, but seemingly no more or less so than other "named" patterns like the Muskrat, Moose, Copperhead, and Canoe. The "prestige" Case patterns in those days for collectors were mainly the large "folding hunter" patterns like the 65, the 050, and the 72, along with the 6250 Elephant Toe Nail pattern.

The 54 gained a lot of collector momentum beginning in the late 1970s. At that time, many variations of the pattern had been documented and the 54 pattern became the focus of a number of Case collectors. Due to its practical size, the 54 pattern became a knife that many knife clubs ordered with special handle materials and blade etches for use as limited edition annual releases. The large blades on the 54 pattern were ideal for etching. These many SFO variations fueled collector interest in the pattern.

Beginning in the 1970s and into the 1980s, tastes changed among the general "knife-using" public. Fewer people were carrying pocket knives and those who did were increasingly changing from the traditional patterns to the modern single-blade stainless steel lockback knives. Many cutlery companies, Case included, cut back on their lines of the older pocket knife patterns by the early 1980s. However, the "Trapper" pattern, in particular the Case 54, seemed to emerge as one of the favorite of the remaining older patterns and enjoyed a resurgence of popularity among knife users as some of the older jack and pen patterns disappeared from the market.

Blade and handle variations: The basic 54 "Trapper" pattern had traditionally always been made with a "California clip" as the master blade and a long spay as the secondary blade. During the Case XX era, the following principal "catalog" variations of the 54 pattern were made, each with the traditional blade configuration:

- 3254, with yellow composition handles.
- 5254, with stag handles.
- 6254, with bone handles.

In 1965, a new stainless steel version of the 54 pattern was introduced as part of a line of six stainless steel pocket knives introduced that year with the CASE XX USA tang stamping:

- 6254 SSP, with bone handles, glazed finished stainless steel blades with polished edges, main blade etched "TESTED XX RAZOR EDGE."

During the Case XX era, Case factory price lists beginning in 1949 and into the 1950s all show only the 3254 and the 5254. The 6254 does not appear in the price lists I have available from 1949 through 1957 but it shows up in the Sept. 1, 1958 price list. From that point on and into the Case XX USA era, all three are shown in every price list, with the 6254 SSP added as of the Feb. 1, 1965 price list. Given the popularity of the 54 pattern in recent years and the many variations produced, many Case collectors would be surprised to find out that these four were the only

Case XX USA 6254 SSP Trapper pattern main blade variations, from left: glazed finish main blade and polished main blade.

"standard product" 54 pattern variations in the Case line from 1965 until 1984.

The 3254 will be found with the CASE XX stamping with yellow composition handles but I have never observed an example with the older yellow celluloid (with white liner). Later examples made from the CASE XX era into the 1970s and to the present day will have yellow delrin handles. The 3254 has been in continuous production since the Case XX era and in recent years the 3254 with chrome vanadium blade steel has been the #1 selling pattern in the Case pocket knife line.

Production of the 5254 continued through the Case XX USA years and the pattern was discontinued in 1970 when Case stopped regular production of stag-handled pocket knives. In 1976, 1977, 1978 and 1981, Case made limited production runs of the 5254 with stag handles and with glazed finish stainless steel blades (5254 SSP) as part of annual stag collector's sets released during those years.

The bone-handled 54 pattern in the CASE XX stamping will be found in several of the Case XX era bone color variations including green bone, "regular" bone and red bone, as well as in "early Rogers" bone. I have never observed a Case XX 6254 handled in black.

The use of bone handles on the 6254 and the 6254 SSP continued through the Case XX USA era and into the 1970s. During the 1970s, delrin was substituted for bone on all Case bone-handled knives on a random basis. From 1972-1977, some examples of the 6254 and the 6254 SSP were handled in delrin, but delrin-handled "trappers" seem to be relatively scarce. My observation is that starting in 1978, the 6254 and the 6254 SSP were switched back to being handled 100 percent in bone.

The 6254 with chrome vanadium blades has remained in the Case product line up to the present day. All "generic" Case bone was dropped in 1996 and replaced with brown bone in the Case catalog descriptions. Then in 1997, the brown bone was changed to chestnut bone in the Case catalog. After 2000, the chestnut bone was replaced with amber bone. During these changes, the pattern number, 6254, and the product code number, 163, have remained the same.

The 6254 SSP also remained in the standard pocket

Case Tested 5254, "Trapper," 4-1/8", $6,000.

Case XX USA 9 Dot, 1971, 6254, Red Bone, 4-1/8", $150.

Case XX USA 7 Dot, 1973, 3254, 4-1/8", $100.

knife line and was gradually changed over to mirror finished stainless blades with no blade etching, and this pattern is still in the Case line today as the 6254 SS in amber bone. Case dropped the etching TESTED XX RAZOR EDGE on the 6254 SSP at some point in the late 1980s, but the glazed blade finish remained in use. In the mid-1990s, the "SSP" suffix was changed simply to "SS." Beginning in 1997, Case dropped the use of the glazed finished blades on the "premium" natural handled pocket knives in the Case line, so the blades on the 6254 SS were changed to the mirror polished finish.

On the 54 Trapper pattern, the bolster will often hide some or all of the dots, so it is easy to mistake a dotted 54 for a Case XX USA example. This 6254 SSP actually has three dots, but they are almost impossible to see.

Blade steel and liner material: The 54 pattern was offered only with chrome vanadium blade steel until 1965, when the first stainless steel version was put into production. From the Case XX era through the 1970s, the liner material for all of the 54 patterns was nickel silver. Beginning circa 1978, Case began changing all pocket knife patterns with nickel silver liners to the standard use of brass as the lining material. This change was complete by 1980.

Other variations: A number of variations in the 54 pattern knives made during the Case XX and the Case XX USA eras will be observed. These all seemed to be "random" manufacturing variations as the changes were never noted in catalogs. Unless otherwise noted, these variations will be found in the 54 patterns will all handle variations.

Frame style: As noted earlier, the Case Tested-era 54 patterns had a slightly slimmer frame and as compared to the later 54s, had a very narrow lower bolster. The Tested-era 54s also had relatively narrow blades and the master California clip blade would transition to an elegant narrow point.

During the Case XX era, the 54 pattern tooling was

Case 5254, "Case Brothers" stamping, 4-1/8", $225. Note: SFO knife made in 1992; no pattern number stamped.

Case 6254, "Case Brothers" stamping, 4-1/8", $150. Note: SFO knife made in 1992; no pattern number stamped.

Case XX 3254, yellow composition, "first model," 4-1/8", $350.

gradually changed to a slightly beefier frame shape, with the blades slightly wider and the main blade having less of a "needle" point. The lower bolster also became significantly longer meaning a shorter handle material slab was required. However, some Case XX-stamped 54 patterns will be found made with the older Tested-era tooling. Collectors refer to these knives as having a "Tested Frame," and these knives are very rare.

Case XX-era 54 pattern trappers with the newer XX-era tooling were made in two variations. The earlier version is referred to by collectors as the "First Model XX" and these knives will have a slightly narrower bolster as compared to later XX-era 54 patterns. This is only a small difference in bolster width, not the significant difference seen when comparing the Tested-era 54 with the XX and later 54 patterns.

I have measured the bolsters on a few of my XX-era 54 patterns and the difference in width seems to be about 1/32 of an inch. I have measured some XX 54s and found the lower bolster width to be 11/32", while others measure 3/8". I also measured the lower bolster on some Case XX USA- and 1970s-era 54 patterns and found them to be 7/16" wide. So apparently the lower bolsters continued to grow. By comparison, the Tested frame has a lower bolster width of 9/32" (based on one example that I measured).

Rare handle materials: Some Case XX-era 6254 patterns will be found in "early Rogers" bone and some 5254s will be found in red stag. Both of these handle materials are rare and desirable on Case 54s. Some XX and USA era 3254s will have "flat yellow" handles, which are scarce. CASE XX USA-stamped 54 patterns will be found in "second-cut" stag handles. These variations are also rare. Some second cut stag was used on 5254s; this material will have a yellow color; 6254s were also made in second-cut stag which was dyed a reddish or wine color.

"Muskrat" master blade: A relatively small number of 54 patterns with the CASE XX USA tang stamping will be found with what collectors refer to as a "muskrat" master blade. While all 54 patterns were made with a "California clip" master blade, the "muskrat"-style blade was slightly narrower. The

Case XX 6254, red bone, 4-1/8", $750.

Case XX 5254, 4-1/8", $900.

Case XX 5254, 4-1/8", $900.

variation is subtle and best detected by a comparison of the blade edge and where it meets the tang, at the "choil." On a "muskrat" blade, the choil will be further back on the tang.

The use of the "muskrat" master blade on the 54 pattern was evidently a random tooling variation as this blade style was never cataloged in Case factory catalogs or price lists. Collectors should be wary since sometimes a used 54 pattern master blade will have the appearance of a "muskrat" blade due to blade wear.

6254 SSP variations: When Case introduced the SSP line of stainless steel pocket knives in 1965, there were a number of variations made early on before the final configurations were adopted. The Case factory catalog from the era shows the 6254 SSP as having glazed finish blades with the main blade etched lengthwise with "TESTED XX RAZOR EDGE." This is the "basic" and most common variation of the 6254 SSP and the knife was made this way from the Case XX USA era and into the 1970s. On these knives, that pattern number 6254 SSP will be on the spay blade.

Some scarce variations of the 6254 SSP with the CASE XX USA stamping include mirror polished, rather than glazed, blades, and the alternate etching CASE XX STAINLESS. While the 6254 SSP was made as standard with concave ground blades, I have observed sporadic examples with flat ground blades made from the Case XX USA era into the 1970s.

Newer variations: In 1984, Case reintroduced stag as a "standard product" handle material and a new 5254 SS was included as one of the six patterns introduced. These knives were initially introduced with "jigged stag" handles. This was a new stag variation for Case and it resembled "second cut" stag but with a tighter and more consistent jig pattern. The "jigged stag" only lasted for about two years then Case went back to the use of traditionally processed stag.

The 5254 SS with polished stainless blades has remained in the Case pocket knife line until the present day, with the exception of a few years after 2000 when stag was again embargoed. A 5254 CV in chrome vanadium was also introduced in 1997 as a catalog product. This represented the first production of a Case stag "Trapper" in chrome vanadium since 1970; however,

Case XX 5254, red stag, 4-1/8", $2,000. Note: the spay blade on this knife was reshaped by a previous owner.

Case XX USA 3254, 4-1/8", $100.

Case XX USA 5254, 4-1/8", $250.

the pattern was discontinued after 1998.

In 1989-1990, Case produced the 5254 and the 6254, with new style "Rogers bone" handles, with Damascus steel blades. These were part of a line of 24 Damascus-bladed patterns introduced in 1989 that represented Case's first use of Damascus steel.

In the late 1970s and through the 1980s, Case produced a virtually countless number of 54 patterns as SFO releases.

Many of these were made as annual club knives for individual knife clubs or as private label SFO releases. Case used a wide variety of handle materials on these SFO "Trappers" including stag, various bone colors, pearl, and synthetics.

Beginning in 1991, Case began to add many 54 pattern variations to the standard product line. Some of these were in production for only a year or two; so many scarce variations can be found (see chart below).

Case XX USA 5254, "Muskrat" blade, 4-1/8", $900.

Case 54 Trapper Pattern - 1990's Standard "Catalog" Variations Introduced 1991-2000

Note - "Last Year Offered" is shown only for those patterns that were discontinued before 2000.

Pattern	Handle		Year Introduced	Last Year Offered
DR 6254 SS	Dark Red Bone		1991	1998
7254 SS	Curly Maple		1991	1993
LT 254 SS	Lightweight Thermoplastic	Caliber Series	1992	1996
9254 SS	Imitation Pearl		1992	1993
I254 SS	Imitation Ivory		1992	1993
7254 SS	Rosewood		1993	1994
2254 SS	Smooth Black		1993	1995
PW 6254 SS	Old Red Bone	Pocket Worn	1996	
6254 SS	Purple Bone		1996	1998
8254 SS	Pearl		1996	
R5254 SS	Red Stag		1996	1998
5254 CV	Stag	Chrome Vanadium	1997	1998
PW 6254 SS	Classic Green Bone	Pocket Worn	1998	
V5254 HB SS	Vintage Stag	Hobo Pattern	1999	
6254 HB SS	Chestnut Bone	Hobo Pattern	1999	
6254 HB SS	Natural Bone	Hobo Pattern	2000	
7254 HB SS	Rosewood	Hobo Pattern	2000	

Case XX USA 6254 SSP, bone, satin finish blades, 4-1/8", $275.

In the years since 2000, Case has produced the 54 "Trapper" in many additional new bone colors and jig patterns, and some new blade configurations.

All of the standard product catalog variations of the 54, combined with numerous SFOs in this pattern, combine for a truly mind boggling array of Case "Trappers." All of the new knives SFOs combined with all of the older 54 pattern variations that have been documented, would together fill a volume larger than this book.

Case XX USA 6254 SSP, red bone, polished blades, 4-1/8", $350.

Case XX USA 6254, second cut bone, 4-1/8", $1,000.

Back of the 6254 second cut bone Trapper.

Case XX USA 10 Dot, 1970, 3254, 4-1/8", $125.

Case XX USA 9 Dot, 1971, 6254 SSP, bone, small stamp, 4-1/8", $150.

Case XX USA 10 Dot, 1970, 6254, 4-1/8", $225.

Case XX USA 8 Dot, 1972, 6254 SSP, bone, large stamp, 4-1/8", $250.

Case XX USA 9 Dot, 1971, 6254, dark red bone, 4-1/8", $150.

Back of the 6254.

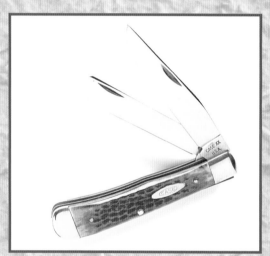

Case XX USA 6 Dot, 1974, 6254, red bone, 4-1/8", $125.

Case XX USA 6 Dot, 1974, 6254, Delrin, 4-1/8", $90.

Case XX USA 3 Dot, 1977, 5254 SSP, "blue scroll," 4-1/8", $140.

Case XX USA 7 Dot, 1983, 6254 SS, bone, 4-1/8", $125. Note: Has new grind.

Back of the 6254 SS.

Case Long Tail C, 1998 Stamp, 6254 SS, chestnut bone, 4-1/8", $50.

Case XX USA 10 Dot, 1980, lightning S, 6254, bone, 4-1/8", $90.

Case XX USA 1 Dot, 1989, lightning S, 5254 SS, 4-1/8", $80.

Case 1995 stamp, 6254 SS, "antique bone," 4-1/8", $60.

Case XX USA 2 Dot, 1978, 6254 bone, 4-1/8", $100.

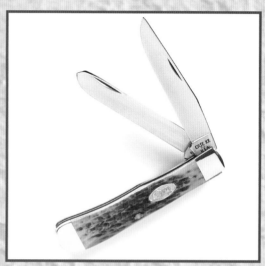

Case XX USA 3 Dot, 1987, lightning S, 6254, bone, 4-1/8", $75.

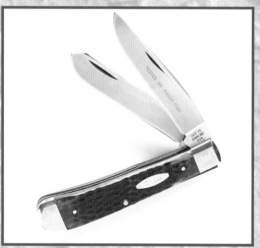

Case XX USA 2 Dot, 1978, 6254 SSP, bone with light edges, 4-1/8", $100.

Case XX USA 4 Dot, 1986, lightning S, 6254 SSP, bone, 4-1/8", $75. Note the small case oval shield.

Case XX USA 3 Dot, 1977, 6254 SSP, red bone, 4-1/8", $125.

Case XX USA 5 Dot, 1975, 6254, red bone, 4-1/8", $125.

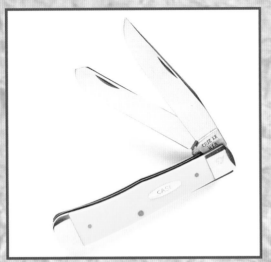

Case XX USA 5 Dot, 1985, lightning S, 3254, 4-1/8", $75.

Case XX USA 6 Dot, 1984, 6254, new grind, 4-1/8", $125.

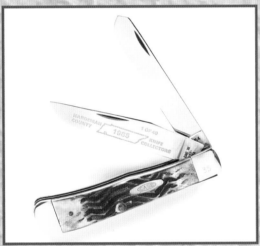

Case XX USA 5 Dot, 1985, lightning S, 5254 SS, "jigged stag" handles, 4-1/8", $150.

Case XX USA 6 Dot, 1984, lightning S, 6254 SSP, 4-1/8", $100.

Case XX USA 5 Dot, 1985, Lightning S, 7254 SS, curly maple, 4-1/8", $75.

Case XX USA 7 Dot, 1983, lightning S, 6254 SSP, new grind, 4-1/8", $150.

Case XX USA 7 Dot, 1983, lightning S, 6254, 4-1/8", $100.

Case XX USA 8 Dot, 1982, lightning S, 6254 SSP, red bone, 4-1/8", $100. Note: This was an SFO overrun.

Case XX USA 7 Dot, 1983, lightning S, 6254 SSP, 4-1/8", $100.

Case XX USA 9 Dot, 1981, lightning S, 6254, 4-1/8", $100.

Case XX USA 8 Dot, 1972, 6254 SSP, dark reddish bone, 4-1/8", $125.

Case XX USA New-1998 stamping, 6254 SS, red bone, 4-1/8", $55.

PATTERN 055

The basic pattern: The 055 pattern is a "cigar" jack knife, with two blades and two backsprings. Closed length is 3-1/2". The 055 pattern goes back to the Case Tested era and earlier and is a "capped" jack knife, meaning there are bolsters at each end of the knife. The 055 pattern is sometimes referred to by collectors as the "small cigar."

Blade and handle variations: During the Case XX era, the following principal variations of the 052 pattern were made:

- 22055, with smooth black handles, clip master blade and pen blade.
- 62055, with bone handles, clip master blade and pen blade.

The 62055 in the CASE XX stamping will be found in several of the Case XX-era bone color variations including green, regular and red, and in rough black. Based on older Case factory price lists, it appears that the 22055 was discontinued as of Jan. 1, 1967.

The use of bone handles on the 62055 continued into the 1970s. During the 1970s, delrin was substituted for bone on the 62055 on a random basis. The 62055 was discontinued as of Nov. 1, 1978.

Blade steel and liner material: From the XX era through the time the pattern was discontinued, all 055 patterns were only offered with chrome vanadium as the blade steel. The liner material during these years was brass.

Other variations: Some 055 patterns with the CASE XX tang stamping were made with a "long pull" nail pull on the master clip blade. These examples were made early in the Case XX era and are fairly rare.

The 055 pattern was also produced as a "junior cattle knife" with three and four blades. The 23055 P with clip, spay, and punch blades and the 64055 with four blades were both produced during the Case XX era. These patterns are quite rare and were apparently only produced for a short period during the XX years. The 055 cigar pattern has never been reintroduced. Case has introduced a new pattern, the Seahorse Whittler, using the 055 pattern number.

Case XX 22055, "small cigar jack," 3-1/2", $90.

Case XX 62055, bone, 3-1/2", $100. *Back of the 62055.*

Case XX 23055P, "junior cattle knife," 3-1/2", $350. Note: Rare variation not shown in XX era catalogs or price lists.

Case Tested 64055P, "junior cattle knife," green bone, 3-1/2", $600.

PATTERN 58 AND 59

The basic patterns: The 58 and the 59 patterns are modern lockback pattern knives both introduced into the Case line in 1978. The P197 L SSP Shark Tooth, introduced in 1975, was the first modern stainless steel lockback in the Case product line. Case built upon the success of the Shark Tooth with the introduction of the 58 and 59 lockback knives in 1978:

- P158 L SSP, with glazed finish stainless steel clip blade and smooth black Pakkawood handles, 4-1/4" closed length.
- P159 L SSP, with glazed finish stainless steel blade and smooth black Pakkawood handles, 5" closed length.

The P158 L SSP was dubbed the "Mako" and the blade was etched with MAKO inset into a shark. The P159 L SSP was dubbed the "Hammerhead" and the blade was etched with HAMMERHEAD inset into a shark. These two new knives, along with the P197 L SSP Shark Tooth, gave Case a trio of "shark"-themed lockback folding knives.

The new Mako and Hammerhead were each configured with a clip point blade with a long nail pull. Each was designed with a brass frame with the CASE logo engraved in the brass bolster. Each knife was sold with a leather belt sheath and individually gift boxed.

The Hammerhead was the same size and style as the Shark Tooth and the two knives shared the same master blade, with only the blade etching changed. The difference is that the brass frame on the Shark Tooth was contoured and rounded for comfort while the frame on the Hammerhead was flat with no contouring. The Mako was a smaller knife with some rounding of the edges of the frame and handles.

Variations: After a few years of production, the P159 L SSP Hammerhead was discontinued (1981) and a new version of the knife was introduced:

- 2159 L SSP, with glazed finish stainless steel blade (no etch) and smooth black delrin handles, 5" closed length.

The 2159 L SSP was introduced in 1981. I believe that the changes to the pattern were made to reduce the retail price of the knife. The suggested retail price

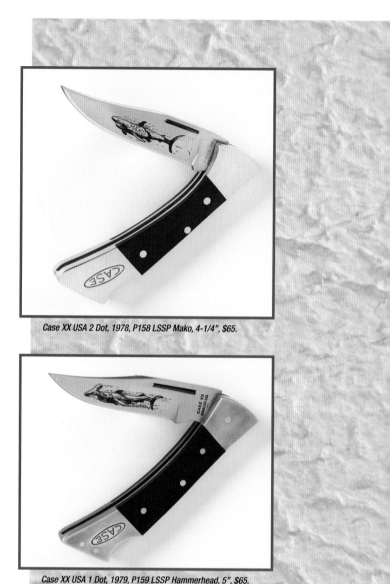

Case XX USA 2 Dot, 1978, P158 LSSP Mako, 4-1/4", $65.

Case XX USA 1 Dot, 1979, P159 LSSP Hammerhead, 5", $65.

for the P159 L SSP Hammerhead at the time that it was discontinued was $55. (Source: Case factory price list October 1981). The following excerpt is from the *Case Collectors Club Newsletter* from September 1981:

The 2159L SSP is another addition to the Case Lock-Back line of knives. The 2159L SSP will be much like the Hammerhead (P159LSSP) with the exception of the handle material, blade and price. The handle is a smooth black plastic and the blade, although the same type as the Hammerhead, has no nail mark or etching. Our sales reps have been instructed to start taking orders for these knives. The suggested retail price is $35.

Another variation to note is that the P158 L SSP Mako was originally designed and manufactured with three brass handle pins. At some point, the design was changed

PATTERN 61

to eliminate the handle pins, with the handle material glued on. I have observed both variations with the 1983 tang stamping, so it is possible that the change was made during that year. The Mako is still in the Case line today and still made without handle pins.

The initial design of the blade on the 2159 L SSP included a semicircle cutout on the tang of the blade to facilitate placement of the index finger for "choking up" on the blade during use. In 1991, the blade design was changed to a more conventional squared off design. The 2159 L SSP has always shared its main blade designs with the P197 L SSP Shark Tooth.

The 2159 L SSP has continued to be part of the Case line until the present day. In the time period of 1984-1986, the blade design was changed back to include the long nail pull. Beginning in 1996, Case returned the HAMMERHEAD etching to the main blade of the 2159 L SSP.

Limited production runs of stag-handled versions of both knives, 5158 L SSP and 5159 L SSP, were made from 1979-1981.

The basic pattern: The 61 pattern goes back to the early years of Case and is a small senator or equal end penknife, constructed with a single backspring and blade at each end. The 61 pattern has "tip" bolsters. Closed length is 2-7/8".

The 61 pattern has always been made with a spear master blade and cuticle blade. During the Case XX era, the following principal variations of the 61 pattern were made:

- 8261, with pearl handles.
- 9261, with imitation pearl handles.

The 9261 in the CASE XX stamping will be found with both the older "cracked ice" imitation pearl handles and with "regular" imitation pearl. Cracked ice was not used on the 9261 after the CASE XX era so later examples made from the CASE XX USA era and into the 1970s will have "regular" imitation pearl handles.

The 9261 was discontinued in mid-1974. The 8261 was produced into the 1970s. Genuine pearl-handled pocket knives were not listed in Case factory catalogs or price lists from about 1967 through the 1970s even though they were in production. Based on my observations, I believe that the 8261 was discontinued circa 1974.

From the XX era through the time that the pattern was discontinued in the 1970s, all 61 patterns were only offered with chrome vanadium as the blade steel. The liner material during these years was nickel silver. One unusual aspect of the 61 pattern is that it was the only modern (post-WWII) Case pocket knife pattern that included the cuticle blade.

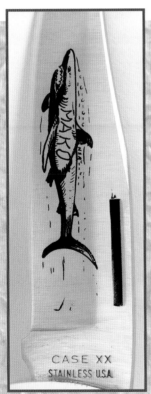

"Mako" blade etching on P159 L SSP.

"Hammerhead" blade etching on P159 LSSP.

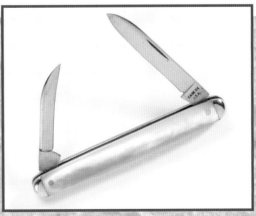

Case XX USA 7 Dot, 1973, 8261, 2-7/8", $75.

PATTERN 63

The basic pattern: The 63 pattern is a pen knife that has been made in two different designs. It is an example of a pattern where two distinctly different design variations were differentiated by the placement of "zeros" in the pattern number. I will use bone-handled models as an example to illustrate the pattern differences.

The 06263 is a "senator" or equal-end pen knife style with a spear master blade and pen blade operating on a single backspring. The 06263 has a closed length of 3-1/8" and distinctive elongated bolsters. This pattern is similar to the 79 pen knife pattern in that both are of the senator style and have a closed length of 3-1/8". The differences are the elongated bolsters on the 63 pattern and the fact that the 79 pattern is "flatter" in terms of the handle shape, while the 63 pattern has handles that are more rounded.

Many collectors refer to the "senator" style of the 63 pattern pen knife as the *Eisenhower*. The story goes that president Dwight D. Eisenhower favored this pattern and purchased them to give as gifts. Beginning in the 1990s, Case adopted the *Eisenhower* name for the 63 senator pattern and most examples manufactured since that time have had a facsimile of president Eisenhower's signature as a blade etching.

The second Case 63 pattern variation is a small two-blade "sleeveboard" pen knife pattern made with a clip master blade at one end and a pen blade at the other end. This pattern has a closed length of 3-1/16". This variation of the 63 pen knife pattern has a zero in the middle of the pattern number (example: 62063 1/2).

Blade and handle variations: During the Case XX era, the following principal variations of the 63 and 063 were made:

- 05263 senator pen knife pattern with stag handles, spear master blade and secondary pen blade.
- 05263 SS with stag handles, polished stainless steel spear master blade and secondary pen blade.
- 06263 senator pen knife pattern with bone handles, spear master blade and secondary pen blade.
- 06263 SS with bone handles, polished stainless steel spear master blade and secondary pen blade.
- 06263 F SS senator pen knife with bone handles, polished stainless steel spear master blade and secondary long file blade.
- 62063 1/2 sleeveboard pen knife pattern with bone handles, polished stainless steel clip master blade and

Case XX 62063-1/2, green bone, 3-1/16", $200.

Case XX 05263 SS, 3-1/8", $140.

Case XX 06263, red bone, 3-1/8", $275. Note: Early XX era version with chrome vanadium blades.

Back of the 06263.

secondary pen blade.

- 62063 1/2 SS sleeveboard pen knife pattern with bone handles, polished stainless steel clip master blade and secondary pen blade.
- 82063 Shad SS sleeveboard pen knife, polished stainless steel spear master blade and secondary pen blade, made as a "shadow" pattern with no bolsters.

In 1965, an additional stainless steel version of the 06263 pattern was introduced as part of a line of six stainless steel pocket knives introduced that year with the CASE XX USA tang stamping:

- 06263 SSP, with bone handles, spear master blade and pen blade. Glazed finished stainless steel blades with polished edges; main blade etched, "TESTED XX RAZOR EDGE."

Circa 1971, a second version of the 06263 SSP was introduced:

- 06263 F SSP, with bone handles, spear master blade and secondary long file blade. Glazed finished stainless steel blade with polished edge; spear blade etched "TESTED XX RAZOR EDGE."

The 05263, 06263 and 62063 1/2 in the Case XX era were all made with both chrome vanadium and stainless steel as the blade material. Based on a review of available Case factory catalogs and price lists, it appears that chrome vanadium was the only blade steel choice offered on these three knives from the first use of the CASE XX tang stamp until the mid-1950s. By about 1955, the blade steel for all three patterns had been changed over to stainless steel. It appears that the 82063 SHAD and the 06263 F were only offered in stainless steel.

The 05263 SS with stainless steel blades was made through the Case XX and Case XX USA eras and into 1970. In mid-1970, the 05263 SS pattern was discontinued when Case stopped regular production of stag-handled pocket knives. During these years, the 05263 SS was made with a polished finish on the blades.

The 06263 and the 62063 1/2 in the CASE XX stamping will be found in several of the Case XX-era bone color variations including green, regular and red. I do not believe the 63 patterns were made in rough black. The 06263 F SS was introduced in 1961 and will be found in red and regular bone. The 62063 1/2

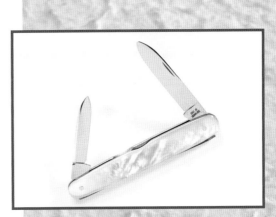

Case XX 82063 S SS "shadow," 3-1/16", $125.

Case XX USA 10 Dot, 1980, lightning S, 05263 R SSP, 3-1/8", $65.

Case XX USA 6 Dot, 1984, lightning S, 05263 SSP, 3-1/8", $55.

Case XX USA 7 Dot, 1973, 06263 SSP, bone, 3-1/8", $60.

SS was discontinued as of Jan. 1, 1966. The 62063 1/2 pattern has never been reintroduced.

The 82063 SHAD SS was discontinued as of Jan. 1, 1966; however, it is believed none were made with the CASE XX USA tang stamping.

The 06263 SS and the 06263 F SS with polished finish stainless steel blades were replaced with the 06263 SSP and the 06263 F SSP with glazed finish stainless steel blades. There was a period of a few years where the 06263 SS with polished blades and 06263 SSP with glazed blades were both offered. The 06263 SS was discontinued in 1971; production of the 06263 SSP continued into the 1980s. The 06263 F SS was transitioned to the 06263 F SSP circa 1971 and this pattern was discontinued as of May 1, 1974.

The use of bone handles on the 06263 SSP continued into the 1970s. During the 1970s, delrin was substituted for bone on the 06263 SSP on a random basis. Beginning in 1978, it appears that Case began handling the 06263 SSP 100 percent in delrin. The 06263 SSP was discontinued in 1985.

Blade steel and liner material: See above for a discussion of the use of stainless steel and chrome vanadium on the 63 pattern. The liner material for the 63 patterns up until the late 1970s was nickel silver. Beginning circa 1978, Case began changing all pocket knife patterns with nickel silver liners to the standard use of brass as the lining material. This change was complete by 1980.

Newer variations: A new version of the 63 pattern was reintroduced in 1980 as part of the Gentlemen's Line. The following variation was introduced:

- 05263 R SSP, a single clip blade with stag handles (no shield) and a bail.

This knife had stainless steel blades with a glazed finish and brass liners. The Gentlemen's Line knives were only made for a few years. However, the 05263 SSP was kept in the Case pocket knife line into the 1980s; the bail was dropped in 1982. In 1987, Case dropped the 05263 SSP and added the 05263 SS with polished stainless steel blades and a shield to the line.

Beginning in the 1990s, Case introduced many additional variations of the 63 "Eisenhower" pattern. In 1996, both red bone-handled and stag-handled versions were introduced with the Eisenhower signature blade etching. The "Eisenhower" pattern has since been offered in many different handle materials with polished stainless steel blades.

PATTERN 64

The basic pattern: The 64 pattern is a "senator" or equal end pen knife pattern with a closed length of 3-1/8". It has a somewhat wide frame and was generally made with tip bolsters. During the Case Tested era, the 64 pattern was made as a two-blade pen knife in several handle materials (pearl, imitation pearl, bone) and with both a pen and file as secondary blade variations. The 64 pattern in those years was also offered in three blades.

Blade and handle variations: During the Case XX era, the following principal variations of the 64 senator pen knife pattern were made:

- 8364 T SS senator pen knife pattern with pearl handles, spear master blade and secondary long file blade and pen blade.
- 8364 Scis SS senator pen knife pattern with pearl handles, spear master blade and secondary long file blade scissors.

Both of the above knives were made with tip bolsters although the "T" suffix for indication of tip bolsters does not appear on the pattern number for the scissors variation. The 8364 T SS was discontinued in 1961.

The 8364 Scis SS was produced into the 1970s. Genuine pearl-handled pocket knives were not listed in Case factory catalogs or price lists from about 1967 through the 1970s even though they were in production. Based on my observations, I believe that the 8364 Scis SS was discontinued in 1973.

Liner material: The standard liner material for the 64 patterns up until the time the 8364 Scis SS was discontinued in the 1970s was nickel silver.

Newer variations: The 64 pattern has never been reintroduced.

Case Tested 9264T, cracked ice, 3-1/8", $100.

Case XX USA 7 Dot, 1973, 8364 Scis SS, 3-1/8", $125.

PATTERN 65

The basic pattern: The 65 pattern is the classic Case "folding hunter" and is a large jack knife pattern made in both one-blade and two-blade variations. The pattern was widely produced beginning in the Case Tested era and a few examples have been seen with the CASE BRADFORD tang stamping.

From the early years of its production and up into the 1970s, the basic two-blade version, the 6265 SAB, was popular with knife users and produced in large quantities. I recall hearing that in the mid-1970s, Case produced the 6265 SAB in quantities approaching 200,000 per year and for a number of years, it was the number-one-selling Case pocket knife pattern.

Blade and handle variations: The 65 pattern has always had a clip as the main blade. Two-blade versions have always had a skinner blade as the secondary blade. During the Case XX era, the following principal variations were made:

- 5165 with stag handles, single clip blade.
- 5265 with stag handles, master clip blade and skinner blade.
- 6165 with bone handles, single clip blade.
- 6265 with bone handles, master clip blade and skinner blade.

The above knives were all made with chrome vanadium as the only blade steel option. In 1972, a stainless steel version of the 6265 was introduced:

- 6265 SAB Dr SSP with jigged brown Pakkawood handles, glazed finish stainless steel master clip blade and skinner blade.

In 1977, a stainless steel lockback version of the 6165 was introduced:

- 6165 SAB Dr L SSP with jigged brown Pakkawood handles, and glazed finish stainless steel master clip blade.

The 5165 SAB DR was discontinued as of Jan. 1, 1966. The 5165 SAB DR was made with the CASE XX USA tang stamping but this knife is quite rare. The 5265 SAB DR was made through the Case XX and the Case XX USA eras and into 1970. In mid-1970, the 5265 pattern was discontinued when Case stopped regular production of stag-handled pocket knives. The 5265 was later brought back with stainless steel blades, 5265 SAB SSP, for inclusion in the 1976 and

Case XX 6265 SAB, "Folding Hunter," red bone, 5-1/4", $450.

Case XX 6165 SAB, red bone, 5-1/4", $450. Note: This is a used knife which has been polished.

Case XX 5265 SAB, red stag, 5-1/4", $600.

1977 annual limited production stag sets.

The 6165 and 6265 in the CASE XX stamping will be found in several of the Case XX-era bone color variations including green, regular and red, as well as rough black. The use of bone handles on the 6165 and the 6265 continued into the 1960s. During the CASE XX and CASE XX USA eras, jigged laminated wood, or Pakkawood, was substituted for bone on the 65 patterns on a random basis.

It is believed the 6165 and 6265 patterns were changed over to being handled in Pakkawood 100 percent at some point early in the CASE XX USA era. It is rare to see a CASE XX USA-stamped 6165 or 6265 in genuine bone, though some were produced. After that point and into the 1970s, Pakkawood was used 100 percent on all standard production 6165 and 6265 patterns.

The 6165 SAB DR L SSP was made through the 1970s and into the 1980s and discontinued as of 1990. The 6265 SAB with chrome vanadium blade steel was also discontinued as of 1990. The 6265 SAB SS with glazed finish stainless steel blades has remained in the Case product line up to the present day.

Liner material: The liner material for all standard production 65 patterns from the Case XX era onward has been brass.

Other variations: A number of variations in the 65 pattern will be observed. Some of these were intended manufacturing changes or product variations, while others were "random" manufacturing variations. Unless otherwise noted here, these variations will be found in both single-bladed and double-bladed 65 patterns and in both bone- and stag-handled versions.

Master blade grind: Some early Case XX-era examples of the 65 pattern will be found with flat ground master blades. All Case XX-era price lists that I have observed from 1940 to 1965 consistently list the 65 patterns with the SAB suffix indicating the saber ground master blade. Therefore, it is probable that the use of the flat blade was for knives on special order or was a "random" manufacturing variation. The flat ground master blade was not used after the Case XX era.

Drilled bolster: The 65 pattern is well known as one of the few Case pocket knife patterns that has the lower bolster drilled to accept a lanyard. Early XX-era variations of the 65 pattern did not have drilled bolsters. It appears based on a review of Case catalogs that the manufacturing

Case XX 5265, Flat Ground, 5-1/4", $750.

Case XX 6265, folding hunter, serrated edge, 5-1/4", $800. Note: Skinner blade etching says, "New Miracle Edge Elto Skinner Dog Supply House."

Case XX USA 3 Dot, 1977, 5265 SAB SSP, "blue scroll," 5-1/4", $150.

change to the drilled lower bolster was made in the late Case XX era. From that point on and for many years, all 65 patterns were made with the drilled lower bolster, with the exception of the 1976 and 1977 limited-production stag handled 5265 models. In the early 1980s, a manufacturing change was made and the drilled bolster was dropped from the 65 pattern, as explained in this excerpt from the *Case Collector's Club Newsletter* of December 1982:

Production Changes – *'65 SAB* – *A production change has just been ordered that will eliminate the Lanyard Hole on the 65 (Folding Hunter) patterns. The first knives without the hole will probably be on the market by February or March.*

A survey indicated that this pattern was carried mainly in a belt sheath and that the Lanyard Hole was a functional feature. The removal of the Lanyard Hole will not affect the functionability, strength or durability of the knife in any way.

Frame change: The 65 pattern frame style was changed in the mid-1960s. The older frame style has an extended bolster at the blade end, and is referred to by collectors as the "XX frame." In about 1965, the frame style was changed so that the raised hump on the front bolster was eliminated, leaving the pattern with a more gradual transition from handle to bolster. This change apparently took some time to complete, as there are examples of the 65 pattern found with the older "XX" frame and with CASE XX USA-stamped blades. These USA 65 patterns with the "XX" frame are scarce.

Serrated edge skinner blade: During the 1960s and into the 1970s, some 6265 SAB patterns were made with serrations on the edge of the skinner blade. Case used its "Miracl-Edge" process, normally used only for kitchen cutlery, to produce the serrated edges. These knives were made on contract as special factory order knives. My understanding is that they were initially designed and produced for the Dog Supply Company of Detroit, Michigan. After a few years, the Dog Supply Company was purchased by the Bill Boatman Company of Bainbridge, Ohio.

Case continued to make these knives on special order for the Bill Boatman Company until the late 1970s. The knives made for each of the two companies were etched with the company name as part of the blade etching on the skinner blade. The Bill Boatman Company marked knives are rare, and the earlier Dog Supply Company knives are rarer still. In 1991, Case modified the standard production

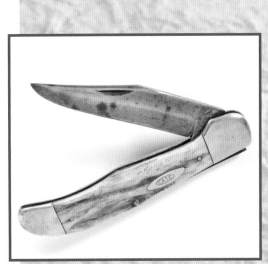

Case XX 5165 SAB, 5-1/4", $400.

Case XX 6165, flat ground bone, 5-1/4", $450.

Case XX USA 1 Dot, 1979, 6165 SAB DR, Pakkawood, 5-1/4", $80.

Serrated skinner blade, typical for the 6265 SAB pattern knives that were made on special order for the Dog Supply Company and the Bill Boatman Company.

6265 SAB SS to include serrations on the skinner blade. This was continued for several years; then in 1993, the plain blade and serrated blade versions were brought back. After that the serrated skinner blade version seemed to be offered sporadically as a standard product knife but the 6265 SAB SS with Pakkawood handles has remained in production until the present day as part of the "Working Knives" series.

Bails: I have observed one example of a Case XX 6265 SAB with a factory-installed bail. This particular knife was part of an intact Case counter display and still wired to the display board just as it had left the Case factory. Since this variation, 6265 SAB R, was never shown in any Case catalog or price list, I believe it was an option offered as a special factory order for individual retailers. I have a copy of a Case factory sheet from 1966 that lists sales aids available. One of the items listed on the sheet is that a "shackle" (bail) could be added to any pocket knife pattern on special order for $0.50 per knife, with a minimum order of 1/3 dozen knives. This would explain the custom bail installation on the 6265 SAB and on other Case XX-era pocket knives.

Mariner's Knife Set: During the Case XX era, Case introduced the Mariner's Knife Set that included a 6265 SAB folding hunter with a separate stainless steel marlin spike and a leather belt sheath designed to hold the knife and spike. The set first appeared in the September 1959 Case factory price list (Catalog #67). It then seems to disappear but appears again in the price lists for Catalog #70 (1967). From this point on, it was offered every year. In 1973 or 1974, a second set was added, the Mariner's Set SS. This set included the (then newly introduced) 6265 SAB SS.

The 6265 SAB folding hunters that were included in the Mariner's Knife Sets were not specially marked, so if an intact set is found it is impossible to tell whether the knife that is included is original to the set. Both Mariner's Knife Sets were still in production in 1982. The chrome vanadium set was discontinued as of Sept. 1, 1983, and the Mariner's Knife Set SS was discontinued in 1985.

Case XX USA 10 Dot, 1980, lightning S, 6165 LSSP, Pakkawood, 5-1/4", $80.

Case XX USA 4 Dot, 1976, 5165 SSP, "Bicentennial Knife," 5-1/4", $225.

Case XX USA 8 Dot, 1972, 6265 SAB DR, Pakkawood, 5-1/4", $100.

PATTERN 67

The basic pattern: The 67 pattern is a "swell-center" or "balloon center" pen knife, with a closed length of 3-1/4" and goes back to the early years of Case. During the Case Tested years and earlier, the 67 pattern was made in both two- and three-blade variations and in bone and various celluloid handle materials.

Beginning with the CASE XX tang stamp after WWII, the 67 pattern was made only as a pen knife, with a clip master blade and a pen blade operating on one backspring, and pattern number 06267. The 06267 was produced during the Case XX era in several bone handle variations including green bone, red bone, and "regular" bone, and in rough black.

Most if not all of the CASE XX stamped 06267 patterns will be found with a long nail pull on the master clip blade. By the Case XX USA era, the long pull was eliminated and the main blade tooling was changed to a slightly modified clip blade shape with a regular nail pull. The 06267 was discontinued as of April 1, 1967. Since this was in the middle of the Case XX USA era, examples of the 06267 with the CASE XX USA tang stamping are relatively rare.

Newer variations: The 67 pattern has never been reintroduced.

PATTERN 69

The basic pattern: The 69 pattern is a "congress" pen knife, with a closed length of 3", and goes back to the early years of Case. Beginning with the CASE XX tang stamp after WWII, the 69 pattern was made only as a pen knife, with a sheepfoot master blade and a pen blade operating on one backspring, and pattern number 6269. The 6269 was produced during the Case XX era in several bone handle variations including green, red and regular, and in rough black.

The use of bone handles on the 6269 continued into the 1970s. During the 1970s, delrin was substituted for bone on the 6269 on a random basis. The 6269 was discontinued as of Nov. 1, 1978. During all years of production from the Case XX era until the time it was discontinued, the only blade steel offered on the 6269 was chrome vanadium. The standard liner material was nickel silver during the Case XX era, but later catalogs from 1968 through 1974 list the 6269 as having brass liners. Oddly enough, the 1977 catalog indicates that the pattern had nickel silver liners.

Newer variations: The 69 pattern has never been reintroduced. Case introduced a different pattern of small congress knife, the 68 pattern, which has been widely produced in recent years in both two- and four-blade variations and in various handle materials.

Case XX 06267, red bone, long pull, 3-1/4", $200.

Case XX 6269, "Small Congress," rough black, 3", $150.

Case XX USA, 06267, red bone, regular pull, 3-1/4", $150.

Case XX 6269, red bone, 3", $225.

PATTERN 71

The basic pattern: The 71 pattern is a "senator" or equal end-style pen knife, with two blades and a single backspring. It has a slim rounded handle shape and the closed length is 3-1/4".

The 71 pattern is similar to the 79 pen knife pattern, but the 71 is 1/8" longer and has a slightly more rounded shape. It goes back to the early years of Case.

Blade and handle variations: During the Case XX era, the following principal variations were made:

- 6271 SS, with bone handles, spear master blade and pen blade.
- 8271 SS, with pearl handles, spear master blade and pen blade.
- 8271 F SS, with pearl handles, spear master blade and file blade.

The 6271 SS in the CASE XX stamping will be found in several of the Case XX-era bone color variations including green, regular and red. Some early XX examples of the 6271 were made with chrome vanadium steel blades, but most will be found in stainless steel. The 6271 SS was discontinued as of Feb. 1, 1964.

As with the 6271, some early XX examples of the 8271 will be found with chrome vanadium steel blades. The unique feature of the 8271 is that the pearl handles were attached by "dovetailing" the pearl under the bolsters at each end of the knife, eliminating the need for handle pins. The 8271 SS was discontinued in 1961. The standard liner material for the 71 pattern was nickel silver.

Newer variations: The 71 pattern has never been reintroduced.

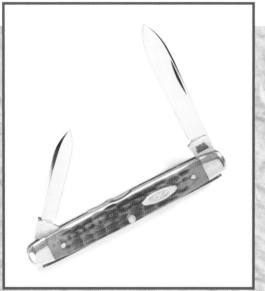

Case XX 6271 SS, red bone, 3-1/4", $250.

Case Tested 8271, pearl, 3-1/4", $400

PATTERN 72

The basic pattern: The 72 pattern is a large folding hunting knife with a single clip blade and is the largest folding hunting knife pattern in the Case line. Some early catalogs refer to the 72 pattern as a "clasp" knife. The pattern goes back to the Case Tested era, when it was made in various handle materials including bone, stag, and various celluloids.

Blade and handle variations: The 72 pattern has always been made as a single-bladed knife with a clip blade. It was discontinued prior to WWII but then was later reintroduced in the following versions:

- 5172 "Bulldog" with stag handles, introduced in the early 1960s.
- P172 "Buffalo" with smooth brown Pakkawood handles, introduced in the late 1960s.

Case XX USA 10 Dot, 1980, lightning S, P172 "Buffalo," 5-1/2", $250.

Case Tested 6172, "Clasp Knife," green bone, 5-1/2", $3,000.

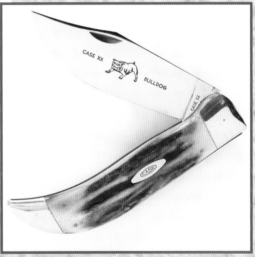

Case XX USA 5172, "Bulldog" transition stamping, 5-1/2", $450.

Case XX USA 5172, Bulldog, "USA" stamping, 5-1/2", $375.

Case Tested 6172, "Clasp Knife," green bone, 5-1/2", $3,000.

The two knives were both made with chrome vanadium as the only blade steel option. In 1980, a stainless steel lockback version of the 72 pattern was introduced:

- P172 L SSP "Boss" with jigged brown Pakkawood handles, a glazed finish stainless steel blade with "BOSS" etching, introduced in 1980.

Both the 5172 "Bulldog" and the P172 "Buffalo" have been popular with knife collectors and each was shipped in a walnut storage/display box. The Bulldog and the Buffalo were considered to be Case's premier folding knives for many years. Based on the information obtained from Case factory price lists, the 5172 was introduced to the Case line sometime between March 1, 1962 and July 1, 1963. The P172 was introduced in 1969. An interesting fact is that at the time it was introduced, the 5172 had a suggested retail price of $10.

In mid-1970, the 5172 pattern was discontinued when Case stopped regular production of stag-handled pocket knives, but was later brought back with a stainless steel blade for inclusion in the 1976 and 1977 annual limited production stag sets, 5172 SSP. Display boxes were not included with these 5172 SSP variations.

The P172 was made through the 1970s and into the 1980s and discontinued as of Oct. 1, 1981. The P172 L SSP "Boss" was still in production as of Jan. 15, 1985, but was discontinued sometime thereafter but prior to March 1, 1986. The Boss did not include a wooden display box but each knife was individually gift boxed with a cordovan leather belt sheath.

The liner material for all standard production 72 patterns from the Case XX era onward has been brass.

Tang stamping variations: The 5172, P172, and P172 L SSP were marked differently as compared to other Case pocket knives. On all XX era and later 72 patterns, the words "HAND MADE IN USA" or "HAND MADE USA" will be found.

There were three different marking variations used on the 5172 "Bulldog":

- The "XX" stamping has CASE XX on the front of the tang, 5172 on the back of the tang and "HAND MADE IN U.S.A." etched on the back of the blade.
- The "Transition" stamping has CASE XX U.S.A. on

the front of the tang, 5172 on the back of the tang and "HAND MADE IN U.S.A." etched on the back of the blade.

- The "USA" stamping has CASE XX 5172 on the front of the tang, HAND MADE USA on the back of the blade and no etching.

There were two initial marking variations used on the P172 "Buffalo" as shown in this table:

Stamping Variation	Front of Tang	Back of Tang
"USA" Stamping	CASE XX P172	HAND MADE USA
1971 to 1979 Stamping	CASE XX P172	HAND MADE USA . . . . Nine Dots (1971) to One Dot (1979)
1980 Stamping "Error" Stamp (see below)	CASE XX P172 (regular S)	HAND MADE USA . . . . (Ten Dots)
1980 to 1981 Stamping	CASE XX P172 ("lightning" S)	HAND MADE USA . . . . Ten Dots (1980) to Nine Dots (1981)

One important thing to note for both the P172 and 5172 is that while both patterns were in production in 1970 (the 5172 for only part of the year), there were *no* examples of either pattern made with the 1970 dating

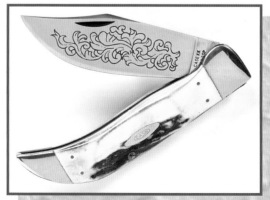

Case XX USA 3 Dot, 1977, 5172SSP, "blue scroll," 5-1/2", $150.

system (ten dots). I believe that the lack of the 10-dot markings on the 72 patterns in 1970 is most likely due to the fact that these knives are marked in a non-standard manner, and with 1970 being the first use of the "dots" dating system, Case may have simply neglected to change the stampings for the 72 pattern when this new marking system was introduced.

There was a 10-dot version of the P172 made in 1980. Many collectors mistakenly assume this knife is a 10-dot 1970 example. The problem is that the initial run of 1980 P172 patterns were stamped with the older tang stamping die that did *not* have the "lightning" S in the word CASE. This is explained in the following excerpt from the *Case Collector's Club Newsletter* issued in December 1981:

Oops – We Goofed!!! 10 dot – P172s??

The P172 (Buffalo) has been in production since 1969. Even though Case started their dating system, using dots, in 1970, a 1970 – 10 dot Buffalo was never made. The knives that were made that year had the CASE XX P172 stamping. Because of this there shouldn't any 10 dot P172s with the old style stamp in existence. But there are!!!

In 1980, when Case went back to 10 dots with the new lightning "S" stamp, the P172 was finally made with 10 dots. However, some blades with the old style stamp went through production with the new blades and were stamped with 10 dots. On these knives the dots will appear on the pile side of the blade tang above the "Hand made in USA."

Because of this there are approximately 600 P172s on the market with 10 dots and the old style stamp. This slight "Slip-Up" has made yet another collectors item out of regular production item.

With only 600 of these on the market, make sure you check the stamps on the P172s you come across. These are sure to become very sought after knives.

Based on the above, evidently the error was corrected and the remaining P172 patterns made during 1980 and 1981 will have markings similar to those found on the 1970s P172 patterns but with a "lightning" S in the word CASE on the front of the tang. The Boss was marked as follows in the chart at top right (note the row of dots on top of the HAND MADE USA).

One quirk of the P172 tang stamping is that due to the shape of the bolster on this pattern, the dots will sometimes be fully or partially hidden by the bolster. This is particularly true on many later 1970s examples since the row of

Stamping Variation	Front of Tang	Back of Tang
1980 to 1985 Stamping	CASE XX P172L SSP ("lightning" S)	. . . . HAND MADE USA Ten Dots (1980) To Five Dots (1985)

dots will be shorter. One way to assist in approximating the age of a P172 is to look at the shield. The P172 being a wood-handled knife, was changed over to the "composition" shield in 1974. So if the shield is old style with the oval around CASE, the knife will be a 1974 (six dot) or earlier example. If the knife has a "composition" shield (without the oval) then the knife is from 1974 or later.

Boxes: The 5172 and the P172 were shipped from the factory including wooden storage/display boxes. The more common box for the 5172 was made with a dark walnut-stained wood finish. There was also a black painted wood box used. The black box seems to be somewhat scarcer though it is not considered rare. Both style boxes for the 5172 had the CASE XX (long tail C) logo and the word "BULLDOG" painted on in gold paint. The P172 "Buffalo" boxes were all dark stained wood and had a metal logo plate with the CASE logo and the word "BUFFALO." I believe that some of the later 5172 boxes were also made with a metal logo plate rather than the painted logo.

Newer variations: Case has recently reintroduced the 72 pattern with a polished stainless steel blade and in a number of bone handle variations.

Case XX USA 10 Dot, P172 L SSP, "Boss" with box, 1980, lightning S, 5-1/2", $100.

PATTERN 75

The basic pattern: The 75 pattern is a large serpentine stockman pattern with square bolsters; closed length is 4-1/4". The pattern goes back to the early years of Case and has been manufactured as a two-blade pattern and three-blade stockman pattern. The two-blade version of the 75 pattern is known to collectors as the "Moose"; the three-blade 75 stockman is often referred to as the "Jumbo Stockman."

Blade and handle variations: The 75 pattern has always been made with a standard clip as the main blade. During the Case XX era, the following principal variations of the 75 pattern were made:

Two blades, "standard" clip master blade:

- 6275 Sp, with bone handles with long spay secondary blade.

Three-blade variations, "standard" clip master blade:

- 5375, with stag handles, secondary blades sheepfoot and spay.
- 6375, with bone handles, secondary blades sheepfoot and spay.

Production of the 5375 continued through the Case XX USA years and the pattern was discontinued in 1970 when Case stopped regular production of stag-handled pocket knives.

The bone-handled 75 pattern variations in the CASE XX stamping will be found in several of the Case XX-era bone color variations including green, regular and red, as well as in rough black.

The 6275 Sp was constructed with two blades operating on two backsprings, with no center liner. Both the 6275 Sp "Moose" and 6375 "Jumbo Stockman" were mainstays in the Case product line and both continued in production through the 1970s and 1980s.

During the 1970s, delrin was substituted for bone on the 6275 and the 6375 on a random basis. Both delrin and bone examples will be found; however, my observation is that starting in 1978, the 6275 and the 6375 were both switched back to being handled 100 percent in bone. Production of the 6275SP in bone was continued until the end of 1990, when the pattern was discontinued. The 6375 has remained in the standard Case product line to the present day.

Blade steel and liner material: From the Case XX era through the 1970s, the liner material for all of the 75 pat-

Case XX 6275 SP, "Moose," red bone-long pull, 4-1/4", $500.

Case XX 6275 SP, "Moose," red bone, 4-1/4", $250.

Case XX 6375, red bone, light color, 4-1/4", $450.

terns was nickel silver. Beginning circa 1978, Case began changing all pocket knife patterns with nickel silver liners to the standard use of brass as the lining material. This change was complete by 1980. During these years, chrome vanadium was the only blade steel offered on standard product examples of the 6275 Sp, 5375, and 6375.

Other variations: The 6275, 5375, and 6375 patterns were all made with both long pull and regular pull master blades during the Case XX era. The long-pull versions were made early in the Case XX years and are fairly rare.

Newer variations: The 6275 Sp "Moose" pattern was reintroduced by Case in recent years. Both the 6275 and the 6375 have been made in a wide variety of bone handle variations and with stainless steel blades.

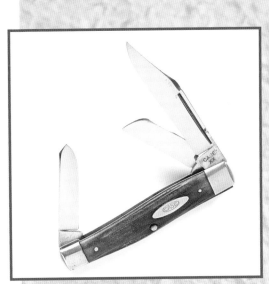

Case XX 5375 LP, dark color red stag, 4-1/4", $1,200.

Case XX 6375, dark bone, 4-1/4", $300.

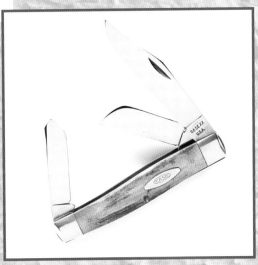

Case XX USA 5375, 4-1/4", $300.

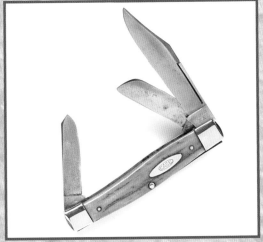

Case XX 5375 LP, light color red stag, 4-1/4", $1,200.

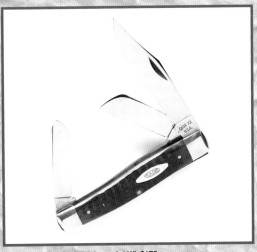

Case XX USA 6375, bone, 4-1/4", $175.

Case XX USA 10 Dot, 1970, 5375, 4-1/4", $350.

Case XX USA 10 Dot, 1980, lightning S, 6275SP, bone, 4-1/4", $80.

Case XX USA 2 Dot, 1978, 6375, bone, 4-1/4", $80.

Case XX USA 4 Dot, 1986, lightning S, 6375, dark bone, 4-1/4", $60.

Case XX USA 9 Dot, 1981, 6375, bone, 4-1/4", $100.

Case XX USA 4 Dot, 1986, lightning S, 6375, light bone, 4-1/4", $65.

PATTERN 78

The basic pattern: The 78 pattern is a "coffin"-style pen knife pattern with two blades operating on a single backspring; closed length is 3-1/16". This is a relatively new Case pattern, having been introduced in 1979. It is unusual in that it is sometimes referred to as a "skeleton" knife, a pocket knife with unfinished metal handle scales, configured so that various handle slabs can be glued or otherwise attached to the scales without the need for visible handle pins.

The Case 78 pattern has been made with various plastic and metal handle coverings. The only blade configuration that has been offered on the 78 pattern is a master spear blade and pen blade, both of stainless steel with a glazed finish.

Case XX USA 8 Dot, 1972, 6275SP, reddish bone, 4-1/4", $125.

The pattern number on a Diamond Jubilee knife. Note that most 78 patterns simply used the pattern number "278."

Case XX USA 1 Dot, 1979, 5275 SSP, Bradford Centennial, 4-1/4", $125.

The 78 pattern was introduced as part of the Gentlemen's Line of pocket knives, first produced in 1979, and the following variations were included:

- E278 SS, with solid brass scales engraved with a Florentine scroll design on the front handle.
- I278 SS, brass scales with plastic imitation ivory handles.
- IS278 SS, brass scales with plastic imitation ivory handles imprinted with a "scrimshaw" seacoast scene on the front handle.
- S278 SS, brass scales with plastic imitation tortoise shell handles.

The above knives represented a departure from

Case XX USA 10 Dot, 1980, lightning S, 5275 SSP, Case 75th, 4-1/4", $125.

the usual Case pattern numbering scheme, since "I" was used instead of the digit "4" to indicate smooth white plastic handles. Many examples of the 78 pattern do not have the full pattern number stamped on the blade but instead simply have "278."

The 78 pattern was also utilized for several limited-edition releases and was popular as an advertising or premium knife with various handle imprints. It was initially made with brass liners and in 1981, the lining material was changed over to stainless steel.

The IS278 SS and the E278 SS were discontinued in 1982, as the Gentlemen's Line was gradually dissolved as a separate product line. The S278 was discontinued in 1986 while the I278 SS remained in the Case standard product line until it was discontinued after 1990.

Case XX USA 1 Dot, 1979, 278 SS, "Diamond Jubilee," 3-1/16", $30.

Case XX USA 1 Dot, 1979, I278 SS, "City of Bradford," 3-1/16", $20.

PATTERN 79

The basic pattern: The 79 pattern is a pen knife pattern made in two different designs and is an example of a pattern where a distinctly different design variation is differentiated by the placement of a "zero" in the pattern number.

The 79 pattern is a "senator" or equal-end pen knife-style with a spear master blade and a pen blade (also made with a file secondary blade) operating on a single backspring; it has a closed length of 3-1/8". This pattern is similar to the 63 "senator" pen knife pattern in that both are of the senator style and have a closed length of 3-1/8". The differences are the elongated bolsters on the 63 pattern and the fact that the 79 pattern is "flatter" in terms of the handle shape, while the 63 pattern has handles that are more rounded.

The second Case 79 pattern variation is the 079 which is a two-blade "sleeveboard" pen knife pattern made with a clip master blade at one end and a pen blade at the other end. This pattern has a closed length of 3-1/4", which is 1/8" longer than the 079.

Blade and handle variations: During the Case XX era, the following principal variations of the 79 and 079 pen knife pattern were made:

Senator pen knife variations with bolsters:

- 5279 senator pen knife pattern with stag handles, spear master blade and secondary pen blade.
- 5279 SS with stag handles, polished stainless steel spear master blade and secondary pen blade.
- 6279 senator pen knife pattern with bone handles, spear master blade and secondary pen blade.
- 6279 SS with bone handles, polished stainless steel spear master blade and secondary pen blade.
- 6279 F SS senator pen knife with bone handles, polished stainless steel spear master blade and secondary long file blade.
- 8279 with pearl handles, spear master blade and secondary pen blade.
- 8279 SS with pearl handles, polished stainless steel spear master blade and secondary pen blade.

Senator pen knife variations without bolsters (shadow):

- 2279 SS with smooth black handles, polished stainless steel spear master blade and secondary pen blade.
- 9279 SS with smooth black handles, polished stainless steel spear master blade and secondary pen blade.

Senator pen knife variations with stainless steel handles:

- M279 SS, polished stainless steel spear master blade and secondary pen blade.
- M279 F SS, polished stainless steel spear master blade and secondary file blade.
- M279 Scis SS, polished stainless steel spear master blade and scissors.

Sleeveboard pen knife variations:

- 82079 1/2 sleeveboard pen knife with pearl handles, clip master blade and secondary pen blade.
- 82079 1/2 SS sleeveboard pen knife with pearl handles, polished stainless steel clip master blade and secondary pen blade.

The 5279, 6279, 8279, and 82079 1/2 patterns in the Case XX era were all made with both chrome vanadium and stainless steel as the blade material. Based on a review of available Case factory catalogs and price lists, it appears chrome vanadium was the only blade steel choice offered on these knives early in the Case XX era. By about 1955, the blade steel for all four patterns had been changed over to stainless steel. It appears that the 6279 F with the file secondary blade was a later introduction and only offered in stainless steel.

The bone-handled 79 patterns in the CASE XX stamping will be found in several of the Case XX-era bone color variations including green, regular and red, and in rough black. The 6279 F SS was discontinued as of April 1, 1957 and the 8279 SS in 1959.

The 5279 SS was discontinued as of Jan. 1, 1966 and examples will be found with the CASE XX USA tang stamping but are rare. The Case XX-era price lists and catalogs I have available do not show the "shadow" patterns (2279 SS and 9279 SS) and I believe neither was produced beyond the Case XX era. All examples of the 9279 SS that I have observed have had handles of yellowish "cracked ice."

Production of the 6279 SS, 82079 1/2 SS, and the M279 SS, M279 F SS, and M279 Scis SS continued into the 1970s. During the 1970s, delrin was substituted for bone on the 6279 SS on a random basis. Beginning in 1978, it appears that Case began handling the 6279 SS 100 percent in delrin. The M279 Scis SS was discontinued as of May 1974. The 6279 SS was discontinued in 1982. The M279 F SS was discontinued as of December

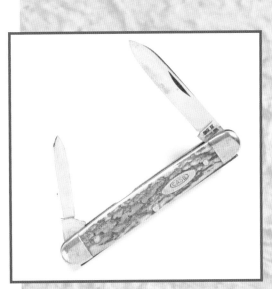

Case XX 5279 SS, 3-1/8", $125.

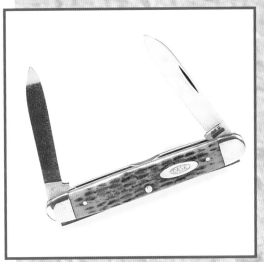

Case XX 6279 F SS, "faded green bone front"/red bone back, 3-1/8", $125.

Case XX 6279 SS, red bone, 3-1/8", $125.

1982 and the M279 SS was discontinued in 1985.

The 82079 1/2 was produced into the early 1980s. Genuine pearl-handled pocket knives were not listed in Case factory catalogs or price lists from about 1967 through the 1970s even though they were in production. I believe the 82079 1/2 was generally in production from 1970 through 1985 when it was discontinued, though it may not have been made every year. Beginning in 1981, the pearl handles on the 82079 1/2 were glued on (no pins). The pattern was shown in the 1983 Case factory catalog and in price lists from 1983 to 1985.

Liner material: The liner material for the 79 patterns up until the late 1970s during the Case XX era was nickel silver. Beginning circa 1978, Case began changing all pocket knife patterns with nickel silver liners to the standard use of brass as the lining material. This change was complete by 1980. Later

catalogs from 1968 and 1974 indicated brass as the liner material, but the 1977 catalog again shows the 6279 SS as having nickel silver liners. The M279 variations did not have liners; the handle slabs of stainless steel also served as liners.

Other variations: During the Case XX era, the 6279 SS and all of the M279 SS variations were made with polished stainless steel blades. Starting in the mid-1970s, the blade finish on the M279s was changed to a glazed finish. The blades on the 6279 SS were also made with both polished and glazed finished blades during the mid-1970s and were changed over to 100 percent glazed finish circa 1978. Likewise the handles on Case XX era M279 patterns were polished. Starting in the Case XX USA era or possibly earlier, the handle finish was changed to a brushed finish.

The 82079 1/2 SS was made with pinned on pearl handles

Case XX 6279 F SS, rough black, 3-1/8", $125.

Case XX 82079-1/2, "sleeveboard," 3-1/4", $150. Note: Early XX-era version with chrome vanadium blades.

The back of the 6279 F SS.

The 79 and the 079 patterns have primarily been made as two-blade pen knife patterns. During the Case Tested era, the 079 was made as a split backspring "whittler" pattern with green bone handles, pattern number 63079 1/2; closed length is 3-1/8", $750.

until 1981, when Case began gluing the pearl handles on (no pins). It was manufactured this way until discontinued in 1985.

Newer variations: Two versions of the 79 pattern were introduced in 1979 as part of the Gentlemen's Line. The following variations were introduced:

- M279 R SS, glazed finish stainless steel spear master blade and secondary pen blade, with a bail.
- M279 F R SS, glazed finish stainless steel spear master blade and secondary file blade, with a bail.

The Gentlemen's Line knives were only made for a few years. Both of these 79 pattern variations were discontinued as of Oct. 15, 1982. In 1989-1990, Case reintroduced the 79 pattern in limited production runs and it has not been manufactured since that time.

Case XX USA 1 Dot, 1979, M279 F SS, 3-1/8", $40.

Case XX 9279 SS "Shadow," cracked ice, 3-1/8", $75.

Case XX USA 5 Dot, 1975, 82079-1/2 SS, 3-1/4", $75.

Case XX M279 Scis SS, 3-1/8", $75.

Case XX USA 8 Dot, 1972, M279 SS, 3-1/8", $50.

PATTERN 80

The basic pattern: The 80 pattern is referred to by collectors as the "Carpenter's Whittler" pattern. It is a 3-7/8" (closed length) serpentine-style handle frame and was introduced during the Case XX era as the 6380. The 6380 pattern is a "split-back whittler," with three blades and two backsprings.

The "split-back" or "split-backspring" designation is used by collectors to refer to a specific blade and backspring arrangement. The 6380 has a relatively thick master clip blade at one end with a small clip blade and a coping blade at the opposite end. The 6380 has two backsprings, with the main blade riding on both springs. Each of the two smaller blades rides on one spring. In order to provide space for the main blade to fall between the two small blades, a partial center liner or "wedge" is installed between the backsprings at the small blade end of the knife.

The 6380 in the CASE XX stamping will be found in several of the Case XX-era bone color variations including green, regular and red. I do not believe the 6380 was produced in rough black. The CASE XX-stamped 6380 will also be found in "early Rogers" bone.

During the 1970s, delrin was substituted for bone on the 6380 on a random basis. Both delrin and bone examples will be found; however, my observation is that starting in 1978, the pattern was switched back to 100 percent production in bone, though the pattern was discontinued in that year. During all of the years of production, chrome vanadium was the only blade steel offered on the standard production model of the 6380. The lining material was nickel silver.

During the early 1980s, a few limited edition and SFO versions of the 80 whittler pattern were made, including one with second cut stag handles and stainless steel blades. The 80 pattern has not been produced since that time. However, Case has in recent years produced a "split backspring whittler variation of the 47 pattern with three blades. This knife has a closed length of 3-7/8" and is similar in appearance to the 80 pattern.

Case XX 6380, reddish bone, light accents, 3-7/8", $450.

Case XX 6380, dark red bone, 3-7/8", $450.

Case XX 6380, red bone, used pocket worn handles, 3-7/8", $750.

Case XX 6380, green bone front, red bone back, 3-7/8", $2,500.

Case XX 6380, early rogers bone, 3-7/8", $2,000.

PATTERN 83

The basic pattern: The 83 is a "swell center whittler" or "balloon whittler" pattern that goes back to the early years of Case. It is a "split-back whittler," with three blades and two backsprings.

The "split-back" or "split-backspring" designation is used by collectors to refer to a specific blade and backspring arrangement.

The 83 pattern has a relatively thick master clip blade at one end with a small clip blade and a pen blade at the opposite end; closed length is 3-1/2". It has two backsprings, with the main blade riding on both springs.

Each of the two smaller blades rides on one spring. In order to provide space for the main blade to fall between the two small blades, a partial center liner or "wedge" is installed between the backsprings at the small blade end of the knife.

Blade and handle variations: The 83 pattern was always made with a clip master blade, and with small clip and pen secondary blades.

During the Case XX era, the following principal variations were made:

- 5383, with stag handles.
- 6383, with bone handles.
- 9383, with imitation pearl handles.

Production of the 5383 continued through the Case XX USA years and the pattern was discontinued in 1970 when Case stopped regular production of stag-handled pocket knives.

The 6383 in the CASE XX stamping will be found in several of the Case XX-era bone color variations including green, regular and red, and in rough black.

During the 1970s, delrin was substituted for bone on the 6383 on a random basis. Both delrin and bone examples will be found; however, my observation is that starting in 1978, the 6383 was switched back to being handled 100 percent in bone and production continued until 1981, when the pattern was discontinued.

The 9383 is a relatively scarce variation of the 83 pattern. It was made early in the Case XX era and discontinued in 1958. All examples of the 9383 that I have observed have had "cracked ice" handles.

Blade steel and liner material: From the XX era through the early 1980s, all 83 patterns were only offered with chrome vanadium as the blade steel. The standard liner material for the 83 pattern was nickel silver.

Beginning circa 1978, Case began changing all pocket knife patterns with nickel silver liners to the standard use of brass as the lining material. This change was complete by 1980.

Other variations: During the Case XX era, a number of 83 patterns were made with saber ground master blades.

I was unable to locate the saber blade versions in any catalog or price list so the years of manufacture are not known. The saber master blade variations are rare.

Newer variations: Case reintroduced the 83 "split backspring whittler" pattern in 2000. It has since been offered in a wide variety of handle materials with stainless steel blades.

Case XX 2383, "Whittler," smooth black, 3-1/2", $200.

Case XX 5383, "Whittler," 3-1/2", $600.

Case XX 2383 SAB, "Whittler," main blade is a saber ground master clip blade, 3-1/2", $350.

Case XX 6383, "Whittler," dark bone, 3-1/2", $300.

Case XX 6383, "Whittler," red bone, 3-1/2", $450.

Case XX USA 10 Dot, 5383, "Whittler," 3-1/2", $325.

Case XX 6383, "Whittler," green bone, 3-1/2", $1,000.

Case XX USA 5383, "Whittler," 3-1/2", $275.

Case Tested 5383, "Whittler," 3-1/2", $2,500.

PATTERN 85

The basic pattern: The 85 pattern is a slim jack knife pattern that collectors refer to as the "doctor's knife." This is a traditional name for this style of slim jack knife and comes from the fact that in times past, a physician would use the squared-off butt end of the handle to crush pills, and the long slim blade could be used to reach into a medicine vial. In the early years of Case, the 85 pattern was made as a one-blade and two-blade jack. Closed length is 3-5/8".

Blade and handle variations: Beginning with the CASE XX tang stamp, the 85 pattern was made only as a single-blade jack with a spear master blade. The following variations were made during the Case XX era:

- 3185, with yellow composition handles.
- 6185, with bone handles.

The 3185 will be found with the CASE XX stamping in both the older yellow celluloid, with white liner, and yellow composition handles. Later examples made from the CASE XX USA era and into the 1970s will have yellow delrin handles. Many 3185s were made without shields but some were made with shields. This seems to be a random variation. The 3185 was discontinued in 1975.

The 6185 in the CASE XX stamping will be found in several of the Case XX-era bone color variations including green, regular and red. The use of bone handles on the 6185 continued into the 1970s. During the 1970s, delrin was substituted for bone on the 6185 on a random basis. It is possible the 6185 was changed to being handled 100 percent in delrin after 1972. I have personally never seen a bone-handled 6185 example from the 1970s made after 1972. The 6185 was discontinued as of Jan. 1, 1977.

Blade steel and liner material: From the XX era through the time the pattern was discontinued in the 1970s, all 85 patterns were only offered with chrome vanadium as the blade steel. The liner material during these years was brass.

Newer variations: In recent years, Case reintroduced the 85 pattern and it has been made in a variety of handle materials and stainless steel blades, and in both one- and two-blade variations.

Case Tested 6383, "Whittler," green bone, 3-1/2", $2,200.

Case Tested 6383 SAB, "Whittler," green bone, saber ground clip blade, 3-1/2", $2,200.

Case XX USA 2 Dot, 1978, 6383, bone, 3-1/2", $100.

Case XX 6185, "doctor's knife," red bone, 3-3/4", $350.

Case XX 6185, green bone, 3-5/8", $500.

Case XX USA 6 Dot, 1974, 6185, delrin, 3-5/8", $60.

PATTERN 087

The basic pattern: The 087 pattern is a medium stockman pattern with round bolsters; closed length is 3-1/4". It goes back to the early years of Case. During the Case XX years and later, it has been manufactured as both a three-blade "stockman" pattern and two-blade jack pattern.

Blade and handle variations: The 087 pattern has always been made with a clip as the main blade. During the Case XX era, the following principal variations of the 087 jack and stockman pattern were made:

- 22087 jack pattern with smooth black handles; secondary pen blade.
- 52087 jack pattern with stag handles; secondary pen blade.
- 62087 jack pattern with bone handles; secondary pen blade.
- 23087 stockman pattern with smooth black handles; secondary sheepfoot and pen blades.
- 53087 stockman pattern with stag handles; secondary sheepfoot and pen blades.
- 63087 stockman pattern with bone handles; secondary spay and pen blades.

Production of the 52087 and the 53087 continued through the Case XX USA years and the patterns were discontinued in 1970 when Case stopped regular production of stag-handled pocket knives.

The 62087 and the 63087 in the CASE XX stamping will be found in several of the Case XX era bone-color variations including green, regular and red, as well as rough black and "late Rogers" bone. The use of bone handles on the 62087 and 63087 continued until mid-1970. The 62087 and 63087 were two of a number of patterns that were changed to being handled 100 percent in delrin in 1970, so both bone and delrin examples were made in that year.

Production of the 62087 and 63087 in delrin, along with the 22087 and 23087, continued through the 1970s and into the 1980s in chrome vanadium blade steel. In 1981, Case changed the blade steel on all of these patterns to stainless steel with a glazed finish. This change was announced in June of 1981. The 23087 Sh Pen SS was discontinued as of Sept. 1, 1983.

Production of the 22087 SS, 62087 SS, and 63087 SS continued into the 1990s as these three patterns became part of Case's "Working Knives" series. The 62087 SS was discontinued after 1998. The 22087 SS and 63087 SS (delrin) are still in the Case line today.

Blade steel and liner material: From the XX era through 1981, chrome vanadium was the only blade steel offered on the 087 stockman and jack patterns. The standard lining material for the 087 "stockman" and "jack" patterns during the Case XX era was nickel silver.

The 1968 catalog shows that the "jack" patterns were lined in brass; however, the 1974 catalog shows the 22087 and 62087 as having nickel silver liners. The 087 "stockman" patterns continued with nickel silver liners during these years but in the 1977 catalog all 087 patterns had been switched over to brass liners.

Newer variations: During the 1980s, a stag-handled version of the two-bladed 087 pattern was introduced as a standard product knife. The 52087 SS was introduced in 1987 as part of Case's standard line of stag-handled pocket knives and was discontinued after 1990.

Up into the 1980s, Case manufactured a two-blade pen knife that had the pattern number 03244 even though the pattern used the 087-style frame.

Circa 1987, Case changed the pattern number of the 03244 to the correct number (32087 Pen) so in effect, another 87 pattern was added to the line at that time. The 32087 Pen is till in the Case standard product line in both chrome vanadium and stainless steel versions.

The 087 pattern is a mainstay in the line and in recent years, many variations of the two- and three-bladed 087 patterns have been offered in a variety of handle materials and stainless steel blades.

Case XX 62087, red bone, 3-1/4", $140.

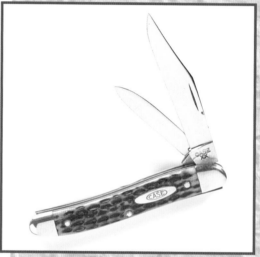

Case XX 62087, green bone, 3-1/4", $225.

Case XX 62087, jack, late rogers bone, 3-1/4", $140.

The back of the Case XX 62087.

Case XX 63087, dark red bone, 3-1/4", $150.

Case XX 23087 Sh Pen, 3-1/4", $100.

Case XX USA 52087, 3-1/4", $140.

Case XX USA New-1990 stamping, 62087 SS, faded delrin, 3-1/4", $30.

Case XX USA 3 Dot, 1977, 52087 SSP, "blue scroll," 3-1/4", $80.

Case XX USA 2 Dot, 1978, 52087 SSP, 3-1/4", $75.

PATTERN 88

The basic pattern: The 88 pattern is a large "congress" pattern with square bolsters; closed length is 4-1/8".

It goes back to the early years of Case and during the Case Tested era, it was manufactured as a two-blade and four-blade pattern.

Blade and handle variations: Beginning with the CASE XX tang stamp, the 88 pattern was offered as a four-blade "congress" pattern with a large sheepfoot blade, a large spear blade, and small coping and pen blades.

The following handle variations were offered during the Case XX era:

- 5488, with stag handles.
- 6488, with bone handle.

These 88 patterns were made with the four blades operating on two backsprings, and with a thick center liner. The extra thick center liner performed two functions. It added rigidity to the knife for extra strength, and it acted as a spacer, providing room for the blades to fall into the handle.

Production of the 5488 continued through the Case XX USA years and the pattern was discontinued in 1970 when Case stopped regular production of stag-handled pocket knives.

The 6488 in the CASE XX stamping will be found in several of the Case XX-era bone color variations including green, regular and red, as well as in rough black.

During the 1970s, delrin was substituted for bone on the 6488 on a random basis. Both delrin and bone examples will be found; however, my observation is that starting in 1978, the 6488 was switched to being handled 100 percent in delrin, though the pattern was discontinued in that year.

Blade steel and liner material: From the Case XX era through the 1970s, the liner material for all of the 88 patterns was brass. The only blade steel option was chrome vanadium.

Other variations: The 5488 and 6488 were made with both long pull and regular pull master blades during the Case XX era.

The long-pull versions were made early in the Case XX years and are very rare. The long pulls on the 88 pattern will be found on the large sheepfoot blade and the long spear blade. The smaller blades will still have "regular" nail pulls.

The 88 pattern is unusual in that both the large sheepfoot blade and the long spear blade are considered as "master" blades and each will have the Case logo tang stamping. Due to this fact, some "transition" examples that have a different logo stamp on each blade will be observed.

Transition models are a result of blades from one year that are left over and used up prior to new blades being stamped out for a particular year. For example, some 88 patterns will be found with the CASE XX tang stamp on one large blade and the CASE XX USA tang stamp on the other large blade.

There are also transition models with CASE XX USA and CASE XX USA (ten dots) for the 5488 and the 6488 and with various "dots" combinations during the 1970s for the 6488. Transition models are scarce.

Newer variations: The 6488 "congress" pattern was reintroduced by Case in recent years. It has been made in a wide variety of bone-handle variations and with stainless steel blades.

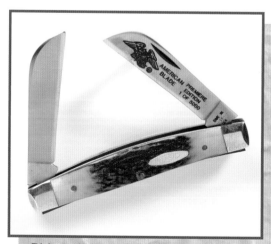

This is a two-blade variation of the 88 pattern made in 1982 as an SFO. The shield is glued on and the knife is double lined on both sides; 5288 SSP, 4-1/8", $80.

Case XX 6488, "Large Congress," red bone, 4-1/8", $1,200.

Back of the 6488.

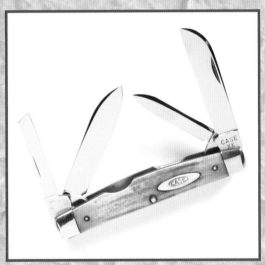

Case XX 5488, "Large Congress," 4-1/8", $1,250.

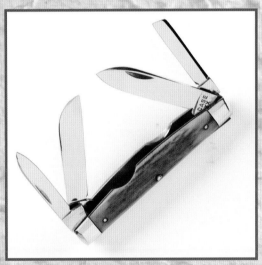

Back of the 5488.

Case XX 6488, red bone, long pull blades, 4-1/8", $2,000.

Case XX 6488, bone, 4-1/8", $600.

PATTERN 92

The basic pattern: The 92 pattern is a large stockman pattern with squared bolsters; closed length is 4". It goes back to the early years of Case, and during the Case XX years and later, it has been manufactured as a both a three-blade "stockman" pattern and two-blade jack pattern. Collectors sometimes refer to the 92 pattern with two blades as a "Texas Jack." In the cutlery industry, square-bolstered larger premium stockman patterns were traditionally referred to as "Texas pattern" stockman knives. This may explain the origin of the name "Texas Jack" for this pattern.

Blade and handle variations: The 92 pattern has always been made with a clip as the main blade. During the Case XX era, the following principal variations of the 92 jack and stockman pattern were made:

- 6292 jack pattern with bone handles; secondary pen blade.
- 5392 stockman pattern with stag handles; secondary sheepfoot and spay blades.
- 6392 stockman pattern with bone handles; secondary sheepfoot and spay blades.
- 33092 stockman pattern with yellow handles; secondary sheepfoot and spay blades. This is the "Large Birdseye" pattern with no bolsters.

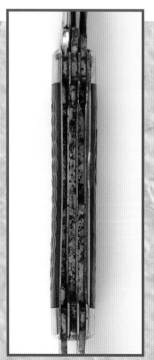

Inside view of the 6592 stock knife, with three backsprings.

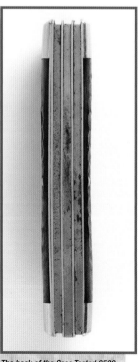

The back of the Case Tested 6592 five-blade stock knife showing the three-backspring construction.

The 33092 is a knife made with no bolsters and with large nickel silver washers anchoring the blade pins at each end. This pattern is referred to by collectors as the "large birdseye" pattern due the oversized pins; the 33044 Sh Sp is a similar knife but at 3-1/4" long closed, it is referred to as the "small birdseye." The 33092 in yellow composition was first produced with the Case XX stamping in 1950. The pattern was produced through the Case XX USA era and through the 1970s. Many 33092s were made without shields, but the pattern was also made with a shield. This seems to be a random variation. The 33092 was discontinued in 1981.

Production of the 5392 continued through the Case XX USA years and the pattern was discontinued in 1970 when Case stopped regular production of stag-handled pocket knives.

The 6292 and 6392 in the CASE XX stamping will be found in several of the Case XX-era bone color variations including green, regular and red, as well as in rough black. The use of bone handles on the 6292 and 6392 continued into the 1970s. During the 1970s, delrin was substituted for bone on the 6292 and 6392 on a random basis. Beginning in 1978, it appears that Case went back to handling the 92 patterns 100 percent in bone.

The 6392 was discontinued after 1990 and has never been reintroduced. The 6292 "Texas Jack" remained in the Case product line until after 2000 but has also been discontinued.

Blade steel and liner material: From the XX era through the 1970s, chrome vanadium was the only blade steel offered on the 92 stockman and jack patterns. The standard lining material for the 92 "stockman" patterns during these years from the XX era through 1977 was nickel silver. Beginning circa 1978, Case began changing all pocket knife patterns with nickel silver liners to the standard use of brass as the lining material. This change was complete by 1980. The 6292 "Texas Jack" was also made with nickel silver liners as standard for most of these years; however, the 1968 catalog lists the 6292 as having brass liners.

Newer variations: Beginning in the 1980s, the two-bladed 92 "Texas Jack" pattern has been made for some limited editions and offered in a variety of handle materials and stainless steel blades.

Case Tested 6592, Five-Blade Stock Knife, green bone, 4", $3,000.

Back of the 6592.

Case XX USA 5392, $550.

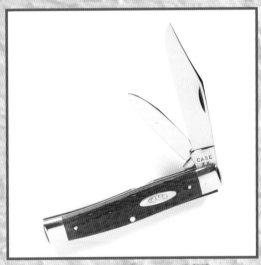

Case XX 6292, "Texas jack knife," red bone, 4", $200.

Case Tested 6392, green bone, 4, $500.

Case XX 6392, dark red bone, 4", $225.

Case XX USA 5392, 4", $275.

Case XX USA 5 Dot 6392, 1985, lightning S, 4", $55.

Case XX 6392, red bone, 4", $350. This is a used knife that has been polished.

Case XX USA 9 Dot 6392, 1981, lightning S, 4", $75.

Case XX USA 3 Dot 33092, 1977, 4", $90.

Case XX USA 1 Dot, 5292 SSP, 1979, Bradford Centennial, 4", $125.

PATTERN 093

The basic pattern: The 093 pattern is a long slim "tickler" or "toothpick" pattern, often referred to by collectors as the "Texas Toothpick"; closed length is 5". It goes back to the early years of Case.

During the pre-WWII era, it was made in various celluloid handle materials and in bone.

Blade and handle variations: The 093 pattern has always been made with a single clip blade. During the Case XX era, the following principal variations were made:

- 31093, with yellow composition handles.
- 61093, with bone handles.

The 31093 was introduced in 1961 and will be found with the CASE XX-era yellow composition handles. It was listed in Case factory price lists until being shown as discontinued as of April 1, 1967. However, the 31093 was not made with the CASE XX USA tang stamping, so evidently it was still in the price lists until the residual stock (with the CASE XX tang stamping) was exhausted.

The 61093 in the CASE XX stamping will be found in several of the Case XX-era bone color variations including green, regular and red. I do not believe the 61093 was ever made in rough black.

The use of bone handles on the 61093 continued into the 1970s. During the 1970s, delrin was substituted for bone on the 61093 on a random basis.

The 61093 was discontinued in 1975. For some unknown reason, examples of the 61093 with the 1973 tang stamping (seven dots) are very scarce.

Blade steel and liner material: From the XX era through the time the pattern was discontinued in the 1970s, all 093 patterns were only offered with chrome vanadium as the blade steel. The liner material during these years was brass.

Case XX 61093, reddish bone, 5", $250.

Case XX 61093, green bone, 5", $650.

Case XX USA 7 Dot, 1983, lightning S, 6254, 4-1/8", $100.

PATTERN 94

The basic pattern: The 94 pattern is referred to by collectors as the "big cigar" pattern. The frame predates WWII and is an equal-end design with rounded bolsters and a closed length of 4-1/4". During the Case XX era, the following principal variations were made:

- 6294, a two-blade jack knife pattern with a master spear blade and a secondary pen blade.
- 6394 1/2, a three-blade "jumbo cattle" knife pattern with a master clip blade and secondary sheepfoot and spay blades.

The 6294 and the 6394 1/2 in the CASE XX stamping will be found in several of the Case XX-era bone color variations including green, regular and red. I do not believe the 94 pattern was produced in rough black. The 94 patterns were made with chrome vanadium blade steel and the jack patterns were made with brass liners.

The 6394 1/2 is a rare Case pattern and was made with a "long pull" nail mark on the master clip blade. Early catalog cuts show the 6394 1/2 as having a nickel silver lining. Case factory price lists show that the 6394 1/2 was in production during 1949 and 1950. It was not listed in the next available price list (1955) and later, so evidently it was discontinued in the early 1950s.

The 6294 will be found in the CASE XX stamping with both the "long pull" nail mark and the regular pull. The 6294 was listed as discontinued as of Jan. 1, 1966 but was never made with the CASE XX USA tang stamping. The 94 pattern has never been reintroduced.

Case XX 6294, "Large Cigar Jack," red bone, 4-1/4", $600.

Case Tested 6294J, "Large Cigar Texas Jack," green bone, 4-1/4", $3,000.

Case Tested 6294, "Large Cigar Jack," green bone-long pull, 4-1/4", $2,500.

Case XX 6294, dark red bone, 4-1/4", $400.

PATTERN 095

The basic pattern: The 095 pattern is a long slim "tickler" or "toothpick" pattern with a closed length of 5".

The pattern was made during the Case Tested era as both a single-blade knife and two-bladed "fisherman's" knife, the 32095 F SS.

Production of the 32095 F SS "Fisherman's Knife" continued into the Case XX era and was one of a very few Case pocket knives made with stainless steel blades during the Case Tested era and the early Case XX era. The "F" was normally used on Case pocket knife pattern numbers to designate a file blade.

In the case of the 32095 F SS, the "F" designated the fish hook sharpening stone that was inset into the front handle.

The 32095 F SS was configured with a clip master blade and with a secondary fish scaler blade that had a hook disgorger at the tip.

The end of the bolster on the knife had a small hole that was designed for use in straightening bent fish hooks.

The 32095 F SS was made with yellow composition handles and will be found with the CASE XX stamping in both the older yellow celluloid (with white liner) and with yellow composition handles.

Later examples made from the CASE XX USA era and into the 1970s will have yellow delrin handles.

The 32095 F SS was made with mirror polished stainless steel blades and with brass liners.

Some examples made during the 1970s and early

Case XX 32095, 5", $125.

1980s will be found with glazed finished blades.

This seems to be a random variation on late 1970s examples but was made a permanent change in mid-1980. The pattern was discontinued as of September 1981.

Newer variations: The 32095 pattern has never been reintroduced. Case has recently introduced a scaled-down version of a "Fisherman's Knife," the 320094 F SS with a closed length of 4-1/4".

PATTERN 96

The basic pattern: The 96 pattern is a two-bladed knife with a slim handle and square bolsters, with a closed length of 4-1/4". The pattern goes back to the Case Tested era.

The only principal variation of the 96 pattern made during the Case XX era was a "Citrus Knife" with a long spear blade at one end and a long pen blade at the other end.

The 6296 X SS was made with polished stainless steel blades and nickel silver liners, and was offered from early in the Case XX era and will be found in several of the bone variations of those years including green, regular and red.

On some Case pocket knife patterns, the "X" suffix has been used to designate "extension" bolster, as on the 62109 X pen knife pattern.

Since the 96 pattern has no extension bolster, it is a mystery as to what the "X" was intended to designate on this pattern.

The 6296 X SS was discontinued as of Jan. 1, 1966. It was produced with the CASE XX USA tang stamping; however, these examples are rare. The 96 "Citrus Knife" pattern has never been reintroduced.

Case XX 6296 X SS, "citrus knife," red bone, 4-1/4", $600.

PATTERN 97

The basic pattern: The P197 L SSP Shark Tooth is a modern lockback pattern folding knife that was introduced into the Case line in the mid-1970s. The Shark Tooth was the first modern stainless steel lockback in the Case product line. The basic production model of the P197 L SSP has a glazed finish stainless steel clip blade and smooth black Pakkawood handles, with a closed length of 5". The blade is etched with "SHARK TOOTH" inset into a shark. Each knife was sold with a leather belt sheath and individually gift boxed.

The history: The Shark Tooth has an interesting history. The knife was first conceived and produced in 1972; however, it was not released to the market at that time. The Case factory catalog that was released in 1974 (Catalog #71) had a picture and specifications for the Shark Tooth but the words "NOT AVAILABLE" were stamped over the catalog image.

News and rumors regarding the potential introduction of the new Shark Tooth knife generated significant excitement among Case pocket knife collectors in the early to mid-1970s. To understand the high level of "buzz" generated by this knife requires some understanding of the type of company that Case was at that time.

From the immediate post-WWII years and into the mid-1960s, Case was a conservative company, as were most other "old-line" cutlery manufacturers at the time. Case was used to supplying knives to knife users, and knife users of the time tended to be conservative and preferred the older "tried and true" patterns.

At that time, the collecting field was still largely limited to antique knives. In particular, for users of conventional (slipjoint) pocket knives, tradition played a huge role in the selection of a new one to replace a favorite worn out one.

Most knife users wanted the traditional pocket knife patterns made with good old fashioned carbon steel. Case was a favored provider in this market place with its vast line of old-style pocket knives in chrome vanadium steel. As late as 1974, the Case pocket knife line was made up almost 100 percent of patterns that were carryovers from the Case Tested era prior to WWII. This is in no way a criticism of Case, as its conservatism in sticking with the older patterns and the older slower ways of cutlery manufacture is what has made Case special.

A few knife companies did succeed in shaking up the cutlery industry in the 1960s and early 1970s. Most knife collectors are familiar with *Buck Knives* and their revolutionary introduction of the famous Buck 110 Folding Hunter in the mid-1960s. This knife, a beefy folder with a single stainless steel locking blade and brass frame, almost single handedly turned the tide of preference among knife users.

By the early to mid-1970s, most of the older American cutlery firms were scrambling to introduce new "flagship" locking blade knives in response to the market popularity of the Buck 110. Some companies chose to copy the 110 almost exactly. Case took a different route and set out to design a folding knife that improved on the design of the Buck 110.

The result was the *Shark Tooth*, first conceived and produced in 1972 with the pattern number 7197 L SSP. The unique design feature is that the brass frame and handle was contoured and rounded for comfort, while the frame and handles on most competing lockback knives of the Buck 110 variety were flat with no contouring. This contouring required more intensive hand labor to accomplish but it made the Shark Tooth more comfortable in the hand of the knife user.

The original handle material used was curly maple, which is the reason for the "7" in the pattern number, which had been used by Case prior to WWII to denote imitation tortoise shell (celluloid) handle material. Since imitation tortoise shell as a handle material had long been discontinued, Case brought back the "7" for use on some knives with smooth wood handles.

Apparently after production of the 7197 L SSP Shark Tooth began, a problem developed with the curly maple handle material and production was halted to find a solution. CASE made the decision to discontinue the use of curly maple and to use a laminated hardwood (Pakkawood). When finished, the Pakkawood handles on the Shark Tooth have a smooth, black, glossy appearance.

Because a large number of blades had already been stamped with the original pattern number 7197 L SSP,

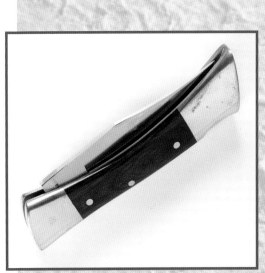

Case XX USA 7 Dot, 1973, P197 L SSP, "Shark's Tooth," 5", $60.

"Shark Tooth" blade etching on the P197 L SSP.

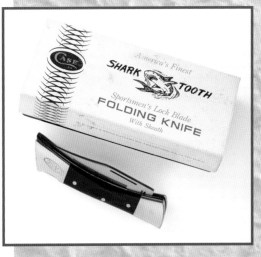

P197 L SSP "Shark Tooth" with box .

Case continued to use these blades even though the handle material had been changed. Blades with the pattern number 7197 L SSP were used in eight dot (1972) and seven dot (1973) knives with the polished black Pakkawood handles.

When new blades had to be made, the prefix "P" replaced the first "7" in the pattern number. The pattern number P197 L SSP first appeared on knives with the six dot (1974) tang stamping and the pattern number has remained that way.

The Shark Tooth was finally released to Case dealers in December of 1975. Each knife was shipped individually boxed with a leather belt sheath, which for the first few years were made of black leather with a smooth surface and the sheath design was "round toe" with a rounded design at the lower end.

Beginning in 1978, the sheath was changed to a different design, which had a squared off lower end and was made of cordovan colored leather with a "basketweave" design.

One interesting note about the Shark Tooth was that at the time it was released, it had a very high retail price as compared to most Case folding knives. In the Case factory price list dated Jan. 1, 1976, the retail price for the Shark Tooth was $50. At that time, the P172 Buffalo retailed for $30 and the 6265 SAB Dr SS "Folding Hunter" with stainless steel blades retailed for $22.50. The P197 L SSP Shark Tooth has remained in the Case product line ever since its introduction and is still offered today.

In the mid-1980s, the Shark Tooth received some positive publicity when it was tested against competing lockback knives by the Montana Outfitters and Guides Association. The following excerpt is from a Case magazine advertisement circa 1986:

Tested Best.

An independent research company conducted an objective test to determine which knives best suited the needs of professional sportsmen, including the prestigious Montana Outfitters and Guides Association. Lock blade knives from Case and two leading competitors were tested in the field for an entire hunting season.

CASE. "The Overwhelming Choice Of Professional Outfitters And Guides"

When the season was over, the guides decided that: 1. Case is a "clearly superior" knife for sportsmen. 2. The Case blade offers superior sharpness. 3. The Case blade is easier to resharpen. 4. In terms of overall preference – which includes workmanship, ease of operation, functional features – Case is the overwhelming choice.

In fact, the choice was so overwhelming that the Montana Outfitters and Guides Association selected Case as the official knife of their prestigious organization.

While the Shark Tooth knife was not specifically mentioned in the text, the advertisement included an image of the knife, so the inference is that it was the Case knife pattern that was used in the testing.

Other variations: There were approximately 1,800 pieces manufactured of the original Shark Tooth that had the curly maple handles and eight dot (1972) blades. These knives were held in stock at Case and were released to dealers beginning in October of 1977. Due to the few pieces released, these original Shark Tooth knives with curly maple handles are relatively rare.

Other examples of the Shark Tooth with curly maple handles have been produced as SFO knives; however, these will have 1980s tang stampings. Limited production runs of the Shark Tooth with stag handles (5197 L SSP) were made during the years of 1979 to 1981.

Newer variations: The initial design of the blade on the Shark Tooth included a semicircle cutout on the tang of the blade to facilitate placement of the index finger for "choking up" on the blade during use. Circa 1991, the blade design was changed to a more conventional squared off design for the tang.

PATTERN 99

The basic pattern: The 99 pattern is a jumbo "swell end" or "torpedo" jack pattern that has been made in one- and two-blade variations. It is a "capped" jack knife, meaning that it has bolsters at both ends; closed length is 4-1/8". The 99 pattern goes back to the early years of Case. When I started collecting Case pocket knives in the mid-1970s, the two-blade 99 pattern was very popular with knife users and was referred to by the "old timers" as the "Rail Splitter." This was probably due to its large size. The 99 pattern was the largest basic two-blade jack knife pattern in the Case line. The 99 pattern really fills the hand. Case sometimes refers to the pattern as an "Uneven Jack."

Blade and handle variations: During the Case XX era, the following principal variations were made:

- 3299 1/2, two-blade jack knife with clip master blade, pen blade and yellow composition handles.
- 5299 1/2, two-blade jack knife with clip master blade, pen blade and stag handles.
- 6299, two-blade jack knife with clip master blade, pen blade and bone handles.

In 1964, another version of the 99 pattern was put into production:

- 1199 Sh R SS, the Whaler, with smooth walnut handles. This is a single-blade version with a polished stainless steel sheepfoot master blade and a bail. The front wood handle was heat stamped "CASE XX WHALER."

The 3299 1/2 will be found with the CASE XX stamping in both the older yellow celluloid (with white liner) and with yellow composition handles. Later examples made from the CASE XX USA era and into the 1970s will have yellow delrin handles. The 3299 1/2 was discontinued in 1978.

Production of the 5299 1/2 continued through the Case XX USA years and the pattern was discontinued in 1970 when Case stopped regular production of stag-handled pocket knives.

The 6299 in the CASE XX stamping will be found in several of the Case XX-era bone color variations including green, regular and red, and in rough black. Rough black examples are fairly common. The 6299 was discontinued as of Jan. 1, 1967; however, it was not made with the CASE XX USA tang stamping. It is probable that after Case stopped production on the 6299, it took some time for stocks to be exhausted.

The 1199 Sh R SS Whaler pattern remained in the Case product line into the early 1980s. Beginning circa 1979, the heat stamping "CASE XX WHALER" on the front handle was dropped and Case began etching the blade with a picture of a whale and the words "CASE XX WHALER." Prior to that time, the blade had a mirror finish. When Case went to the new etched blade version, the blade finish was changed to a glazed finish.

Blade steel and liner material: From the XX era through the time that the patterns were discontinued, chrome vanadium was the only blade steel offered on the 99 two-blade jack patterns. The single-blade Whaler was made with a stainless steel blade. The standard liner material for all 99 patterns was brass.

Other variations: During the Case Tested era and into the Case XX era, the main blade shape on the clip blade versions of the 99 pattern had a shape that collectors refer to as the "A" blade. This blade shape has a distinctive upsweep of the blade pack forming a peak above the nail pull. Circa the early 1960s, the tooling was changed for the main clip blade of the 99 pattern and the blade became slightly narrower without the upsweep. This would be considered the "regular" clip blade. The "A" blade versions of the 3299 1/2 and the 5299 1/2 are somewhat scarcer than the "regular" blade versions.

Newer variations: In 1986, a run of 3299 1/2 jack patterns were made on special order for one of Case's dealers. During the late 1980s and the 1990s, Case reintroduced the 99 pattern and brought out a number of limited production variations of the 99 jack pattern in both bone and stag handles and with a single clip blade or with clip and pen blades. The 99 pattern is still manufactured by Case today in various handle configurations and with polished stainless steel blades.

Case XX USA 5299-1/2, "Rail Splitter," 4-1/8", $175.

Case Tested 5299-1/2, "Rail Splitter," 4-1/8", $650.

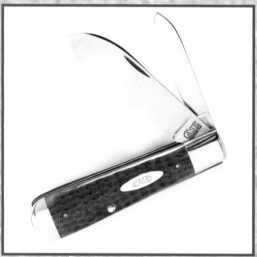

Case Tested 6299, "Rail Splitter," green bone, 4-1/8", $550.

Case XX 6299 "rail splitter," rough black, 4-1/8", $275.

Case Tested 5299-1/2, "Rail Splitter," without shield, 4-1/8", $600.

Case Tested 6299, "Rail Splitter," dark green bone, 4-1/8", $550.

Case XX USA 5 Dot, 1975, 3299-1/2, 4-1/8", $60.

Case Tested 6299-1/2, "Rail Splitter," green bone, 4-1/8", $750.

Case XX USA 4 Dot, 1976, 1199 SH R SS, "Whaler," 4-1/8", $50.

Case XX USA 9 Dot, 1981, lightning S, 1199 Sh R SS, "Whaler," etched blade, 4-1/8", $50.

PATTERN 102

The basic pattern: The 102 pattern is a three-blade "lobster"-style pattern knife and goes back to the early days of Case. It has a distinctive "sleeve-board"-style frame with a master spear blade and a pen blade on the top of the knife and a long "pick" file with a nail cleaner tip that folds along the bottom. The 102 is a relatively small pattern with a closed length of 2-3/4".

Blade and handle variations: During the Case XX era, the following principal variations were made:

- 83102 SS with stainless steel blades; spear master blade and secondary pen blade and long file blade. This is a "shadow" pattern, made without bolsters.
- M3102 R SS with stainless steel handles; stainless steel spear master blade and secondary pen blade and long file blade, with bail.

The 83102 SS was discontinued as of Jan. 1, 1966. It was not made with the CASE XX USA tang stamping. Production of the M3102 R SS continued into the 1970s and the pattern was discontinued circa 1973. The 83102 SS was made with nickel silver as the standard liner material, while the M3102 R SS had no liners since it was made with solid stainless steel handles. The handles on early Case XX examples of the M3102 R SS had a polished finish. Later examples had a "brushed" finish. The 102 pattern has never been reintroduced.

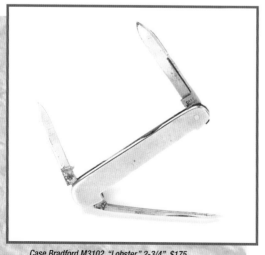

Case Bradford M3102, "Lobster," 2-3/4", $175.

PATTERN 105

The basic pattern: The 105 pattern is a three-blade "lobster"-style pattern knife and was introduced during the Case XX era. It has a rectangular-shaped frame with a master spear blade and a pen blade on the top of the knife and a long flat file with a nail cleaner tip that folds along the bottom. The knife has a closed length of 3-1/8".

The 105 pattern was made only in one variation. The T3105 SS was made during the Case XX era with polished stainless steel blades and with patterned brass handles. The T3105 SS is referred to by collectors as the "Toledo Scale" pattern and was not found listed in any of the available Case factory price lists so the exact years of production are not known.

The handle designation "T" is unique to this knife and refers to the patterned brass handles. Apparently the particular style and coloring of the brass handles resembles patterns of artwork that originated in Toledo, Spain. Similar metal handle scales have been widely used by pocket knife manufacturers in Solingen, Germany; however, I have never seen any other American cutlery firm use this type of handle.

Newer variations: At the time that the T3105 SS was discontinued during the Case XX era, Case had a number of blades and files left over for this pattern. These blades and files (with the CASE XX STAINLESS tang stamping) remained stored at Case for many years. In the early 1970s, Case obtained new "Toledo scale" handles that were similar to the originals. At that time, approximately 2,000 of the knives were assembled with the old mint XX era blades and the new handles. These new T3105 SS knives were then sold through Case dealers.

Since the older blades were used in assembling the new T3105 SS knives, there is only one way to tell the difference between the original XX-era T3105 SS and the new 1970s-era T3105 SS: The new handles will have a series of "dots" outlining the interior scroll patterns on the handles; the older XX era knives do not have these dots on the handles.

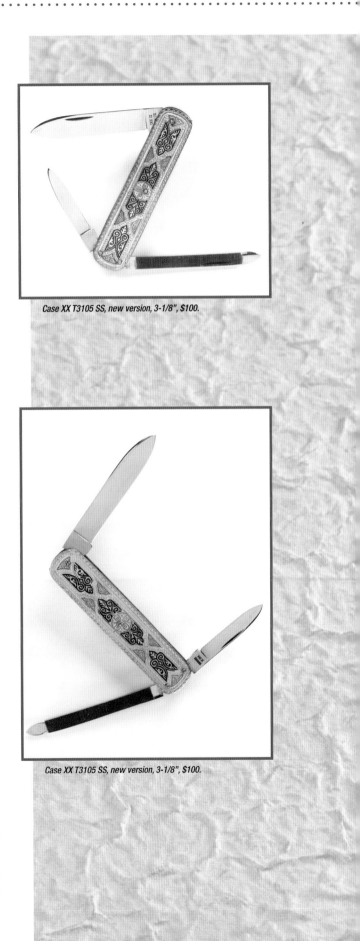

Case XX T3105 SS, new version, 3-1/8", $100.

Case XX T3105 SS, new version, 3-1/8", $100.

PATTERN 109X

The basic pattern: The 109X pattern is referred to by collectors as the "Baby Copperhead" pattern. It is a 3-1/8" (closed length) pen knife with a clip master blade and a pen secondary blade operating on a single backspring.

The pattern is known for the distinctive shape of the "extension" bolster at the pen blade end; the bolster extends upward to cover the sharp corner at the back of the pen blade tang.

The 109X pattern goes back to the early years of Case and is believed that the "X" suffix designates the "extension" bolster on this pattern.

The 62109X in the CASE XX stamping will be found in several of the Case XX-era bone color variations including green, regular and red, and in rough black. Production of the 62109X in bone handles continued into the 1970s.

During the 1970s, delrin was substituted for bone on the 62109X on a random basis. Both delrin and bone examples will be found; however, my observation is that starting in 1978, the pattern was switched back to 100 percent production in bone. The 62109X was discontinued circa 1985.

During all years of production from the Case XX era through 1985, chrome vanadium was the only blade steel offered on the standard production model of the 62109X. The lining material was nickel silver until the late 1970s when it was transitioned over to brass.

Newer variations: The 109X pattern was used for some SFO releases in the 1980s. Beginning in the 1990s, Case reintroduced the 109X pattern to the standard product line. Many recent examples have been produced with stainless steel blade material and in various handle materials including stag.

Case XX 62109X, "Baby Copperhead," red bone, 3-1/8", $250.

Case XX 62109X, "Baby Copperhead," rough black, 3-1/8", $200.

Case XX 62109X, bone, 3-1/8", $150.

PATTERN 131

Case XX USA 7 Dot, 1983, 62109X, 3-1/8", $60.

Case 1996 stamping, 52109X SS, 3-1/8", $60.

Case XX USA 10 Dot, 1980, lightning S, 52109X SSP, Case 75th Anniversary, 3-1/8", $80.

The basic pattern: The 131 pattern is well known to Case pocket knife collectors as the "Canoe" and is an equal end-style frame with distinctive "extension" bolsters at both ends. The extension bolsters cover the sharp corners at the back of each blade tang and provide a "cutout" for better grip and for ease of blade opening. Closed length is 3-5/8". The 131 pattern goes back to the Case Tested era, when it was made in both two- and three-blade variations.

Blade and handle variations: Beginning with the CASE XX tang stamp, the 131 pattern was offered as a two-blade "double end" knife with a master spear blade at one end and a pen blade at the other end, operating on a single backspring. The following handle variations were offered during the Case XX era:

- 52131, with stag handles.
- 62131, with bone handle (introduced late in the XX era).

Production of the 52131 continued through the Case XX USA years and the pattern was discontinued in 1970 when Case stopped regular production of stag handled pocket knives.

The 62131 deserves a special note here. While the 52131 was made throughout the entire Case XX era, the 62131 was introduced during the time period that the CASE XX tang stamping was being changed over to the CASE XX USA tang stamping. The Case factory price list dated Feb. 1, 1965 does not list the 62131, but it is listed in the price list dated Jan. 1, 1966. A very few examples of the 62131 were produced with the CASE XX tang stamping. This may have been a pilot run from 1964 or 1965. The 62131 with the CASE XX tang stamping is extremely rare and quite frankly it is a commonly counterfeited knife.

Production of the 62131 in bone handles continued through the Case XX USA era and into the 1970s. During the 1970s, delrin was substituted for bone on many Case pocket knife patterns on a random basis. I personally have never seen a 62131 handed in delrin; however, I have heard that they exist and if so, they should be considered as a rare variation.

In 1974, a change was made and an etching of a canoe was added to the main blade of the 62131. Blade etchings on Case pocket knives are common on current production knives, but at that time, very few Case pocket knives were made with etched blades. The ad-

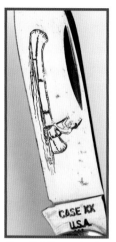

"Canoe" etching used on the 62131 starting in 1974.

dition of the etching to the main blade of the 62131 represented one of Case's early efforts to cater to knife collectors. The 62131 will be found both with and without the canoe etching in the 1974 tang stamping, but examples of the plain blade version from that year are scarce. The "canoe" blade etching on the 62131 has continued until the present day on the basic bone handled standard production 62131 with chrome vanadium blades.

Blade steel and liner material: From the Case XX era through the present day, the liner material for all 131 patterns has been brass (some examples with pearl and exotic materials may use nickel silver). Traditionally, the only blade steel option on standard product versions of the 131 was chrome vanadium. The first stainless steel version of the 131 was the 52131 SSP that was produced in 1977 as part of the limited production "Blue Scroll" stag set. Beginning in the late 1980s, SFO versions with polished stainless blades were made. Beginning in the 1990s, a number of standard product 131 patterns with polished stainless steel blades were introduced.

Other variations: The 52131 was made with both a "long pull" and a "regular pull" on the master blade during the Case XX era. The long pull examples were made early in the Case XX years and are quite rare.

The 131 pattern with two blades was traditionally made with both blades operating on a single backspring. Beginning in 1985, the tooling was changed to a two-backspring design, with each blade operating on its own backspring. I believe that both variations were produced in 1985, but by 1986 the change was complete. Manufacture of the 131 pattern with two backsprings has continued to the present day.

Newer variations: The 131 "Canoe" pattern has been widely produced by Case in recent years. It has been made in a wide variety of handle variations and with stainless steel blades.

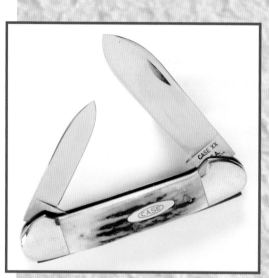

Case XX USA 10 Dot 52131, 1970, "Canoe," 3-5/8", $275.

Case XX 52131, "Canoe," red stag, 3-5/8", $750.

Case XX USA 52131, "Canoe," 3-5/8", $250.

Case XX USA 3 Dot 62131, 1977, "Canoe," red bone, 3-5/8", $80.

Case XX USA 10 Dot 62131, 1980, 3-5/8", $65.

Case XX USA 3 Dot, 1977 52131 SSP, "blue scroll," 3-5/8", $125.

Case 1996 stamping, 62131 SS, red bone, 3-5/8", $45.

Case XX 52131, 3-5/8", $500.

Case XX USA 7 Dot, 1973, 62131 bone, 3-5/8", $80.

MUSKRAT PATTERN

The basic pattern: The Muskrat is a well-known Case pocket knife pattern that is made with the 47 "stockman" frame or handle die, with a closed length of 3-7/8". The standard Case Muskrat has always been constructed with two identical "California clip"-style blades, each operating on its own backspring.

The Muskrat is one of a very few Case pocket knife patterns that never had a pattern number. The knife was always listed in Case price lists simply as "Muskrat" and goes back to the Case Tested era. When Case began stamping pattern numbers on pocket knives consistently during the Case XX era, the Muskrat was made with the word "MUSKRAT" stamped on the tang of the rear blade.

The basic two-blade knife as described with bone handles and with chrome vanadium blades was the only version of the Muskrat made in the Case standard pocket knife line from the Case XX era through the 1980s. The Muskrat in the CASE XX stamping will be found in several of the Case XX-era bone color variations including green, "early Rogers," regular and red, and in "late Rogers" bone and rough black.

The use of bone on the standard Muskrat continued through the Case XX USA era. During the 1970s, delrin was substituted for bone on the Muskrat on a random basis. Both delrin and bone examples will be found; however my observation is that starting in 1978 the Muskrat pattern was switched back to being handled 100% in bone. The basic Muskrat pattern in chrome vanadium with bone handles remained in the Case line as a standard pattern into the 1990s. In 1997, it became part of the "Chestnut Bone" series but was discontinued in the early 2000s.

Blade steel and liner material: From the XX era through the time that the pattern was discontinued, the standard product Muskrat was only offered with chrome vanadium as the blade steel. The liner material during these years was nickel silver. Beginning circa 1978, Case began changing all pocket knife patterns with nickel silver liners

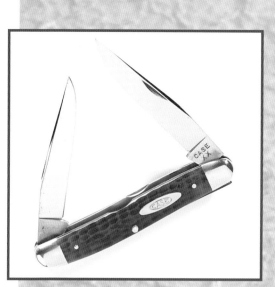

Case XX Muskrat, red bone, 3-7/8", $600.

Case XX USA 3 Dot, 1977, Muskrat, dark bone, 3-7/8", $100.

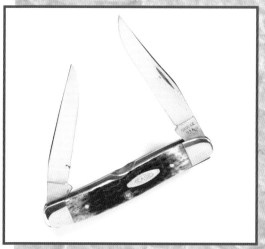

Case XX USA 2 Dot, 1978, Muskrat, bone, 3-7/8", $100.

to the standard use of brass as the lining material. This change was complete by 1980.

Other variations: The first use of stainless steel blades in the Muskrat pattern was in 1978, when Case made the Stag Muskrat SSP pattern with stag handles and glazed finished stainless steel blades for inclusion in the limited production 1978 "Red Scroll" stag sets.

A standard production stainless steel Muskrat variation in bone handles (Muskrat SS) was added to the Case pocket knife line in 1991 but was only made for the years of 1991-1992. This knife had glazed finish stainless steel blades.

Traditionally, the Muskrat pattern was tooled with two backsprings and with no center liner between the two springs. Since the two blades sit in a parallel position in the closed knife, a center liner is not necessary. However, beginning circa 1981, Case added a center brass liner to the Muskrat pattern and it was made this way for awhile. Later the construction was changed again to delete the center liner. I do not know the exact years that the center liner was used, but by 1986 the change was complete and the center liner had been deleted from the Muskrat pattern.

Hawbaker's Special Muskrat: This version was made as a "special factory order" or SFO knife for S. Stanley Hawbaker and Sons, a trapping supply company located in Pennsylvania. The so-called "Hawbaker Muskrat" or "Hawbaker's Special" will have the normal "California clip" blade in the front of the knife but the back blade will be a long sheepfoot blade with a straight cutting edge and a sharp point. The blades will be etched "HAWBAKER'S SPECIAL" and "IMPROVED MUSKRAT KNIFE." There were many variations of the "Hawbaker's Special" pattern made from the Case XX era until 1982.

Newer variations: The Muskrat in recent years has been widely produced both in the Case standard product line and for SFOs and has been offered in a variety of handle materials with polished stainless steel blades

Case XX USA 8 Dot, 1982, Muskrat "Hawbaker's Special," 3-7/8", $200.

Case XX, Muskrat, bone, 3-7/8", $350.

Case XX USA 2 Dot, 1978, stag MUSKRAT SSP, 3-7/8", $175.

FLY FISHERMAN PATTERN

The basic pattern: The "Fly Fisherman" pattern is a four-blade "lobster"-style pattern knife with flat metal handles. This knife is one of a very few Case pocket knife patterns that never had a pattern number. The knife was listed in Case price lists simply as Fly Fisherman but the full pattern name was Fly Fisherman SS and the name was abbreviated Fly Fish on the blade tang in blade in place of a pattern number. Closed length is 3-7/8" and the pattern goes back to the Case Tested era.

The Fly Fisherman was always made with flat metal handles and had a main clip blade, a scissors, a long file (for sharpening hooks) with a hook remover tip, and a long "pick" that could be used to untie knots in fishing line. The handle was equipped with a bale at one end and a screwdriver tip at the other end. The front handle was engraved with "CASE'S (long tail C) FLY FISHING KNIFE." The back handle had a ruler scale in inches engraved.

Early versions of the Fly Fisherman with the "CASE TESTED" tang stamping will sometimes be found with a spear master blade, though most will have the clip blade. During that era, the Fly Fisherman was made with a nickel silver handle. It was listed in Case XX era Case factory price lists beginning in September 1949 and discontinued as of Jan. 1, 1976.

An interesting fact is that for all of the years that it was part of the Case pocket knife line, the Fly Fisherman was Case's most expensive pocket knife. For example, the Case factory price list from 1970 indicates a retail price of $18 for the Fly Fisherman; the same price lists shows the stag-handled 5172 Bulldog retailing at $13 and the 5488 "large congress" with stag handles retailing at $12. During its last year of production in 1975, the retail price of the Fly Fisherman had risen to $27.50. This is not a lot of money for a knife by today's standards, but consider that the 6254 "Trapper" retailed for $11.50 at that time.

Another interesting fact is that Case was one of only two American cutlery firms to offer a Fly Fisherman pattern pocket knife. Union Cutlery Company (Kabar) produced a similar fly fishing knife pattern with celluloid handles. The fly fishing knife in general seems to be an English knife pattern and numerous variations were made by Sheffield cutlery firms.

Other variations: The Fly Fisherman pattern is unusual in that both the clip blade and the long file blade are considered as "master" blades and each will have the Case logo tang stamping. Due to this fact, some "transition" examples that have a different logo stamp on each blade will be observed.

Transition models are a result of blades from one year that are left over and are used up prior to new blades being stamped out for a particular year. For example, some Fly Fisherman patterns will be found with the CASE XX tang stamp on one blade and the CASE XX USA tang stamp on the other large blade. There are also transition models with CASE XX USA and CASE XX USA (ten dots) and with various "dots" combinations during the 1970s. Transition models are somewhat scarcer than "regular" models; however, the Fly Fisherman pattern was not produced in large numbers so all models are scarce.

Case apparently intended to reintroduce the Fly Fisherman pattern in the mid-1980s. I have seen a copy of a Case new product sheet that shows a new Fly Fisherman pattern along with some other new pocket knife and filet knife patterns. The knife was listed as being "available in 1986." I have never observed an example of one of these new Fly Fisherman pocket knives, and it was not listed in the 1985 or 1986 Case factory price lists or in the 1986 Case factory catalog, so I do knot know whether it was actually put into production.

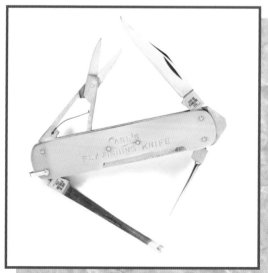

Case XX USA 10 Dot/9 Dot, "Fly Fisherman," 3-7/8", $250.

PATTERN S-2

The basic pattern: The S-2 is a small two-blade "lobster"-style pattern pen knife. The S-2 is an unusual Case pocket knife pattern in that it really has no pattern number. The handle code "S" designates the patterned sterling silver handles that were used on this pattern. To the best of my knowledge the S-2 is the only standard product Case pocket knife pattern to be made with sterling silver handles. The S-2 has a closed length of 2-1/4" and has a spear master blade of polished stainless steel and a file blade. The S-2 pattern was always made with a bail.

Case factory price lists first show the S-2 as of Feb. 1, 1965. It was produced with the CASE XX STAINLESS tang stamping, so production apparently began prior to 1965. The S-2 was made through April 1, 1967 and was produced with the CASE XX USA tang stamping. Some examples of the S-2 will be found with a "long pull" master blade while others will have "regular pull." The S-2 has never been reintroduced.

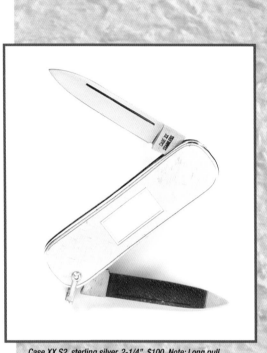

Case XX S2, sterling silver, 2-1/4", $100. Note: Long pull.

Case XX USA-S-2, sterling silver, 2-1/4", $100. Note: Regular pull.

SIDEWINDER PATTERN

The basic pattern: The Sidewinder is a large Case locking blade folding knife that was designed with an unusual "side lock" locking mechanism and introduced in 1980. Both the handle pattern and the shape of the blade are quite unusual. The Sidewinder is one of a very few Case pocket knife patterns that never had a pattern number. The knife was listed in Case price lists simply as Sidewinder. The Sidewinder was shipped individually boxed with a leather belt sheath. The handle material is polished brown Pakkawood. Closed length is 5-1/4" and blade material is stainless steel and the liner material is brass.

The usually shaped clip blade on the Sidewinder locks open and is released by depressing the CASE shield on the front of the handle. The glazed finish blade has an etching of a picture of a snake with the word SIDEWINDER. Case literature states that the Sidewinder could be closed with one hand due to the side lock mechanism and the definite half stop on the blade; Case received a patent for the locking mechanism. The Sidewinder was apparently never produced in large numbers and was discontinued in 1985.

Variations: During the years that the Sidewinder was produced, a number of manufacturing changes were made in particular as to how the knives were marked. The following excerpts from 1981 and 1982 editions of the *Case Collectors' Club Newsletter* explain some of these changes.

Case Collectors' Club Newsletter, June 1981:

Sidewinder Stampings

On the original factory order of 5,000 pieces, The Sidewinder was stamped as follows: CASE XX SS U.S.A. and 10 dots. The words PAT. PEND. are engraved above the stamp. This was done on the Pile side of the blade tang, which is the reverse of our normal stamping procedures. This was done to accommodate the possible stamping of the pattern name (SIDEWINDER) on the Mark side of the blade tang.

As it turned out, the SIDEWINDER name was incorporated into the photo-etching on the blade. Because of this, the stamp will be changed. The 9 dot stamp will be on the Mark side of the blade tang and the PAT. PEND. will be stamped on the Pile Side.

With the first 5,000 knives having the reversed stamping on them, they will probably become a much sought after item by the collector.

Case Collectors' Club Newsletter, December 1981:

Production Changes

Sidewinders – *You may be noticing a very prominent change in the appearance of the Sidewinder. Manufacturing has changed the bolster pins from nickel-silver to brass. The change to brass is to afford smoother action in blade movement and to lessen galling. While the change will not effect the cost of the knife, the brass pins will be very noticeable.*

Case Collectors' Club Newsletter, December 1982:

What's New

SIDEWINDER PATENT – *We finally received our patent number for the Sidewinder. We will now be stamping blades with "PAT. NO. 4274200." This will be in the location previously occupied by "PAT. PEND." Although this is in process it may be a few months before it is seen on the market.*

Case XX USA 8 Dot, 1982, lightning S, "Sidewinder," 5-1/4", $250.

"Sidewinder" with box (8 dot, 1982).

TEXAS LOCKHORN PATTERN

The basic pattern: The Texas Lockhorn is a large Case locking blade folding knife that was designed with two identical locking clip blades. It was introduced in 1980 and is in some respects a jumbo version of the Muskrat pattern with locking blades. The closed length of the Texas Lockhorn is 4-1/2" and the blades are stainless steel with a glazed finish. Each of the two identical "California clip" blades operates on its own backspring locking mechanism. Handle material is smooth white composition and liner material is brass.

The Texas Lockhorn is one of a very few Case pocket knife patterns that never had a pattern number. The knife was listed in Case price lists simply as Texas Lockhorn and was shipped individually boxed with a leather belt sheath. The Texas Lockhorn was discontinued in 1985.

Variations: The Texas Lockhorn was manufactured with two different handle materials: a yellowish white Micarta handles that resembled ivory and a smooth white delrin. The use of Micarta on the Texas Lockhorn represented the first use of Micarta as a handle material on a Case folding knife. The years of use for each of the two materials is unknown. However, the 1980 Case factory catalog indicates the handle material on the Texas Lockhorn as "smooth Ivory plastic." The 1983 Case factory catalog is less specific but lists the material as "smooth imitation ivory." The white delrin was subject to cracking around the four-corner handle pins on the Texas Lockhorn.

Some Texas Lockhorn knives were made on special order with one of the blades having a serrated edge.

Case XX USA 9 Dot, 1981, lightning S, "Texas Lockhorn," ivory micarta, made for Cabela's, one blade serrated, 4-1/2", $250.

Case XX USA 9 Dot, 1981, lightning S, Texas Lockhorn, white delrin, 4-1/2", $200.

CASE POCKET KNIVES VALUE GUIDE

When buying and selling antique pocket knives, there are many factors that determine the final sale price for a particular knife. Knife prices can rise and fall based on collecting trends and economic factors.

In most transactions, the final sale price depends primarily on the dynamics between the individual buyer and seller. How badly does the buyer want the knife? And how motivated is the seller? The dynamic in buying and selling pocket knives is in some respects no different from that involved in any other transaction, whether it is the purchase and sale of a house, an automobile, or commodities.

The big difference in a pocket knife sale is that there is often a sentimental or emotional component. Every knife collector has different preferences as to pattern, condition, the exact coloring of handle material, etc. For each knife, there are intangible factors that may affect a buyer's enthusiasm to make the purchase. Likewise, some knife sellers are attached to their knives and not strongly motivated to sell, while another seller may want to quickly divest knives to obtain cash.

The values shown in this guide should be used as just that – a guide. It is up to each individual buyer and seller to determine an exact price for any knife transaction.

Values are for knives in mint condition, unused, unsharpened, never carried and with no significant rust spots. On Case pocket knives with chrome vanadium blades, a knife with a few minor specks or "pepper spots" may still be considered "mint" by most collectors. Likewise, some degree of blade rub or very minor blade wobble may be acceptable on a mint knife if the knife came from the factory that way. On older and rarer knives, these minor issues may not affect the value much. The newer a knife is, the more the expectation that a mint knife will be "perfect" in order to be considered as truly mint.

However, handle cracks or handle shrinkage (on composition handled knives) even on an unused knife will significantly reduce the value, as will lazy blades. It is rare to find an unused mint older Case pocket knife with lazy or slow blades, but it does happen. Handle cracks (hairlines) are commonly seen on older Case bone-handled knives, as are cracks at the pins on composition- and pearl-handled knives.

If a knife is sharpened, used, stained, tarnished, or cleaned and buffed, the value of the knife will drop exponentially, though all used and sharpened older Case pocket knives do have some value. Again, the older and rare knives tend to retain a higher percentage of their mint value when used. Newer knives that have been sharpened or carried often have value not as a collectible but for resale as a "using" knife.

ADDITIONAL NOTES ON VALUES

All values shown are for MINT knives with no cracks.

For bone-handled knives, the values shown are for basic or "dark" bone handles or for handles with very minor coloring.

For Case XX stamped knives with "true" green bone handles, values will be from about 50 percent higher than shown, for common or less desired patterns, to up to three to four times the values shown, for very desirable patterns with medium to lighter colored green bone. The tinting or coloring of the bone often has an impact on value. Similar multipliers apply for Case XX-stamped knives with "early Rogers" bone handles.

For Case XX-stamped knives with reddish or red bone handles, values will increase from about a 25 percent addition to the values shown, for darker red bone, up to double the values shown, for nice evenly matched blood red or lighter red bone. In general for the Case XX era, there are far more specimens of reddish or red bone handled knives as compared to those handled in green bone. The "red bone" multipliers also apply to knives handled with "late Rogers" bone. Likewise, "late Roger" bone is significantly more often observed than is "early Rogers" bone.

Case XX-stamped knives with rough black handles will generally be valued according to the values shown for the "basic bone" handles. For some patterns, rough black examples may command a slight premium, in the range of 25 percent, if the knife is scarce in rough black. There are a few patterns that are rare in rough black; these can be worth significantly more. On the other hand, some basic jack knife patterns (examples are the 35 and 99 patterns) were widely produced in rough black, lowering the values for these specimens by about 25 percent, as compared to bone.

Case XX-stamped knives with red stag handles command significant premiums as compared to those with regular stag handles. However, there are many shades and variations in color on red stag. Generally, a nicely colored red stag will have up to twice the value of the same knife in basic stag, or up to three times the value for very desirable patterns (examples: 5254 and 5488).

Some Case XX patterns were made with both regular pull and long pull master blades. Those with long pull blades were made early in the Case XX era, so these examples are often found with "premium" handle materials like red stag and green bone. For very desirable patterns (examples are the 6275, 6375, 5375, 5488 and 6488), examples with long pull will be valued at from double to triple that of the same knife with "regular" pulls. For less desirable patterns (6231 and 92042, for example), the value premium for a long pull example will be in the 25 percent range.

Case XX and Case XX USA-stamped knives with "flat yellow" handles are generally valued somewhat higher as compared to "regular" yellow composition handles. The value premium for "flat yellow" ranges in general from 10 percent for less collected patterns (like the 3318) to 40 percent or more for patterns that are more widely collected (like the 54 pattern).

For Case pocket knives made during the 1970s, a set of nice red bone handles can increase the value of a knife by 25-40 percent, as compared to the "basic bone" values shown. Again for more desirable patterns, the percentage increase will be in the higher end of the range.

For 1970s delrin-handled knives, where the knife was normally handled in bone, the delrin-handled specimen will be about equal in value to the "basic" bone-handled knife, or up to 20 percent lower for some patterns that were widely produced in delrin. The values in the table shown for delrin-handled knives are specific to knives that were switched 100 percent to production in delrin. If a pattern is particularly desirable or widely collected, certain delrin examples may have higher values if fewer were produced in delrin (examples: 6254 and 6254 SSP).

For Case XX-stamped knives with imitation pearl handles, a knife handled in "cracked ice" may command a slight premium over a "regular" imitation pearl-handled knife; however, collector interest in imitation pearl-handled knives is generally low, other than for rare patterns (examples: 9383 and 93047). Often these rarer patterns will only be found in cracked ice.

This value guide does not include a number of rare and obscure Case XX patterns, and likewise there are many minor variations of the patterns included that are not shown or valued. Generally these rarer patterns and minor variations are only noticed by assiduous collectors who may be specialists in a particular pattern.

There are other Case pocket knife variations, second cut stag handles for example, that are better known and more valuable; however, these knives are often so rarely found in mint condition that the establishment of a value is difficult if not impossible. In some instances, the word "RARE" is inserted in place of a price; these are knives that are so rare that the market for them is very limited, and they are frequently counterfeited.

The best advice I can give to the Case pocket knife collector in establishing values of individual knives is to learn the "basic" patterns and variations and then gain experience through study and observation, which are the best teachers.

VALUE GUIDE, CASE XX THROUGH 1989

4100 SS, WHITE COMPOSITION HANDLES

CASE XX	$250
CASE XX USA	$125
10 Dot, 1970	$150
Dots 1971-1979	$100
10 Dot, 1980	—
Dots 1981-1989	—

4200 SS, WHITE COMPOSITION HANDLES

CASE XX	Rare
CASE XX USA	$175
10 Dot, 1970	$200
Dots 1971-1979	$125
10 Dot, 1980	—
Dots 1981-1989	—

3201, YELLOW COMPOSITION HANDLES

CASE XX	$75
CASE XX USA	$60
10 Dot, 1970	$75
Dots 1971-1979	$60
10 Dot, 1980	—
Dots 1981-1989	—

6201, BONE HANDLES

CASE XX	$90
CASE XX USA	$75
10 Dot, 1970	$75
Dots 1971-1979	$60
10 Dot, 1980	—
Dots 1981-1989	—

6201 R SS, DELRIN HANDLES

CASE XX —	
CASE XX USA	—
10 Dot, 1970	—
Dots 1971-1979	$30
10 Dot, 1980	$30
Dots 1981-1989	$30

9201, IMITATION PEARL HANDLES

CASE XX	$75
CASE XX USA	$60
10 Dot, 1970	$60
Dots 1971-1979	$30
10 Dot, 1980	—
Dots 1981-1989	—

9201 R SS, IMITATION PEARL HANDLES

CASE XX	—
CASE XX USA	—
10 Dot, 1970	
Dots 1971-1979	$30
10 Dot, 1980	$30
Dots 1981-1989	$30

6202 1/2, BONE HANDLES

CASE XX	$125
CASE XX USA	$75
10 Dot, 1970	$100
Dots 1971-1979	$60

10 Dot, 1980	—
Dots 1981-1989	—

6201 1/2, DELRIN HANDLES

CASE XX	—
CASE XX USA	—
10 Dot, 1970	—
Dots 1971-1979	$45
10 Dot, 1980	—
Dots 1981-1989	—

6205, BONE HANDLES

CASE XX	$225
CASE XX USA	—
10 Dot, 1970	—
Dots 1971-1979	—
10 Dot, 1980	—
Dots 1981-1989	—

6205 RAZ, BONE HANDLES

CASE XX	$300
CASE XX USA	$225
10 Dot, 1970	$250
Dots 1971-1979	$125
10 Dot, 1980	—
Dots 1981-1989	—

2207, BLACK COMPOSITION HANDLES

CASE XX	$250
CASE XX USA	—
10 Dot, 1970	—
Dots 1971-1979	—
10 Dot, 1980	—
Dots 1981-1989	—

6207, BONE HANDLES

CASE XX	$200
CASE XX USA	$125
10 Dot, 1970	$125
Dots 1971-1979	$75
10 Dot, 1980	—
Dots 1981-1989	—

6207 SP SSP, BONE HANDLES

CASE XX	—
CASE XX USA	—
10 Dot, 1970	—
Dots 1971-1979	$75
10 Dot, 1980	$75
Dots 1981-1989	$50

6208, BONE HANDLES

CASE XX	$150
CASE XX USA	$100
10 Dot, 1970	$100
Dots 1971-1979	$60
10 Dot, 1980	—
Dots 1981-1989	—

A6208, APPALOOSA BONE HANDLES

CASE XX	—
CASE XX USA	—
10 Dot, 1970	—
Dots 1971-1979	$55

10 Dot, 1980	$55
Dots 1981-1989	$55

A6208 SS, APPALOOSA BONE HANDLES

CASE XX	—
CASE XX USA	—
10 Dot, 1970	—
Dots 1971-1979	—
10 Dot, 1980	—
Dots 1981-1989	$55

6208 SS, DELRIN HANDLES

CASE XX	—
CASE XX USA	—
10 Dot, 1970	—
Dots 1971-1979	—
10 Dot, 1980	—
Dots 1981-1989	$35

6308, BONE HANDLES

CASE XX	$275
CASE XX USA	$225
10 Dot, 1970	$250
Dots 1971-1979	$75
10 Dot, 1980	$75
Dots 1981-1989	$75

62009, BONE HANDLES

CASE XX	$125
CASE XX USA	$80
10 Dot, 1970	$80
Dots 1971-1979	—
10 Dot, 1980	—
Dots 1981-1989	—

62009, DELRIN HANDLES

CASE XX	—
CASE XX USA	—
10 Dot, 1970	$60
Dots 1971-1979	$50
10 Dot, 1980	—
Dots 1981-1989	—

62009 1/2, BONE HANDLES

CASE XX	$125
CASE XX USA	$75
10 Dot, 1970	$100
Dots 1971-1979	—
10 Dot, 1980	—
Dots 1981-1989	—

62009 1/2, DELRIN HANDLES

CASE XX	—
CASE XX USA	—
10 Dot, 1970	$60
Dots 1971-1979	$50
10 Dot, 1980	—
Dots 1981-1989	—

A62009 1/2, APPALOOSA BONE HANDLES

CASE XX	—
CASE XX USA	—
10 Dot, 1970	—

Dots 1971-1979 $60
10 Dot, 1980 $60
Dots 1981-1989 $60

A62009 1/2 SS, APPALOOSA BONE HANDLES
CASE XX   —
CASE XX USA   —
10 Dot, 1970   —
Dots 1971-1979   —
10 Dot, 1980   —
Dots 1981-1989 $60

62009 1/2 SS, DELRIN HANDLES
CASE XX   —
CASE XX USA   —
10 Dot, 1970   —
Dots 1971-1979   —
10 Dot, 1980   —
Dots 1981-1989 $40

62009 RAZ, BONE HANDLES
CASE XX $150
CASE XX USA $100
10 Dot, 1970 $120
Dots 1971-1979   —
10 Dot, 1980   —
Dots 1981-1989   —

62009 RAZ, DELRIN HANDLES
CASE XX   —
CASE XX USA   —
10 Dot, 1970 $75
Dots 1971-1979 $60
10 Dot, 1980   —
Dots 1981-1989   —

6111 1/2 L, BONE HANDLES
CASE XX $500
CASE XX USA $300
10 Dot, 1970 $300
Dots 1971-1979 $140
10 Dot, 1980 $150
Dots 1981-1989 $150

11011, WALNUT HANDLES
CASE XX $80
CASE XX USA $65
10 Dot, 1970 $75
Dots 1971-1979 $60
10 Dot, 1980   —
Dots 1981-1989   —

61011, BONE HANDLES
CASE XX $110
CASE XX USA $150
10 Dot, 1970   —
Dots 1971-1979   —
10 Dot, 1980   —
Dots 1981-1989   —

61011, PAKKAWOOD HANDLES
CASE XX $75
CASE XX USA $60
10 Dot, 1970 $75

Dots 1971-1979 $50
10 Dot, 1980 $50
Dots 1981-1989   —

61011, DELRIN HANDLES
CASE XX   —
CASE XX USA   —
10 Dot, 1970   —
Dots 1971-1979   —
10 Dot, 1980   —
Dots 1981-1989 $35

6214, BONE HANDLES
CASE XX $125
CASE XX USA $90
10 Dot, 1970 $100
Dots 1971-1979   —
10 Dot, 1980   —
Dots 1981-1989   —

6214, DELRIN HANDLES
CASE XX   —
CASE XX USA   —
10 Dot, 1970 $65
Dots 1971-1979 $50
10 Dot, 1980   —
Dots 1981-1989   —

6214 1/2, BONE HANDLES
CASE XX $125
CASE XX USA $90
10 Dot, 1970 $100
Dots 1971-1979   —
10 Dot, 1980   —
Dots 1981-1989   —

6214 1/2, DELRIN HANDLES
CASE XX   —
CASE XX USA   —
10 Dot, 1970 $65
Dots 1971-1979 $50
10 Dot, 1980   —
Dots 1981-1989   —

1116 SP, WALNUT HANDLES
CASE XX $80
CASE XX USA $60
10 Dot, 1970 $80
Dots 1971-1979 $60
10 Dot, 1980   —
Dots 1981-1989   —

6216, BONE HANDLES
CASE XX $140
CASE XX USA   Rare
10 Dot, 1970   —
Dots 1971-1979   —
10 Dot, 1980   —
Dots 1981-1989   —

6216 1/2, BONE HANDLES
CASE XX $140
CASE XX USA $65
10 Dot, 1970   —

Dots 1971-1979   —
10 Dot, 1980   —
Dots 1981-1989   —

2217, BLACK COMPOSITION
CASE XX $175
CASE XX USA   —
10 Dot, 1970   —
Dots 1971-1979   —
10 Dot, 1980   —
Dots 1981-1989   —

6217, BONE HANDLES
CASE XX $250
CASE XX USA $125
10 Dot, 1970 $150
Dots 1971-1979   —
10 Dot, 1980   —
Dots 1981-1989   —

6217, PAKKAWOOD HANDLES
CASE XX   —
CASE XX USA   —
10 Dot, 1970 $100
Dots 1971-1979 $80
10 Dot, 1980   —
Dots 1981-1989   —

3318 SH PEN, YELLOW COMPOSITION HANDLES
CASE XX $125
CASE XX USA $90
10 Dot, 1970 $125
Dots 1971-1979 $60
10 Dot, 1980 $60
Dots 1981-1989 $50

3318 SH SP, YELLOW COMPOSITION HANDLES
CASE XX   —
CASE XX USA   —
10 Dot, 1970   —
Dots 1971-1979   —
10 Dot, 1980   —
Dots 1981-1989 $45

4318 SH SP, WHITE COMPOSITION HANDLES
CASE XX $125
CASE XX USA $90
10 Dot, 1970 $125
Dots 1971-1979 $75
10 Dot, 1980   —
Dots 1981-1989   —

5318 SH SP SS, STAG HANDLES
CASE XX   —
CASE XX USA   —
10 Dot, 1970   —
Dots 1971-1979   —
10 Dot, 1980   —
Dots 1981-1989 $65

6318 Sh Sp, BONE HANDLES

CASE XX	$175
CASE XX USA	$125
10 Dot, 1970	$125
Dots 1971-1979	$75
10 Dot, 1980	$60
Dots 1981-1989	$50

6318 Sh PEN, BONE HANDLES

CASE XX	$175
CASE XX USA	$125
10 Dot, 1970	$125
Dots 1971-1979	$80
10 Dot, 1980	$60
Dots 1981-1989	$50

6318 Sp Pu, BONE HANDLES

CASE XX	$200
CASE XX USA	$125
10 Dot, 1970	$125
Dots 1971-1979	$80
10 Dot, 1980	$60
Dots 1981-1989	$50

5120 RSS, STAG HANDLES

CASE XX	—
CASE XX USA	—
10 Dot, 1970	—
Dots 1971-1979	$50
10 Dot, 1980	$45
Dots 1981-1989	$45

5120 R SS, STAG HANDLES

CASE XX	—
CASE XX USA	—
10 Dot, 1970	—
Dots 1971-1979	—
10 Dot, 1980	—
Dots 1981-1989	$45

2220, BLACK COMPOSITION HANDLES

CASE XX	$80
CASE XX USA	$60
10 Dot, 1970	$65
Dots 1971-1979	$55
10 Dot, 1980	—
Dots 1981-1989	—

3220, YELLOW COMPOSITION HANDLES

CASE XX	$90
CASE XX USA	$75
10 Dot, 1970	$90
Dots 1971-1979	$60
10 Dot, 1980	—
Dots 1981-1989	—

5220, STAG HANDLES

CASE XX	$175
CASE XX USA	$125
10 Dot, 1970	$125
Dots 1971-1979	—
10 Dot, 1980	—
Dots 1981-1989	—

5220 SS, STAG HANDLES

CASE XX	—
CASE XX USA	—
10 Dot, 1970	—
Dots 1971-1979	—
10 Dot, 1980	—
Dots 1981-1989	$60

6220, BONE HANDLES

CASE XX	$110
CASE XX USA	$100
10 Dot, 1970	$100
Dots 1971-1979	—
10 Dot, 1980	—
Dots 1981-1989	—

6220, DELRIN HANDLES

CASE XX	—
CASE XX USA	—
10 Dot, 1970	$65
Dots 1971-1979	$50
10 Dot, 1980	—
Dots 1981-1989	—

SR6220, SATIN ROSE BONE HANDLES

CASE XX	—
CASE XX USA	—
10 Dot, 1970	—
Dots 1971-1979	$60
10 Dot, 1980	$60
Dots 1981-1989	$60

6220 SS, DELRIN HANDLES

CASE XX	—
CASE XX USA	—
10 Dot, 1970	—
Dots 1971-1979	—
10 Dot, 1980	—
Dots 1981-1989	$25

8220 SS, PEARL HANDLES

CASE XX	—
CASE XX USA	—
10 Dot, 1970	—
Dots 1971-1979	—
10 Dot, 1980	—
Dots 1981-1989	$75

9220, IMITATION PEARL HANDLES

CASE XX	$150
CASE XX USA	—
10 Dot, 1970	—
Dots 1971-1979	—
10 Dot, 1980	—
Dots 1981-1989	—

220024 Sp, BLACK COMPOSITION HANDLES

CASE XX	$250
CASE XX USA	—
10 Dot, 1970	—
Dots 1971-1979	—
10 Dot, 1980	—
Dots 1981-1989	—

31024 1/2, YELLOW COMPOSITION HANDLES

CASE XX	$50
CASE XX USA	—
10 Dot, 1970	—
Dots 1971-1979	—
10 Dot, 1980	—
Dots 1981-1989	—

32024 1/2, YELLOW COMPOSITION HANDLES

CASE XX	$60
CASE XX USA	$50
10 Dot, 1970	—
Dots 1971-1979	—
10 Dot, 1980	—
Dots 1981-1989	—

61024 1/2, BONE HANDLES

CASE XX	$65
CASE XX USA	$60
10 Dot, 1970	—
Dots 1971-1979	—
10 Dot, 1980	—
Dots 1981-1989	—

62024 1/2, BONE HANDLES

CASE XX	$75
CASE XX USA	$60
10 Dot, 1970	—
Dots 1971-1979	—
10 Dot, 1980	—
Dots 1981-1989	—

5225 1/2 SS, STAG HANDLES

CASE XX	—
CASE XX USA	—
10 Dot, 1970	—
Dots 1971-1979	—
10 Dot, 1980	—
Dots 1981-1989	$60

6225 1/2, BONE HANDLES

CASE XX	$175
CASE XX USA	$90
10 Dot, 1970	$90
Dots 1971-1979	$65
10 Dot, 1980	—
Dots 1981-1989	—

SR6225 1/2, SATIN ROSE BONE HANDLES

CASE XX	—
CASE XX USA	—
10 Dot, 1970	—
Dots 1971-1979	$55
10 Dot, 1980	$55
Dots 1981-1989	$55

SR6225 1/2 SS, SATIN ROSE BONE HANDLES

CASE XX	—
CASE XX USA	—
10 Dot, 1970	—
Dots 1971-1979	—

10 Dot, 1980 —
Dots 1981-1989 $55

62027 1/2, BONE HANDLES
CASE XX $125
CASE XX USA —
10 Dot, 1970 —
Dots 1971-1979 —
10 Dot, 1980 —
Dots 1981-1989 —

6227, BONE HANDLES
CASE XX $100
CASE XX USA $75
10 Dot, 1970 $75
Dots 1971-1979 —
10 Dot, 1980 —
Dots 1981-1989 —

6227, DELRIN HANDLES
CASE XX —
CASE XX USA —
10 Dot, 1970 $60
Dots 1971-1979 $40
10 Dot, 1980 —
Dots 1981-1989 —

62027, DELRIN HANDLES
CASE XX —
CASE XX USA —
10 Dot, 1970 —
Dots 1971-1979 $40
10 Dot, 1980 —
Dots 1981-1989 —

SR62027, SATIN ROSE BONE HANDLES
CASE XX —
CASE XX USA —
10 Dot, 1970 —
Dots 1971-1979 $45
10 Dot, 1980 $45
Dots 1981-1989 $45

6327 SH SP, BONE HANDLES
CASE XX $150
CASE XX USA $90
10 Dot, 1970 $100
Dots 1971-1979 —
10 Dot, 1980 —
Dots 1981-1989 —

6327 SH SP, DELRIN HANDLES
CASE XX —
CASE XX USA —
10 Dot, 1970 $60
Dots 1971-1979 $45
10 Dot, 1980 —
Dots 1981-1989 —

63027 SH SP, DELRIN HANDLES
CASE XX —
CASE XX USA —
10 Dot, 1970 —
Dots 1971-1979 $40

10 Dot, 1980 —
Dots 1981-1989 —

9327 SH SP, IMITATION PEARL HANDLES
CASE XX $75
CASE XX USA $65
10 Dot, 1970 $74
Dots 1971-1979 $45
10 Dot, 1980 —
Dots 1981-1989 —

22028, BLACK COMPOSITION HANDLES
CASE XX $200
CASE XX USA —
10 Dot, 1970 —
Dots 1971-1979 —
10 Dot, 1980 —
Dots 1981-1989 —

62028, BONE HANDLES
CASE XX $300
CASE XX USA —
10 Dot, 1970 —
Dots 1971-1979 —
10 Dot, 1980 —
Dots 1981-1989 —

2229 1/2, BLACK COMPOSITION HANDLES
CASE XX $150
CASE XX USA —
10 Dot, 1970 —
Dots 1971-1979 —
10 Dot, 1980 —
Dots 1981-1989 —

6229 1/2, BONE HANDLES
CASE XX $175
CASE XX USA $225
10 Dot, 1970 —
Dots 1971-1979 —
10 Dot, 1980 —
Dots 1981-1989 —

11031 SH, WALNUT HANDLES
CASE XX $60
CASE XX USA $50
10 Dot, 1970 $60
Dots 1971-1979 $45
10 Dot, 1980 —
Dots 1981-1989 —

12031 L R, WALNUT HANDLES
CASE XX $65
CASE XX USA $50
10 Dot, 1970 $65
Dots 1971-1979 $45
10 Dot, 1980 $45
Dots 1981-1989 $40

12031 L H R, WALNUT HANDLES
CASE XX —
CASE XX USA —

10 Dot, 1970 —
Dots 1971-1979 $45
10 Dot, 1980 $45
Dots 1981-1989 $40

13031 L R, WALNUT HANDLES
CASE XX $75
CASE XX USA $60
10 Dot, 1970 $75
Dots 1971-1979 $55
10 Dot, 1980 —
Dots 1981-1989 —

2231 1/2, BLACK COMPOSITION HANDLES
CASE XX $140
CASE XX USA —
10 Dot, 1970 —
Dots 1971-1979 —
10 Dot, 1980 —
Dots 1981-1989 —

2231 1/2 SAB, BLACK COMPOSITION HANDLES
CASE XX $125
CASE XX USA $65
10 Dot, 1970 $75
Dots 1971-1979 $50
10 Dot, 1980 —
Dots 1981-1989 —

22031 1/2, BLACK COMPOSITION HANDLES
CASE XX $140
CASE XX USA —
10 Dot, 1970 —
Dots 1971-1979 —
10 Dot, 1980 —
Dots 1981-1989 —

6231, BONE HANDLES
CASE XX $250
CASE XX USA Rare
10 Dot, 1970 —
Dots 1971-1979 —
10 Dot, 1980 —
Dots 1981-1989 —

62031, BONE HANDLES
CASE XX $175
CASE XX USA —
10 Dot, 1970 —
Dots 1971-1979 —
10 Dot, 1980 —
Dots 1981-1989 —

6231 1/2, BONE HANDLES
CASE XX $175
CASE XX USA $80
10 Dot, 1970 $90
Dots 1971-1979 $65
10 Dot, 1980 $50
Dots 1981-1989 $50

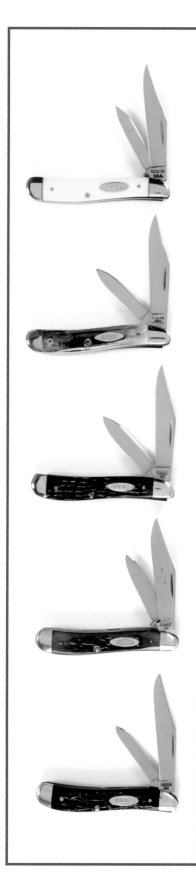

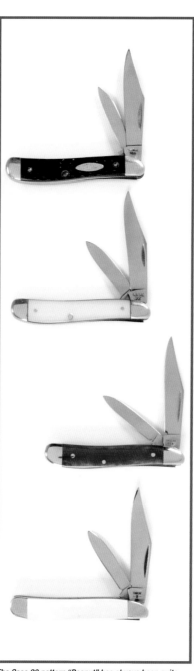

The Case 20 pattern "Peanut" has always been quite popular with both collectors and users. At left, from top: Case XX USA 3220, yellow composition; 10 dot, 1970, 5220 stag; Case XX 6220, "regular" bone; Case XX 6220, "late Rogers" bone; and Case XX 6220, rough black. Above, from top: 6 dot, 1974, 6220, delrin; Case XX 9220, imitation pearl; 1 dot, 1979, SR6220, Satin Rose smooth bone; and 8 dot, 1982, genuine pearl. Closed length is 2-3/4".

62031 1/2, BONE HANDLES

CASE XX	$175
CASE XX USA	—
10 Dot, 1970	—
Dots 1971-1979	—
10 Dot, 1980	—
Dots 1981-1989	—

62031 L H R, DELRIN HANDLES

CASE XX	—
CASE XX USA	—
10 Dot, 1970	—
Dots 1971-1979	—
10 Dot, 1980	—
Dots 1981-1989	$35

5232, STAG HANDLES

CASE XX	$250
CASE XX USA	$130
10 Dot, 1970	$150
Dots 1971-1979	—
10 Dot, 1980	—
Dots 1981-1989	—

52032 SS, STAG HANDLES

CASE XX	—
CASE XX USA	—
10 Dot, 1970	—
Dots 1971-1979	—
10 Dot, 1980	—
Dots 1981-1989	$65

5332, STAG HANDLES

CASE XX	$300
CASE XX USA	$150
10 Dot, 1970	$200
Dots 1971-1979	—
10 Dot, 1980	—
Dots 1981-1989	—

53032 SS, STAG HANDLES

CASE XX	—
CASE XX USA	—
10 Dot, 1970	—
Dots 1971-1979	—
10 Dot, 1980	—
Dots 1981-1989	$65

6232, BONE HANDLES

CASE XX	$140
CASE XX USA	$85
10 Dot, 1970	$125
Dots 1971-1979	$50
10 Dot, 1980	—
Dots 1981-1989	—

62032, BONE HANDLES

CASE XX	—
CASE XX USA	—
10 Dot, 1970	—
Dots 1971-1979	$45
10 Dot, 1980	$55
Dots 1981-1989	$40

6332, BONE HANDLES

CASE XX	$175
CASE XX USA	$100
10 Dot, 1970	$150
Dots 1971-1979	$65
10 Dot, 1980	—
Dots 1981-1989	—

63032, BONE HANDLES

CASE XX	—
CASE XX USA	—
10 Dot, 1970	—
Dots 1971-1979	$50
10 Dot, 1980	$55
Dots 1981-1989	$40

3233, YELLOW COMPOSITION HANDLES

CASE XX	$80
CASE XX USA	$65
10 Dot, 1970	$75
Dots 1971-1979	$50
10 Dot, 1980	—
Dots 1981-1989	—

5233, STAG HANDLES

CASE XX	$125
CASE XX USA	$100
10 Dot, 1970	$100
Dots 1971-1979	—
10 Dot, 1980	—
Dots 1981-1989	—

52033 SSP, STAG HANDLES

CASE XX	—
CASE XX USA	—
10 Dot, 1970	—
Dots 1971-1979	—
10 Dot, 1980	—
Dots 1981-1989	$45

52033 R SSP, STAG HANDLES

CASE XX	—
CASE XX USA	—
10 Dot, 1970	—
Dots 1971-1979	$45
10 Dot, 1980	$45
Dots 1981-1989	$45

53033 SS, STAG HANDLES

CASE XX	—
CASE XX USA	—
10 Dot, 1970	—
Dots 1971-1979	—
10 Dot, 1980	—
Dots 1981-1989	$55

6233, BONE HANDLES

CASE XX	$90
CASE XX USA	$75
10 Dot, 1970	$80
Dots 1971-1979	—
10 Dot, 1980	—
Dots 1981-1989	—

6233, DELRIN HANDLES

CASE XX	—
CASE XX USA	—
10 Dot, 1970	$60
Dots 1971-1979	$45
10 Dot, 1980	—
Dots 1981-1989	—

62033, DELRIN HANDLES

CASE XX	—
CASE XX USA	—
10 Dot, 1970	—
Dots 1971-1979	$40
10 Dot, 1980	$40
Dots 1981-1989	$35

A62033, APPALOOSA BONE HANDLES

CASE XX	—
CASE XX USA	—
10 Dot, 1970	—
Dots 1971-1979	$45
10 Dot, 1980	$45
Dots 1981-1989	$45

A62033 SS, APPALOOSA BONE HANDLES

CASE XX	—
CASE XX USA	—
10 Dot, 1970	—
Dots 1971-1979	—
10 Dot, 1980	—
Dots 1981-1989	$45

62033 SS, DELRIN HANDLES

CASE XX	—
CASE XX USA	—
10 Dot, 1970	—
Dots 1971-1979	—
10 Dot, 1980	—
Dots 1981-1989	$25

6333, BONE HANDLES

CASE XX	$125
CASE XX USA	$85
10 Dot, 1970	$90
Dots 1971-1979	—
10 Dot, 1980	—
Dots 1981-1989	—

6333, DELRIN HANDLES

CASE XX	—
CASE XX USA	—
10 Dot, 1970	$60
Dots 1971-1979	$45
10 Dot, 1980	—
Dots 1981-1989	—

63033, DELRIN HANDLES

CASE XX	—
CASE XX USA	—
10 Dot, 1970	—
Dots 1971-1979	$40
10 Dot, 1980	$40
Dots 1981-1989	$35

63033 SS, DELRIN HANDLES

CASE XX	—
CASE XX USA	—
10 Dot, 1970	—
Dots 1971-1979	—
10 Dot, 1980	—
Dots 1981-1989	$25

8233, PEARL HANDLES

CASE XX	$110
CASE XX USA	$80
10 Dot, 1970	$80
Dots 1971-1979	$65
10 Dot, 1980	—
Dots 1981-1989	—

9233, IMITATION PEARL HANDLES

CASE XX	$60
CASE XX USA	$50
10 Dot, 1970	$50
Dots 1971-1979	$40
10 Dot, 1980	—
Dots 1981-1989	—

92033, IMITATION PEARL HANDLES

CASE XX	—
CASE XX USA	—
10 Dot, 1970	—
Dots 1971-1979	$40
10 Dot, 1980	$40
Dots 1981-1989	$40

92033 SS, IMITATION PEARL HANDLES

CASE XX	—
CASE XX USA	—
10 Dot, 1970	—
Dots 1971-1979	—
10 Dot, 1980	—
Dots 1981-1989	$40

6235, BONE HANDLES

CASE XX	$140
CASE XX USA	—
10 Dot, 1970	—
Dots 1971-1979	—
10 Dot, 1980	—
Dots 1981-1989	—

6235 1/2, BONE HANDLES

CASE XX	$125
CASE XX USA	$65
10 Dot, 1970	$75
Dots 1971-1979	$50
10 Dot, 1980	—
Dots 1981-1989	—

A6235 1/2, APPALOOSA BONE HANDLES

CASE XX	—
CASE XX USA	—
10 Dot, 1970	—
Dots 1971-1979	$60
10 Dot, 1980	$60
Dots 1981-1989	$60

A6235 1/2 SS, APPALOOSA BONE HANDLES

CASE XX	—
CASE XX USA	—
10 Dot, 1970	—
Dots 1971-1979	—
10 Dot, 1980	—
Dots 1981-1989	$60

6235 1/2 SS, DELRIN HANDLES

CASE XX	—
CASE XX USA	—
10 Dot, 1970	—
Dots 1971-1979	—
10 Dot, 1980	—
Dots 1981-1989	$40

620035, COMPOSITION HANDLES

CASE XX	$75
CASE XX USA	—
10 Dot, 1970	—
Dots 1971-1979	—
10 Dot, 1980	—
Dots 1981-1989	—

620035 1/2, COMPOSITION HANDLES

CASE XX	$75
CASE XX USA	—
10 Dot, 1970	—
Dots 1971-1979	—
10 Dot, 1980	—
Dots 1981-1989	—

2137, BLACK COMPOSITION HANDLES

CASE XX	—
CASE XX USA	—
10 Dot, 1970	$40
Dots 1971-1979	$30
10 Dot, 1980	$30
Dots 1981-1989	$25

2137 SS, BLACK COMPOSITION HANDLES

CASE XX	—
CASE XX USA	—
10 Dot, 1970	$40
Dots 1971-1979	$30
10 Dot, 1980	$30
Dots 1981-1989	$25

2138, BLACK COMPOSITION HANDLES

CASE XX	—
CASE XX USA	$50
10 Dot, 1970	$45
Dots 1971-1979	$30
10 Dot, 1980	$30
Dots 1981-1989	$25

2138 SS, BLACK COMPOSITION HANDLES

CASE XX	—
CASE XX USA	—
10 Dot, 1970	$50
Dots 1971-1979	$30
10 Dot, 1980	$30
Dots 1981-1989	$25

2138 L SS, BLACK COMPOSITION HANDLES

CASE XX	—
CASE XX USA	—
10 Dot, 1970	$60
Dots 1971-1979	$35
10 Dot, 1980	$35
Dots 1981-1989	$30

52042 SS, STAG HANDLES

CASE XX	—
CASE XX USA	—
10 Dot, 1970	—
Dots 1971-1979	—
10 Dot, 1980	—
Dots 1981-1989	$50

52042 R SS, STAG HANDLES

CASE XX	—
CASE XX USA	—
10 Dot, 1970	—
Dots 1971-1979	$50
10 Dot, 1980	$50
Dots 1981-1989	$50

62042, BONE HANDLES

CASE XX	$75
CASE XX USA	$60
10 Dot, 1970	$65
Dots 1971-1979	$50
10 Dot, 1980	—
Dots 1981-1989	—

62042 R, BONE HANDLES

CASE XX	$100
CASE XX USA	$65
10 Dot, 1970	$75
Dots 1971-1979	$65
10 Dot, 1980	—
Dots 1981-1989	—

A62042, APPALOOSA BONE HANDLES

CASE XX	—
CASE XX USA	—
10 Dot, 1970	—
Dots 1971-1979	$40
10 Dot, 1980	$40
Dots 1981-1989	$40

A62042 SS, APPALOOSA BONE HANDLES

CASE XX	—
CASE XX USA	—
10 Dot, 1970	—
Dots 1971-1979	—
10 Dot, 1980	—
Dots 1981-1989	$45

62042 SS, DELRIN HANDLES

CASE XX	—
CASE XX USA	—
10 Dot, 1970	—
Dots 1971-1979	—
10 Dot, 1980	—
Dots 1981-1989	$25

92042, IMITATION PEARL HANDLES

CASE XX	$50
CASE XX USA	$50
10 Dot, 1970	$50
Dots 1971-1979	$35
10 Dot, 1980	$35
Dots 1981-1989	$35

92042 R, IMITATION PEARL HANDLES

CASE XX	$60
CASE XX USA	$50
10 Dot, 1970	$50
Dots 1971-1979	$40
10 Dot, 1980	$40
Dots 1981-1989	$30

92042 SS, IMITATION PEARL HANDLES

CASE XX	—
CASE XX USA	—
10 Dot, 1970	—
Dots 1971-1979	—
10 Dot, 1980	—
Dots 1981-1989	$30

92042 R SS, IMITATION PEARL HANDLES

CASE XX	—
CASE XX USA	—
10 Dot, 1970	—
Dots 1971-1979	—
10 Dot, 1980	—
Dots 1981-1989	$30

6143, BONE HANDLES

CASE XX	$125
CASE XX USA	$75
10 Dot, 1970	$75
Dots 1971-1979	$60
10 Dot, 1980	$60
Dots 1981-1989	$50

03244, YELLOW COMPOSITION HANDLES

CASE XX	—
CASE XX USA	—
10 Dot, 1970	—
Dots 1971-1979	$30
10 Dot, 1980	$30
Dots 1981-1989	$30

03244 R, YELLOW COMPOSITION HANDLES

CASE XX	—
CASE XX USA	—
10 Dot, 1970	—
Dots 1971-1979	$35
10 Dot, 1980	$35
Dots 1981-1989	$35

06244, BONE HANDLES

CASE XX	$100
CASE XX USA	$75
10 Dot, 1970	$80
Dots 1971-1979	—
10 Dot, 1980	—
Dots 1981-1989	—

06244, DELRIN HANDLES

CASE XX	—
CASE XX USA	—
10 Dot, 1970	$60
Dots 1971-1979	$40
10 Dot, 1980	—
Dots 1981-1989	—

6244, BONE HANDLES

CASE XX	$100
CASE XX USA	$75
10 Dot, 1970	$80
Dots 1971-1979	—
10 Dot, 1980	—
Dots 1981-1989	—

6244, DELRIN HANDLES

CASE XX	—
CASE XX USA	—
10 Dot, 1970	$60
Dots 1971-1979	$40
10 Dot, 1980	—
Dots 1981-1989	—

SR6244, SATIN ROSE BONE HANDLES

CASE XX	—
CASE XX USA	—
10 Dot, 1970	—
Dots 1971-1979	$45
10 Dot, 1980	$45
Dots 1981-1989	$45

SR6244 SS, SATIN ROSE BONE HANDLES

CASE XX	—
CASE XX USA	—
10 Dot, 1970	—
Dots 1971-1979	—
10 Dot, 1980	—
Dots 1981-1989	$45

6244 SS, DELRIN HANDLES

CASE XX	—
CASE XX USA	—
10 Dot, 1970	—
Dots 1971-1979	—
10 Dot, 1980	—
Dots 1981-1989	$30

33044 SH SP, YELLOW COMPOSITION HANDLES

CASE XX	$150
CASE XX USA	$90
10 Dot, 1970	$100
Dots 1971-1979	$65
10 Dot, 1980	—
Dots 1981-1989	—

6344 SH PEN, BONE HANDLES

CASE XX	$140
CASE XX USA	$80
10 Dot, 1970	$100
Dots 1971-1979	—
10 Dot, 1980	—
Dots 1981-1989	—

6344 SH PEN, DELRIN HANDLES

CASE XX	—
CASE XX USA	—
10 Dot, 1970	$75
Dots 1971-1979	$45
10 Dot, 1980	—
Dots 1981-1989	—

6344 SH SP, BONE HANDLES

CASE XX	$150
CASE XX USA	$90
10 Dot, 1970	$120
Dots 1971-1979	—
10 Dot, 1980	—
Dots 1981-1989	—

6344 SH SP, DELRIN HANDLES

CASE XX	—
CASE XX USA	—
10 Dot, 1970	$85
Dots 1971-1979	$45
10 Dot, 1980	—
Dots 1981-1989	—

2345 1/2, BLACK COMPOSITION HANDLES

CASE XX	$175
CASE XX USA	$175
10 Dot, 1970	—
Dots 1971-1979	—
10 Dot, 1980	—
Dots 1981-1989	—

2345 1/2 SP PU, BLACK COMPOSITION HANDLES

CASE XX	$275
CASE XX USA	—
10 Dot, 1970	—
Dots 1971-1979	—
10 Dot, 1980	—
Dots 1981-1989	—

6345 1/2, BONE HANDLES

CASE XX	$275
CASE XX USA	$500
10 Dot, 1970	—
Dots 1971-1979	—
10 Dot, 1980	—
Dots 1981-1989	—

6445 R, BONE HANDLES

CASE XX	$225
CASE XX USA	$125
10 Dot, 1970	$140
Dots 1971-1979	$75
10 Dot, 1980	—
Dots 1981-1989	—

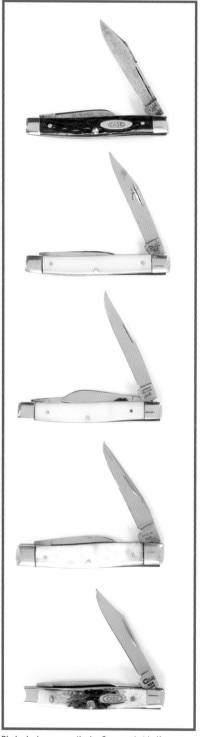

Blade designs on particular Case pocket knife patterns often evolved over time, as illustrated by these 33 pattern pen knife patterns, 2-5/8", from top: Case XX 6233, green bone with long pull clip blade; Case XX 9233, imitation pearl, with wide clip blade with regular pull; 7 dot, 1973, 9333, imitation pearl with slim clip blade; 3 dot, 1977, 92033, with redesigned clip blade; and 1995 stamping 5233, with retooled older style clip blade.

640045 R, BLACK COMPOSITION HANDLES

CASE XX	$45
CASE XX USA	$45
10 Dot, 1970	$45
Dots 1971-1979	$35
10 Dot, 1980	$35
Dots 1981-1989	$30

3246 R SS, YELLOW COMPOSITION HANDLES

CASE XX	$140
CASE XX USA	—
10 Dot, 1970	—
Dots 1971-1979	—
10 Dot, 1980	—
Dots 1981-1989	—

6246 R SS, BONE HANDLES

CASE XX	$250
CASE XX USA	$100
10 Dot, 1970	$150
Dots 1971-1979	$100
10 Dot, 1980	—
Dots 1981-1989	—

6246 L R SS, DELRIN HANDLES

CASE XX	—
CASE XX USA	—
10 Dot, 1970	—
Dots 1971-1979	$35
10 Dot, 1980	$40
Dots 1981-1989	$35

04247 SP, WHITE COMPOSITION HANDLES

CASE XX	$250
CASE XX USA	$175
10 Dot, 1970	—
Dots 1971-1979	—
10 Dot, 1980	—
Dots 1981-1989	—

05247 SP, STAG HANDLES

CASE XX	$375
CASE XX USA	$375
10 Dot, 1970	—
Dots 1971-1979	—
10 Dot, 1980	—
Dots 1981-1989	—

06247 PEN, BONE HANDLES

CASE XX	$140
CASE XX USA	$90
10 Dot, 1970	$125
Dots 1971-1979	$75
10 Dot, 1980	$75
Dots 1981-1989	$65

3347 SH SP, YELLOW COMPOSITION HANDLES

CASE XX	$140
CASE XX USA	$100
10 Dot, 1970	$125
Dots 1971-1979	$65

10 Dot, 1980 — $65
Dots 1981-1989 — $60

5347 SH SP, STAG HANDLES

CASE XX	$350
CASE XX USA	$225
10 Dot, 1970	$275
Dots 1971-1979	—
10 Dot, 1980	—
Dots 1981-1989	—

5347 SH SP SS, STAG HANDLES

CASE XX	$450
CASE XX USA	$250
10 Dot, 1970	$450
Dots 1971-1979	—
10 Dot, 1980	—
Dots 1981-1989	—

53047, STAG HANDLES

CASE XX	$350
CASE XX USA	$225
10 Dot, 1970	$275
Dots 1971-1979	—
10 Dot, 1980	—
Dots 1981-1989	—

6347 SH SP, BONE HANDLES

CASE XX	$200
CASE XX USA	$140
10 Dot, 1970	$175
Dots 1971-1979	$75
10 Dot, 1980	$75
Dots 1981-1989	$60

6347 SH SP SS, BONE HANDLES

CASE XX	$350
CASE XX USA	—
10 Dot, 1970	—
Dots 1971-1979	—
10 Dot, 1980	—
Dots 1981-1989	—

6347 SH SP SSP, BONE HANDLES

CASE XX	—
CASE XX USA	$150
10 Dot, 1970	$150
Dots 1971-1979	$65
10 Dot, 1980	$65
Dots 1981-1989	$55

6347 SP PEN, BONE HANDLES

CASE XX	$225
CASE XX USA	$225
10 Dot, 1970	$225
Dots 1971-1979	$75
10 Dot, 1980	—
Dots 1981-1989	—

6347 SH PU, BONE HANDLES

CASE XX	$250
CASE XX USA	—
10 Dot, 1970	—
Dots 1971-1979	—

10 Dot, 1980 — —
Dots 1981-1989 — —

6347 SP PU, BONE HANDLES

CASE XX	$225
CASE XX USA	$175
10 Dot, 1970	$175
Dots 1971-1979	$75
10 Dot, 1980	—
Dots 1981-1989	—

63047, BONE HANDLES

CASE XX	$200
CASE XX USA	$140
10 Dot, 1970	$175
Dots 1971-1979	$65
10 Dot, 1980	—
Dots 1981-1989	—

SR6347 1/2, SATIN ROSE BONE HANDLES

CASE XX	—
CASE XX USA	—
10 Dot, 1970	—
Dots 1971-1979	$55
10 Dot, 1980	$55
Dots 1981-1989	$55

SR6347 1/2 SS, SATIN ROSE BONE HANDLES

CASE XX	—
CASE XX USA	—
10 Dot, 1970	—
Dots 1971-1979	—
10 Dot, 1980	—
Dots 1981-1989	$55

6347 1/2 SS, DELRIN HANDLES

CASE XX	—
CASE XX USA	—
10 Dot, 1970	—
Dots 1971-1979	—
10 Dot, 1980	—
Dots 1981-1989	$35

93047, IMITATION PEARL HANDLES

CASE XX	$300
CASE XX USA	—
10 Dot, 1970	—
Dots 1971-1979	—
10 Dot, 1980	—
Dots 1981-1989	—

64047 P, BONE HANDLES

CASE XX	$325
CASE XX USA	$175
10 Dot, 1970	$175
Dots 1971-1979	$100
10 Dot, 1980	—
Dots 1981-1989	—

31048, YELLOW COMPOSITION HANDLES

CASE XX	$75
CASE XX USA	$65

10 Dot, 1970 $65
Dots 1971-1979 $50
10 Dot, 1980 $45
Dots 1981-1989 $40

31048 SP, YELLOW COMPOSITION HANDLES
CASE XX $85
CASE XX USA $75
10 Dot, 1970 $75
Dots 1971-1979 $60
10 Dot, 1980   —
Dots 1981-1989   —

31048 SH R, YELLOW COMPOSITION HANDLES
CASE XX $150
CASE XX USA   —
10 Dot, 1970   —
Dots 1971-1979   —
10 Dot, 1980   —
Dots 1981-1989   —

32048 SP, YELLOW COMPOSITION HANDLES
CASE XX $125
CASE XX USA $85
10 Dot, 1970 $85
Dots 1971-1979 $55
10 Dot, 1980 $50
Dots 1981-1989 $45

61048, BONE HANDLES
CASE XX $110
CASE XX USA $85
10 Dot, 1970   —
Dots 1971-1979   —
10 Dot, 1980   —
Dots 1981-1989   —

61048, DELRIN HANDLES
CASE XX   —
CASE XX USA $50
10 Dot, 1970 $60
Dots 1971-1979 $40
10 Dot, 1980 $40
Dots 1981-1989 $30

61048 SP, BONE HANDLES
CASE XX $125
CASE XX USA $125
10 Dot, 1970   —
Dots 1971-1979   —
10 Dot, 1980   —
Dots 1981-1989   —

61048 SP, DELRIN HANDLES
CASE XX   —
CASE XX USA $60
10 Dot, 1970 $60
Dots 1971-1979 $50
10 Dot, 1980   —
Dots 1981-1989   —

61048 SSP, BONE HANDLES
CASE XX   —
CASE XX USA $85
10 Dot, 1970 $100
Dots 1971-1979   —
10 Dot, 1980   —
Dots 1981-1989   —

61048 SSP, DELRIN HANDLES
CASE XX   —
CASE XX USA $50
10 Dot, 1970 $60
Dots 1971-1979 $40
10 Dot, 1980 $40
Dots 1981-1989 $30

62048 SP, BONE HANDLES
CASE XX $140
CASE XX USA $125
10 Dot, 1970   —
Dots 1971-1979   —
10 Dot, 1980   —
Dots 1981-1989   —

62048 SP, DELRIN HANDLES
CASE XX   —
CASE XX USA $60
10 Dot, 1970 $75
Dots 1971-1979 $45
10 Dot, 1980 $45
Dots 1981-1989 $35

62048 SP SSP, BONE HANDLES
CASE XX   —
CASE XX USA $125
10 Dot, 1970   —
Dots 1971-1979   —
10 Dot, 1980   —
Dots 1981-1989   —

62048 SP SSP, DELRIN HANDLES
CASE XX   —
CASE XX USA $60
10 Dot, 1970 $75
Dots 1971-1979 $45
10 Dot, 1980 $45
Dots 1981-1989 $35

6249, BONE HANDLES
CASE XX $200
CASE XX USA $140
10 Dot, 1970 $175
Dots 1971-1979 $125
10 Dot, 1980 $90
Dots 1981-1989 $80

6250, BONE HANDLES
CASE XX $400
CASE XX USA $750
10 Dot, 1970   —
Dots 1971-1979   —
10 Dot, 1980   —
Dots 1981-1989   —

6250, PAKKAWOOD HANDLES
CASE XX $275
CASE XX USA $150
10 Dot, 1970 $150
Dots 1971-1979 $125
10 Dot, 1980   —
Dots 1981-1989   —

C61050 SAB, BONE HANDLES
CASE XX $250
CASE XX USA   —
10 Dot, 1970   —
Dots 1971-1979   —
10 Dot, 1980   —
Dots 1981-1989   —

C61050 SAB, PAKKAWOOD HANDLES
CASE XX $125
CASE XX USA $90
10 Dot, 1970 $90
Dots 1971-1979 $65
10 Dot, 1980   —
Dots 1981-1989   —

21051 L SSP, BLACK COMPOSITION HANDLES
CASE XX   —
CASE XX USA   —
10 Dot, 1970   —
Dots 1971-1979 $45
10 Dot, 1980 $40
Dots 1981-1989 $40

61051 L SSP, PAKKAWOOD HANDLES
CASE XX   —
CASE XX USA   —
10 Dot, 1970   —
Dots 1971-1979 $45
10 Dot, 1980 $40
Dots 1981-1989 $40

M1051 L SSP, METAL HANDLES
CASE XX   —
CASE XX USA   —
10 Dot, 1970   —
Dots 1971-1979 $40
10 Dot, 1980 $35
Dots 1981-1989 $35

P1051 1/2 L SSP, PAKKAWOOD HANDLES
CASE XX   —
CASE XX USA   —
10 Dot, 1970   —
Dots 1971-1979   —
10 Dot, 1980 $35
Dots 1981-1989 $35

P10051 L SSP, PAKKAWOOD HANDLES
CASE XX   —
CASE XX USA   —
10 Dot, 1970   —
Dots 1971-1979   —
10 Dot, 1980 $40
Dots 1981-1989 $40

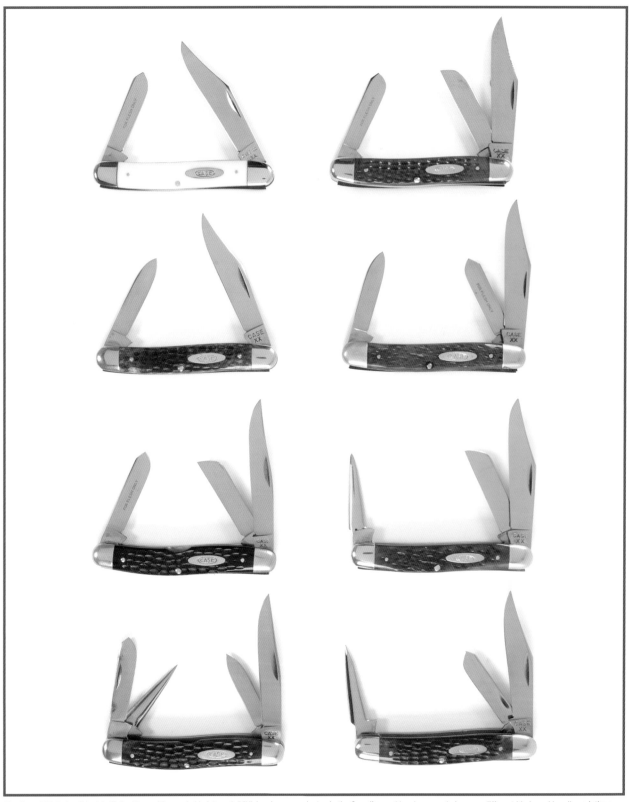

The Case 47 full-size "stock knife" pattern with rounded bolsters, 3-7/8", has been a mainstay in the Case line and has been made in many different blade and handle variations. This group of eight knives illustrates different blade combinations used over the years. Left row, from top: Case XX USA 04247, white composition, "two-blade stockman" (single backspring); Case XX 06247 PEN, bone, "double-end knife" (single backspring); Case XX 63047, three-blade stock, bone; and Case XX 64047 P, four-blade stock, reddish bone. Right row, from top: Case XX 6347 Sh Sp, red bone; Case XX 6347 Sp Pen, late Rogers bone; Case XX 6347 Sh Pu, late Rogers bone; Case XX 6347 Sp Pu, reddish bone.

62052, BONE HANDLES

CASE XX	$150
CASE XX USA	$100
10 Dot, 1970	$125
Dots 1971-1979	$75
10 Dot, 1980	—
Dots 1981-1989	—

54052, STAG HANDLES

CASE XX	$450
CASE XX USA	$275
10 Dot, 1970	$300
Dots 1971-1979	—
10 Dot, 1980	—
Dots 1981-1989	—

64052, BONE HANDLES

CASE XX	$350
CASE XX USA	$150
10 Dot, 1970	$225
Dots 1971-1979	$125
10 Dot, 1980	—
Dots 1981-1989	—

62053 SS, BONE HANDLES

CASE XX	$125
CASE XX USA	—
10 Dot, 1970	—
Dots 1971-1979	—
10 Dot, 1980	—
Dots 1981-1989	—

82053 SS, PEARL HANDLES

CASE XX	$125
CASE XX USA	—
10 Dot, 1970	—
Dots 1971-1979	—
10 Dot, 1980	—
Dots 1981-1989	—

82053 S R, PEARL HANDLES

CASE XX	$125
CASE XX USA	—
10 Dot, 1970	—
Dots 1971-1979	—
10 Dot, 1980	—
Dots 1981-1989	—

82053 S R SS, PEARL HANDLES

CASE XX	$90
CASE XX USA	$80
10 Dot, 1970	$100
Dots 1971-1979	$60
10 Dot, 1980	—
Dots 1981-1989	—

3254, YELLOW COMPOSITION HANDLES

CASE XX	$300
CASE XX USA	$100
10 Dot, 1970	$125
Dots 1971-1979	$80
10 Dot, 1980	$80
Dots 1981-1989	$75

5254, STAG HANDLES

CASE XX	$650
CASE XX USA	$275
10 Dot, 1970	$275
Dots 1971-1979	—
10 Dot, 1980	—
Dots 1981-1989	—

5254 SS, STAG HANDLES

CASE XX	—
CASE XX USA	—
10 Dot, 1970	—
Dots 1971-1979	—
10 Dot, 1980	—
Dots 1981-1989	$80

6254, BONE HANDLES

CASE XX	$400
CASE XX USA	$225
10 Dot, 1970	$250
Dots 1971-1979	$125
10 Dot, 1980	$100
Dots 1981-1989	$80

6254 SSP, BONE HANDLES

CASE XX	—
CASE XX USA	$225
10 Dot, 1970	$250
Dots 1971-1979	$125
10 Dot, 1980	$100
Dots 1981-1989	$80

22055, BLACK COMPOSITION HANDLES

CASE XX	$100
CASE XX USA	$100
10 Dot, 1970	—
Dots 1971-1979	—
10 Dot, 1980	—
Dots 1981-1989	—

62055, BONE HANDLES

CASE XX	$140
CASE XX USA	$100
10 Dot, 1970	$125
Dots 1971-1979	$60
10 Dot, 1980	—
Dots 1981-1989	—

P158 L SSP, PAKKAWOOD HANDLES

CASE XX	—
CASE XX USA	—
10 Dot, 1970	—
Dots 1971-1979	$50
10 Dot, 1980	$50
Dots 1981-1989	$45

2159 L SSP, BLACK COMPOSITION HANDLES

CASE XX	—
CASE XX USA	—
10 Dot, 1970	—
Dots 1971-1979	—
10 Dot, 1980	—
Dots 1981-1989	$45

P159 L SS, PAKKAWOOD HANDLES

CASE XX	—
CASE XX USA	—
10 Dot, 1970	—
Dots 1971-1979	$50
10 Dot, 1980	$50
Dots 1981-1989	$45

8261, PEARL HANDLES

CASE XX	$75
CASE XX USA	$75
10 Dot, 1970	$75
Dots 1971-1979	$60
10 Dot, 1980	—
Dots 1981-1989	—

9261, IMITATION PEARL HANDLES

CASE XX	$50
CASE XX USA	$50
10 Dot, 1970	$50
Dots 1971-1979	$30
10 Dot, 1980	—
Dots 1981-1989	—

05263, STAG HANDLES

CASE XX	$225
CASE XX USA	—
10 Dot, 1970	—
Dots 1971-1979	—
10 Dot, 1980	—
Dots 1981-1989	—

05263 SS, STAG HANDLES

CASE XX	$140
CASE XX USA	$100
10 Dot, 1970	$125
Dots 1971-1979	—
10 Dot, 1980	—
Dots 1981-1989	—

05263 SSP, STAG HANDLES

CASE XX	—
CASE XX USA	—
10 Dot, 1970	—
Dots 1971-1979	—
10 Dot, 1980	—
Dots 1981-1989	$45

05263 R SSP, STAG HANDLES

CASE XX	—
CASE XX USA	—
10 Dot, 1970	—
Dots 1971-1979	$45
10 Dot, 1980	$45
Dots 1981-1989	$45

06263, BONE HANDLES

CASE XX	$150
CASE XX USA	—
10 Dot, 1970	—
Dots 1971-1979	—
10 Dot, 1980	—
Dots 1981-1989	—

06263 SS, BONE HANDLES

CASE XX	$110
CASE XX USA	$75
10 Dot, 1970	$100
Dots 1971-1979	$75
10 Dot, 1980	—
Dots 1981-1989	—

06263 F SS, BONE HANDLES

CASE XX	$110
CASE XX USA	$75
10 Dot, 1970	$100
Dots 1971-1979	$75
10 Dot, 1980	—
Dots 1981-1989	—

06263 SSP, BONE HANDLES

CASE XX	—
CASE XX USA	$75
10 Dot, 1970	$85
Dots 1971-1979	$50
10 Dot, 1980	$35
Dots 1981-1989	$30

06263 F SSP, BONE HANDLES

CASE XX	—
CASE XX USA	—
10 Dot, 1970	—
Dots 1971-1979	$75
10 Dot, 1980	—
Dots 1981-1989	—

62063 1/2, BONE HANDLES

CASE XX	$150
CASE XX USA	—
10 Dot, 1970	—
Dots 1971-1979	—
10 Dot, 1980	—
Dots 1981-1989	—

62063 1/2 SS, BONE HANDLES

CASE XX	$125
CASE XX USA	—
10 Dot, 1970	—
Dots 1971-1979	—
10 Dot, 1980	—
Dots 1981-1989	—

82063 SHAD SS, PEARL HANDLES

CASE XX	$125
CASE XX USA	—
10 Dot, 1970	—
Dots 1971-1979	—
10 Dot, 1980	—
Dots 1981-1989	—

8364 T SS, PEARL HANDLES

CASE XX	$150
CASE XX USA	—
10 Dot, 1970	—
Dots 1971-1979	—
10 Dot, 1980	—
Dots 1981-1989	—

8364 SCIS SS, PEARL HANDLES

CASE XX	$150
CASE XX USA	$110
10 Dot, 1970	$125
Dots 1971-1979	$85
10 Dot, 1980	—
Dots 1981-1989	—

5165 SAB, STAG HANDLES

CASE XX	$500
CASE XX USA	—
10 Dot, 1970	—
Dots 1971-1979	—
10 Dot, 1980	—
Dots 1981-1989	—

5165 SAB DR, STAG HANDLES

CASE XX	$500
CASE XX USA	$500
10 Dot, 1970	—
Dots 1971-1979	—
10 Dot, 1980	—
Dots 1981-1989	—

5265 SAB, STAG HANDLES

CASE XX	$500
CASE XX USA	—
10 Dot, 1970	—
Dots 1971-1979	—
10 Dot, 1980	—
Dots 1981-1989	—

5265 SAB DR, STAG HANDLES

CASE XX	$500
CASE XX USA	$225
10 Dot, 1970	$250
Dots 1971-1979	—
10 Dot, 1980	—
Dots 1981-1989	—

6165 SAB, BONE HANDLES

CASE XX	$325
CASE XX USA	—
10 Dot, 1970	—
Dots 1971-1979	—
10 Dot, 1980	—
Dots 1981-1989	—

6165 SAB DR, BONE HANDLES

CASE XX	$300
CASE XX USA	$350
10 Dot, 1970	—
Dots 1971-1979	—
10 Dot, 1980	—
Dots 1981-1989	—

6165 SAB DR, PAKKAWOOD HANDLES

CASE XX	$125
CASE XX USA	$100
10 Dot, 1970	$100
Dots 1971-1979	$65
10 Dot, 1980	$65
Dots 1981-1989	$50

6165 SAB DR L SSP, PAKKAWOOD HANDLES

CASE XX	—
CASE XX USA	—
10 Dot, 1970	—
Dots 1971-1979	$60
10 Dot, 1980	$60
Dots 1981-1989	$55

6265 SAB, BONE HANDLES

CASE XX	$275
CASE XX USA	—
10 Dot, 1970	—
Dots 1971-1979	—
10 Dot, 1980	—
Dots 1981-1989	—

6265 SAB DR, BONE HANDLES

CASE XX	$275
CASE XX USA	$400
10 Dot, 1970	—
Dots 1971-1979	—
10 Dot, 1980	—
Dots 1981-1989	—

6265 SAB DR, PAKKAWOOD HANDLES

CASE XX	$125
CASE XX USA	$100
10 Dot, 1970	$100
Dots 1971-1979	$85
10 Dot, 1980	$65
Dots 1981-1989	$50

06267, BONE HANDLES

CASE XX	$140
CASE XX USA	$90
10 Dot, 1970	—
Dots 1971-1979	—
10 Dot, 1980	—
Dots 1981-1989	—

6269, BONE HANDLES

CASE XX	$125
CASE XX USA	$75
10 Dot, 1970	$75
Dots 1971-1979	$65
10 Dot, 1980	—
Dots 1981-1989	—

6271 SS, BONE HANDLES

CASE XX	$125
CASE XX USA	—
10 Dot, 1970	—
Dots 1971-1979	—
10 Dot, 1980	—
Dots 1981-1989	—

8271 SS, PEARL HANDLES

CASE XX	$150
CASE XX USA	—
10 Dot, 1970	—
Dots 1971-1979	—
10 Dot, 1980	—
Dots 1981-1989	—

8271 F SS, PEARL HANDLES

CASE XX	$150
CASE XX USA	—
10 Dot, 1970	—
Dots 1971-1979	—
10 Dot, 1980	—
Dots 1981-1989	—

5172, STAG HANDLES

CASE XX	$500
CASE XX USA	$350
10 Dot, 1970	—
Dots 1971-1979	—
10 Dot, 1980	—
Dots 1981-1989	—

5172 (TRANSITION), STAG HANDLES

CASE XX	—
CASE XX USA	$450
10 Dot, 1970	—
Dots 1971-1979	—
10 Dot, 1980	—
Dots 1981-1989	—

P172, PAKKAWOOD HANDLES

CASE XX	—
CASE XX USA	$140
10 Dot, 1970	—
Dots 1971-1979	—
10 Dot, 1980	—
Dots 1981-1989	—

P172 L SSP, PAKKAWOOD HANDLES

CASE XX	—
CASE XX USA	—
10 Dot, 1970	—
Dots 1971-1979	—
10 Dot, 1980	$140
Dots 1981-1989	$140

5375, STAG HANDLES

CASE XX	$500
CASE XX USA	$250
10 Dot, 1970	$275
Dots 1971-1979	—
10 Dot, 1980	—
Dots 1981-1989	—

6275 SP, BONE HANDLES

CASE XX	$175
CASE XX USA	$125
10 Dot, 1970	$140
Dots 1971-1979	$75
10 Dot, 1980	$75
Dots 1981-1989	$65

6375, BONE HANDLES

CASE XX	$250
CASE XX USA	$175
10 Dot, 1970	$200
Dots 1971-1979	$95
10 Dot, 1980	$95
Dots 1981-1989	$75

E278 SS, PATTERNED BRASS HANDLES

CASE XX	—
CASE XX USA	—
10 Dot, 1970	—
Dots 1971-1979	$60
10 Dot, 1980	$60
Dots 1981-1989	—

I278 SS, WHITE COMPOSITION HANDLES

CASE XX	—
CASE XX USA	—
10 Dot, 1970	—
Dots 1971-1979	$30
10 Dot, 1980	$30
Dots 1981-1989	$25

S278 SS, IMITATION TORTOISE HANDLES

CASE XX	—
CASE XX USA	—
10 Dot, 1970	—
Dots 1971-1979	$30
10 Dot, 1980	$30
Dots 1981-1989	$25

5279, STAG HANDLES

CASE XX	$175
CASE XX USA	—
10 Dot, 1970	—
Dots 1971-1979	—
10 Dot, 1980	—
Dots 1981-1989	—

5279 SS, STAG HANDLES

CASE XX	$125
CASE XX USA	$225
10 Dot, 1970	—
Dots 1971-1979	—
10 Dot, 1980	—
Dots 1981-1989	—

6279, BONE HANDLES

CASE XX	$125
CASE XX USA	—
10 Dot, 1970	—
Dots 1971-1979	—
10 Dot, 1980	—
Dots 1981-1989	—

6279 SS, BONE HANDLES

CASE XX	$85
CASE XX USA	$85
10 Dot, 1970	$85
Dots 1971-1979	$45
10 Dot, 1980	$30
Dots 1981-1989	$30

6279 F SS, BONE HANDLES

CASE XX	$85
CASE XX USA	—
10 Dot, 1970	—
Dots 1971-1979	—
10 Dot, 1980	—
Dots 1981-1989	—

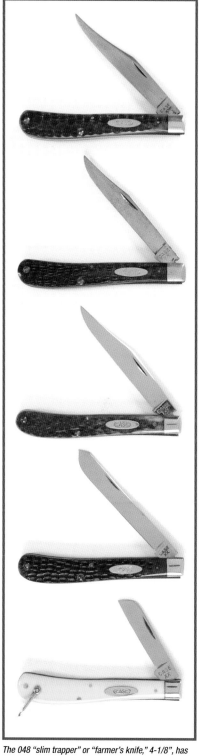

The 048 "slim trapper" or "farmer's knife," 4-1/8", has been a popular and widely produced Case pocket knife pattern. From top: 61048 Case XX, green bone; Case XX 61048, red bone; Case XX 61048, late Rogers bone; Case XX 61048 Sp, red bone; and Case XX 31048 Sh R, "florist's knife," yellow composition..

8279, PEARL HANDLES

CASE XX	$125
CASE XX USA	—
10 Dot, 1970	—
Dots 1971-1979	—
10 Dot, 1980	—
Dots 1981-1989	—

8279 SS, PEARL HANDLES

CASE XX	$100
CASE XX USA	—
10 Dot, 1970	—
Dots 1971-1979	—
10 Dot, 1980	—
Dots 1981-1989	—

M279 SS, STAINLESS STEEL HANDLES

CASE XX	$35
CASE XX USA	$35
10 Dot, 1970	$40
Dots 1971-1979	$30
10 Dot, 1980	$25
Dots 1981-1989	$25

M279 F SS, STAINLESS STEEL HANDLES

CASE XX	$35
CASE XX USA	$35
10 Dot, 1970	$40
Dots 1971-1979	$30
10 Dot, 1980	$25
Dots 1981-1989	$25

M279 R SS, STAINLESS STEEL BLADES

CASE XX	—
CASE XX USA	—
10 Dot, 1970	—
Dots 1971-1979	$30
10 Dot, 1980	$25
Dots 1981-1989	$25

M279 F R SS, STAINLESS STEEL BLADES

CASE XX	—
CASE XX USA	—
10 Dot, 1970	—
Dots 1971-1979	$30
10 Dot, 1980	$25
Dots 1981-1989	$25

M279 Scis SS, STAINLESS STEEL HANDLES

CASE XX	$50
CASE XX USA	$45
10 Dot, 1970	$50
Dots 1971-1979	$40
10 Dot, 1980	—
Dots 1981-1989	—

2279 SHAD SS, BLACK COMPOSITION HANDLES

CASE XX	$75
CASE XX USA	—
10 Dot, 1970	—
Dots 1971-1979	—
10 Dot, 1980	—
Dots 1981-1989	—

9279 SHAD SS, IMITATION PEARL HANDLES

CASE XX	$75
CASE XX USA	—
10 Dot, 1970	—
Dots 1971-1979	—
10 Dot, 1980	—
Dots 1981-1989	—

82079 1/2, PEARL HANDLES

CASE XX	$150
CASE XX USA	—
10 Dot, 1970	—
Dots 1971-1979	—
10 Dot, 1980	—
Dots 1981-1989	—

82079 1/2 SS, PEARL HANDLES

CASE XX	$100
CASE XX USA	$85
10 Dot, 1970	$100
Dots 1971-1979	$75
10 Dot, 1980	$60
Dots 1981-1989	$60

6380, BONE HANDLES

CASE XX	$450
CASE XX USA	$275
10 Dot, 1970	$300
Dots 1971-1979	$175
10 Dot, 1980	—
Dots 1981-1989	—

2383, BLACK COMPOSITION HANDLES

CASE XX	$200
CASE XX USA	$225
10 Dot, 1970	—
Dots 1971-1979	—
10 Dot, 1980	—
Dots 1981-1989	—

5383, STAG HANDLES

CASE XX	$450
CASE XX USA	$250
10 Dot, 1970	$300
Dots 1971-1979	—
10 Dot, 1980	—
Dots 1981-1989	—

9383, IMITATION PEARL HANDLES

CASE XX	$375
CASE XX USA	—
10 Dot, 1970	—
Dots 1971-1979	—
10 Dot, 1980	—
Dots 1981-1989	—

6383, BONE HANDLES

CASE XX	$350
CASE XX USA	$225
10 Dot, 1970	$275
Dots 1971-1979	$125

10 Dot, 1980	$100
Dots 1981-1989	$100

3185, YELLOW COMPOSITION HANDLES

CASE XX	$150
CASE XX USA	$150
10 Dot, 1970	$250
Dots 1971-1979	$125
10 Dot, 1980	—
Dots 1981-1989	—

6185, BONE HANDLES

CASE XX	$250
CASE XX USA	$150
10 Dot, 1970	$175
Dots 1971-1979	$85
10 Dot, 1980	—
Dots 1981-1989	—

22087, BLACK COMPOSITION HANDLES

CASE XX	$75
CASE XX USA	$75
10 Dot, 1970	$75
Dots 1971-1979	$45
10 Dot, 1980	$45
Dots 1981-1989	$40

22087 SS, BLACK COMPOSITION HANDLES

CASE XX	—
CASE XX USA	—
10 Dot, 1970	—
Dots 1971-1979	—
10 Dot, 1980	—
Dots 1981-1989	$30

23087 SH Pen, BLACK COMPOSITION HANDLES

CASE XX	$85
CASE XX USA	$85
10 Dot, 1970	$100
Dots 1971-1979	$45
10 Dot, 1980	$45
Dots 1981-1989	$40

23087 SH Pen SS, BLACK COMPOSITION HANDLES

CASE XX	—
CASE XX USA	—
10 Dot, 1970	—
Dots 1971-1979	—
10 Dot, 1980	—
Dots 1981-1989	$35

52087, STAG HANDLES

CASE XX	$150
CASE XX USA	$125
10 Dot, 1970	$125
Dots 1971-1979	—
10 Dot, 1980	—
Dots 1981-1989	—

52087 SS, STAG HANDLES

CASE XX	—
CASE XX USA	—
10 Dot, 1970	—
Dots 1971-1979	—
10 Dot, 1980	—
Dots 1981-1989	$60

53087 SH PEN, STAG HANDLES

CASE XX	$225
CASE XX USA	$150
10 Dot, 1970	$175
Dots 1971-1979	—
10 Dot, 1980	—
Dots 1981-1989	—

62087, BONE HANDLES

CASE XX	$90
CASE XX USA	$75
10 Dot, 1970	$90
Dots 1971-1979	—
10 Dot, 1980	—
Dots 1981-1989	—

62087, DELRIN HANDLES

CASE XX	—
CASE XX USA	—
10 Dot, 1970	$65
Dots 1971-1979	$45
10 Dot, 1980	$45
Dots 1981-1989	$40

62087 SS, DELRIN HANDLES

CASE XX	—
CASE XX USA	—
10 Dot, 1970	—
Dots 1971-1979	—
10 Dot, 1980	—
Dots 1981-1989	$30

63087 SP PEN, BONE HANDLES

CASE XX	$140
CASE XX USA	$90
10 Dot, 1970	$125
Dots 1971-1979	—
10 Dot, 1980	—
Dots 1981-1989	—

63087 SP PEN, DELRIN HANDLES

CASE XX	—
CASE XX USA	—
10 Dot, 1970	$75
Dots 1971-1979	$45
10 Dot, 1980	$45
Dots 1981-1989	$40

63087 SP PEN SS, DELRIN HANDLES

CASE XX	—
CASE XX USA	—
10 Dot, 1970	—
Dots 1971-1979	—
10 Dot, 1980	—
Dots 1981-1989	$30

5488, STAG HANDLES

CASE XX	$1,250
CASE XX USA	$550
10 Dot, 1970	$950
Dots 1971-1979	—
10 Dot, 1980	—
Dots 1981-1989	—

6488, BONE HANDLES

CASE XX	$750
CASE XX USA	$300
10 Dot, 1970	$375
Dots 1971-1979	—
10 Dot, 1980	—
Dots 1981-1989	—

33092, YELLOW COMPOSITION HANDLES

CASE XX	$225
CASE XX USA	$140
10 Dot, 1970	$150
Dots 1971-1979	$80
10 Dot, 1980	$80
Dots 1981-1989	$80

5392, STAG HANDLES

CASE XX	$450
CASE XX USA	$250
10 Dot, 1970	$300
Dots 1971-1979	—
10 Dot, 1980	—
Dots 1981-1989	—

6292, BONE HANDLES

CASE XX	$125
CASE XX USA	$90
10 Dot, 1970	$125
Dots 1971-1979	$75
10 Dot, 1980	$75
Dots 1981-1989	$60

6392, BONE HANDLES

CASE XX	$250
CASE XX USA	$150
10 Dot, 1970	$150
Dots 1971-1979	$85
10 Dot, 1980	$85
Dots 1981-1989	$60

31093, YELLOW COMPOSITION HANDLES

CASE XX	$225
CASE XX USA	—
10 Dot, 1970	—
Dots 1971-1979	—
10 Dot, 1980	—
Dots 1981-1989	—

61093, BONE HANDLES

CASE XX	$225
CASE XX USA	$125
10 Dot, 1970	$150
Dots 1971-1979	$85
10 Dot, 1980	—
Dots 1981-1989	—

6294, BONE HANDLES

CASE XX	$375
CASE XX USA	—
10 Dot, 1970	—
Dots 1971-1979	—
10 Dot, 1980	—
Dots 1981-1989	—

6394 1/2, BONE HANDLES

CASE XX	$2,500
CASE XX USA	—
10 Dot, 1970	—
Dots 1971-1979	—
10 Dot, 1980	—
Dots 1981-1989	—

32095 F SS, YELLOW COMPOSITION HANDLES

CASE XX	$100
CASE XX USA	$100
10 Dot, 1970	$100
Dots 1971-1979	$65
10 Dot, 1980	$65
Dots 1981-1989	$65

6296 X SS, BONE HANDLES

CASE XX	$450
CASE XX USA	$650
10 Dot, 1970	—
Dots 1971-1979	—
10 Dot, 1980	—
Dots 1981-1989	—

P197 L SSP, PAKKAWOOD HANDLES

CASE XX	—
CASE XX USA	—
10 Dot, 1970	—
Dots 1971-1979	$55
10 Dot, 1980	$55
Dots 1981-1989	$50

1199 SH R SS, WALNUT HANDLES

CASE XX	$75
CASE XX USA	$75
10 Dot, 1970	$85
Dots 1971-1979	$50
10 Dot, 1980	$50
Dots 1981-1989	$50

3299 1/2, YELLOW COMPOSITION HANDLES

CASE XX	$140
CASE XX USA	$90
10 Dot, 1970	$110
Dots 1971-1979	$65
10 Dot, 1980	—
Dots 1981-1989	—

5299 1/2, STAG HANDLES

CASE XX	$400
CASE XX USA	$175
10 Dot, 1970	$250
Dots 1971-1979	—
10 Dot, 1980	—
Dots 1981-1989	—

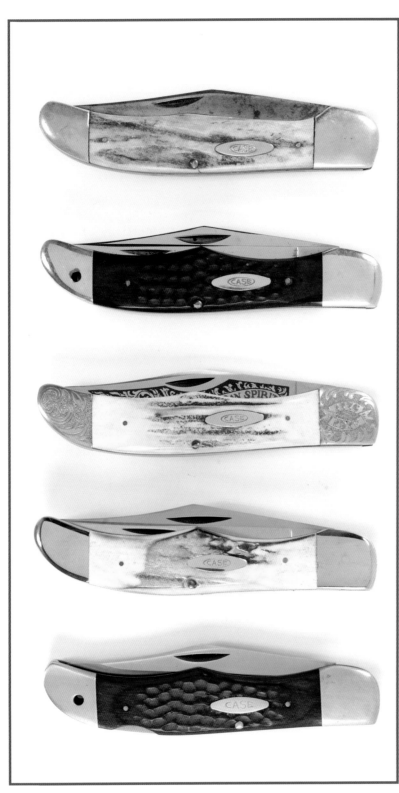

The 65 "folding hunter" pattern was traditionally Case's most popular pattern among knife users. At 5-1/4," it is a robust pattern that has been made in both one- and two-blade variations. From the top: Case XX 5165 SAB, 8 dot 1972 6265 SAB DR, Pakkawood; 4 dot 1976 5165 SAB SSP Bicentennial Knife; 3 dot 1977 5265 SAB SSP (Blue Scroll); and 10 dot 1980 6165 SAB DR L SSP (lockback), Pakkawood.

6299, BONE HANDLES

CASE XX	$350
CASE XX USA	—
10 Dot, 1970	—
Dots 1971-1979	—
10 Dot, 1980	—
Dots 1981-1989	—

83102 SS, PEARL HANDLES

CASE XX	$175
CASE XX USA	—
10 Dot, 1970	—
Dots 1971-1979	—
10 Dot, 1980	—
Dots 1981-1989	—

M3102, STAINLESS STEEL HANDLES

CASE XX	$60
CASE XX USA	$60
10 Dot, 1970	$75
Dots 1971-1979	$40
10 Dot, 1980	—
Dots 1981-1989	—

T3105 SS, PATTERNED METAL HANDLES

CASE XX	$225
CASE XX USA	—
10 Dot, 1970	—
Dots 1971-1979	—
10 Dot, 1980	—
Dots 1981-1989	—

T3105 SS (NEW), PATTERNED METAL HANDLES

CASE XX	$125
CASE XX USA	—
10 Dot, 1970	—
Dots 1971-1979	—
10 Dot, 1980	—
Dots 1981-1989	—

62109 X, BONE HANDLES

CASE XX	$125
CASE XX USA	$75
10 Dot, 1970	$90
Dots 1971-1979	$50
10 Dot, 1980	$45
Dots 1981-1989	$45

52131, STAG HANDLES

CASE XX	$500
CASE XX USA	$250
10 Dot, 1970	$275
Dots 1971-1979	—
10 Dot, 1980	—
Dots 1981-1989	—

62131, BONE HANDLES

CASE XX	Rare
CASE XX USA	$125
10 Dot, 1970	$150
Dots 1971-1979	$65
10 Dot, 1980	$65
Dots 1981-1989	$50

FLY FISHERMAN, STAINLESS STEEL HANDLES

CASE XX	$300
CASE XX USA	$250
10 Dot, 1970	$250
Dots 1971-1979	$175
10 Dot, 1980	—
Dots 1981-1989	—

S-2, STERLING SILVER HANDLES

CASE XX	$100
CASE XX USA	$100
10 Dot, 1970	—
Dots 1971-1979	—
10 Dot, 1980	—
Dots 1981-1989	—

MUSKRAT, BONE HANDLES

CASE XX	$300
CASE XX USA	$200
10 Dot, 1970	$225
Dots 1971-1979	$125
10 Dot, 1980	$100
Dots 1981-1989	$80

SIDEWINDER, PAKKAWOOD HANDLES

CASE XX	—
CASE XX USA	—
10 Dot, 1970	—
Dots 1971-1979	—
10 Dot, 1980	$225
Dots 1981-1989	$225

TEXAS LOCKHORN, WHITE COMPOSITION HANDLES

CASE XX	—
CASE XX USA	—
10 Dot, 1970	—
Dots 1971-1979	—
10 Dot, 1980	$175
Dots 1981-1989	$175

TEXAS LOCKHORN, IVORY MICARTA HANDLES

CASE XX	—
CASE XX USA	—
10 Dot, 1970	—
Dots 1971-1979	—
10 Dot, 1980	$175
Dots 1981-1989	$175

NEW CASE POCKET KNIFE PATTERNS INTRODUCED IN 1989, MADE FOR 1989 AND 1990

CURLY MAPLE-HANDLED POCKET KNIVES, 1989 AND 1990

711010L SS	$125
71405 L SS	$60
7207 Sp SS	$65
7215 SS	$50
7220 SS	$50
7225 1/2 SS	$50
72033 SS	$45
72042 SS	$40
7254 SS	$65
072087 SS	$45
7344 Sh Pen SS	$45
73087 Sp Pen SS	$45

POCKET KNIVES WITH DAMASCUS BLADES, ROGERS BONE HANDLES, 1989 AND 1990

ROG6120 D	$75
ROG6125 1/2 D	$75
ROG61059 L D	$100
ROG611098 D	$100
ROG61405 L D	$80
ROG6207 Sp D	$125
ROG6215 D	$85
ROG62033 D	$75
ROG62042 D	$85
ROG6254 D	$150
ROG62131D	$100
ROG6247 Sh Sp D	$150

POCKET KNIVES WITH DAMASCUS BLADES, STAG HANDLES, 1989 AND 1990

5120 D	$75
5125 1/2 D	$75
51059 L D	$125
511098 D	$75
51405 L D	$80
5207 Sp D	$125
5215 D	$85
52033 D	$75
52042 D	$85
5254D	$150
52131 D	$100
5347 Sh Sp D	$150

POCKET KNIVES, NEW PATTERNS, 1989 AND 1990

R611010 L SS	$125
R611098 SS RAZ	$50
511098 SS RAZ	$60
61139 L SS	$60
51139 L SS	$75
R61225 L SS	$50
51225 L SS	$60
R61405 L SS	$50
51405 L SS	$60
R62005 RAZ SS	$60
52005 RAZ SS	$80

CASE VINTAGE CATALOG PAGES

This section includes the cover (below) and all of the pocket knife pages from the Case factory catalog #67 (through P. 294), which was in use from early 1957 through mid-1959. The pocket knives pictured will have the CASE XX tang stamping. I wanted to include this in the book since these older catalogs are rare and seldom seen today. In those days, only authorized Case dealers received a catalog, so the number of each catalog printed was relatively low. I especially enjoy the small line drawings that are located on the cover and on various pages.

After the end of catalog #67, there are included two pages from the Case factory catalog #81 (P. 295-296), which was issued in 1980. These pages show the Case Gentlemen's Line of pocket knives. Due to space constraints, I could not include more pages from this or other Case catalogs, but I wanted to show the Gentlemen's Line since it is an unusual and little known piece of Case history.

After that is one page showing the stag handled pocket knives in Damascus steel (P. 297) that were produced from 1989-1990. These are significant, being the first knives produced by Case with Damascus steel blades.

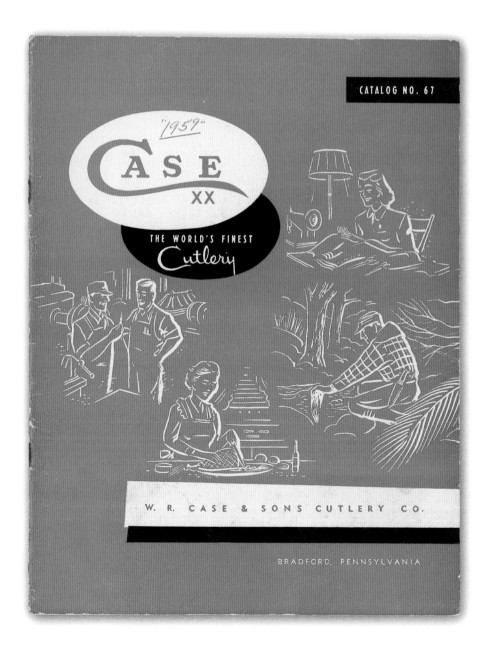

W. R. CASE & SONS CUTLERY CO.

ONE BLADE JACKS

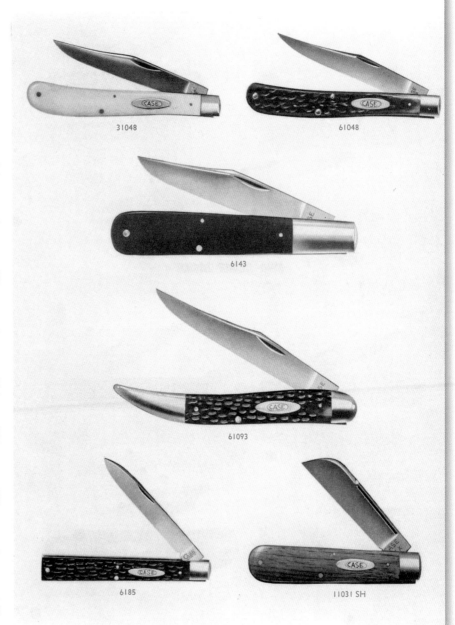

No. 31048
   Length closed 4⅛''. Cream colored composition handle. Brass lining. Nickel silver bolster.

No. 31048 SP
   Same as 31048 except spay blade instead of clip blade.

No. 61048
   Length closed 4⅛''. Bone stag handle. Brass lining. Nickel silver bolster.

No. 61048 SP
   Same as 61048 except spay blade instead of clip blade.

No. 6143
   Length closed 5''. Bone stag handle. Iron lining and bolster.

No. 61093
   Length closed 5''. Bone stag handle. Brass lining. Nickel silver bolsters.

No. 6185
   Length closed 3⅝''. Bone stag handle. Brass lining. Nickel silver bolster.

No. 3185
   Same as 6185 except has cream colored composition handle.

No. 11031 SH
   Length closed 3¾''. Walnut handle. Brass lining. Nickel silver bolster.

31048

61048

6143

61093

6185

11031 SH

W. R. CASE & SONS CUTLERY CO.

ONE BLADE JACKS

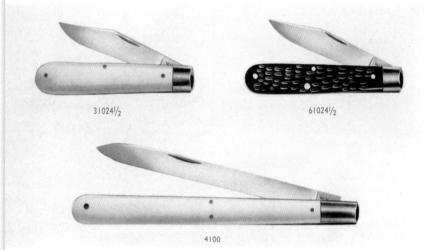

31024½

61024½

4100

No. 31024½

Length closed 3". Cream composition handle. Brass lining. Nickel silver bolster.

No. 61024½

Length closed 3". Bone stag handle. Brass lining. Nickel silver bolster.

No. 4100

Length closed 5½". White composition handle. Nickel silver bolster and lining.

TWO BLADE JACKS

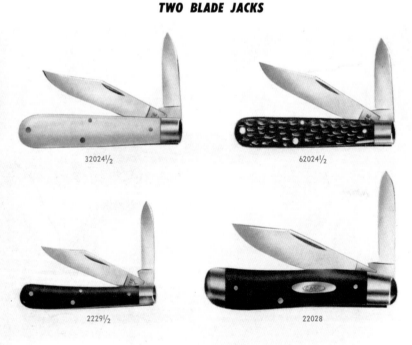

32024½

62024½

2229½

22028

No. 32024½

Length closed 3". Cream composition handle. Brass lining. Nickel silver bolster.

No. 62024½

Length closed 3". Bone stag handle. Brass lining. Nickel silver bolster.

No. 2229½

Length closed 2½". Black composition handle. Brass lining. Nickel silver bolster.

No. 22028

Length closed 3½". Black composition handle. Nickel silver bolsters and lining.

4

WORLD'S FINEST CUTLERY

W. R. CASE & SONS CUTLERY CO.

TWO BLADE JACKS

No. 6202½
Length closed 3⅜". Bone stag handle. Brass lining. Nickel silver bolster.

No. 6214
Length closed 3⅜". Bone stag handle. Brass lining. Nickel silver bolsters.

No. 2220
Length closed 2¾". Black composition handle. Brass lining. Nickel silver bolsters.

No. 3220
Length closed 2¾". Cream composition handle. Brass lining. Nickel silver bolsters.

No. 5220
Length closed 2¾". Genuine stag handle. Brass lining. Nickel silver bolsters.

No. 6220
Length closed 2¾". Bone stag handle. Brass lining. Nickel silver bolsters.

No. 9220
Length closed 2¾". Imitation pearl handle. Brass lining. Nickel silver bolsters.

No. 6225½
Length closed 3". Bone stag handle. Brass lining. Nickel silver bolsters.

6202½

6214

2220

3220

5220

6220

9220

6225½

W. R. CASE & SONS CUTLERY CO.

TWO BLADE JACKS

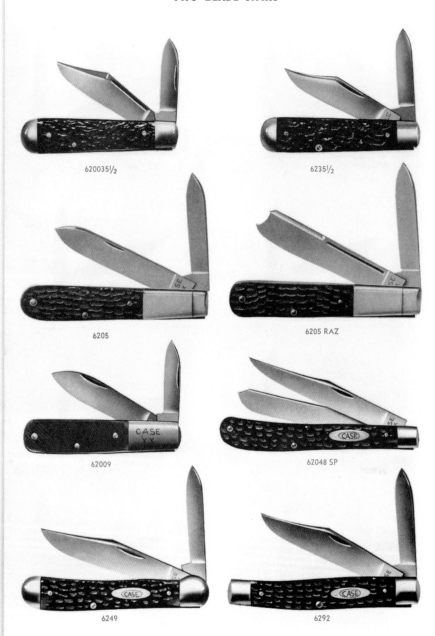

620035¹/₂

6235¹/₂

6205

6205 RAZ

62009

62048 SP

6249

6292

No. 620035¹/₂
  Length closed 3¹/₄". Composition handle. Brass lining. Nickel silver bolsters.
No. 620035
  Same as 620035¹/₂ except with spear and pen blades.
No. 6235¹/₂
  Length closed 3¹/₄". Bone stag handle. Brass lining. Nickel silver bolsters.
No. 6235
  Same as 6235¹/₂ except with spear and pen blades.
No. 6205
  Length closed 3³/₄". Bone stag handle. Brass lining. Nickel silver bolster.
No. 6205 RAZ
  Length closed 3³/₄". Bone stag handle. Brass lining. Nickel silver bolster.
No. 62009
  Length closed 3³/₈". Smooth bone stag handle. Brass lining. Nickel silver bolster.
No. 62009¹/₂
  Same as 62009 except with clip and pen blades.
No. 62048 SP
  Length closed 4¹/₈". Bone stag handle. Brass lining. Nickel silver bolster.
No. 32048 SP
  Same as 62048 SP except with cream composition handle.
No. 6249
  Length closed 3¹⁵/₁₆". Bone stag handle. Brass lining. Nickel silver bolsters.
No. 6292
  Length closed 4". Bone stag handle. Nickel silver lining and bolsters.

WORLD'S FINEST CUTLERY

W. R. CASE & SONS CUTLERY CO.

TWO BLADE JACKS

No. 22031½
Length closed 3¾". Black composition handle. Brass lining. Nickel silver bolster.

No. 62031½
Length closed 3¾". Bone stag handle. Brass lining. Nickel silver bolster.

No. 62031
Same as 62031½ except with spear and pen blades.

No. 2231½ SAB
Length closed 3¾". Black composition handle. Brass lining. Nickel silver bolsters. Clip blade saber ground.

No. 2231½
Same as 2231½ SAB except clip blade is regular grind.

No. 6231½
Length closed 3¾". Bone stag handle. Brass lining. Nickel silver bolsters.

No. 6231
Same as 6231½ except with spear and pen blades.

No. 62055
Length closed 3½". Bone stag handle. Brass lining. Nickel silver bolsters.

No. 22055
Same as 62055 except with black composition handle.

No. 62087
Length closed 3¼". Bone stag handle. Nickel silver lining and bolsters. Concave ground blades.

No. 22087
Same as 62087 except with black composition handle.

No. 6232
Length closed 3⅝". Bone stag handle. Brass lining. Nickel silver bolsters.

No. 6207
Length closed 3½". Bone stag handle. Brass lining. Nickel silver bolsters.

220031½

62031½

2231½ SAB

6231½

62055

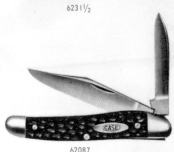

62087

6232

6207

W. R. CASE & SONS CUTLERY CO.

TWO BLADE JACKS

6217

6294

3299½

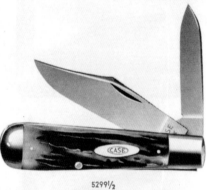

5299½

3254

5254

No. 6217

Length closed 4". Bone stag handle. Brass lining. Nickel silver bolster.

No. 6294

Length closed 4¼". Bone stag handle. Brass lining. Nickel silver bolsters.

No. 3299½

Length closed 4⅛". Cream colored composition handle. Brass lining. Nickel silver bolsters.

No. 5299½

Length closed 4⅛". Genuine stag handle. Brass lining. Nickel silver bolsters.

No. 6299

Same as 5299½ except with spear blade instead of clip blade and bone stag handle.

No. 3254

Length closed 4⅛". Cream colored composition handle. Nickel silver lining and bolsters.

No. 5254

Length closed 4⅛". Genuine stag handle. Nickel silver lining and bolsters.

8

W. R. CASE & SONS CUTLERY CO.

PEN KNIVES

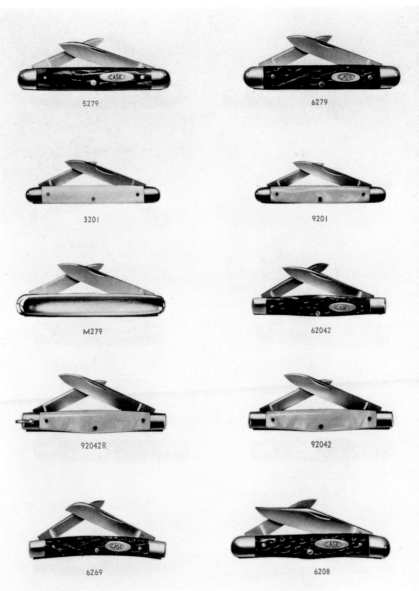

No. 5279
Length closed 3¹⁄₈". Genuine stag handle. Nickel silver lining and bolsters. Concave ground stainless steel blades. Stainless spring.

No. 6279
Length closed 3¹⁄₈". Bone stag handle. Nickel sliver lining and bolsters. Concave ground stainless steel blades. Stainless spring.

No. 3201
Length closed 2⁵⁄₈". Cream colored composition handle. Nickel silver lining and bolsters. Concave ground blades.

No. 9201
Length closed 2⁵⁄₈". Imitation pearl handle. Nickel silver lining and bolsters. Concave ground blades.

No. M279
Length closed 3¹⁄₈". Polished stainless steel handle. Concave ground stainless steel blades. Stainless spring.

No. 62042
Length closed 3". Bone stag handle. Nickel silver lining and bolsters. Concave ground blades.

No. 62042R
Same as 62042 with bail.

No. 92042R
Same as 92042 with bail.

No. 92042
Length closed 3". Imitation pearl handle. Nickel silver lining and bolsters. Concave ground blades.

No. 6269
Length closed 3". Bone stag handle. Nickel silver lining and bolsters. Concave ground blades.

No. 6208
Length closed 3¹⁄₄". Bone stag handle. Nickel silver lining and bolsters.

W. R. CASE & SONS CUTLERY CO.

PEN KNIVES

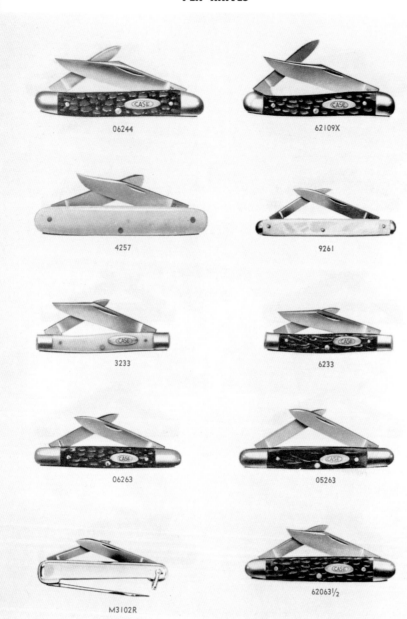

06244

62109X

4257

9261

3233

6233

06263

05263

M3102R

62063½

No. 06244
Length closed 3¼". Bone stag handle. Nickel silver lining and bolsters. Concave ground blades.

No. 62109X
Length closed 3⅛". Bone stag handle. Nickel silver lining and bolsters.

No. 4257
Office Knife. Length closed 3¾". White composition handle. Nickel silver lining.

No. 9261
Length closed 2⅞". Imitation pearl handle. Nickel silver lining and tips. Concave ground blades.

No. 3233
Length closed 2⅝". Cream colored composition handle. Nickel silver lining and bolsters. Concave ground blades.

No. 9233
Same as 3233 except with imitation pearl handle.

No. 6233
Length closed 2⅝". Bone stag handle. Nickel silver lining and bolsters. Concave ground blades.

No. 06263
Length closed 3⅛". Bone stag handle. Nickel silver lining and bolsters. Stainless steel, concave ground blades. Stainless steel springs.

No. 05263
Length closed 3⅛". Genuine stag handle. Nickel silver lining and bolsters. Stainless steel concave ground blades. Stainless steel springs.

No. M3102R
Length closed 2¾". Polished stainless steel handle. Concave ground stainless steel blades. Stainless spring. Pick type file.

No. 62063½
Length closed $3\frac{1}{16}$". Bone stag handle. Nickel silver lining and bolsters. Concave ground stainless steel blades. Stainless spring.

WORLD'S FINEST CUTLERY

W. R. CASE & SONS CUTLERY CO.

POCKET KNIVES

PEN KNIVES AND DOUBLE END KNIVES

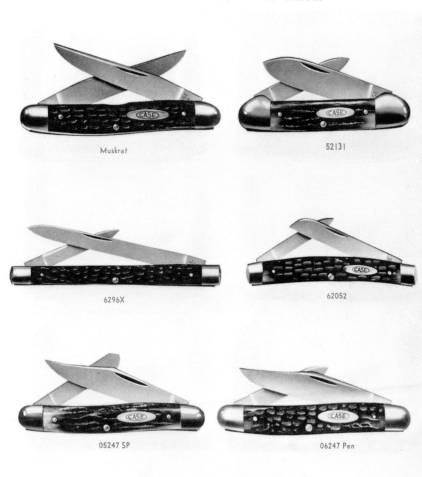

Muskrat

52131

6296X

62052

05247 SP

06247 Pen

6275 SP

Muskrat
> Length closed 3⅞". Bone stag handle. Nickel silver lining and bolsters.

No. 52131
> Length closed 3⅝". Genuine stag handle. Brass lining. Nickel silver bolsters.

No. 6296X
> Citrus Knife. Length closed 4¼". Bone stag handle. Nickel silver lining and bolsters. Stainless steel blades and springs.

No. 62052
> Length closed 3½". Bone stag handle. Nickel silver lining and bolsters.

No. 05247 SP
> Length closed 3⅞". Genuine stag handle. Nickel silver lining and bolsters. Spay blade concave ground.

No. 04247 SP
> Same as 05247 SP except white composition handle.

No. 06247 PEN
> Length closed 3⅞". Bone stag handle. Nickel silver lining and bolsters. Pen blade concave ground.

No. 6275 SP
> Length closed 4¼". Bone stag handle. Nickel silver lining and bolsters.

W. R. CASE & SONS CUTLERY CO.

THREE BLADES

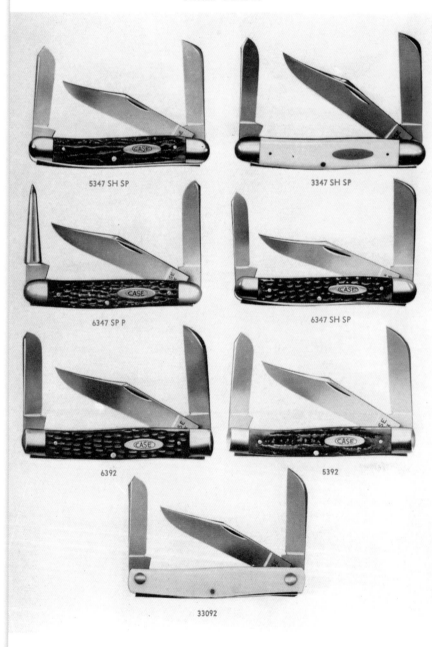

5347 SH SP

3347 SH SP

6347 SP P

6347 SH SP

6392

5392

33092

No. 5347 SH SP
Length closed 3⅞". Genuine stag handle. Nickel silver lining and bolsters. Spay blade concave ground.

No. 5347 SH SP SS
Same as 5347 SH SP except stainless steel blades and springs.

No. 6347 SH SP SS
Same as 5347 SH SP except bone stag handle and stainless steel blades and springs.

No. 3347 SH SP
Length closed 3⅞". Cream composition handle. Nickel silver lining and bolsters. Spay blade concave ground.

No. 6347 SP P
Length closed 3⅞". Bone stag handle. Nickel silver lining and bolsters. Spay blade concave ground.

No. 6347 SH P
Same as 6347 SP P except sheep blade in place of spay blade.

No. 6347 SH SP
Length closed 3⅞". Bone stag handle. Nickel silver lining and bolsters. Spay blade concave ground.

No. 6347 SP Pen
Same as 6347 SH SP except with pen blade in place of sheep blade.

No. 6392
Length closed 4". Bone stag handle. Nickel silver lining and bolsters.

No. 5392
Length closed 4". Genuine stag handle. Nickel silver lining and bolsters.

No. 33092
Length closed 4". Cream composition handle. Nickel silver lining.

12

W. R. CASE & SONS CUTLERY CO.

THREE BLADES

No. 6380
Length closed 3⅞". Bone stag handle. Nickel silver lining and bolsters.

No. 53047
Length closed 4". Genuine stag handle. Nickel silver lining and bolsters. Spay blade, concave ground.

No. 63047
Same as 53047 except with bone stag handle.

No. 6375
Length closed 4¼". Bone stag handle. Nickel silver lining and bolsters.

No. 5375
Same as 6375 except with genuine stag handle.

No. 6308
Length closed 3¼". Bone stag handle. Nickel silver lining and bolsters.

No. 6332
Length closed 3⅝". Bone stag handle. Brass lining. Nickel silver bolsters. Concave ground blades.

No. 2345½ SH
Length closed 3⅝". Black composition handle. Nickel silver lining and bolsters.

No. 6345½ SH
Same as 2345½ SH except with bone stag handle.

No. 6333
Length closed 2⅝". Bone stag handle. Nickel silver lining and bolsters. Concave ground blades.

No. 9333
Same as 6333 except with imitation pearl handle.

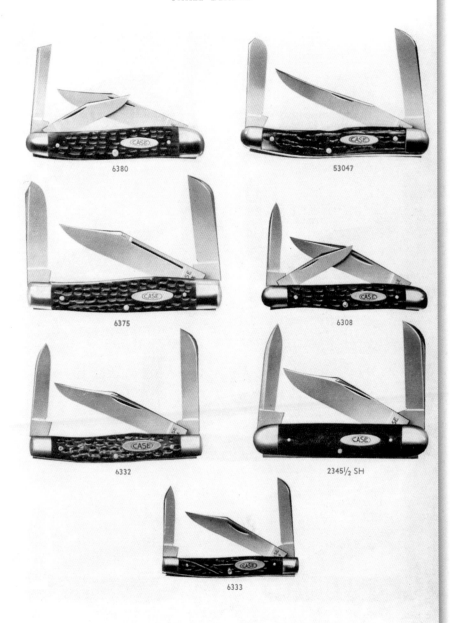

6380

53047

6375

6308

6332

2345½ SH

6333

W. R. CASE & SONS CUTLERY CO.

THREE BLADES

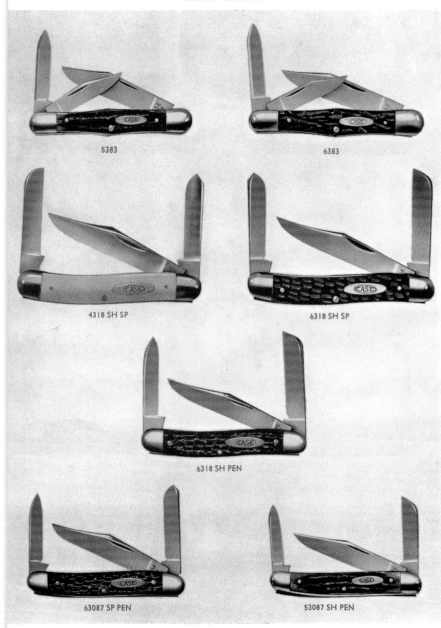

5383

6383

4318 SH SP

6318 SH SP

6318 SH PEN

63087 SP PEN

53087 SH PEN

No. 5383
Length closed 3½". Genuine stag handle. Nickel silver lining and bolsters.

No. 9383
Same as 5383 except imitation pearl handle.

No. 6383
Length closed 3½". Bone stag handle. Nickel silver lining and bolsters.

No. 2383
Same as 6383 except with black composition handle.

No. 4318 SH SP
Length closed 3½". White composition handle. Nickel silver lining and bolsters. Spay blade, concave ground.

No. 6318 SH SP
Length closed 3½". Bone stag handle. Nickel silver lining and bolsters. Spay blade, concave ground.

No. 6318 SH PEN
Same as 6318 SH SP except with pen blade instead of spay blade.

No. 3318 SH PEN
Same as 6318 SH PEN except with cream composition handle.

No. 63087 SP PEN
Length closed 3¼". Bone stag handle. Nickel silver lining and bolsters. Concave ground blades.

No. 53087 SH PEN
Length closed 3¼". Genuine stag handle. Nickel silver lining and bolsters. Concave ground blades.

No. 23087 SH PEN
Same as 53087 SH PEN except with black composition handle.

W. R. CASE & SONS CUTLERY CO.

POCKET KNIVES

FOUR BLADES

No. 5488
Length closed 4⅛". Genuine stag handle. Brass lining. Nickel silver bolsters.

No. 6488
Same as 5488 except with bone stag handle.

No. 6445 R
Length closed 3¾". Bone stag handle. Brass lining. Nickel silver bolsters.

No. 64047 P
Length closed 4". Bone stag handle. Nickel silver lining and bolsters. Spay and pen blades, concave ground.

No. 640045 R
Length closed 3¾". Composition handle. Brass lining. Nickel silver bolsters.

No. 54052
Length closed 3½". Genuine stag handle. Nickel silver lining and bolsters.

No. 64052
Length closed 3½". Bone stag handle. Nickel silver lining and bolsters.

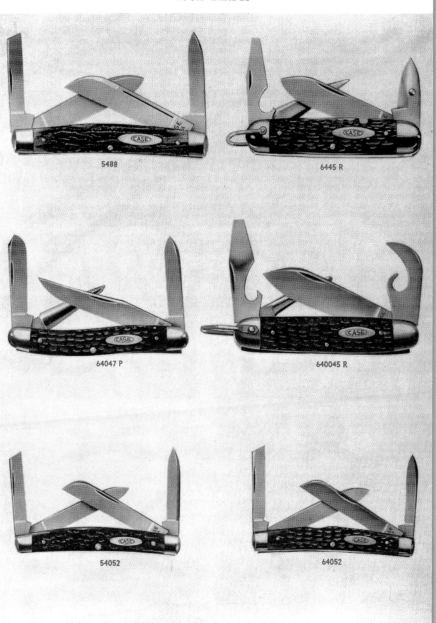

5488

6445 R

64047 P

640045 R

54052

64052

WORLD'S FINEST CUTLERY

W. R. CASE & SONS CUTLERY CO.

FINE PEARL

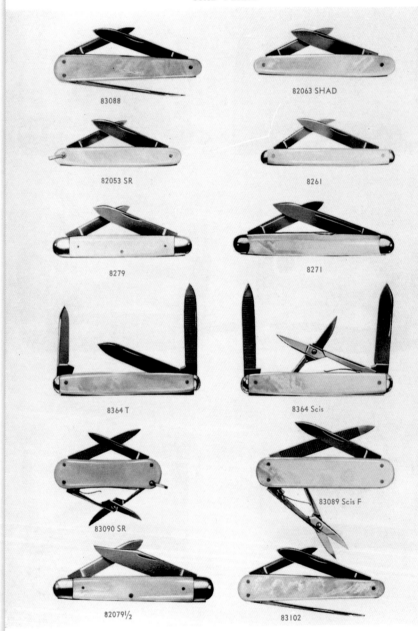

83088

82063 SHAD

82053 SR

8261

8279

8271

8364 T

8364 Scis

83090 SR

83089 Scis F

82079½

83102

No. 83088
Length closed 3⅛". Genuine pearl handle. Nickel silver lining. Stainless steel, concave ground blades. Stainless steel springs. Pick file.

No. 82063 SHAD
Length closed 3-1/16". Genuine pearl handle. Nickel silver lining. Stainless steel, concave ground blades. Stainless steel springs.

No. 82053 SR
Length closed 2-13/16". Genuine pearl handle. Nickel silver lining. Concave ground blades.

No. 8261
Length closed 2⅞". Genuine pearl handle. Nickel silver lining and tips. Concave ground blades.

No. 8279
Length closed 3⅛". Genuine pearl handle. Nickel silver lining and bolsters. Stainless steel, concave ground blades. Stainless steel springs.

No. 8271
Length closed 3¼". Genuine pearl handle. Nickel lining and bolsters. Stainless steel, concave ground blades. Stainless steel springs.

No. 8271F
Same as 8271 except file instead of small spear blade.

No. 8364 T
Length closed 3⅛". Genuine pearl handle. Nickel silver lining and tips. Stainless steel, concave ground blades. Stainless steel springs.

No. 8364 Scis
Length closed 3⅛". Genuine pearl handle. Nickel silver lining and tips. Stainless steel concave ground blades. Stainless steel springs. Scissors.

No. 83090 SR
Length closed 2¼". Genuine pearl handle. Nickel silver lining. Stainless steel, concave ground blades. Stainless steel springs.

No. 83089 Scis F
Length closed 3-1/16". Genuine pearl handle. Nickel silver lining. Stainless steel, concave ground blades. Stainless steel springs.

No. 82079½
Length closed 3¼". Genuine pearl handle. Nickel silver lining and bolsters, concave ground blades.

No. 83102
Genuine pearl handle. Nickel silver lining. Concave ground stainless steel blades. Stainless springs.

WORLD'S FINEST CUTLERY

W. R. CASE & SONS CUTLERY CO.

POCKET KNIVES

SPECIAL PURPOSE AND FISH KNIVES

No. 2109B
Length closed 3¼" (Budding knife). Black composition handle. Brass lining. Nickel silver bolster.

No. C61050 SAB
Length closed 5½". Bone stag handle. Nickel silver bolsters. Brass lining. Saber ground blade.

No. 6165 SAB
Length closed 5¼". Bone stag handle. Brass lining. Nickel silver bolsters. Saber ground blade.

No. 32095F
Length closed 5". Cream colored composition handle. Nickel silver bolsters. Brass lining. Fish hook sharpening stone on side of handle. Stainless steel blades and springs.

No. 6265 SAB
Length closed 5¼". Bone stag handle. Brass lining. Nickel silver bolsters. Master blade saber ground.

No. 5265 SAB
Same as 6265 SAB except with genuine stag handle.

No. 5165 SAB
Length closed 5¼". Genuine stag handle. Brass lining. Nickel silver bolsters. Saber ground blade.

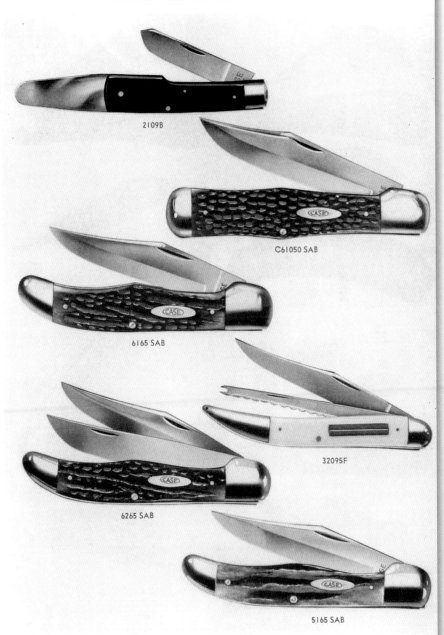

2109B

C61050 SAB

6165 SAB

32095F

6265 SAB

5165 SAB

WORLD'S FINEST CUTLERY

W. R. CASE & SONS CUTLERY CO.

SPECIAL PURPOSE AND FISH KNIVES

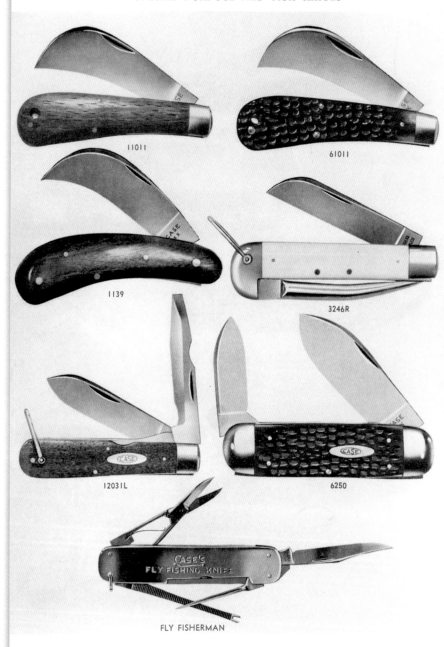

11011

61011

1139

3246R

12031L

6250

FLY FISHERMAN

No. 11011
Length closed 4". Walnut handle. Brass lining. Nickel silver bolster.

No. 61011
Length closed 4". Bone stag handle. Brass lining. Nickel silver bolster.

No. 1139
Length closed 4¼". Walnut handle. Extra heavy brass lining.

No. 3246R
Length closed 4⅜". Cream colored composition handle. Brass lining. Nickel silver bolsters. Marlin spike is stainless steel, also blade and spring.

No. 12031L
Length closed 3¾". (Electrician's knife) Walnut handle. Brass lining. Nickel silver bolster. Screwdriver blade locks into open position.

No. 6250
Length closed 4⅜". Bone stag handle. Brass lining. Nickel silver bolsters.

FLY FISHERMAN
Length closed 3⅞". Stainless steel handle with cutting blade and scissors on one side and pick and file on other side. Screwdriver on one end. Stainless steel blades, scale in inches on opposite side. Concave ground blade.

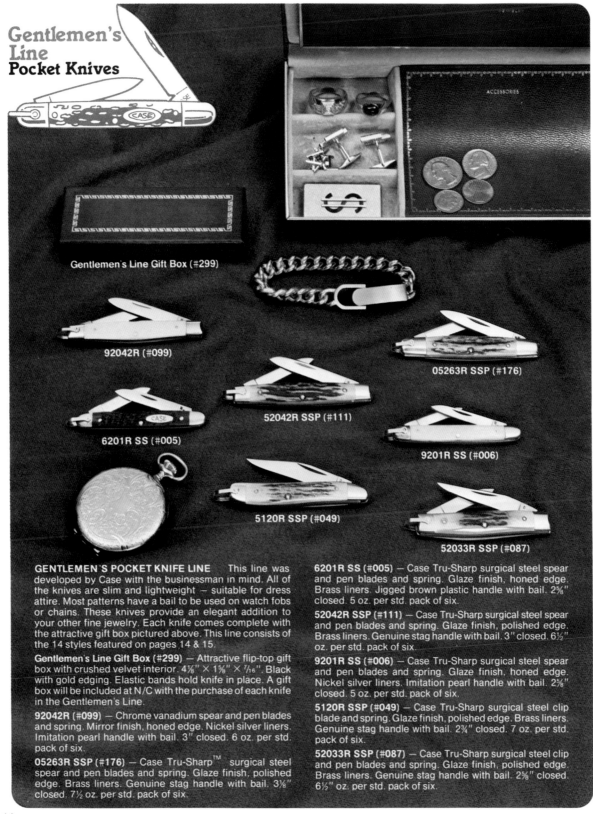

Gentlemen's Line Pocket Knives

Gentlemen's Line Gift Box (#299)

92042R (#099)

05263R SSP (#176)

6201R SS (#005)

52042R SSP (#111)

9201R SS (#006)

5120R SSP (#049)

52033R SSP (#087)

GENTLEMEN'S POCKET KNIFE LINE   This line was developed by Case with the businessman in mind. All of the knives are slim and lightweight — suitable for dress attire. Most patterns have a bail to be used on watch fobs or chains. These knives provide an elegant addition to your other fine jewelry. Each knife comes complete with the attractive gift box pictured above. This line consists of the 14 styles featured on pages 14 & 15.

Gentlemen's Line Gift Box (#299) — Attractive flip-top gift box with crushed velvet interior. 4⅛" × 1⅝" × ⁷⁄₁₆". Black with gold edging. Elastic bands hold knife in place. A gift box will be included at N/C with the purchase of each knife in the Gentlemen's Line.

92042R (#099) — Chrome vanadium spear and pen blades and spring. Mirror finish, honed edge. Nickel silver liners. Imitation pearl handle with bail. 3" closed. 6 oz. per std. pack of six.

05263R SSP (#176) — Case Tru-Sharp™ surgical steel spear and pen blades and spring. Glaze finish, polished edge. Brass liners. Genuine stag handle with bail. 3⅛" closed. 7½ oz. per std. pack of six.

6201R SS (#005) — Case Tru-Sharp surgical steel spear and pen blades and spring. Glaze finish, honed edge. Brass liners. Jigged brown plastic handle with bail. 2⅝" closed. 5 oz. per std. pack of six.

52042R SSP (#111) — Case Tru-Sharp surgical steel spear and pen blades and spring. Glaze finish, polished edge. Brass liners. Genuine stag handle with bail. 3" closed. 6½ oz. per std. pack of six.

9201R SS (#006) — Case Tru-Sharp surgical steel spear and pen blades and spring. Glaze finish, honed edge. Nickel silver liners. Imitation pearl handle with bail. 2⅝" closed. 5 oz. per std. pack of six.

5120R SSP (#049) — Case Tru-Sharp surgical steel clip blade and spring. Glaze finish, polished edge. Brass liners. Genuine stag handle with bail. 2¾" closed. 7 oz. per std. pack of six.

52033R SSP (#087) — Case Tru-Sharp surgical steel clip and pen blades and spring. Glaze finish, polished edge. Brass liners. Genuine stag handle with bail. 2⅝" closed. 6½ oz. per std. pack of six.

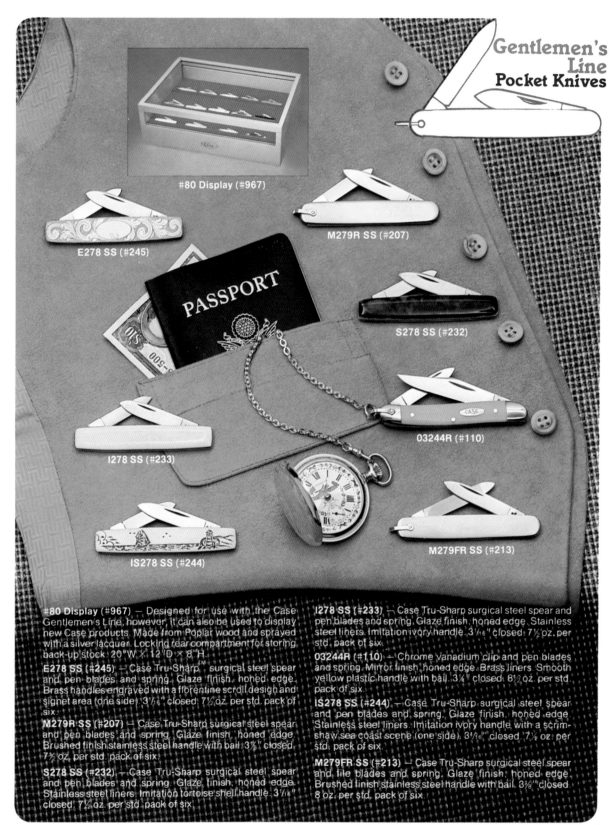

Gentlemen's Line
Pocket Knives

#80 Display (#967)

E278 SS (#245)

M279R SS (#207)

S278 SS (#232)

I278 SS (#233)

03244R (#110)

IS278 SS (#244)

M279FR SS (#213)

#80 Display (#967) — Designed for use with the Case Gentlemen's Line; however, it can also be used to display new Case products. Made from Poplar wood and sprayed with a silver lacquer. Locking rear compartment for storing back-up stock. 20"W X 12"D × 8"H.

E278 SS (#245) — Case Tru-Sharp™ surgical steel spear and pen blades and spring. Glaze finish, honed edge. Brass handles engraved with a florentine scroll design and signet area (one side). 3¹⁄₁₆" closed. 7½ oz. per std. pack of six.

M279R SS (#207) — Case Tru-Sharp surgical steel spear and pen blades and spring. Glaze finish, honed edge. Brushed finish stainless steel handle with bail. 3⅜" closed. 7½ oz. per std. pack of six.

S278 SS (#232) — Case Tru-Sharp surgical steel spear and pen blades and spring. Glaze finish, honed edge. Stainless steel liners. Imitation tortoise shell handle. 3¹⁄₁₆" closed. 7½ oz. per std. pack of six.

I278 SS (#233) — Case Tru-Sharp surgical steel spear and pen blades and spring. Glaze finish, honed edge. Stainless steel liners. Imitation ivory handle. 3¹⁄₁₆" closed. 7½ oz. per std. pack of six.

03244R (#110) — Chrome vanadium clip and pen blades and spring. Mirror finish. Honed edge. Brass liners. Smooth yellow plastic handle with bail. 3¼" closed. 8½ oz. per std. pack of six.

IS278 SS (#244) — Case Tru-Sharp surgical steel spear and pen blades and spring. Glaze finish, honed edge. Stainless steel liners. Imitation ivory handle with a scrimshaw sea coast scene (one side). 3¹⁄₁₆" closed. 7½ oz. per std. pack of six.

M279FR SS (#213) — Case Tru-Sharp surgical steel spear and file blades and spring. Glaze finish, honed edge. Brushed finish stainless steel handle with bail. 3⅜" closed. 8 oz. per std. pack of six.

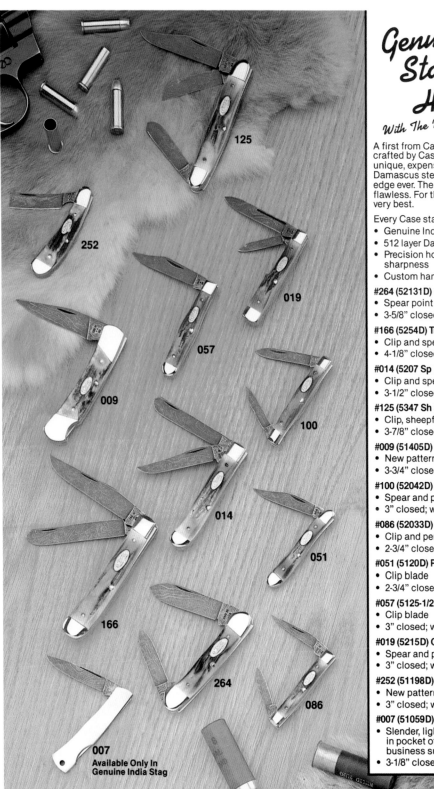

Genuine India Stag Horn Handles

With The Ultimate Damascus Steel

A first from Case. Rare India Stag horn crafted by Case into knives that resemble unique, expensive jewelry. Durable 512 layer Damascus steel blades for the keenest edge ever. The feel is "rich," the function flawless. For the person who insists on the very best.

Every Case stag handle knife features:
- Genuine India stag horn handles
- 512 layer Damascus steel blades
- Precision honed edges for superior sharpness
- Custom hand-crafted details

#264 (52131D) Canoe Handle Knife
- Spear point and pen blades
- 3-5/8" closed; weighs 2.7 oz.

#166 (5254D) Trapper
- Clip and spey blades
- 4-1/8" closed; weighs 3.5 oz.

#014 (5207 Sp D) Mini Trapper
- Clip and spey blades
- 3-1/2" closed; weighs 2.2 oz.

#125 (5347 Sh Sp D) Stock Knife
- Clip, sheepfoot and spey blades
- 3-7/8" closed; weighs 2.7 oz.

#009 (51405D) Lockback
- New pattern with special-design blade
- 3-3/4" closed; weighs 4.0 oz.

#100 (52042D) Pen Knife
- Spear and pen blades
- 3" closed; weighs 1.0 oz.

#086 (52033D) Mini Texas Jack
- Clip and pen blades
- 2-3/4" closed; weighs 1.0 oz.

#051 (5120D) Peanut
- Clip blade
- 2-3/4" closed; weighs 1.0 oz.

#057 (5125-1/2D) Swell Center
- Clip blade
- 3" closed; weighs 1.0 oz.

#019 (5215D) Gunstock
- Spear and pen blades
- 3" closed; weighs 1.5 oz.

#252 (51198D) Mini Razor
- New pattern with small razor blade
- 3" closed; weighs 2.0 oz.

#007 (51059D) Executive's Knife
- Slender, lightweight and fits comfortably in pocket of the most conservative business suit
- 3-1/8" closed; weighs 1.0 oz.

125

252

019

057

009

100

014

051

166

264

086

007
Available Only In Genuine India Stag

INDEX

MORE BEAUTIFUL BLADES TO BEHOLD

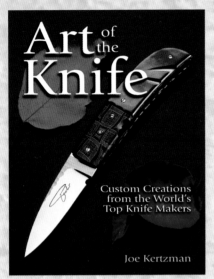

By Joe Kertzman
Enjoy the creativity and study the craftsmanship of knifemaking with each of the 350 brilliant color photos of highly engraved folders, engraved fixed blades, wire-wrapped knives and more in this one-of-a-kind book. Each photo includes with a basic explanation of materials used to make these stunning pieces of art and strength.
Hardcover • 8-¼ x 10-⅞ • 256 pages
350 color photos
Item# Z0733 • $35.00

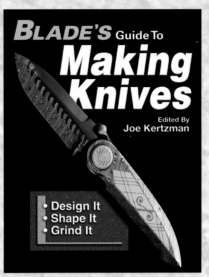

Edited by Joe Kertzman
Explore the creativity and craftsmanship of knifemaking in 350 brilliant color photos of highly engraved folders, engraved fixed blades, wire-wrapped knives and more, with a basic explanation of materials.
Softcover • 8-¼ x 10-⅞ • 160 pages
250 color photos
Item# BGKFM • $24.99

By Joe Kertzman
This easy-to-use CD contains 10 years of BLADE magazine issues – every issue, every article, every beautiful photograph of knives from 1997-2007 are waiting for you! This 2-CD set features each issue as it appeared in print, with the added benefit of being able to search for topics, knives, makers using the key word or index for searching. In addition you also can enlarge pages on screen by 400% for a closer view of the stunning knives.
As a special bonus, this spectacular set of CDs also includes all of the 2008 issues as well! That's 132 issues on 2-CDs.
Format: CD-PDF
Item# Z5686 • $39.99

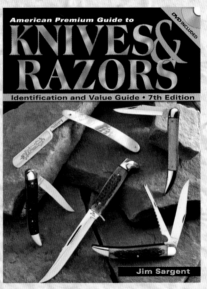

By Jim Sargent
Keeping your knife collecting and identifying skills sharp is a snap, with the new edition of the premiere guide to collectible cutlery. You will find updated prices and manufacturer data, along with extensive details about patterns, blade styles, handle materials, tang stamps, and company histories, plus thousands of photos for accurately assessing pocketknives and straight razors from legendary makers.
Softcover • 8-¼ x 10-⅞ • 504 pages
250 color and 2,200 b&w photos
Item# Z2189 • $27.99

Order directly from the publisher at www.krausebooks.com

Krause Publications, Offer **KNB9**
P.O. Box 5009
Iola, WI 54945-5009
www.krausebooks.com

Call **800-258-0929** 8 a.m. - 5 p.m. to order direct from the publisher, or visit booksellers nationwide or antiques and hobby shops.

Please reference offer **KNB9** with all direct-to-publisher orders

Expert References for Knife Making and Collecting